THE FUTURE OF ELECTION STUDIES

Other titles of interest:

Sociological Views on Political Participation in the 21st Century
Research in Political Sociology, Volume 10
Dobratz, Buzzell and Waldner

Theoretical Directions in Political Sociology for the 21st Century
Research in Political Sociology, Volume 11
Dobratz, Buzzell and Waldner

Political Power and Social Theory, Volume 14
Davis

Related Journals:

Electoral Studies

Orbis

For further information on all these titles please visit: www.elsevier.com

THE FUTURE OF ELECTION STUDIES

EDITED BY

MARK N. FRANKLIN

Trinity College, Connecticut, USA

CHRISTOPHER WLEZIEN

Nuffield College, Oxford, UK

2002

Pergamon
An imprint of Elsevier Science

Amsterdam – Boston – London – New York – Oxford – Paris
San Diego – San Francisco – Singapore – Sydney – Tokyo

ELSEVIER SCIENCE Ltd
The Boulevard, Langford Lane
Kidlington, Oxford OX5 1GB, UK

First edition 2002

Reprinted from: Electoral Studies, Volume 21, Issue 2.

Library of Congress Cataloging in Publication Data
A catalog record from the Library of Congress has been applied for.

British Library Cataloguing in Publication Data
A catalogue record from the British Library has been applied for.

ISBN: 0–08–044174–2

∞ The paper used in this publication meets the requirements of ANSI/NISO Z39.48–1992 (Permanence of Paper).
Printed in The Netherlands.

Contents

Contributors

Jake Bowers will receive his Ph.D. in Political Science from the University of California, Berkeley, and will take up an appointment as Assistant Professor of Political Science at the University of Michigan. He is currently working in the Political Science Department and the Center for Political Studies at the University of Michigan.

Henry E. Brady is Professor of Political Science and Public Policy at the University of California, Berkeley where he directs the university's Survey Research Center. His co-authored writings include *Letting the People Decide: The Dynamics of a Canadian Election* (which won the Harold Adams Innis award for the best book in the social sciences published in Canada in 1992-93) and *Voice and Equality: Civic Voluntarism in American Politics* (1995). His co-authored monographs include *Counting All The Votes: The Performance of Voting Technology in the United States* (2001) and *Expensive Children in Poor Families: The Intersection of Childhood Disabilities and Welfare* (2000). Professor Brady has also written numerous articles on statistical methods and research design and on politics and policy in Canada, the United States, Russia, and Estonia.

John Curtice is Professor of Politics at Strathclyde University, Glasgow, and Deputy Director of the ESRC Centre for Research into Elections and Social Trends. He was co-director of the four British Election Studies conducted between 1983 and 1997, resulting in co-authorship of *How Britain Votes* (1985), *Understanding Political Change* (1991), *On Message* (1999) and *The Rise of New Labour* (2001). He is also a member of the Planning Committee of the Comparative Study of Electoral Systems project, which undertakes comparative electoral research based on national election studies.

Cees van der Eijk is Professor of Political Science at the University of Amsterdam. He has been a Principal Investigator of a number of the Dutch Parliamentary Election Studies, and of the European Election Studies in 1989, 1994 and 1999. He is the author or co-author of a dozen books, including *Electoral Change in the Netherlands, Choosing Europe?* and *In Search of Structure;* and has also written numerous articles in professional journals such as *Acta Politica*, the *British Journal of Political Science, Electoral Studies,* the *European Journal of Political Research* and *Quality and Quantity*. The topics of his research are mainly in comparative politics, political behavior, and methodology.

Robert S. Erikson is Professor of Political Science at Columbia University, New York. He previously taught at Florida State University and the University of Houston. His has co-authored *The Macro Polity* (2002: Cambridge University Press), *Statehouse Democracy* (1993: Cambridge University Press) and *American Public Opinion* (updated 6th edition, 2003: Longman). He has written numerous articles in scholarly journals, mostly about U.S. electoral politics and political behavior. He has won the Heinz Eulau Award of the American Political Science Association and the Pi Sigma Alpha Award of the Midwest Political Science Association. He is the past editor of the *American Journal of Political Science* and past president of the Southwest Political Science Association.

Mark Franklin is the Reitemeyer Professor of International Politics at Trinity College, Hartford Connecticut. He has been a Principal Investigator of European Election Studies since 1989 and is the author or co-author of seven books, including *Choosing Europe?* (1996), *Electoral Change* (1992), *The Community of Science in Europe* (1987), and *The Decline of Class Voting in Britain* (1985). He also has articles in the *American Journal of Political Science*, the *American Political Science Review*, the *British Journal of Political Science*, *Comparative Political Studies*, *Electoral Studies*, the *European Journal of Political Research*, the *Journal of Theoretical Politics*, *Legislative Studies Quarterly*, *Political Behavior*, and other journals; and has served on several of their editorial boards. He has been a Guggenheim Fellow and a member of the Advisory Board for the British Election Studies.

Martin Johnson (Ph.D., Rice University, 2002), is Assistant Professor of political science at the University of California, Riverside. He studies the influence of social context and other sources of political information on public opinion, political behavior, and public policy. His research has appeared in the *American Journal of Political Science*, *Legislative Studies Quarterly*, and *State Politics and Policy Quarterly*.

Richard Johnston is Professor and Head of Political Science at the University of British Columbia and an Associate Member of Nuffield College, Oxford. He is author or co-author of *Public Opinion and Public Policy in Canada: Questions of Confidence*, *Letting the People Decide: Dynamics of a Canadian Election*, *The Challenge of Direct Democracy: The 1992 Canadian Referendum*, and of numerous book chapters and journal articles. He was Principal Investigator of 1998 and 1992–3 Canadian Election Studies, and co-investigator and director of survey for the UBC-based "Equality, Security, Community" group and for the 2000 US Campaign Study at the Annenberg School for Communication, University of Pennsylvania.

Kathleen Knight is Senior Lecturer at Barnard College, Columbia University. Her research interests include American public opinion and ideology, political psychology, mass media, and women in politics. Her recent publications include: "Liberalism and Conservatism" in *Measuring Political Attitudes* (Academic Press, 1999), "Public Opinion and Talk Radio" with David Barker in *Public Opinion Quarterly*, 2000, and

"Pathways to Power: Women in the Oireachtas 1919-2000" with Yvonne Galligan and Una Nic Giolla Choille in *Women in Parliament: Ireland* (Wolfhound Press, 2000). She has served on Planning Committee of the American National Election Studies.

Michael Marsh is Associate Professor of Political Science at Trinity College Dublin. His core teaching and research interests are parties, elections and public opinion in Ireland and other advanced industrial societies. He is presently co-principal investigator of the first ever election study for the Republic of Ireland, studying the recent 2002 election. He has published a number of books and articles, most recently *Days of blue loyalty: the politics of membership of the Fine Gael party*, PSAI Press, 2002 and *How Ireland Voted 2002*, Palgrave, (Forthcoming 2003).

W. Phillips Shively received his PhD from the University of North Carolina in 1969. He has served on the faculty of the University of Oregon, Yale University, the University of Minnesota, and the University of Oslo (visitor). He has been a member of the faculty of the University of Minnesota for 30 years, and has served that institution as Provost for Arts, Sciences and Engineering. Among various professional duties, he has served as editor of *The American Journal of Political Science*, and he is currently chair of the planning committee for the Comparative Study of Electoral Systems project. His research interests include methods for multi-level analysis, the role of parties in the voter's electoral decision, and the functioning of representative institutions.

Robert M. Stein is the Lena Gohlman Fox Professor of Political Science and Dean, School of Social Sciences at Rice University. He is author of *Urban Alternatives* (Pittsburgh 1990) and co-author of *Perpetuating the Pork Barrel* (Cambridge 1995). His current research focuses on metropolitan governance and the distribution of federal assistance to metropolitan area governments.

Laura Stoker is Associate Professor of Political Science at the University of California, where she has been teaching since receiving her Ph. D. (Political Science, 1990, University of Michigan). She has served on the Board of Overseers of the American National Election Studies (1994–2002, Chair 2000–2002), on the Electorial Board of the American Political Science Review (1997–2001) and is a former fellow of the Centre for Advanced Study in the Behavioral Sciences (1993–1994, 1997–1998). Her research focused on the development and change of political beliefs, attitudes, and behavior, and employs data drawn from surveys and experiments. Specific topics include the moral basis of citizens' opinions on public policies; sources of short- and long-run change in interpersonal political influence within the family; and intergenerational political change.

Christopher Wlezien is Reader in of quantitative methods and comparative politics and a fellow of Nuffield College at the University of Oxford. He previously was professor of political science and Founding Director of the Institute for the Study of Political Economy at the University of Houston. His research and teaching interests encompass a range of fields in American and Comparative politics, including political behavior, public opinion, political institutions and public policy, and his articles have appeared in numerous journals and edited volumes. Wlezien has served on the Planning Committee of the American National Election Study and on a number of editorial boards, including *Electoral Studies* and *Social Science Quarterly*.

John Zaller is professor of Political Science at UCLA where he specializes in public opinion, the mass media, and electoral politics. He has written *Nature and Origins of Mass Opinion* and is currently finishing *A Theory of Media Politics* and (with Marty Cohen, David Karol, and Hans Noel) *Beating Reform: The Resurgence of Parties in Presidential Nominations, 1980 to 2000*. He has been a Fellow at the Center for Advanced Study at Stanford, a Guggenheim Fellow, and a member of American Academy of Arts and Sciences since 1998. He also served on the Board of Overseers of National Election Studies.

Preface

Christopher Wlezien and Mark N. Franklin

It has been just over 50 years since the first election study was conducted in the United States. Since that time we have extensively studied voting behavior and election outcomes in a large and growing number of countries. Studying elections and electoral behavior has required us to learn, first and foremost, how to conduct election studies; and it is certainly true that we have learned a lot about how to do this. But there is always more to learn. What problems still remain? Perhaps most importantly, what changes in the design and conduct of election studies show promise of opening up new avenues of research or of improving the way in which research opportunities are grasped?

In March, 1999, a conference was held at the University of Houston to consider these questions. The conference brought together scholars who have directed (and continue to direct) election studies in Britain, Canada, Ireland, the Netherlands, and the United States, along with scholars who direct the European Elections Studies (EES) and the Comparative Study of Electoral Systems (CSES). The agenda for the conference had been developed over an extended period of e-mail communication during which prospective participants employed a discussion list to share their views about the topics that the conference should address.[1]

At the conference, we discovered that election studies in these countries (and presumably elsewhere) are facing similar fundamental methodological problems. Moreover, the problems are primarily intellectual. Election studies designed on the

[1] Aside from the individuals whose chapters are included in this book, two others participated in the conference; namely Richard Murray, and Kent Tedin. We also want to recognize Arthur Miller and Warren Miller for their contribution to planning the conference. Unfortunately, neither could attend. It was just days before the conference that Warren met his untimely death. The conference was largely supported by an endowment from the John and Rebecca Moores Scholar fund at the University of Houston. Other support was provided by the University's Center for Public Policy and College of Social Sciences. The event was organized through the Institute for the Study of Political Economy. We want to specifically thank Christopher Carman, Jenny Hill, Richard Murray, Pam Rossman, Richard Rozelle, Adrian Shepherd, Kent Tedin, and Phyllis Van Horn for their assistance.

Michigan model are reaching the limit of what they can achieve, above all because the calls on questionnaire space have far outstripped our ability to include all desired questions without jeopardizing the study. Moreover, many of the research questions now on the agenda of those who study voting and elections simply do not lend themselves to being investigated by means of such studies, at least as traditionally designed and conducted. Happily, solutions to the problem of adequately addressing new research questions offer a potential solution to the problem of questionnaire space to the extent that new research questions are 'hived off' to special-purpose studies while election studies themselves focus on what one author calls their 'core business.'

This collection of chapters considers the nature of the new research questions facing electoral scholars, why conventional pre- and/or post-election studies are ill-equipped to address these questions, and how such studies are being adapted and might be further adapted in order to meet the challenges they face.

Before turning to the chapters, let us mention that the future is now - as far as the ideas underlying this book are concerned. For once, these are not chapters written by policy advisors in the hopes that those who make policy may take notice. The contributors to this book are the directors of national election studies: they are policy-makers when it comes to the conduct of these studies. So it should come as no surprise to learn that some of the ideas contained in this symposium already have found their way (and others are even now finding their way) into the design of election studies in the United States and elsewhere. Some of the respects in which this has already happened at the time of writing are elaborated in our concluding chapter.

The collection consists of nine chapters of varying length (some as short as eight pages, others stretching beyond 25 pages) that lay out the problems and proposed solutions in the form of a quasi-dialog between contributors, and ends with a conclusion. The chapters do not reproduce the dialog that took place in Houston, but are more properly seen as a recapitulation, continuation, and development of those discussions. The chapters all start from ideas broached at the conference but take those ideas further and develop their implications in a way that could not be done in Houston. This is not a conventional symposium consisting of papers that were taken to a conference, but a rather unusual collection of chapters exploring ideas spawned by the conference itself.[2]

The nine chapters cluster neatly into three groups. The first set offers broad perspectives on election studies. Those by John Curtice and by Kathleen Knight and Michael Marsh set the scene by surveying what election studies have achieved and where they currently stand, in all their varieties (and similarities). John Curtice focuses particularly on the continuities that these studies evince, and the achievements that continuities make possible. He ends with a plea that these achievements not be jeopardized by any reforms that might be thought desirable on other grounds. Kathleen Knight and Michael Marsh look rather more deeply into the specifics of different studies so as to show how contrasting (and perhaps even incompatible) their objectives have often been. Cees van der Eijk builds on these different appraisals to develop ideas that formed the

---

[2] Drafts of the papers were circulated among contributors who were given the chance to comment on each others' papers. Contributors had the opportunity to respond to, or develop, the ideas in other papers.

core of the conference proceedings: ideas about the challenges now facing election studies together with a proposal that election studies *per se* should focus on their own core business of properly studying the dependent phenomena while leaving to other (linked) studies the job of measuring independent variables. His essay provides an intellectual framework for understanding the issues addressed in the remaining chapters.

The chapters 'addressing space' look at ways in which the conventional national election study is being, and might further be, elaborated as a vehicle for studying contextual effects of various kinds. Michael Marsh introduces the topic and describes the growing importance of context and its measurement. He then proceeds to describe the rationale behind, and the organization of, the European Election Studies and (more briefly) the Comparative Study of Electoral Systems projects; and shows how these studies focus on the collection and analysis of contextual information. The chapter by Martin Johnson, W. Phillips Shively, and Robert Stein studies some of the problems that arise when we attempt to embed individuals in their context and suggests an innovative strategy for determining the extent to which respondents react to the context in which they find themselves. The final chapter in the group, by Laura Stoker and Jake Bowers, considers a different set of problems that arise when we try to investigate the individual contests that occur in particular districts or constituencies during a national legislative election. In the process, these two authors address some sampling and analysis issues that are relevant to the EES and CSES as well.

The final group of chapters is concerned with 'addressing time.' Among those papers, Robert Erikson's considers ways in which individual-level characteristics can be used in aggregated form to address macro-level concerns such as the determinants of election outcomes over time, and the implications of these concerns for questionnaire design. Richard Johnston and Henry Brady describe a particular sample design, the rolling cross-section, that permits the investigation of changes in context as an election campaign proceeds. Finally, John Zaller considers the limited power of election studies of conventional size to assess campaign effects, or the effects of other political events, and suggests the need for larger samples if any but the most gross campaign effects are to be found.

These nine chapters reinforce each other in important ways. A recurring theme of the chapters in Part II and Part III is the realization that the sample sizes of contemporary election studies are quite inadequate for the purposes to which they are increasingly being put. But the logic of the chapters in Part I leads us in the direction of proposing 'core' election studies for which larger sample sizes would not be out of the question because they involve many fewer variables. The chapters in Parts II and III are also linked to those in Part I in a different way, since they spell out some of the ways in which separate data collection efforts can complement each other if small 'core' election studies are provided with adequate linkage variables. These chapters also focus on some of the problems that will still need to be addressed by such studies.

In a concluding essay we, the editors, reiterate some of the recommendations made by the contributors to this book for reforming the way in which election studies are conducted and offer a general assessment of the prospects for such reforms. We also provide an overview of the likely future development of election studies in the light of the concerns and ideas expressed at the conference and in the pages of this volume.

Acknowledgements

We thank Harold Clarke, Geoff Evans, and especially Elinor Scarbrough, for their input and guidance, not just regarding this introductory essay but the entire symposium. We also thank two anonymous reviewers, who put us all through our paces and helped us to produce a more interesting and important product.

Chapter 1

The state of election studies: Mid-life crisis or new youth?

John Curtice

Michigan-style national election studies have now been conducted for around 40 years or more in a number of countries. Given their relative inattention to context and difficulties in disentangling cause and effect, it might be considered time for radical change to, or even abandonment of, such studies. However, the longevity of the studies coupled with a growing programme of comparative research means that it is only now beginning to be possible to address some key questions about the impact of context on voting behaviour. What is required in order to take advantage of this newly emerging opportunity is a change to the way we analyze data from national election studies; and it is important that this opportunity not be jeopardized by ill-considered changes in their design.

National election studies have reached middle age. The first of the pioneer Michigan US studies was undertaken in 1952; the Swedish series began in 1956, while Norway was not far behind with its first study in 1957. Studies in Britain and Germany will soon be celebrating their 40th birthday (Mochmann et al., 1998; Thomassen, 1994a). So this is clearly an appropriate moment to evaluate their legacy. Are election studies approaching a mid-life crisis? Or are they perhaps not quite so old as they seem?

Michigan-style national election studies have one important distinguishing characteristic: they endeavour to understand elections and electoral behaviour by interviewing as close to polling day as possible a nationally representative sample of the population eligible to vote. Elections are examined primarily through the prism of voters. What does and does not influence voters is ascertained by comparing the behaviour and attitudes of one group of voters at a particular election with that of another group at the same election. It is assumed that if we can understand what accounts for differences between voters at an election we can understand what accounts for the outcome and key characteristics of elections in general.

In practice, of course, voters are far from being the only actors in an election. Parties and candidates issue appeals and make attempts to get their supporters to the polls.

The media report what parties and candidates say and may also offer their own interpretations. And events, whether the state of the economy, foreign wars, or a simple gaffe, may take on an importance that no one can control. The behaviour and attitudes of voters are, of course, the end product of these influences, but whether we can adequately understand the electoral process by looking at the end product alone is, at least, open to question. This was certainly the view of the authors of the Columbia local studies that were in vogue before the Michigan model became the dominant approach in survey-based electoral research (Benney et al., 1956; Berelson et al., 1954; Lazarsfeld et al., 1948; Milne and Mackenzie 1954, 1958; Valen and Katz, 1964). The content of the media, what parties and candidates did, and how voters interacted with each other socially and politically, were all commonly of as much interest to these authors as were the reactions and behaviour of voters.

Even if we leave aside these considerations, there is good reason to question the power of the Michigan approach. At the heart of any research enterprise is a wish to be able to say something about causation. We may, for example, wish to take a social psychological approach and ask whether the absence of party identification means that voters are more likely to switch their votes (Campbell et al. 1960, 1966). Or we may be concerned about the rationality of the electorate and enquire whether voters vote for the party closest to them on the issues they consider important (Downs, 1957; Key, 1966). Such questions have been central to scholarly debate about the electoral process for the last fifty years. Yet all too often in Michigan-style survey research we are left wondering whether a correlation between party identification and volatility shows that party identification influences vote or whether, in fact, it indicates that vote influences party identification (Butler and Stokes, 1974; Crewe et al., 1977; Thomassen, 1976). Equally, we often find it difficult to tell whether voters, in fact, vote for the party that is closest to them on the issues that matter to them or whether they are simply inclined to think that the party they have decided to vote for anyway must be closest to them on the issues (Miller, 1976; Morris, 1995).

There are, then, two important limitations to Michigan-style national election studies. They pay too little attention to the context in which a vote is cast. And even when they do find groups of voters that behave differently from one another, they can still find it difficult to disentangle cause and effect. Little wonder that some might suppose national election studies to be approaching a mid-life crisis. After fifty years of apparently ascertaining associations rather than causation, the law of diminishing returns might be thought to have set in for what, within political science at least, is often seen as a relatively expensive research resource.

The case is exaggerated, of course. Michigan-style national election studies have attempted to rise to the challenges of studying context and of ascertaining cause and effect. Perhaps the clearest example of the former is the use of the so-called 'rolling thunder' design, in which a small representative sample of voters is interviewed on each day of the election campaign. Coupled with analysis of the content of the media and the speeches and actions of politicians, this design enables us to examine whether the aggregate distribution of party support changes in response to media output and campaign events. At the same time, by bringing together all the interviews undertaken during the campaign, we also have access to a large national representative sample.

This rolling thunder design has been used to particular effect in Canada (Bartels, 1988; Johnston et al., 1992).

Meanwhile, Michigan-style election studies have never been entirely without the means to unravel causation. Here the most valuable tool is time. If an attitude is measured at time t and a behaviour at time $t+1$, the attitude is evidently a potential influence on the behaviour, whereas the opposite cannot be the case. Many national election studies have introduced time into their designs either by deploying a so-called pre-post design in which the same group of voters is interviewed both before and after polling day, or by employing an inter-election panel design in which voters interviewed at the last election are contacted again at the next (Curtice and Semetko, 1994; Miller and Shanks, 1996). While potentially subject to problems of conditioning and attrition, these panel designs also have the advantage that they reduce our reliance on respondents' memory of past attitudes or behaviour, thereby giving us, for example, more reliable estimates of the volatility of voting behaviour (Himmelweit et al., 1978).

Even so, these variations on the Michigan approach still have important limitations (see also chapter 5). True, there is considerable value in knowing that voters' attitudes or behaviour can be changed by campaign events or the messages of the media. We may learn, for example, that the election campaign is not simply a ritual (Butler, 1952). However, it may well be that what matters most in an election campaign is not variation in the content of the messages received by the electorate from one day to the next but, rather, what is said consistently during the entire election campaign. After all, parties will usually decide what their policy stance on a particular issue is for an election and then stick with it for the whole of the campaign. If so, the content of the campaign may be a constant rather than a variable, making it difficult to assess its impact. True, attempts are sometimes made to get around this problem by, for example, looking for differences between those who say they have followed the campaign or the media closely and those who say they have not (Norris et al., 1999). But these attempts always suffer from the problem that if the media or election campaigns have truly been influential, then their message will have reached not only those who followed the election closely but also percolated through to those who did not.

However, while parties may consistently deliver the same message at any one election, it is not uncommon for them to change their policy stance from one election to the next (Budge et al., 1987; Klingemann et al., 1994). So, while there may be little variance in the messages transmitted to voters during a campaign, we can certainly anticipate variance in their content between campaigns. This implies that if we wish to understand the impact of election campaigns, we should often be comparing across elections rather than dissecting only what happens during a particular campaign.

It is not that users of national election studies have failed to look at changes between elections. What is striking, however, is the predominantly apolitical nature of the main relationships addressed by such work and the emphasis on linear developments. The dominant concept has been dealignment. This is the suggestion that, as a result of changes in the nature of society (such as rising education levels, rising affluence, and the advent of television), the bonds between parties and voters are in long-term secular decline; the bonds referred to are either social-psychological (partisan dealignment) or sociological (class dealignment) (Clark and Lipset, 1991; Crewe, 1984; Dalton, 1996; Dalton et al., 1984; Evans, 1999; Franklin et al., 1992; Miller and Shanks, 1996; Nieuwbeerta, 1995; Wattenberg, 1996). In other words, long-term change in electoral behaviour is regarded as the product of long-term gradual secular social change without reference to potentially fluctuating political circumstances.

If we believe that election campaigns matter, a very different approach seems in order. Perhaps the relationship between social background and vote depends not so much on social change as on the kind of election campaign that is waged. We might, for example, expect there to be a stronger relationship between social background and vote if the parties put forward very different policy programmes than if they all propose very similar programmes (Evans, 1999; Kitschelt, 1994). There is certainly some evidence to suggest that, from 1970 onwards, the strength of the relationship between class and vote in Britain has fluctuated in line with the varying policy distance between the Conservative and Labour parties (Evans et al., 1999). So, rather than simply looking for linear trends over time we should regard elections as independent events whose political context needs to be measured and impact evaluated.

Nevertheless, it may well be the case that some important influences on voting behaviour in a country do not in fact change much from one election to the next. One obvious candidate in this respect is a country's constitutional structure and electoral system. Yet while these rarely change between elections, there is every reason to believe that they have an important influence on the way people vote. We might, for example, expect the traits of individual candidates to matter more to voters in a presidential rather than a parliamentary system (McAllister, 1996). We might expect the incidence and character of strategic voting to be different under a single member plurality electoral system from what it is under a party list system without a significant de facto or de jure threshold (Blais and Massicotte, 1996). And we might anticipate that prospective voting is more common under a proportional rather than a majoritarian electoral system (Schumpeter, 1976). Unless the same country uses a different electoral system for different elections, however, it is difficult to assess the validity of such propositions through single country analysis. Rather we need to compare what happens across countries.

To do this, of course, the same survey questions need to be asked in a similar manner in different countries. In other words, it is not sufficient that election studies are national in scope; they need also to incorporate an international dimension (Granberg and Holmberg, 1988; Thomassen, 1994b). Yet, until recently, there was no forum in which national election studies systematically collaborated in the collection of comparable data, although the European Election Study, which covers all European Union countries on the occasion of European parliamentary elections, has shown the potential of such endeavours (van der Eijk and Franklin, 1996; Katz and Wessels, 1999; Schmitt and Thomassen, 1999). This significant omission is now being corrected through the Comparative Study of Electoral Systems Project (CSES) which, since 1996, has seen at least two dozen countries administer a common module of questions designed to facilitate the examination of the impact of constitutional and electoral systems on voting behaviour (Comparative Study of Electoral Systems, 1996).

As might already be apparent, our argument implies more than just the deployment of a temporal and comparative framework. It also requires three other important if related changes to our traditional approach towards election studies. The first is that we cannot expect to understand elections and electoral behaviour simply by looking at them through the prism of the voter. Rather, we need also to measure the macro-context within which electoral behaviour takes place, be this the policy platforms of the parties, the output of the media, or a country's political or economic structure.

The reason why we want to measure the environment is in order to assess its impact. This brings us to our second change. As we have noted, much research based on election studies has hitherto consisted of identifying associations measured at the level of the individual voter, associations that, with varying degrees of success, may be taken to denote causation. But once we decide to bring context into the picture, we are often no longer simply interested in whether A causes B. Rather, we are interested in whether the relationship between A and B varies according to the context, C. For example, is the relationship between social background and vote stronger when parties make ideologically more differentiated appeals? Or is the association between candidate evaluations and vote choice stronger in presidential systems than in parliamentary ones? In short, we become interested in the conditions under which relationships exist, or become stronger, rather than just establishing the general validity or otherwise of particular individual level associations.

Such considerations apply even if panel data are available. We have noted that panels are better placed to measure volatility, that is, the extent of switching electoral preferences between two points in time. Volatility is often regarded as an attribute of voters, the product of a low level of psychological attachment to parties. Yet, in truth, volatility may also be an attribute of elections. Voters might, for example, be more likely to change their preferences during an election campaign if the policy positions of the parties are close to each other rather than if they are far apart. Or voters may be thought more likely to switch their votes from one election to the next if one or more parties adopt significantly different policy positions at succeeding elections. Thus, just as we may be interested in the contexts under which the association between two variables in a single- wave survey may be weaker or stronger, we can also be concerned to establish the conditions under which the relationship between variables collected in different waves of a panel are weaker or stronger.

From this flows our third change of approach. If each election potentially provides a unique context, then what determines the power of our research is not simply the number of respondents interviewed at any particular election (or, indeed, over how many years election studies have been conducted), but rather how many elections (of differing character) have been covered. It is only when a number of elections have been studied, some of them taking on one character, some another, that we can begin to assess whether there any general statements can be made about the relationship between context and voter behaviour. And, of course, we have to bear in mind that more than one potentially significant aspect of context may vary between elections, so it is relatively easy for the number of theoretically relevant variables to be greater than the number of elections for which we have data.

If we look at national election studies in terms of the number of elections studied, rather than the number of years over which they have been studied, we see them in a new light. We discover that, rather than being middle-aged, they are at most only now coming of age. The US study of the 2000 presidential election was but the 18th such study. The Swedish study is no more than a teenager, having conducted its 14th study in 1998, whilst the British study, with just eleven elections studied so far, is only now reaching adolescence. Far from approaching a mid-life crisis, our national election time series are in truth only just beginning to make it possible to address some of the questions raised about the possible influence of political context.

Consider, again, the claim that the strength of the class cleavage, or any other cleavage, depends on the ideological distance between the parties, a distance that may fluctuate from election to election. That claim appears to fit the evidence well in Britain from 1970 onwards, but it seems incapable of accounting for the strength of the association between class and vote at the two elections covered by the British Election Study series prior to that date (1964 and 1966). The claim can, thus, only be considered plausible rather than proven. Meanwhile the relationship between class and vote proved to be at its weakest to date at the 1997 election, a finding that is consistent both with the argument that a secular process of class dealignment is in operation and with the claim that what matters is the ideological distance between the parties. Quite evidently, the relative merits of the respective theories cannot be determined without evidence from further elections.

National election studies are, then, in fact, about to present us with an important new opportunity to advance our understanding of electoral behaviour. By exploiting the developing time series within countries, and by engaging in systematic programmes of international collaboration between countries, they are beginning to make it possible to turn elections and systems from constants into variables. Not least of the attractions of this development is that a field of scientific endeavour that has hitherto been dominated by theories derived from social psychology (party identification), economics (rational choice theory), and sociology (class dealignment) may at last begin to explore the role that politics plays in voting behaviour.

To exploit this potential we do not need to change the design of election studies so much as the way we approach their conceptualisation and analysis (although we may want to change the design for other reasons, see chapter 3). We need to regard any particular election study as an instance of context and to introduce into our analyses measures of what we think are the theoretically important features of that context (see, for example, Weakliem and Heath, 1999). Yet our ability to do this rests on our willingness to be patient. We can only understand how elections differ from one another if, indeed, we have collected the same information at each election. Asking the same old questions in the same old election study using the same old research design might appear to be a symptom of a research endeavour approaching sclerotic old age. In truth, such an approach is vital to our ability to understand the electoral process. Having nurtured election studies through their youth, we should certainly ensure that we do not now miss out on the fruits of their young adulthood through ill-considered change or retirement.

References

Bartels, L.M. 1988. Presidential primaries and the dynamics of public choice. Princeton University Press, Princeton, NJ.

Benney M., Gray A., Pear R. 1956. How people vote. Routledge and Kegan Paul, London.

Berelson B., Lazarsfeld, P.F., McPhee, W.V. 1954. Voting: A study of opinion formation in a presidential campaign. University of Chicago Press, Chicago.

Blais A., Massicotte L. 1996. Electoral systems. In: LeDuc L., Niemi, R.G., Norris P. (eds), Comparing democracies: elections and voting in global perspective, pp. 49–81. Sage, Thousand Oaks, CA.

Budge, I., Robertson D., Hearl D. (eds). 1987. Ideology, strategy and party change: spatial analyses of post-war election programmes in 19 democracies. Cambridge University Press, Cambridge.

Butler, D.E. 1952. The British General Election of 1951. Macmillan, London.

Butler, D.E., Stokes, D.E. 1974. Political change in Britain: the evolution of electoral choice, 2nd ed. Macmillan, London.

Campbell, A., Converse, P.E., Miller, W.E., Stokes, D.E. 1960. The American voter. Wiley, New York.

Campbell, A., Converse, P.E., Miller, W.E., Stokes, D.E. 1966. Elections and the political order. Wiley, New York.

Clark, T.N., Lipset, S.M. 1991. Are social classes dying? International Sociology 6(4), pp. 397–410.

Comparative Study of Electoral Systems. 1996. http://www.umich.edu:80/~nes/cses/cses.htm

Crewe, I. 1984. The electorate: partisan dealignment ten years on. In: Berrington, H. (eds), Change in British politics, pp. 183–215. Frank Cass, London.

Crewe, I., Särlvik, B., Alt, J. 1977. Partisan dealignment in Britain 1964–1974, British Journal of Political Science 7, pp. 129–190.

Curtice, J., Semetko, H. 1994. Does it matter what the papers say? In: Heath, A., Jowell, R., Curtice, J., Taylor, B. (eds), Labour's last chance? the 1992 election and beyond, pp. 43–63. Dartmouth, Aldershot.

Dalton, R., Flanagan, S., Beck, P. (eds). 1984. Electoral change in advanced industrial democracies. Princeton University Press, Princeton.

Dalton, R.J. 1996. Citizen politics: public opinion and political parties in advanced western democracies, 2nd ed. Chatham House, Chatham, NJ.

Downs, A. 1957. An economic theory of democracy. Harper and Row, New York.

van der Eijk, C., Franklin, M.N. (eds). 1996. Choosing Europe? The European electorate and national politics in the face of union. University of Michigan Press, Ann Arbor.

Evans, G. 1999. The end of class politics? Oxford University Press, Oxford.

Evans, G., Heath, A.F., Payne, C.D. 1999. Class: Labour as a catch-all party? In: Evans, G., Norris, P. (eds). Critical elections: British parties and voters in long-term perspective, pp. 87–101. Sage, London.

Franklin, M., Mackie, T., Valen, H. (eds). 1992. Electoral change: Responses to evolving social and attitudinal structures in western countries. Cambridge University Press, Cambridge.

Granberg, D., Holmberg, S. 1988. The political system matters: social psychology and voting behaviour in Sweden and the United States. Cambridge University Press, Cambridge.

Himmelweit, H.T., Jarger, M., Stockdale, J. 1978. Memory for past vote: implications of a study of bias in recall, British Journal of Political Science 8(4), pp. 365–376.

Johnston, R., Blais, A., Brady, H.E., Crête, J. 1992. Letting the people decide: dynamics of a Canadian election. Stanford University Press, Stanford, CA.

Katz, R., Wessels, B. (eds). 1999. European Parliament and European Integration. Oxford University Press, Oxford.

Key, V.O. 1966. The responsible electorate: rationality in presidential voting 1936–64. Harvard University Press, Cambridge, MA.

Kitschelt, H. 1994. The transformation of European social democracy. Cambridge University Press, Cambridge.

Klingemann H.-D., Hofferbert, R., Budge, I. 1994. Parties, policies and democracy. Westview Press, Boulder, CO.

Lazarsfeld, P.F., Berelson, B., Gaudet, H. 1948. The people's choice: How the voter makes up his mind in a presidential campaign. Columbia University Press, New York.

McAllister, I. 1996. Leaders. In: LeDuc, L., Niemi, R.G., Norris, P. (eds), Comparing democracies: Elections and voting in global perspective. Thousand Oaks, CA, Sage, pp. 280–298.

Miller, W.E. 1976. The cross-national use of party identification as a stimulus to political enquiry. In: Budge, I., Crewe, I., Farlie, D. (eds), Party identification and beyond: representations of voting and party competition. Wiley, London.

Miller, W.E., Shanks, J.M. 1996. The new American voter. Harvard University Press, Cambridge, MA.

Milne, R., Mackenzie, H. 1954. Straight fight 1951. Hansard Society, London.

Milne, R., Mackenzie, H. 1958. Marginal seat 1955. Hansard Society, London.

Mochmann, E., Oedegard, I.C., Mauer, R. 1998. Inventory of national election studies in Europe 1945–1995. Edwin Ferger Verlag, Bergisch Gladbach.

Morris, R. 1995. What informed public? Washington Post National Weekly Edition 10–16 April, 36.

Nieuwbeerta, P. 1995. The democratic class struggle in twenty countries. Thesis Publishers, Amsterdam.

Norris, P., Curtice, J., Sanders, D., Scammell, M., Semetko, H. 1999. On message: Communicating the campaign. Sage, London.

Schmitt, H., Thomassen, J. (eds). 1999. Political representation and legitimacy in the European Union. Oxford University Press, Oxford.

Schumpeter, J.A. 1976. Capitalism, socialism and democracy, 5th ed. Allen and Unwin, London: Allen and Unwin.

Thomassen, J. 1976. Party identification as a cross-national concept: its meaning in the Netherlands. In: Budge, I., Crewe, I., Farlie, D. (eds), Party identification and beyond: Representations of voting and party competition, pp. 63–79. Wiley, London.

Thomassen, J. (ed.). 1994a. Special Issue, The intellectual history of election studies: European Journal of Political Research 25 (3).

Thomassen, J. 1994b. Introduction: the intellectual history of election studies. European Journal of Political Research 25 (3), 239–245.

Valen, H., Katz, D. 1964. Political parties in Norway. Universitetsforlaget, Oslo.

Wattenberg, M. 1996. The decline of American political parties 1952–1994. Harvard University Press, Cambridge, MA.

Weakliem, D., Heath, A. 1999. The secret life of class voting: Britain, France, and the United States since the 1930s. In: Evans, G. (ed.), The end of class politics?, pp. 97–136. Oxford University Press, Oxford.

Chapter 2

Varieties of election studies

K. Knight and M. Marsh

In this chapter we describe the role of national election studies in voting behavior research in Europe and the United States. We begin with an overview of the organizational development of election studies emphasizing those elements that have influenced design and data collection over time. We then consider the theoretical influences reflected in the several sub-fields of electoral behavior research that have been incorporated into the studies and their implications for the nature of inference. The treatment of time in both theoretical and practical terms is given special attention because of its crucial implications for research design and inference. In the final section, we illustrate how these considerations have affected the selection of variables in national election studies and discuss prospects for a greater comparative focus in the future.

1 Introduction

The field of 'election studies' has traditionally been quite broad, and so diverse that the term 'varieties' may suggest more coherence than we are able to portray. In part, this is a tribute to the complexity of electoral phenomena and their centrality in democratic politics. It also results from differences in the social and political contexts of different countries when election studies emerged, the research resources and technological capabilities available to the academic community, and trends in the development of social science theory at the time. Although election studies need not be national in scope to provide important insights into the nature of electoral processes and individual behavior, we restrict our attention in this paper primarily to national studies. As the field has developed, similarities among national-level studies have increased, but this has not necessarily meant that the studies are directly comparable. Here, we delineate some of the major similarities and differences across the field of electoral research at the national level, largely in Europe and the United States.

We first look briefly at some practical and organizational issues that have influenced design and data collection patterns over time. We then consider the theoretical influences that have been incorporated into the studies and their implications for the nature of inference. The treatment of time in both theoretical and practical terms is given special consideration in the next section because of its crucial implications for research design and inference. In the final section, we illustrate how these considerations have affected the selection of variables in national election studies and discuss the prospects for a greater comparative focus in the future.

The field of election studies is certainly bound together by a common focus on elections. Beyond this, it is dominated by a theoretical focus on individual electoral behavior and the methodology of mass survey research. This does not mean that other theoretical foci and methodologies are not used, but that they are usually embedded in an election context that provides measures of individual attitudes through national-level public opinion polls. Such polls may be linked with contextual data reflecting long-term institutional characteristics and social-demographic structure, as well as short-term campaign effects. They may also be augmented with multi-wave interviews, over-sampling of theoretically interesting populations, follow-up investigations of social networks, and they may include imbedded experiments. These days, more frequently than in the past, results from survey research are and analyzed with other aggregate indicators (typically economic performance and consumer sentiment).[1]

The 'classic' national election study requires a nationwide representative sample of the electorate interviewed in some detail about their attitudes concerning a specific national election. Because data collection is resource intensive it generally requires funding, in all or in part, by national-level private or public foundations. Research design and implementation are in the hands of academic social scientists who endeavor to provide a comprehensive inventory of variables that allow for testing alternative hypotheses and aid in theory building. Over time, election studies have ranged from ad hoc opportunities by relatively small scholarly communities (as was the case in the very first 'Michigan' study in 1948) to highly planned and coordinated multi-method enterprises seeking to accommodate the interests of a broad segment of the research community (as with the 1997 and 2001 British Election Studies). Somewhat parallel to this we can distinguish an 'institutionalization' dimension, defined in terms of expectations of long-term research support. Security of long-term funding provides opportunities to operationalize theoretical approaches that require long-term data collection strategies and to coordinate scholarly investigation cross-nationally.

Beyond the organizational dimensions, election studies differ in terms of the object of inference. The essential distinction here lies between studies that seek to explain election outcomes and those that seek to explain the decisions of individual voters (see Miller and Shanks, 1982; Erikson, this volume, chapter 7). A further useful distinction can be drawn in terms of level of generalizability — does the research seek to explain behavior in a particular election, or to draw inferences about electoral behavior

---

[1] Of course, the earliest tradition in electoral research was aggregate (Siegfried, 1913; Key, 1955). So it might be said that the richness of individual level survey data as it has been amassed over time has provided the opportunity to renew this tradition with much more precise observations of complex political phenomena.

in general? Yet another dimension is to consider whether the research attempts to evaluate electoral behavior with reference to normative ideals, such as democracy or rationality, or simply attempts to describe and predict (i.e. model) it.

Research in electoral behavior is both unified and divided by broad theoretical influences in social science that carry major implications for design and data collection strategies. Four general theoretical traditions can be distinguished: sociological, psychological, economic, and communication.[2] These theoretical influences can be seen in the kinds of variables that are emphasized in the data collection and modeling efforts and, to some extent, in the controversies that develop over measurement and inference. While it is useful to distinguish among the various theoretical perspectives, it is also the case that national election studies frequently reflect a blending of theoretical interests. Changes in theoretical fashion are reflected in the addition and deletion of blocks of variables across time. In addition, the cumulative richness of the data collections for secondary research means that items originally intended to operationalize one theoretical concept may later be borrowed to operationalize another.

The treatment of time can be seen as a further major distinction between election studies. The implications of differences in the theoretical and practical effects of time will be considered in some detail below. However, one example of the influence of time can be seen in the predictability of election cycles and the calling of elections. Uncertainty about the timing of the next election, and the relatively brief formal campaign in many parliamentary systems, has encouraged – and, earlier, necessitated – the use of post-election surveys.

All these influences are reflected in the selection of variables included in national election studies. Over time, the scope and complexity of the different national efforts have increased to what many regard as the breaking point. Constant tensions exist between the desire to preserve cross-time comparability of items within countries and the elaboration of new ideas. Efforts at cross-national comparison are most often evident in the borrowing of theories and methods on a 'bilateral' basis. This leads to further difficulties in generalizing across different electoral contexts, and ultimately to increasing demands for the inclusion of more variables. If national election studies are to avoid sinking under the weight of increasing demands, strategies must be found to prioritize and coordinate content.

This is even more true of cross-national elections studies, such as the several European Election Studies (EES) and the current project on the Comparative Study of Electoral Systems (CSES). The EES project used the occasions of simultaneous European Parliament elections first in 12 countries, and now 15 countries, to explore electoral behavior using a comparative design (Schmitt and Mannheimer, 1991; van der Eijk et al., 1996a,b; Marsh and Norris, 1997). The severe resource constraints on the EES forced those involved to target a particular theme in each study. In 1989 it was mobilisation; in 1994 it was representation; and in 1999 it was the impact of the media, The Comparative Study of Electoral Systems project (see Marsh, this volume, chapter 4) has employed a similar strategy.

---

[2] This discussion and its elaboration in later pages is based loosely on a presentation at the University of Houston by Cees Van der Eijk.

2 Organizational characteristics

Election studies are the primary example of 'big science' in modern political research. In essence, they form a part of the research infrastructure. As such, they require the mobilization and coordination of significant human and technological capacities over a relatively short period of time. While advances in computing techniques have made the task much less daunting than it was in the 1940s and 1950s, it is still the case that election studies require the contribution of significant material and intellectual resources. The payoff is that they (should) yield very rich data sets that benefit from the attention of researchers with different theoretical perspectives and substantive concerns. The data from election studies have become more valuable as they have accumulated over time, but this value has only been realized by additional contributions for archiving, updating, and further distribution to the scholarly community. This further emphasizes the collective goods characteristic of the endeavor.

The scale, complexity, and cost of national election studies encourage collaboration, and from the beginning collaboration has been a hallmark of the enterprise. The vast majority of significant publications about elections have been co-authored. In fact, we cannot think of any single authored report from any national election study. Early patterns of cooperation led to the establishment of research centers within universities and across academic institutions. The piecemeal nature of much academic funding also promoted the development of organizations to coordinate academic research endeavors. The 'public/private partnerships', developed primarily between the media and the academy, have also produced a wealth of survey data across time. The developing community of election scholars also provided the major impetus for the creation of significant data archives like the ICPSR (originally ICPR) at Michigan in 1964.

The American National Election Study, originated in 1948, has surveyed cross-sections of the American electorate every two years, or more frequently, since then. Because of its longevity and continuity, it has served as a source of theoretical stimulation and, to a lesser extent, as an organizational model for the major European studies. The other major theoretical and organizational influences on European election studies can be traced to George Gallup's efforts in the 1940s, and to the 'Columbia school' (Lazarsfeld et al., 1948; Berelson et al., 1954). Gallup's influence was particularly evident in early Scandinavian electoral research (Holmberg, 1994; Valen and Aardal, 1994); his preference for simple question design is also still manifest in Swedish election studies. The 'Columbia school' emphasized two distinct ideas that carry through in research up to the present: the 'sociological perspective' with its emphasis on the individual's location in a social context; and, secondly, an interest in campaign dynamics.

Regular programs of election studies have been carried out in Britain, Germany, Netherlands, and the Scandinavian countries since the 1960s, and somewhat more sporadically in Denmark, France, Belgium, and other European countries, as well as in Canada and Australia. Other countries have managed sophisticated studies of electoral behavior without the opportunity for nationwide academic election studies. Noteworthy here is Ireland (Gallagher and Laver, 1993; Marsh and Mitchell, 1999) where recently there has been a financial commitment to a fully funded academic election study. A special issue of the *European Journal of Political Research* on "The Intellectual History of Election Studies" edited by Thomassen (1994) provides a wealth of detail on the development of several national enterprises. Papers from an APSA panel in 1998 (cited separately below) provide more information. These accounts suggest that, while researchers in different countries had the goal of comparative research from the beginning, the development of national election studies in each country was driven primarily by the context of that country's electoral process. Early research yielded important information about the differences among national electoral processes, but little that allowed direct cross-national comparisons. The similarities in question wording that did exist initially between US and 'native' questionnaires owed much to the influence of 'missionaries' from Michigan, who were responsible for much of the 'borrowing' that took place. Recent similarities have been the result of learning from one-another by all election study teams. More importantly, though, there is also the increasing realization that a more comparative focus is worthwhile, and some would say necessary, to any proper understanding of national election processes.

Several models of national-level organization are detailed in the EJPR (1994) accounts. Most common among these is the model of a single lead institution with an advisory board. Early development of, and commitment to, the advisory board model is particularly evident in the case of the Netherlands (van der Eijk and Niemoller, 1994). Competition for funding and change in lead institution was responsible for some discontinuities in the British studies (Curtice, 1994) and in the development of several different centers of electoral research in Germany (Schmitt, 1998). A 'survey' of national election surveys carried out for the British ESRC (Miller and Sinnott, 1998) indicates that the single national survey with single lead institution and advisory board has become even more dominant as the organizational model. In addition, about half of the national election study programs obtain funding exclusively from their respective social science research councils, or the equivalent. The other half receives some degree of government aid combined with resources from private funding agencies and the media.

The ESRC survey (Miller and Sinnott, 1998) suggests the emergence of a typical national election study consisting of personal interviews with a nationally representative sample of the electorate, using a panel study with waves immediately prior to and following the national election. This can be supplemented by a number of different observational strategies, such as inter-election panels, rolling cross-sections, and other elements that will be treated in more detail below. Miller and Sinnott's survey also testifies to the continuing cross-fertilization of ideas and research strategies, and the emergence of a more consciously comparative focus, among those who conduct national election studies.

3 Varieties of inference

Although academic election studies first gained prominence as a result of correctly predicting an election where traditional political pollsters failed (Miller, 1994), predicting the winner is generally not the purpose of election studies. Rather, their purpose, in general, is to explain electoral behavior. In attempting to achieve this general goal a number of 'sub-fields' have developed almost independent lives. The theoretical perspectives represented by the sub-fields influence the object of inference in various studies. Further distinctions can be made in terms of whether the primary emphasis is placed upon explaining the *outcome* of elections, or the *behavior* of voters, the scope of generalization, and the normative implications of the research.

4 Sub-fields of electoral research

As we suggested earlier, the initial theoretical influence on electoral research was sociological. The availability of aggregate election statistics facilitated early efforts to explore the nature of social cleavages and partisan dynamics. As survey research became the major mode for collecting data on elections, the theoretical questions of interest became more social–psychological in nature. Objective observation describing the individual's location in the social structure was augmented by indicators of subjective social class, reference group, and party identification.

This social–psychological perspective dominated early election studies, and publications reflecting this approach — consciously or unconsciously — remain the most numerous in the field of electoral research. In fact, both the communication and economic perspectives can be seen to pre-suppose concepts elaborated in the social–psychological approach. In addition to partisan and group identification, the social–psychological perspective has focused a great deal of attention on questions of citizen competence: knowledge, the organization of 'belief systems', and attitude stability over time. Substantial attention has also been devoted to attitudinal determinants of the vote, including policy preferences, left–right ideological orientations, and candidate and party images. Political socialization, efficacy, tolerance, and support for democratic values have also been included as part of this perspective, although the issues they address are more remote from the act of voting in a particular election. The 1980s witnessed efforts to model information processing in electoral choice that borrowed directly from the field of cognitive psychology (Lau and Sears, 1986; Sniderman et al., 1991; Lodge and McGraw, 1995), while the 1990s, following developments in neuro-psychology (Marcus et al., 2000), yielded renewed attention to the impact of emotional states on political judgment. Finally, the psychological perspective has, in general, encouraged a consciousness of measurement extending not only to matters of question-wording and order effects, but also to issues of social desirability, acquiescence, and other response set biases, and matters of interview context such as interviewer effects.

The third source of electoral behavior theory, political communication, has been recognized as central to the understanding of elections since the early efforts of the 'Columbia school'. More than any other, this sub-field also illustrates that advances in understanding many aspects of electoral behavior can be made without national samples of the electorate. Indeed, understanding the impact of differences in media content, exposure, and information processing requires experimental methodology that has been, until recently, unavailable to survey research. The intersection of psychology and communication research has produced important advances in understanding electoral behavior, including the elaboration of 'framing' and 'priming' effects, and developments in the 'on-line' information processing model of candidate evaluation. Because media effects are frequently conditional, even 'fugitive' (Bartels, 1993), it has been difficult for interested researchers to obtain the space in national election studies necessary to examine them definitively. The 1997 British Election Study design (Curtice, Heath and Jowell, 1998) provides the best opportunity for integrating the study of media effects with the study of national elections.

The fourth sub-field, political economy, has been responsible for the development of several different perspectives in voting research. These can be divided into studies emphasizing the effects of the economy on elections; the application of economic theory to electoral behavior; and methodology. The most obvious of these has to do with the impact of economic conditions on electoral decision-making. Such conditions can be measured either objectively or as matters of perception. The second, less obvious, impact of the economic perspective can be seen in the development of measures of candidate/voter 'issue proximities', which, in effect, operationalize the Downsian spatial model of elections. The third influence of economics on electoral behavior research has been the adoption of a wide variety of econometric modeling techniques, aggregate time-series, game theoretic, and experimental methodologies.

5 Objects of inference

The theoretical perspectives borrowed from the sub-fields listed above provide one strong set of influences on research design and measurement strategies in electoral behavior research. Two other sources of influence are more intrinsic to politics. The first of these stems from the nature of the dependent variable of interest, which cannot be directly observed at the individual level due to the secrecy of the ballot (van der Eijk, this volume, chapter 3). Contextual differences in the construction of electoral choice, however, mean that aspects of the vote may also need to be conceptualized as independent variables. The second intrinsically political influence on election studies is a normative concern centering around concepts such as 'representation', 'participation', and 'system support'.

A number of the most prominent early studies of voting behavior focused a good deal of attention on the intellectual capacities of the electorate and the health of democratic politics. The long-running debate over whether voters could live up to the expectations of democratic theorists is the best example of blending descriptive and normative inference. The basic argument can be paraphrased as follows: for democracy to 'work', citizens must be interested in politics, have stable issue preferences, and know what the current government is doing. Repeated empirical findings from the 1950s and 1960s (Campbell et al., 1960; Converse, 1964; but cf. Key, 1966) suggested that citizens had limited interest in politics, that their opinions on issues tended to vary randomly, and that only a minority could identify the current government's policy with respect to those issues. In such circumstances, not only was there little incentive for democratically elected representatives to respond to the preferences of the public;

it was impossible even for the most well-meaning politician to know, and so follow, the public will.

This pessimistic view stands in stark contrast to 'Downsian' (Downs, 1957) models that seek to explain voters' decision-making in terms of policy preferences, individuals' proximity to party manifestos, and their location in a left–right ideological space. The question of whether the awareness and rationality of the electorate is to be tested or assumed has remained one of the major divisions within the research community. Recent research has continued the challenge to the 'elitist' perspective, suggesting that voters can use a variety of short cuts to make sensible choices (Sniderman et al., 1991; Wlezien, 1995; Lupia and McCubbins, 1998; Zaller, 1992).

Another major focus of electoral research driven by broad normative concerns about democracy is the investigation of political participation, particularly turnout. This area of research also provides an excellent illustration of the need for a comparative perspective to provide insights into the range of mechanisms that affect turnout, and the complexity of design and measurement issues arising from attempts at comprehensive explanation. National-level studies have focused on regional, class, cultural, and 'psychological' differences, whereas cross-national research emphasizes differences in institutional arrangements, such as registration requirements, the timing of elections, and voting rules (Lipjhart, 1994; Powell, 1986). Arguably, given appropriate measures of institutional and other context differences, individual-level differences become irrelevant (Franklin, 1996; 2002).

This is an obvious instance of the way in which national explanations need to be placed in a comparative context. An even more obvious instance — although less attention has been paid to it — is the nature of the vote itself: what choice are voters given?; and how are they asked to express it? The impact of the electoral system on the choice that can be made has, to date, received little systematic study (at least, until the launch of the CSES project); and the link between the voter's preference structure across parties and the vote actually cast has also been neglected. These two themes are illustrated in the growing interest in 'tactical voting' in the UK (Catt, 1996), which has had implications for the design of recent election studies. So also has the growing diversity of the UK party system, where voters in different districts are offered quite different choices with respect to party. Increasing use is made of variables which try to measure the voters preference structure rather than simply the vote, a need underlined by Rivers' (1988) argument that different groups of voters may make their choices in different ways and that different methodologies are required to model those processes (see van der Eijk, this volume, chapter 3).

6 The treatment of time

The classic national election study employed a post-election design. This maximizes flexibility in selecting hypotheses to be examined in explaining the election result. But the post-election design can be contaminated by an un-measurable degree of rationalization by interview subjects. Moreover, its treatment of time is entirely static. It provides a 'snapshot' of the electorate in the context of a particular election. This design is particularly amenable to examination of the structure of political beliefs, and comparisons across sub-populations, but is probably the least adequate in terms of explaining why people came to have those beliefs. This is particularly so when the focus of interest is on short-term influences and the impact of the electoral campaign.

The pre-election interview with a post-election follow-up has, thus, become the preferred design of election studies. This design provides important leverage from explanatory variables measured prior to the outcome they are hypothesized to cause. The two-wave (pre-post) design also allows rudimentary consideration of opinion change over time. Even so, some attitudes of most interest may still appear to change simultaneously between the first and second waves. Where resources permit, examination of attitude stability and change over time is substantially enhanced by a multi-wave panel design. The 1980 American election study, for instance, included a four-wave panel. An alternative used in, among others, Canadian election studies and described elsewhere (Johnston and Brady, this volume, chapter 8) is a rolling set of cross-sectional samples. Each has provided evidence to address important questions of attitude change.

The availability of multi-wave panel data provided the 'measurement error' response (Erikson, 1979; Achen, 1975; Cassel, 1984; Feldman, 1989) to the 'non-attitudes' thesis (Converse 1964, 1970). As its name suggests, the measurement error thesis attributes most of the response instability observed in individual-level opinions to the instrument used to obtain them rather than to fickleness on the part of respondents. Like the earlier 'elite/populist' debate, this one is clearly fueled by the normative inferences drawn about the political competence of a large part of the mass electorate. Rolling cross-section data have been used to provide a better grip on the general problem of endogeneity in models of electoral explanation. This problem has bedeviled attempts to show that the electorate is motivated by issue concerns rather than that it employs issue concerns as a rationalization for more habitual behavior (van der Eijk, this volume, chapter 3).

A concern with change that predates the election campaign has prompted the inclusion of long-term panel components (with re-interviews after 2–6 years) starting in the 1950s and 1960s. The panel sample is typically augmented, and in some cases supplemented, by a fresh cross-section sample of respondents during each election period to control for testing effects and to compensate for panel attrition. These remain major elements of the American, British, Dutch, and German election studies to the present day. In addition, scholars particularly interested in campaign effects have fielded more frequent inter-election panels. While several recent studies have uncovered more by way of campaign effects, it has been difficult to generalize findings from elections cross-nationally, or over time (Semetko et al., 1994; Semetko, 1996). One reason for the difficulty in establishing the nature of campaign effects is explored by Zaller (this volume, chapter 9). Where there is a predictable long lead-up to the election, some potential control over campaign events that occur over time can also be obtained by releasing interview assignments for random half or quarters of sampled respondents across the period of the campaign period. This method was used in most of the American National Election Studies of Presidential elections since the late 1960s. It prefigures the rolling cross-section design pioneered by campaign firms that have become common in academic election studies.

The rolling cross-section design trades off the ability to investigate attitude stability at the individual level for the opportunity to examine attitude change over time. In doing so, it implicitly assigns random instability in attitudes to measurement error. In this design, small new representative samples are obtained at short regular intervals. These small cross-sections can be aggregated to obtain moving averages of political opinion about a particular issue or political leaders. If a salient event is suspected of having some impact on the electorate, sampled observations before the event can be aggregated and compared with aggregated observations after the event to test for statistically significant differences. Full trend analysis employing the rolling cross-section design is hampered, however, by the relatively large sampling error inherent in the small sample size for any brief period of interviewing.

As techniques were being developed to study change across time over short (single election campaign) or intermediate (two or three election) periods, the longer-term 'time-series' elements of national election studies were also beginning to bear fruit. Long-term analyses of electoral behavior are particularly dependent on the commitment to maintaining comparable questions over time. And this motivation can often conflict with the desire for the theoretical innovation that attracts both funding and professional reputation. Fortunately, the commitment to cross-time continuity of measures has been strongly affirmed in national election studies. Temporal comparisons of national electorates first identified apparent discontinuities in terms of historical periods, contrasting, for example, the 'steady state' of the 1950s with changes in the 1960s and 1970s. The first extended investigations of system dynamics focused on changes in the structure of social cleavages (Dalton et al., 1984; Franklin et al., 1992). The theses of party decline, growth of new parties, and realignment remain the most prominent among these new foci on dynamic phenomena.

The availability of comparable observations over time also rekindled interest in the internal mechanisms of individual decision-making as they might be influenced by structural changes in society. The availability of national data over time allows thorough examination of processes such as generational change and replacement, rising levels of educational attainment, 'cognitive mobilization', ideological polarization, and realignment. The availability of long series of comparable observations over time is also a stimulus for models of electoral behavior that emphasize the importance of events, economic conditions, and other matters of historical context, not least the behavior of the parties.

7 Selection of variables

What is most striking about the variables used in election studies is how many there are, and how they have multiplied over the years. A list of variables common across several election studies is displayed in Table 1.[3] Early questionnaires were very short by contemporary standards, particularly when panel designs and the additional, now

---

[3] The terms variables and questions are used interchangeably here, even though there is no necessary one-to-one relationship between them. Some single variables, such as occupational status, require a large number of questions; in other instances, the same question may be coded in different ways to yield several

Table 1: Varieties of variables used in national election studies

---

Variables

Demographics including occupation of respondent, partner and parents, gender, education, religion, race, length of residence
Group attachments
  - Organisation membership and activity
  - Ethnic and group identity, strength of identity
Respondents' neighbourhood context: socio-political character, actual and perceived.
Respondents' personal context: socio-political characteristics of discussion partners
Socialization — re-socialization
Party attachment
  - Party identification
  - Party closeness
  - Feeling thermometers
  - Probability of voting for
Media consumption and evaluation
Political information and knowledge
Campaign interest and activities
Issues
  - Salience: self and parties
  - Positions: self and parties
  - Competence of parties
Political attitudes including
  - Left–right
  - Efficacy
  - Alienation, anomie
  - Ethnocentrism
  - Authoritarianism
Political values including
  - Social goals and priorities
  - Personal goals and priorities
Government performance
  - Economic change: pocketbook and socio-tropic
  - Credit and blame for change
  - Temporal and/or regional economic context
Party images
  - Likes/dislikes
  - Image differentials: eg honest–dishonest
  - Group related
Leader/candidate images
  - Likes/dislikes
  - Attributes, image differentials: eg honest–dishonest
  - Group related assessments
Voting
  - Choice, and second choices
  - History
  - Government preference
  - Preference voting
  - Voting and non-voting
  - Registration

common, drop-off questionnaire[4] are taken into account. For instance, the SPSS file for the 1952 US national election study contains about 250 variables; that for the 1996 survey contains over 1500. Half a century of academic study has certainly not produced agreement on any parsimonious set of variables necessary for understanding electoral behavior. Studies have generally got larger and even the most limited studies ask around 100 questions of their sample. Nonetheless, there are variations, both within countries over time and between countries, in what are considered to be the more important variables.

In part, the selection of variables is dependent upon theoretical focus and research design. Most obviously, studies with a pre-post design and a drop-off questionnaire ask a lot more questions and consider may more variables. More limited designs mean less space, but also restrict what can usefully be asked. Single post-election studies, for instance, are less equipped to uncover short-term changes, and thus have given far less attention to questions on things such as media influence than have more complex designs.

A second reason for differences is that theoretical concerns vary. Some early researchers expected voting decisions to be made on the basis of the policies and competence of candidates, and designed studies and selected variables accordingly. A later generation of researchers expected choice to be a function of long-term social and political loyalties. Currently many scholars expect that they will have to give more attention to short-term change, whose complex and somewhat idiosyncratic origin will only be captured by an increasingly wide range of variables. This point is developed at greater length below. Theoretical concerns not only affect the choice of variables; they have also had a significant impact on the design of the questions themselves (van der Eijk, this volume, chapter 3).

A third reason for variation, tied to the previous one, is that elections vary in terms of the importance of key factors — such as parties and candidates — depending on voting rules. Different electoral systems demand very different things of voters. For instance, the Swedish voter chooses a party list, the British voter picks a candidate/party, while the Irish voter must rank-order a list of candidates. Different party systems also may require different approaches to understanding the long-term loyalties and short-term considerations of the voter.

A fourth reason for variation is the length of time that a particular series of national election studies have been running. Changes in content, with some exceptions, take place incrementally and slowly. The value of the time-series element may prolong the life of questions and variables that might otherwise not merit inclusion, and may reflect the intellectual fashions of an earlier era. The longer-standing election studies may thus contain a wider range of variables.

Different theoretical perspectives can each prompt the inclusion of a different set of appropriate variables in election studies. Changes in the persuasiveness of different

---

variables. Given concerns about measurement, it is certainly the case that some of the increase in the number of questions represents merely an attempt to measure variables more reliably, rather than an increase in the number of variables of interest.

[4] This is a supplementary questionnaire that may be left with the respondent and either collected later, or returned by post. It can add significantly to the number of questions available for analysis.

perspectives account for new questions. As already noted, however, old questions may be retained, thus gradually enlarging the questionnaire. As illustrated in Table 1, nine clusters of variables present in national election studies in Europe and the United States can be identified. These clusters of variables can be thought of as representing the various threads, or strands, of research attention that have been woven into election studies over time. If it were possible to depict the fabric created from these threads in color, the pattern would approximate an elaborate brocade that changes as various themes are introduced. However, the shape of the garment (our overall understanding of electoral behavior) might not be at all easy to discern.

The first strand, which may be traced back to the sociological perspective of early aggregate research, seeks to explain voting behavior in terms of group interests and attachments. This underpins the wealth of demographic and personal details that form a significant part of all surveys. Essentially, questions according to this perspective tap membership of, and position in, the main social cleavages of a country, with class, religion, race, or ethnic identity the primary elements. The growing ethnic diversity of many European countries has justified increased attention to this aspect. Class is also more diversified now, and, thus, may require many more questions than it used to as researchers try to allow for both status- and authority-based conceptions. The UK studies, which have been heavily influenced by the work of Goldthorpe (1980), devote particular attention to this aspect, with parental occupation and the occupations of other members of the household also being examined in detail. So have French and Dutch studies. In contrast, Swedish, Norwegian, and Danish studies, for instance, pay relatively little attention to class beyond establishing occupation, class identity, education, and income group.

In contrast to the individual-centered bias, a second strand is the recording in many studies of the respondent's social context (Marsh, this volume, chapter 4). Norwegian election studies have a long tradition of linking data on individual respondents to extensive socio-economic and political data on the area in which respondents live and vote. Some other studies have also sought to locate individuals in context, both by including neighborhood information from other sources and by asking the respondent about his or her locality. Contextual data may be justified by the need to understand the individual as part of a local society, and also by the need to know the political choices facing the voter — to understand certain types of tactical voting, for instance.

All studies explore respondent's partisanship. Initially, the US concept of 'party identification' formed the centerpiece of such research. However, the classic operationalizations of the concept traveled poorly outside the US, in countries which had more clearly defined parties (and more of them) and where the absence of party primary elections meant that voters were not required to register as a supporter of one party or another. Comparative use has been made of the 'party attachment' operationalization, but this has some of the same problems. Voters are still seen to have unique attachments. More recently, it has been accepted that people may have some long-term predisposition to vote for a number of parties (van der Eijk and Niemoller, 1983; Esaiasson and Holmberg, 1988). The attachment question may be amended to reflect this, but such multiple attachments or inclinations can be examined more effectively in other ways. Party approval thermometers are now quite widely used. Another alternative is a 'probability of voting' question developed in Dutch election studies and employed in studies of European Parliament elections (van der Eijk et al., 1996a), and in recent German, Spanish, and British election studies. This latter form asks people to assess the probability of ever voting for a particular party. Both probability of support questions and approval scales allow the voter to be mapped onto a party space, which may have one or more dimensions. The latter measure is more closely correlated with actual vote than the former: voters almost invariably vote for the party for which they give the highest probability of voting.

A fourth strand of interest in election studies that requires attention to measuring both individual variation and context focuses on the impact of the media. Extensive data sets on the content of media coverage during elections have been developed and appended to survey data ascertaining patterns of individual media consumption, attention, and interest in the campaign. Careful attention to the range of media variables required for proper model specification and appropriate panel study designs have substantially demystified research in this field (Zaller, 1996).

A fifth strand centers around the importance and nature of issues. These have always featured in election studies. While there have been developments in the theoretical understanding of issue effects, the major change is in the way issues are measured. Variations between studies reflect differences in theoretical emphasis and measurement. Stokes' (1964) classic distinction between position and valence issues has given rise to two different sorts of questions. All surveys contain some questions on issue salience, tapping what issues the respondent feels are the most important in the campaign. This may be couched in personal or in national terms, or both. In some studies (Dutch, Swedish), respondents are also asked what issues are most important for which parties, mapping issue salience in party space. All surveys also contain some measures of the respondent's position on certain issues, though there is some variation in how many such items are used, how the items are phrased, and whether a 5-, 7-, or 11-point scale is used. Again, many studies ask respondents to locate parties on these scales as well, thus mapping parties in issue space. Such data can be used to examine Downsian models as well as more recent variants, such as the theory of directional voting (Rabinowitz and Macdonald, 1989). Issues may also be measured with Likert-type items, asking people to agree/disagree with certain issue-related statements. However, a battery of such items is more often used to tap more general political attitudes, such as left–right, ethnocentrism, authoritarianism, efficacy, and so on. There is some sharing of the positional and the Likert items across countries, but no standardization. The issue-space items may often transfer poorly across countries. Likert items are perhaps more commonly imported, but are not always equivalent. Issues are also examined in terms of competence. Respondents may be asked which parties have the best policies on an issue, or which party has good or bad policies (Norway, Sweden).

Campbell et al. (1960) dismissed the idea that many voters have an ideology, basing this conclusion on the lack of consistent issue positions and the absence of the degree of coherence expected between various issue items. However, ideology remains a sixth important theme in modern studies, whether it is called political principles and measured by scaling Likert items, or whether it is called left–right position and measured through a single left–right self-placement item.[5] Ideology may also be conceived as a set of values. Many studies contain the standard Inglehart battery, but several studies have also made considerable efforts to measure respondent's goals or priorities. The Swedish election studies, for instance, ask a number of questions about the kind of society that should be worked towards.

A seventh set of variables is prompted by the idea that voters choose parties on grounds of performance rather than issue promises. Voters may not be ideological, or even well informed on issues, but they can still hold governments accountable (Key, 1966). The focus here tends to be economic, with voters asked about the record of the previous administration, both in terms of the national well being and their own personal well being. Further questions may also be employed to find out who the respondent credits or blames for improved or worsened well being.

An eighth strand of research in electoral behavior measures the impact of the candidates. The form and focus of these impacts vary very much according to the electoral system, and the wider political system of which elections are a part. Presidential candidates are obviously crucial in presidential systems. In addition to their issue stances and record in office, candidates may be assessed with respect to numerous character traits. Party leaders may be similarly assessed in parliamentary systems. Where the electoral system allows some possibility for personal voting, a variety of questions may tap people's knowledge of, and opinions about, individual candidates. These are extensive in the US, where the personal vote is considered to be particularly important, but it is less extensive elsewhere. Finnish, Swiss, and Japanese election studies, however, contain a number of items to assess the basis of candidate-centred voting, as does the 2000 Irish election study.

Some items tap the images respondents have of candidates, and similar batteries of questions tap party images. An initially popular method here was to ask people their likes and dislikes with respect to candidates and parties. These have thrown up a wide variety of images, which have been further explored with closed-ended questions. Some use is also made of closed items asking people to decide between characterizations such as honest/dishonest, modern/traditional, and so on, and others asking people how much they identify parties or candidates with particular groups or ideas. Although they form a significant part of British and US survey questionnaires, 'image' items are absent from many studies. Heath et al. (1998) suggest that images, particularly in the case of party leaders, are not easily examined with a post-election design as the election result may seriously contaminate the data.

A final set of variables in election studies has to do with the vote itself. Vote choice is the conventional dependent variable in election studies: whether or not the respondent voted,[6] and whom they voted for. Questions are typically asked about personal voting history, if this is not otherwise available from panel data, and sometimes about family voting history. Vote choice is a more complicated to ask about where there is some system of preference voting. In Denmark, Finland, Switzerland, and the

---

[5] See Knight (1999) for details on differences in measurement strategies.
[6] The first item is one of the few that can be validated, although this is legally possible only in some countries.

Netherlands, for instance, this aspect of choice is also explored; and it is a significant feature of analysis of elections in both parts of Ireland where voters are invited to rank all candidates, thus providing potentially rich information on voters' preferences across parties (van der Brug et al., 2000). In addition, as noted above, questions about probability of party support may prove to be a useful way of constructing the dependent variable in cross-national studies. The nature of this measure is discussed in more detail by van der Eijk (this volume, chapter 3).

8 Conclusion

Election studies developed as academics sought to understand the nature of the electoral process in general and the nature of the voter's decision-making process in particular. A more substantive concern with explaining the results of particular elections was also a consideration, and remains crucial to maintaining the linkage between academic and professional interests in this field. While this is probably one of the more cohesive areas of political science, for various reasons the studies themselves remain diverse. The traditions, resources, and political structures characteristic of different countries encourage differences. These differences can only be modified somewhat by the growing linkages of personnel and publications between teams responsible for election studies in their countries. In part this diversity is a good thing, permitting, perhaps even encouraging, innovation. Some other chapters in this volume illustrate ideas developed in particular studies that could be valuable elsewhere. The time-series generated by national election studies are also valuable, and could be compromised in a drive for more comparable measures across countries (see Cortice, this volume, chapter 1).

Even so, there are also benefits to be gained from greater standardization, particularly in terms of questionnaire design. Much diversity in question wording can probably be justified only in terms of tradition; but, in the absence of more work on the consequences of different question wordings, we cannot be sure even of this. The CSES project described elsewhere (Marsh, this volume, chapter 4) is an important step in the direction of justifiable uniformity. The European Election Studies (van der Eijk et al., 1996b) also display the benefits of asking the same questions in different countries. For all their richness and detail, however, single-country single-election surveys provide what are essentially 'case studies' as far as evidence for testing particular theories are concerned.

The basis of the field of study would be much stronger if placed on a more substantial comparative basis. The very cost of election studies may work against this, however. As major infra-structural projects in the social sciences, election studies soak up a significant portion of national social science research budgets. In consequence, a large number of social scientists want to ensure that 'their' questions and concerns are met by the final survey instruments. Unless this problem can be somehow finessed (see van der Eijk, chapter 3; Franklin and Wlezien, chapter 10), pleasing the international community of scholars may take second or third place, particularly where the studies are not the province of a small team. This suggests that continued, and even closer, cooperation among comparative scholars is essential to progress. In addition, sustained cross-national comparative election research will need more by way of multi-national funding.

References

Achen, C. 1975. Mass political attitudes and the survey response, American Political Science Review 69, pp. 1218–1231.

Bartels L. 1993. Message received: the political impact of media exposure, American Political Science Review 87, pp. 267–285.

Berelson, B.R., Lazarsfeld, P.F., McPhee, W.N. 1954. Voting. University of Chicago Press, Chicago.

Campbell, A., Converse, P.E., Miller, W.E., Stokes, D.E. 1960. The American Voter. Wiley, New York.

Cassel, C.A. 1984. Issues in measurement: the "Levels of Conceptualization" index of edeological sophistication, American Journal of Political Science 28, pp. 418–429.

Catt, H. 1996. Voting Behaviour: A Radical Critique. Leicester University Press, London.

Converse, P.E. 1964. The nature of belief systems in mass publics. In: Apter, D.E. (ed.), Ideology and Discontent. Free Press, New York.

Converse, P.E. 1970. Attitudes vs. non-attitudes: the continuation of a dialogue. In: Tufte, E.R. (ed.), The Quantitative Analysis of Social Problems. Addison-Wesley: Reading, MA.

Curtice, J., Heath, A., Jowell, R. 1998. The Design of the British National Election Study: A History and Evaluation. CREST: Centre for Research into Elections and Social Trends. Strathclyde University, Glasgow.

Curtice, J. 1994. Great Britain: imported ideas in a changing political landscape, European Journal of Political Research 25, pp. 267–286.

Dalton, R., Flanagan, S., Beck, P.A. (eds). 1984. Electoral Change in Advanced Industrial Democracies: Realignment or Dealignment? Princeton University Press: Princeton, NJ.

Downs, A. 1957. An Economic Theory of Democracy. Harper, New York.

van der Brug, W., van der Eijk, C., Marsh, M. 2000. Exploring uncharted territory: the Irish presidential election 1997, British Journal of Political Science 30, pp. 631–650.

van der Eijk, C., Niemoller, K. 1983. Electoral Change in the Netherlands. Empirical Results and Methods of Measurement. CT Press, Amsterdam.

van der Eijk, C., Niemoller, K. 1994. Election studies in the Netherlands: pluralism and accommodation, European Journal of Political Research 25, pp. 323–342.

van der Eijk, C., Franklin, M. et al. 1996. Choosing Europe? The European Electorate and National Politics in the Face of Union. University of Michigan Press, Ann Arbor, MI.

van der Eijk, C., Franklin, M., Marsh, M. 1996. What voters teach us about Europe-wide elections: what Europe-wide elections tell us about voters, Electoral Studies 15, pp. 149–166.

Esaiasson, P., Holmberg, S. 1988. Representation from Above: Members of Parliament and Representative Democracy in Sweden. Dartmouth, Aldershot.

Erikson, R.S. 1979. The SRC panel data and mass attitudes, British Journal of Political Science 9, pp. 89–114.

Feldman, S. 1989. Reliability and stability of policy positions: evidence from a five-wave panel, Political Analysis 1, pp. 25–60.

Franklin, M.N., Mackie, T., Valen, H. et al. 1992. Electoral Change: Responses to Evolving Social and Attitudinal Structures in Western Nations. Cambridge University Press, Cambridge.

Franklin, M.N. 1996. Electoral participation. In: LeDuc, L., Niemi, R., Norris, P. (eds), Comparing Democracies. Sage, Beverley Hills, CA.

Franklin, M.N. 2002. Dynamics of Electoral Participation. In: LeDuc, L., Niemi, R., Norris, P. (eds), Comparing Democracies 2. Sage, Beverley Hills, CA.

Gallagher, M., Laver, M. (eds). 1993. How Ireland Voted 1992. Folens/ PSAI Press, Dublin and Limerick.

Goldthorpe, J. 1980. Social Mobility and Class Structure in Modern Britain. Clarendon Press, Oxford.

Heath, A., Jowell, R., Curtice, J. 1998. The design of the British Election Study. Paper presented at the Annual Convention of the American Political Science Association, 3–6 September, Boston, MA.

Holmberg, S. 1994. Election studies the Swedish way, European Journal of Political Research 25, pp. 309–322.

Key, V.O. 1955. A theory of critical elections, Journal of Politics 17, pp. 3–17.

Key, V.O. 1966. The Responsible Electorate. Vintage Books, New York.

Knight, K. 1999. Liberalism and conservatism. In: Robinson, J.P., Shaver, P.R., Wightsman, L.S. (eds), Measures of Political Attitudes. Academic Press, New York.

Lau, R., Sears, D.O. 1986. Political Cognition. Lawrence Erlbaum, Hillsdale, NJ.

Lazarsfeld, P.F., Berelson, B.R., Gaudet, H. 1948. The People's Choice. Columbia University Press, New York.

Lipjhart, A. 1994. Electoral Systems and Party Systems: A Study of Twenty-Seven Democracies, 1945–1990. Oxford University Press, Oxford.

Lodge, M., McGraw, K.M. 1995. Political Judgement. University of Michigan Press, Ann Arbor, MI.

Lupia, A., McCubbins, M. 1998. The Democratic Dilemma: Can Citizens Learn What They Need to Know? Cambridge University Press, New York.

Marcus, G.E., Neuman, W.R., MacKuen, M. 2000. Affective Intelligence and Political Judgment. University of Chicago Press, Chicago IL.

Marsh, M., Norris, P. (eds). 1997. Political Representation in the European Parliament. Special issue of European Journal of Political Research 32 (2).

Marsh, M., Mitchell, P. (eds). 1999. How Ireland Voted 1997. Westview/PSAI Press, Boulder, CO and Limerick.

Miller, W.E., Shanks, J.M. 1982. Policy directions and presidential leadership: alternative interpretations of the 1980 presidential election, British Journal of Political Science 12, pp. 299–356.

Miller, W.E., Sinnott, R. 1998. ESRC Survey of Election Surveys. Mimeo.

Miller, W.E. 1994. An organizational history of the intellectual origins of the American National Election Study, European Journal of Political Research 25, pp. 247–267.

Powell, G.B., Jr. 1986. American voter turnout in comparative perspective, American Political Science Review 80, pp. 17–43.

Rabinowitz, G., Macdonald, S.E. 1989. A directional theory of issue voting, American Political Science Review 83, pp. 93–121.

Rivers, D. 1988. Heterogeneity in models of electoral choice, American Journal of Political Science 32, pp. 737–757.

Schmitt, H. 1998. The design of the German National Election Study. Mannheimer Zentrum fur Europaische Sozialfoeschung. Paper presented at the Annual Convention of the American Political Science Association, Boston, MA, 3–6 September, University of Mannheim, Mannheim.

Schmitt, H., Mannheimer, R. (eds). 1991. The European elections of 1989. Special issue of European Journal of Political Research 19 (1).

Semetko, H.A. 1996. Political balance on television: campaigns in the United States, Britain and Germany, Harvard International Journal of Press and Politics 1, pp. 51–71.

Semetko, H.A., Nossiter, T.J., Scammell, M. 1994. The media's coverage of the campaign. In: Heath, A., Jowell, R., Curtice, J. (eds), Labour's Last Chance? Dartmouth, Aldershot UK.

Siegfried, A. 1913. Tableau Politique de la France d'ouest sur la Troisieme Republique. Colin: Paris.

Sniderman, P.M., Brody, R.A., Tetlock, P.E. 1991. Reasoning and Choice. Cambridge University Press, Cambridge.

Stokes, D.E. 1964. Spatial models of party competition. In: Campbell, A., Converse, P., Miller, W., Stokes. D. (eds), Elections and the Political Order. Wiley, New York.

Thomassen, J. 1994. The intellectual history of election studies, European Journal of Political Research 25, pp. 239–245.

Valen, H., Aardal, B. 1994. The Norwegian program of electoral research, European Journal of Political Research 25, pp. 287–308.

Wlezien, C. 1995. The public as thermostat: dynamics of preferences for spending, American Journal of Political Science 39, pp. 981–1000.

Zaller, J. 1992. The Nature and Origins of Mass Opinion. Cambridge University Press, Cambridge, MA.

Zaller, J. 1996. The myth of massive media impact revived: New support for a discredited idea. In: Mutz, D.C., Sniderman, P.M., Brody, R.A. (eds), Political Persuasion and Attitude Change. University of Michigan Press, Ann Arbor, MI.

Chapter 3

Design issues in electoral research: Taking care of (core) business

Cees van der Eijk

National and other election studies suffer from a number of problems that can be addressed if electoral researchers focus first and foremost on the 'core business' of election studies — measurement of the dependent variable in all its aspects — and allow other concerns (generally associated with measuring independent variables) to be 'hived off' to special-purpose surveys specific to particular sub-fields of electoral studies. These additional surveys can later be linked to the core election study for analysis purposes. This chapter spells out the manner in which such linkages can be implemented, and enumerates a variety of advantages to be gained from splitting up in this way the business of studying voter attitudes and behavior. It elaborates how measurement of the dependent variable, traditionally a straightforward question about party choice, can be improved, and indicates the advantages thereof for improving our understanding of the voter's calculus, and for comparative electoral research.

1 Introduction

The proliferation and maturation of all kinds and varieties of election research (cf. Knight and Marsh, this volume, chapter 2), including perspectives from political economy, political communication, political sociology, and so on, generate demands for questionnaire space which are impossible to accommodate in any single national election study. These different sub-fields all have an interest in measuring what may be called the 'dependent' variables in electoral research: questions relating directly to voting behavior. Their priorities about which 'independent' variables to measure differ, however, since each of the sub-fields emphasizes different phenomena when attempting to understand voters' choices. The scarcity of space in the questionnaires of national election studies has contributed to a burgeoning of 'topical' election

The Future of Election Studies
Copyright © 2002 by Elsevier Science Ltd.
All rights of reproduction in any form reserved.
ISBN: 0-08-044174-2

surveys, each dominated by the questions that are (sometimes exclusively) relevant to a particular sub-disciplinary approach. This development has repeatedly led to the question whether there is still a compelling need for 'national' election studies at all. The main argument of this chapter is that such a need definitely does exist, but that it pertains to a set of core concerns that is considerably narrower than what is usually addressed in national election studies.

Defining the core concerns of election studies clearly opens up the possibility, just as in the case of commercial firms, of downsizing (by outsourcing elements that are important but not of core concern) and of investing more in the core itself, thus attaining higher quality than otherwise would be possible. In this contribution I first expand on what I see as the central concerns of election studies and show how these concerns are inadequately served by many national election studies in their present form. I then show how specialized research interests can be better served by combining (narrowly defined) national election studies with tailor-made proprietary surveys. Such combinations, however, call for the various studies to be linked in productive ways, and the requirements for accomplishing this are discussed. I also argue that this approach can ameliorate persistent problems of endogeneity, which are pervasive in the interpretation of data from national election surveys. But downsizing is not enough. In order to make theoretical progress, election studies also need to re-focus on their core concerns, especially regarding the measurement of party choice — typically regarded as central yet unproblematic. I argue that current practices are inadequate, and that improvements can only be achieved with additional investments in, and expansion of, these core concerns.

2 Core concerns of national election studies

The core business of national election surveys consists of fielding questions relating very directly to electoral behavior. For convenience these are referred to as the dependent variables. They should be measured as extensively as possible. Irrespective of their importance in the research process as a whole, other questions (pertaining to factors that can explain electoral behavior — the independent variables) should be less central in national election surveys. Independent variables can be, and for reasons of space often have to be, measured much more summarily. That is in itself not a problem as long as national election studies contain sufficient devices for productive linking with external data, including other more dedicated surveys.

Surveys are absolutely indispensable for studying electoral behavior. The secrecy of the vote implies that electoral behavior cannot be directly observed, hence the need for indirect measurement. Traditionally, this has taken the form of the respondents reporting their behavior in response to a survey question. Moreover, such surveys have to be fielded very soon after the fact in order to yield valid measurements. It has been repeatedly demonstrated that responses to survey questions regarding electoral behavior are affected, on the one hand, by memory decay, and on the other, by evolving real-world political conditions. This implies that such reports are more valid the sooner they are obtained after the actual behavior being measured. Recalling behavior that is of marginal personal importance for many respondents often requires heuristics that re-enact the decision, which is itself contingent on elements of the context in which the decision was made. Changes in the real world of politics affect the political preferences of respondents, which in turn affect their response regarding which party or candidate they voted for at an earlier moment in time. Questions about electoral behavior also generate different responses if they are fielded outside a real election context (for example, in a controlled experiment). These threats to the validity of the response relate to electoral participation as well as to party choice. They result not only in distortions of univariate distributions, but — and considerably more harmful to academic endeavors aimed at explanation — also of inter-relationships between variables.[1] Even a few months after the fact, questions about electoral behavior can have dubious validity.

In addition to the timely measurement of the 'dependent' variables (electoral participation and party choice), the core concerns of 'national' election studies include fielding questions that are directly related to these, pertaining to such matters as the certainty of the choice, the perception of the options for choice, and the like. Many of these questions can also yield responses that are different when asked in circumstances other than the election in question, so that, for these questions, it is just as imperative that they are included in surveys conducted as soon as possible after an election. The central concern of voter studies consists of the most timely, and most extensive measurement possible of the dependent variable.

For the purpose of explaining electoral behavior, surveys must also contain questions about independent variables, but only in the degree of detail that is productive in view of sample size and of informed expectations about distributions.[2] The real problem with independent variables originates, however, from the multitude of demands that cannot all be accommodated in a single survey. Two ways out of this problem are commonplace, each of which undercuts the legitimacy of the claim that national election studies are multi-purpose infrastructural resources. One is to only allocate space to independent variables that belong to a specific (sub-disciplinary) approach; for example, an economic or a communication-centered explanation. This may provide sufficient questionnaire space to satisfy the needs of that particular approach, but it will limit the extent to which the study can still be regarded as a multi-purpose infrastructural resource. The other way out is to allocate some questionnaire space to each of a number of competing claims. This generally yields a sub-optimal

---

[1] Studies of recall of electoral choice have consistently found that incorrect recall increases with time, and with the extent to which a respondent's political preferences have changed since the time of the election to be recalled (van der Eijk and Niemöller, 1979, van der Eijk and Niemöller, 1983, chap. 4, Granberg and Holmberg, 1988, chap. 9; and other references in these publications). Responses to party choice questions asked outside real election situations are differently related to other variables, such as economic evaluations, than party choice responses obtained in actual election contexts (Paldam and Nannestad, 2000, p. 390). Moreover, choice (and hence recall of choice) is affected by whether there is much or little at stake in an election (van der Eijk et al., 1996). Respondents' reports of their electoral participation display quite different patterns of association with other variables, dependent on whether they are obtained inside or outside real election contexts (Schmitt and Mannheimer, 1991; van der Eijk and Schmitt, 1990).

[2] Irrespective of how important certain distinctions may be thought to be as qualifiers of behavior, when they apply to too few numbers of people to generate propositions with a desired level of confidence, then their importance is small. It makes no sense to include such variables in a survey that does not have an adequate sample size (see Zaller, this volume, chapter 9).

outcome for everyone. The independent variables will not be of much use to analysts who do not belong to a particular sub-field, while they are likely not to be sufficient to satisfy the needs of those who do.

The needs of sub-fields can be better satisfied by fielding dedicated studies in which their own core interests are measured as extensively as possible, and linked to national election studies, which, for their part, optimize the measurement of electoral behavior. The dedicated studies do not have to be restricted to surveys, but may also involve direct observations, experimental studies, content analyses, census-like aggregate data, opinion polls, or whatever. Moreover, such studies need not be (and sometimes are better not) studied at the time of an election, but election study data can be linked to them when appropriate for purposes of analysis.

My arguments in this section, thus, define the core concerns of national election studies as the timely and extensive measurement of individual electoral behavior (electoral participation and party choice) and the immediate concomitants of this behavior (certainty, hesitation, and so on), together with the variables needed for linking this information to data derived from other sources.

As the ability to link a 'core election study' to data from other studies is critical to any new focus on the core business of election studies, in the next section I explain what I mean by linkage and give examples. In subsequent sections I focus on two major problems currently plaguing election studies (endogeneity and the proper measurement of the dependent variable) and show how a focus on the core business of election studies can provide us with solutions to these two problems. It also provides a solution to the problem of overly massive election studies.

3 Linkage

The term 'linking' is used in a generic sense that includes procedures which are sometimes also referred to as merging, adding, pooling, splicing, stacking, imputing, and sometimes in combination with (partial) aggregation. What such procedures lead to is a data matrix that can be analyzed as though it had been derived from a single study whereas, in fact, it has been constructed from a series of separate data sources. In formal terms, it is a projection of an n-dimensional multi-level data structure in fewer than n dimensions, without the need for the n-dimensional structure to be complete (cf. Buss, 1979).

One of the most common procedures is cohort analysis. Information from different individuals at different points in time is linked by partial aggregation to the level of cohorts, which can — on the basis of auxiliary information from censuses — be assumed to be comparable over time at the population level.[3] In that case, the data sets to be linked derive from surveys but the linkage is performed at the level of the cohort, with individual-level data aggregated to the level at which the linkage takes

---

[3] Auxiliary information can also inform us about compositional changes for which corrections have to be made before proper comparison is possible. For example, one can think of the changing gender distribution in cohorts as an effect of the greater longevity of women or of immigration and emigration effects.

place.[4] In an analogous form, partial aggregates other than cohorts can be used to link information from different surveys, at least if it can be assumed that they constitute samples from an unchanging segment of the population.[5] In a different form, surveys can be linked by adding to individual records from one survey information derived from other surveys; for example, when average perceptions of the issue-positions of the parties from one survey are linked to voters' own positions on those issues, and their party preferences, measured in a different survey.[6] To the extent that it is deemed desirable, this can be further refined by taking into account differences in perceptions among groups. The tradition of synthetic matching, which has been developed particularly by census bureaus, provides a rich source of inspiration on possibilities, limitations, and statistical consequences of such kinds of linkage.[7]

A rather different example would be the linking of survey data with economic or social data. In that instance, records derived from survey respondents are supplemented with economic or social data for the geographic area in which those respondents live or the sector in which they work. The economic data are spliced into a survey at the level of the individual, and the data remain at the individual level; alternatively, individual-level data might be aggregated to the level of the geographic unit for which economic or social data are available. Linkages can be performed at the level of any unit that is of interest to a particular sub-field of political science. For example, researchers studying parties might link to data of interest at the level of the party; those studying the media might link to data of interest at the level of the newspaper or television program read or watched by individuals whose characteristics and behavior are derived from survey data.

One could object that such procedures assume the absence of significant higher-order or cross-level interactions, without providing the means to test such assumptions. Such objections are, in principle, correct; in practice, they are often irrelevant. The alternative — starting from the full n-dimensional multi-level data structure — is beyond the financial and logistic reach of even the most ambitious and well-endowed research teams. Moreover, simple spreadsheet-like simulations of the 'what if' type can quickly reveal to what extent violations of such assumptions have appreciable effects on substantive conclusions, while auxiliary information often exists about the real magnitude of such interactions.

---

[4] The aggregation does not have to be explicit. One may, for example, add a cohort-identifier to individual respondents and perform an individual level multivaraiate analysis in which the cohort-identifying variables are amongst the independent variables. The coefficients of these variables then pertain to the cohorts as aggregates, even though no explicit aggregation has been performed.

[5] An example can be found in Franklin (1991) who uses social–structural characteristics (assumed not to change in the period between the studies to be linked) to link two independent cross-sectional surveys in an analysis of the mobilization of partisanship during election campaigns.

[6] Cf. van der Eijk and Franklin (1991). Such linkages always require substantive assumptions, such as, in this example, the assumption that (perceptions of) parties' positions have not changed in the period between the surveys to be linked. Usually, researchers are well able to assess the plausibility of such assumptions, using contextual information or findings from other studies.

[7] Some of this literature is to be found in the context of statistical disclosure control (methods for preventing such matching, at least at a very low level of aggregation), a topic of obvious concern for census bureaus; cf. Willenborg and de Waal (2000).

The most pervasive form of linkage employed in contemporary election studies is between individual-level data and data concerning the contexts within which the individuals reside (Marsh, this volume, chapter 4). Information about contexts can, of course, be gained from the individuals themselves by asking them about their geographic, political, and social situations, but such questions are often subject to the endogeneity problem (discussed in the next section). Information about contexts gleaned from respondents is not independent from other information gleaned from those respondents. For example, information about which political party has most support in the constituency or district can be contaminated by the party preferences of respondents. But if the contextual information is obtained from sources other than the respondents, then such contamination cannot occur. Moreover, information derived from external sources can be far more extensive than can be obtained from the limited number of questions in an election survey. Linkage variables for contextual data often consist of purely geographic information which is often known independently of any questions included in the survey: city, county, and perhaps even ward of residence (and much else) can be gained from the address or postal code of the respondent. These geographic identifiers provide links to many forms of contextual data.[8]

In summary: linkage variables are readily acquired for most types of auxiliary information that a researcher might want to include as independent variables in analyzing voting. Independent variables acquired in this way are inevitably measured at the level of some unit above that of the individual; what is needed is the identity of the specific unit at that level to which the individual belongs. The unit might be a cohort (identified by date of birth),[9] or a geographic entity (identified by postal address), or political party or newspaper (identified by name) or virtually any other unit less numerous than the population being sampled. Moreover, individual-level data for individuals other than those included in the election study can be aggregated to some higher unit (usually geographic or demographic) and linked at that level.

Although the variables being linked to must invariably exist at some higher level of aggregation, the level of analysis of the resulting data can remain that of the individual election study respondent. Data about newspapers read, or party voted for, or any feature of the political, social or economic context of the respondent applies individually to each respondent identified with the unit concerned no less than does the gender or age of that respondent. The fact that many other respondents have the same gender or age does not make these characteristics any less characteristic of specific individuals; nor does the fact that many other respondents read the same newspaper or live in the same city make the characteristics of that newspaper or city any less of an individual-level characteristic. The only difference between asking individuals about

---

[8] Political scientists may, in this respect, learn a lot from consumer market analysts, who have developed extremely profitable (literally) ways of linking individual-level data with information relating to regions of different extent.

[9] Productive linking requires the highest level of specificity of the identifiers used to link studies. Their exact definition, therefore, requires careful consideration. It is obvious, for example, that identification of the cohort to which a respondent belongs, is much more accurate based on date of birth than based on age. In spite of this many surveys only ask about age, thereby greatly diminishing their potential for productive linking.

the ethnic diversity of their neighborhood, or whether there are few or many parties on their ballot, and establishing such facts by reference to external databases, is that the information will often be more accurate when derived from a source other than the respondent.[10]

Linkage, then, can be a powerful means by which researchers in different sub-fields can provide themselves with additional variables, over and above those already contained in the core election study, at low cost and high accuracy. This permits the core election study to focus on taking care of its own (core) business without harm (even perhaps with some gain) to other sub-fields. Researchers in those sub-fields can make use of the core election study to provide them with variables about voting behavior strictly conceived, while acquiring the remainder of their information from studies conducted in other ways. Additional benefits to be gained from focussing in this way upon the core business of election studies are considered in the next two sections.

4 Endogeneity

Focussing election studies on the core business of electoral choice, and leaving the measurement of other concepts to other studies, brings the major benefit of freeing variables measured in those other studies from the taint of endogeneity — an endemic problem in survey research.

The term endogeneity is often used to point to explanatory variables (and their random disturbances) being dependent on the same influences as the dependent variable. This constitutes a violation of standard assumptions in multivariate analysis, which may endanger the consistency of estimators. These statistical consequences of endogeneity (caused particularly by the non-independence of error-terms) are not the major focus of concern here. Rather, our concern is with endogeneity in a somewhat more general sense, referring to doubts about the position of a putative causal factor in explanatory or causal propositions.[11] In this sense, endogeneity problems lie at the heart of many persistent substantive debates in electoral research. These involve questions such as whether issue and policy preferences, economic evaluations, or government approval (co-)*determine* party choice, or whether they are rather *derived* from party choice or party attachments, which themselves are based on entirely

---

[10] This is not to deny the relevance of perceptions — irrespective of their accuracy — in the explanation of individual behavior. When perceptions (and not their real-world referents) are the real phenomena of interest to a researcher, then surveys are indispensable for obtaining them. This does not preclude obtaining them in a dedicated survey rather than in a core election study.

[11] The statistical problems referred to in the more narrow definition of endogeneity can to some extent be handled by methods that allow the modeling of interrelations between error terms. All such models, however, require a specification of causal ordering that is theoretically — not statistically — grounded. The more general formulation of the endogeneity problem involves doubts about exactly such causal orderings. Consequently, many of the advanced statistical approaches that 'solve' endogeneity problems in the first sense of the term, are begging the question in its second sense as they assume that the wider endogeneity questions are solved theoretically.

different grounds (such as parental transmission, or conformity to group pressures). Stated differently, should interrelations between such variables and party choice be seen as evidence of rationality, or as evidence of rationalization?

The proposition that A affects B (i.e. that A is a cause of B) may often be countered by the argument that A can be seen as the effect of B, or that A and B are both subject to other factors. The normal approach to dealing with the latter problem is to take into account potential common antecedent factors, thus distinguishing causal effects from spurious ones.[12] In the case of endogeneity concerns, however, this is often impossible as the potential common factors cannot be simply explicated as variables. When data about A and B come from a single survey, any kind of relationship between the two may have been produced by the measurement procedure itself. The process of being interviewed (and interaction with an interviewer) sets off mental processes that impinge on all responses. All kinds of 'psycho-logics' may be triggered, which generate relationships between different variables. Such psycho-logics cannot be interpreted as causal connections between the constructs that these variables were intended to measure. None of the responses from surveys, and no pattern of responses, can *ipso facto* be taken to be free from processes which include, amongst others, rationalization, white lies, acquiescence tendencies (or their opposite), self-delusion, sensitization, outright deception, and cognitive balancing. Questions about causal orderings become even more problematic in the light of results from studies of medium or long-term individual change, which provide ample evidence of all kinds of reciprocal effects between variables. Such effects, in analyses of short-run developments (such as election campaigns), are often identified as putative causes and putative effects.

Two different, but usually intertwined, problems play a role in situations that give rise to endogeneity concerns. One relates to the *internal validity* of causal propositions: the problem of determining the direction of causal influences. Methods for testing hypothesized causal structures — such as LISREL — may help by rejecting (falsifying) the specific causal ordering of the model being tested.[13] As a recent case in point, Nannestad and Paldam (2000, p. 133) use causal analysis methods to investigate the effects of evaluations of the economy on party preferences, and conclude that "the results are . . . clearly rejecting causality from the retrospective to the prospective" which contributes to rejecting the interpretation that retrospective evaluations of the economy affect party preferences. Accordingly, these same analyses suggest "causality the other way. We hence seem to have a case of adaptive recollections". This is a somewhat veiled way of stating that the retrospective evaluations are not recollections at all, but something else instead.

The second kind of problem underlying many concerns about endogeneity is the *validity of operationalization*: to what extent do our measures reflect the phenomena

---

[12] Obviously, this is only possible when the causal order of the different variables is settled on theoretical grounds. When causal order is the problem at hand, common solutions for dealing with spurious relationships obviously fall short (see also footnote 11).

[13] In line with the previous two footnotes, it must be emphasized that falsification is only conditional;, i.e. resting upon a series of theoretical decisions in the construction of the model to be tested.

they purport to measure, and not something else? Clearly, in Nannestad and Paldam's example, problems of internal validity applying to a specific causal interpretation of the data give rise to doubts about the operationalization of the theoretical constructs. It is obvious that the sequence can also run the other way, from doubts about operationalization to doubts about the internal validity of causal propositions.[14] Just as (indeed, just because) causal ordering is subject to endogeneity problems, hardly any of the measurements obtained from surveys can, a priori, be assumed to be beyond the same endogeneity concerns, if only because the validity of the operationalizations cannot be taken for granted (especially in view of the impact of the interview process on responses).

In spite of the fact that there are no cut-and-dried solutions to endogeneity problems, some strategies may help to mitigate them. In addition to explicit causal analysis, logic helps in assessing whether the variables under consideration actually measure what they were supposed to measure, or whether they actually measure some other phenomenon generated by the measurement process itself.[15] In addition to this, methods for improving the operationalizations of important variables are crucial, especially the combination of multiple-item measurement, and the use of measurement models that test for the presence of non-trivial relationships in the data.[16]

By far the best way to deal with endogeneity problems, however, is to bring 'external' data into play — especially in the context of a comparative perspective. External data are not derived from the survey itself but can be linked to it (in ways discussed above).[17] Such external data can be of various kinds, depending on the problem at hand. It may be other survey data (opinion polls, media audience studies, for example), economic indicators, census data, and so on. Although such external data are obviously not without their own validity problems (see Johnson et al., this volume, chapter 5), the likelihood is small that they will be associated with the dependent variable by virtue of having been derived from the same survey or interview. When combined with a comparative approach, the questions to be addressed change from the relatively sterile 'whether or not' endogeneity problems exist to a much more informative inquiry about the circumstances under which such problems are more or less pronounced.[18] The ease with which external data can be productively combined with

---

[14] See also the extended argument in Wlezien et al. (1997).

[15] As a case in point, when observing left/right proximity between voters and the parties they choose, a traditional discussion is whether this indicates rationalization or (Downsian) rationality. When pursued to its logical extreme, the rationalization argument leads to the expectation that there will be little agreement between voters about where (in left/right terms) the parties they did not vote for are perceived to be. This expectation can be tested empirically (e.g. van der Eijk and Niemöller, 1983; van der Eijk, 1998). Other approaches to this rationality/rationalization controversy are used by Granberg (1983), Judd et al. (1983), Krosnick (1990) and van der Brug (2001).

[16] Cf. Coombs (1964), Mokken (1971), Jöreskog and Sörbom (1983) and van Schuur (1993).

[17] Sometimes, data derived from the survey itself but pertaining to a higher level of aggregation than the one involved in the analysis at hand, can also be regarded as external data. This possibility is not pursued here.

[18] Moreover, when confronted with the possibility that (part of) the relationships observed can be attributed to factors such as rationalization, assimilation, or whatever, it is not very interesting merely to demonstrate that such effects are statistically significant. Much more informative is an estimate of the extent to which this does, or does not, invalidate substantive conclusions.

data from voter surveys depends on factors explored in the previous section: the availability of a sufficient number of well-chosen and well-coded linkage variables, and study designs that, by incorporating contextuality concerns (see Marsh, chapter 4), enhance the pay-off from such linkages.

5   Reconsidering the dependent variable

To judge from their questionnaires, survey practitioners believe that their dependent variable(s) are relatively straightforward and unproblematic. Being interested in explaining the electoral behavior of individual voters, the standard way is to ask respondents whether or not they cast a vote, and, if they did, which party or candidate they voted for (or, in a pre-election survey, which they intend to vote for). Often, additional questions are asked that relate immediately to this behavior, such as how long in advance they decided upon their choice, whether they had been in any doubt about casting their vote, or about who to vote for, and so on. But, at their core, almost all such studies represent the dependent phenomenon by only these two questions. In this section, I argue that the single question about party choice is insufficient for an adequate understanding of voter behavior, and that it should be supplemented by other questions.[19]

Over a century and a half ago, John Stuart Mill (1975, originally published in 1843) formulated his principles of logic, upon which even today much of our thinking about explanation and causation are based. Particularly with respect to the social and political world, he recommended active control over all relevant variables, and the elimination of rival explanations to putative cause–effect relationships. His methods of agreement, of differences, and (most particularly) of concomitant variation were supposed to help analysts achieve this. Although it is clear that Mill did not have anything like election studies in mind, the logic of his argument certainly applies to them. But some of his teachings seem to have been forgotten in the design of most voter surveys in past decades.

The implication of Mill's logic in electoral research is that any observed association between an independent variable and a particular choice can only be interpreted as explanatory to the extent that the same independent variable is not associated in the same fashion with other possible choices a voter could have made. However, we can only test this interpretation empirically (by attempting to falsify it) by 'measuring', in one way or another, voters' relationship to the options that they did not choose. Without such information, the method of concomitant variation is implemented incompletely, weakening the foundations of causal propositions.

[19] The arguments in this section reflect to a large extent the work since 1982 of a number of scholars including, in addition to myself, Kees Niemöller, Rob Mokken, Mark Franklin, Jean Tillie, Wouter van der Brug and Erik Oppenhuis. See, for example, van der Eijk and Niemöller (1984), van der Eijk and Franklin (1996, chap. 20), Tillie (1995), Oppenhuis (1995) and van der Brug et al. (2000a,b). This work has resulted in the development and extensive validation of a straightforward survey question that has been used successfully in a large number of surveys. Other scholars have constructed variations of this survey question, without altering its logic (cf. Maas et al., 1990). Similar arguments about the need to supplement the ubiquitous party/candidate choice question have been made by Burden (1997) and Pappi (1996).

If we are to understand how voters arrive at their choices, we cannot afford to look only at the result of that process (the party or candidate voted for), as it is almost always possible to construct different 'explanations' for that outcome which cannot be adequately tested vis-a-vis each other. Did someone vote for a party because it is a religious party, or because it is middle-of-the-road, or because it pays attention to the needs of the countryside? To select between these alternative explanations, we need to know how that voter evaluates each of the other parties or candidates on offer, each of which can also be characterized as being religious or secular, left/middle/right in orientation, rural or urban. Stated differently, the ubiquitous question about party choice allows only restricted observation of the variation in preferences that is truly there. We see neither the variation (for each respondent) between all the parties that were not chosen, nor the variation (for each party) between all the respondents who did not vote for it.[20]

The major problem with surveys that include only the single question about party choice is that they provide no means to distinguish the *choice* for a party from the *preferences* for the various parties. This distinction would be irrelevant if we are willing to assume that: (1) each voter prefers only one party; (2) each party not chosen is not preferred; and, consequently, (3) there are no differences in preference between the parties not chosen. Although it is possible to conceive of situations in which these assumptions would hold, theoretical and empirical insights argue against them. Empirically, we know, for instance, that during campaigns many people hesitate and waver between parties, that switching from one party to another is patterned according to the similarity between them, and we know also that feelings of identification with parties are not mutually exclusive.[21] These observations suggest the existence of distinct (though sometimes of roughly equal strength) preferences for more than just a single party.[22] Theoretically, not only Downsian reasoning but also social–structural and social–psychological theories lead us to expect that most voters hold multiple preferences (cf. Tillie, 1995, pp. 14–26).

The equation of preference and choice is problematic because of the way electoral choice is institutionalized in most systems: it is dichotomous (a party is either chosen or not), and it is ipsative (choosing one party from the ballot implies that all others are not chosen). The combination of dichotomous choice and (conceivably) continuous preference, risks creating artifacts in the description of the relationship between preference and some other (for example, independent) variable. Depending upon the

---

[20] Some of the methods of multivariate analysis very much in vogue today, such as multinomial or conditional logit and probit analysis, seem to take into account all choice options simultaneously. If they really did so, they would obviate the need to ask survey questions about preferences for parties which were not chosen. Yet, what they actually do is to make assumptions about the strength of (unobserved) individual voter's preferences for the parties not votes for. Without any explicit observation of individual voters' assessment of parties, these assumptions remain unsubstantiated leaps of faith (see below).

[21] The evidence about hesitation and switching is too extensive to mention. With respect to non-exclusive 'identifications', see, for example, Thomassen (1975), Weisberg (1980), van der Eijk and Niemöller (1983, chap. 8).

[22] Even in the two-party case it has been shown that taking account of differences in the level of preferences for the party not voted for yields superior models of voter decision-making (Burden, 1997).

(unknown) level of preference for the party that is chosen, a single relationship will be observed in quite different forms (cf. Cook and Campbell, 1979, pp. 12–13).[23]

The ipsative nature (that is, the enforced mutual exclusivity) of electoral choice on the basis of the standard voting question will under most circumstances lead to incomplete results when investigating the relationship between choice (measured only by the conventional party/candidate choice question) and other factors. For some independent variables, it may be impossible to assess their effect on choice; for others, the estimated effects will commonly be biased (overstating or understating their importance); and, in still other cases, results will be outright incorrect.[24] In order to avoid these problems, the ubiquitous question on party choice should be complemented by questions on (the intensity of) electoral preference that allow a semi-continuous response, and which are, in any case, non-ipsative: that is, not imposing logically mutual constraints on reports of preference for different parties.[25] Ideally, such questions should operationalize *electoral utilities* for each party: that is, the degree of utility a voter would derive from voting for it.[26] Such questions have been included in a limited number of studies, and have successfully survived extensive tests of their validity and practical applicability. The Dutch National Election Studies since 1982, the European Election Studies of 1989, 1994, and 1999 (conducted in all member-states of the European Union (EU)), and the most recent British and Spanish election studies all employ a standard question (the so-called 'probability to vote question') that asks respondents how likely it is (on a 10-point scale from 'certainly never' to 'certainly at some time') that they would ever vote for each of the parties, which are then enumerated one by one.[27] Although rarely used for the purposes advocated here, the so-called

---

[23] Whereas the problems that arise from ipsativity are particularly damaging in multi-party contexts, the problem arising from a dichotomous representation of preference is equally relevant in pure two-party contexts (Burden 1997).

[24] An example of the latter is given by Tillie (1995, pp. 27–28). An example of incomplete results is the inability to assess the impact of party size on (ipsative) choice if no other questions are asked other than party/candidate choice (cf. van der Eijk et al., 1996, p. 352). The inability to assess the effect of this factor results in it being subsumed in the estimated effects of other variables, which are thus biased.

[25] Forms of logical mutual constraint (ipsativity) are not restricted to the standard 'party voted for' question. The same problems apply to a variety of question formats such as pick the k most preferred parties out of a series of n (for all values of k); rank-order a series of n parties according to preference; rank-order the k most preferred parties out of a series of n. By contrast, no logical mutual constraints exist in questions that apply any of the following logics (amongst others): indicate the level of preference for each of a series of n parties; indicate for each pair of parties which of the two is more preferred. Electoral systems that allow a detailed expression of preferences — such as STV — also necessitate more elaborate operationalization of electoral choice. Experience tells us, however, that here too ipsativity in the actual choice situation (rank-ordering implies ipsativity) should *not* be matched by ipsativity in question format but rather by preference ratings (cf. van der Brug et al., 2000a).

[26] Ideal measures of electoral utility fulfill the following criteria: (a) they yield for each respondent a score for each of the parties; (b) empirically, actual party choice coincides with the party that generates the highest utility; and (c) empirically, no factors are found that impinge upon the actual choice after controlling for electoral utilities.

[27] The responses to this question fulfill the requirements mentioned in footnote 26 with flying colors. In a series of EU-wide samples in 1994, the percentage of respondents that actually voted for the party with the highest utility ranges from 93 to 99% (van der Eijk et al., 1999). Similar results were obtained from a comparable study in the EU member-states in 1989 (van der Eijk et al., 1996). The qualifier 'ever' in the

sympathy or thermometer scale, which is included in many election studies (amongst others in the US and Germany), is an acceptable 'poor man's choice' as an electoral utility measure.[28] To arrive at more valid interpretations of the choice process, the core questions of voter surveys should, thus, not only include electoral participation and actual vote-choice, but also questions about the electoral utility for each of the options on offer.[29] Such electoral utility questions — one for each of the parties in the polit-ical system — require a special design for analysis, which is a straightforward extension of regression in space and time (Stimson, 1985).[30] In addition to providing a better basis for understanding electoral choice, these questions offer a number of advantages, which may be crucial for the further development of theories about elec-tions and voter behavior. I list some of these, briefly, and refer to examples that can be found in the literature.

- Most importantly, working with (properly validated) electoral utilities as dependent variables makes it possible to transcend proper names of parties in the analysis of electoral processes. Names of specific parties (Labour, CDU, or whatever) can be replaced by meaningful variables characterizing them (ideological position, stand on issues, esteem their leaders enjoy, size, government status, and the like), thus contributing to the development of more generic theories about electoral processes. This is particularly important in comparative studies, because it makes possible the combining of surveys from different systems in such a way that they can be analysed simultaneously. This, in turn, provides an optimal condition for assessing the ways in which a voter's calculus is (or is not) different in various countries (cf. van der Eijk and Franklin, 1996, chap. 20, van der Brug et al., 2000b).
- Measures of electoral utility permit — when analyzing party preferences and party choice — the introduction of independent variables external to the surveys and related to the characteristics of political parties. This is particularly relevant as these

question wording serves merely as a projective device, inviting respondents to disassociate themselves from the ipsativity usually imposed by the actual ballot (see, for validating analyses, Tillie, 1995). Some researchers have objected that it is not certain that respondents react to the projection as intended, rather than to the literal wording of the question. All empirical tests, however, indicate that respondents under-stand the question not as probing into an unknown future, but as asking about current preferences.

[28] To the extent of my knowledge, only the Dutch Parliamentary Election Study 1994 survey includes both the probability to vote questions and the sympathy scales, thus allowing a comparative assessment of their performance. It turns out that the probability to vote question performs better than the thermometer question in terms of criterion b (and hence also in terms of criterion c) mentioned in footnote 26. This seems to be caused by the stimulus 'sympathy' being less directly linked to electoral choice than 'how likely is it that you will ever vote for this party'. Nevertheless, when only thermometer scales are avail-able, they come a considerable way towards fulfilling the function of electoral utility measures. The only place where thermometer scales have actually been used as the kind of extension of the dependent variable advocated here is in analyses of issue-effects according to the directional paradigm (cf. Rabinowitz and McDonald, 1989).

[29] 'Each' of the parties on offer is often not feasible when taken literally. In much research the parties included are only those present in the awareness of a sufficiently large numbers of voters to warrant analysis.

[30] Detailed descriptions of how to apply this design with standard statistical packages are provided in van der Eijk and Franklin (1996, chap. 20) and Tillie (1995).

characteristics tend to change over time, while such changes can hardly be taken into account on the basis of proper names. This potential offers unique opportunities to link survey data with other data such as, for example, those of the Manifesto Research Group (cf. van der Brug 1997, 1999).

- Measures of electoral utility permit a much richer analysis of electoral competition than is possible with the classic party choice question. (van der Eijk and Niemöller, 1984; Tillie, 1995, chap. 5; van der Eijk and Franklin, 1996, chap. 3 and its subsequent applications). Moreover, using measures of electoral utility makes possible the construction of the kind of counterfactuals that are required for assessing the macro-effects of aspects of an election contest; such as, for example, the bonuses obtained or deficits incurred by parties because of the prominence of specific issues, the characteristics of party leaders, and so on.[31]
- Electoral utility questions allow for more detailed investigation of the basis of support for individual parties than is possible with only party-choice questions. They manifest, in addition to actual choice, strong support, which does not coincide with choice, and choice which does not coincide with strong support. This has proven to be invaluable in the study of small parties (cf. Rüdig and Franklin, 1991; van der Brug et al., 2000b), and in campaign research commissioned by political parties.
- With proper methods of analysis, measures of electoral utility permit the construction of comparable cross-study (often cross-national or longitudinal) measures of other variables, even when those have not been asked in identical terms in the surveys to be compared. Without the loss of information that is entailed by alternative procedures, this yields comparably scaled measures of, for example, income, occupation, and similar variables, which are notoriously difficult to standardize in comparative research (van der Eijk and Franklin, 1996, chaps. 19 and 20, Tillie, 1995, chap. 6).[32]

The use of special-purpose questions to observe the preference structures of voters regarding parties they did not vote for is hugely preferable to any of the methodological 'fixes' currently in vogue for handling polychotomous measures of party choice, most particularly multinomial logistic regression.[33] Such methods have — often unnoticed — the effect of imputing to voters who did not choose a party a derivative of the preferences of the voters who did choose that party. When these assumed preferences are compared with actual observations (in surveys which include the relevant questions) significant differences are commonly found. The truth of the matter is that

---

[31] Counterfactuals based on out-of-survey information are still ideal, but not always easy to construct in view of the implied demands for relevant data; cf. Anker (1992) who presents a generalized method of normal vote analysis applicable to multi-party systems. Yet, when such counterfactuals are not attainable, relevant 'what if' scenarios can be constructed from electoral utility measures (cf. van der Eijk, 1995).

[32] For a more detailed explanation, see Marsh (chapter 4).

[33] As a case in point, see Whitten and Palmer (1996), which is an excellent contribution to the topic of modeling voter choice in comparative research. In spite of their justified critique of existing practices, their own use of multinomial logit analyses implies assumptions about voters' preferences for parties they did not vote for that can be shown to coincide only partially with such preferences when actually observed. I will present relevant comparisons in more detail elsewhere (van der Eijk and Kroh 2002).

sophisticated statistical methods are not a sure means of replacing information that was never measured in the survey or anywhere else; in the case of information about parties not chosen, it is a very unsure method indeed.

6 Concluding remarks

The evolution of election studies into an increasing number of specialized sub-fields makes it progressively more difficult for national election studies to cater to the needs of each of these interests. For good reasons, this void tends to be filled by studies dedicated to these more specialized needs. This generates the question of the relationship between national election studies and other studies relevant to (aspects of) the electoral process. If not addressed, this question may undermine the status of national election studies as infrastructural data collection programs — a detrimental outcome for all concerned. I have argued in this chapter that the solution should not be sought in increasing the scope and detail of national election studies, but, rather, in keeping them lean and as focussed as possible on the 'core business' of election studies: phenomena associated with the election itself.

Such a focus involves the following. First, to measure the 'dependent variables' as extensively as possible, including the various aspects of electoral participation and electoral choice. As I argued, these should also comprise measurements of electoral utilities. Second, national election studies should include as independent variables those that provide maximum linkage potential to specialized studies within the sub-fields of electoral research, and to other kinds of external data (economic indicators, media markets, census information, and so on). This strategy will prevent unnecessary duplication of data collection efforts by national election studies and specialized election studies, while at the same time making it possible to combine creatively their respective data by linking them. This strategy will also make it easier for national election studies to adapt their designs to take better account of relevant contextual differences, as discussed in the next chapter of this volume. Focussing national election studies on these elements will also contribute to mitigating problems in the analyses of electoral processes that are as pervasive for 'mainstream' election studies as for research in sub-fields, most particularly problems associated with endogeneity.

References

Anker, H. 1992. Normal Vote Analysis. Het Spinhuis, Amsterdam.

van der Brug, W. 1997. Where's the Party? Voters' Perceptions of Party Positions. Doctoral Dissertation, University of Amsterdam.

van der Brug, W. 1999, Voters' perceptions and party dynamics, Party Politics 5, pp. 147–169.

van der Brug, W. 2001. Perceptions, opinions, and party preferences in the face of a real world event: Chernobyl as a natural experiment in political psychology, Journal of Theoretical Politics 13, pp. 53–80.

van der Brug, W., van der Eijk, C., Marsh, M. 2000. Exploring uncharted territory: The Irish Presidential Election 1997, British Journal of Political Science 30, pp. 631–650.

van der Brug, W., Fennema, M., Tillie, J. 2000. Anti-immigrant parties in Europe: ideological or protest vote?, European Journal of Political Research 37, pp. 77–102.

Burden, B. 1997. Deterministic and probabilistic voting models, American Journal of Political Science 41, pp. 1150–1169.

Buss, A. 1979. Toward a unified framework for psychometric concepts in the multivariate development situation: intraindividual change and inter- and intraindividual differences. In: Nesselroade, J., Baltes, P. (eds), Longitudinal Research in the Study of Behavior and Development. Academic Press, New York.

Cook, T., Campbell, D. 1979. Quasi-Experimentation. Design and Analysis Issues for Field Settings. Rand McNally, Chicago.

Coombs, C. 1964. A Theory of Data. Wiley, New York.

van der Eijk, C. 1998. Measuring agreement in ordered rating-scales. In: Fennema, M., van der Eijk, C., Schijf, H. (eds), In Search of Structure: Essays in Social Science and Methodology. Het Spinhuis, Amsterdam.

van der Eijk, C. 1995. Strijdpunten en politieke voorkeuren. In: van Holsteyn, J.J.M., Niemoller, B. (eds), De Nederlandse Kiezer 1994. DSWO Press, Leiden.

van der Eijk, C. and Kroh, M. 2002. Alchemy or Science? Discrete choice Models for Analysing Voter choice in Multi-Party Contests. Paper presented at the 2002 Annual Meeting of the American Political Science Association.

van der Eijk, C., Niemöller, K. 1979. Recall accuracy and its determinants, Acta Politica 14, pp. 289–342.

van der Eijk, C., Niemöller, K. 1983. Electoral Change in the Netherlands: Empirical Results and Methods of Measurement. CT Press, Amsterdam.

van der Eijk, C., Niemöller, K. 1984. Het Potentiële Electoraat van de Nederlandse Politieke Partijen, Beleid en Maatschappij 11, pp. 192–204.

van der Eijk, C., Schmitt, H. 1990. The role of the Eurobarometer in the study of European elections and the development of comparative electoral research. In: Reif, K., Inglehart, R. (eds), Eurobarometer: The Dynamics of European Public Opinion. Macmillan, London.

van der Eijk, C., Franklin, M. 1991. European community politics and electoral representation: evidence from the 1989 European Elections Study, European Journal of Political Research 19, pp. 105–128.

van der Eijk, C., Franklin, M. (eds). 1996. Choosing Europe? The European Electorate and National Politics in the Face of Union. University of Michigan Press, Ann Arbor, MI.

van der Eijk, C., Franklin, M., Oppenhuis, E. 1996. The strategic context: party choice. In: van der Eijk, C., Franklin, M. (eds), Choosing Europe? The European Electorate and National Politics in the Face of Union. University of Michigan Press, Ann Arbor, MI.

van der Eijk, C., Franklin, M., van der Brug, W. 1999. Policy preferences and party choice. In: Schmitt, H., Thomassen, J. (eds), Political Representation and Legitimacy in the European Union. Oxford University Press, Oxford.

Franklin, M. 1991. Getting out the vote: social structure and the mobilization of partisanship in the 1989 European elections, European Journal of Political Research 19, pp. 129–148.

Granberg, D. 1983. Preference, expectations and placement judgments: some evidence from Sweden, Social Psychology Quarterly 46, pp. 363–368.

Granberg, D., Holmberg, S. 1988. The Political System Matters: Social Psychology and Voting Behavior in Sweden and the United States. Cambridge University Press, Cambridge, UK.

Jöreskog, K., Sörbom, D. 1983. LISREL VI. Department of Statistics, University of Uppsala, Sweden.

Judd, C., Kenney, D., Krosnick, J. 1983. Judging the positions of political candidates: models of assimilation and contrast, Journal of Personality and Social Psychology 44, pp. 952–963.

Krosnick, J. 1990. Americans' perceptions of presidential candidates: a test of the projection hypothesis, Journal of Social Issues 46, pp. 159–182.

Maas, K., Steenbergen, M., Saris, W. 1990. Vote probabilities, Electoral Studies 9, pp. 91–107

Mill, J. 1975. A System of Logic. In: Collected Works of J.S. Mill. Routledge and Kegan Paul, London.

Mokken, R. 1971. A Theory and Procedure of Scale Analysis. Mouton, The Hague.

Nannestad, P., Paldam, M. 2000. Into Pandora's Box of economic evaluations: a study of the Danish macro VP-function, 1986–1997, Electoral Studies 19, pp. 123–140.

Oppenhuis, E. 1995. Voting Behavior in Europe: A Comparative Analysis of Electoral Participation and Party Choice. Het Spinhuis, Amsterdam.

Paldam, M., Nannestad, P. 2000. What do voters know about the economy? A study of Danish data, 1990–1993, Electoral Studies 19, pp. 363–391.

Pappi, F.-U. 1996. Political behavior: reasoning voters and multi-party systems. In: Goodin, R., Klingemann, H.-D. (eds), A New Handbook of Political Science. Oxford University Press, New York.

Rabinowitz, G., McDonald, S. 1989. A directional theory of issue voting, American Political Science Review 83, pp. 93–121.

Rüdig, W., Franklin, M. 1991. The Greening of Europe: Ecological Voting in the 1989 European Elections. University of Strathclyde Papers in Government and Politics, Glasgow.

Schmitt, H., Mannheimer, R. 1991. About voting and non-voting in the European elections of June 1989, European Journal of Political Research 19, pp. 31–54.

van Schuur, W. 1993. Nonparametric unfolding models for multicategory data, Political Analysis 4, pp. 41–74.

Stimson, J. 1985. Regression in space and time: a statistical essay, American Journal of Political Science 18, pp. 191–214.

Thomassen, J. 1975. Party identification as a cross-cultural concept: its meaning in the Netherlands, Acta Politica 10, pp. 36–56.

Tillie, J. 1995. Party Utility and Voting Behavior. Het Spinhuis, Amsterdam.

Traugott, M., Katosh, J. 1979. Response validity in surveys of voting behavior, Public Opinion Quarterly 43, pp. 359–377.

Weisberg, H. 1980. A multi-dimensional conceptualization of party identification, Political Behavior 2, pp. 33–60.

Willenborg, L., de Waal, T. 2000. Elements of Statistical Disclosure Control. Springer, New York.

Whitten, G., Palmer, H. 1996. Heightening comparativists' concern for model choice: voting behavior in Great Britain and the Netherlands, American Journal of Political Science 40, pp. 231–260.

Wlezien, C., Franklin, M., Twiggs, D. 1997. Economic perceptions and vote choice: disentangling the endogeneity, Political Behavior 19, pp. 7–17.

Chapter 4

Electoral context

M. Marsh

This chapter explores the importance of context in election studies. A distinction is made between global and compositional effects, and those resulting from measurement error. While compositional effects are essentially spatial, global effects may also result from temporal variation. The mechanisms through which such effects come about are outlined and then some different designs for exploring and assessing such effects are considered. Particular attention is paid to work on contextual effects using British election studies, the work of Huckfeldt and Sprague on one US locality, and comparative studies such as the European election studies and the Comparative Study of Electoral Systems project. It is argued that global contextual effects merit more attention than compositional ones.

1 Introduction

Context in election research most often means the locality. The importance of the 'local' in explaining an individual's electoral behaviour is accepted in many countries, although localism might not be as pronounced in all countries as it appears to be in Ireland, where local deviations from national patterns are commonplace and a national election can be described, with only some degree of exaggeration, as '41 local elections'. The importance, such as it is, of 'local' context for understanding individual behaviour stems from several factors.

First, and most obviously, the voter may be faced with a different practical choice, with different names and possibly different parties on the ballot paper according to the constituency. This difference affects all those in an area, and this type of contextual effect for this reason has been called a 'global' effect (Lazarsfeld and Menzel, 1972, p. 228). Continuing the example, one global effect may affect all localities. This is the context of the general election itself: the stances of the parties; the record of the government; and the nature of the issue agenda. All elections, like opinion polls, are in reality snapshots in time and we should take account of this in assessing the electorate's choices. A second reason why local context matters for individual decision-making is that the composition of 'local' units varies with respect to dependent and/or the independent variables.[1] Such an effect is often called 'contextual' (Huckfeldt and Sprague, 1995, pp. 10–11) although this term can be misleading since there are other types of effects deriving from context. I shall call such an effect 'compositional' here. With respect to the dependent variable for instance, parties have more support in some areas than in others, and where a party is strong on the ground, it may have a better chance of converting the undecided and mobilising the faithful. Countless studies in many countries have demonstrated such compositional effects, showing, for instance, that the probability of an individual changing his vote from one election to another may be proportional to the strength of the majority party in an area (see Huckfeldt and Sprague, 1993). In an insightful article, McLean (1973) pointed out that the phenomenon of 'constant swing' at constituency level (a shift in vote support of x% in each constituency) which typically characterised British elections depended, in fact, on such variable probabilities at the individual level. National uniformity thus demanded a local contextual effect!

These two reasons cover the usual applications of the term contextual effect, but there is one other important reason. This is that the local (or temporal) context may be important because factors that are apparently equivalent are not actually equivalent at all. This may be true of individual measures. A small farmer in the west of Ireland may be a very different creature, responding to different markets, or having quite different expectations compared to a small farmer just outside Dublin. Moving to a different level, the nature of a party, or the meaning of an issue, may also vary across time or space sufficiently to undermine assumptions of equivalence.

These different reasons give rise to different uses of the term context but are all potentially important in any explanation of electoral behaviour, threatening to bias any results obtained if they are ignored. This threat comes about for two reasons. First, this is because context is an omitted variable. If a model excludes a variable that is systematically related to the dependent variables as well as an independent variable, estimates will be biased, perhaps alarmingly so. For instance, positive relationships may be estimated as negative or strong relationships estimated as weak. This is always a potential problem, but arguably omitted contextual variables are particularly likely to pose this threat. A second reason stems from false assumptions of equivalence. This leads to systematic measurement error that again may depress, exaggerate, or reverse the signs attached to the estimated coefficients. Ignoring context, then, has potentially invalidating consequences for our results.

Context is also important because, even if our estimates are not biased, we may still misunderstand exactly why our model works. Variables indicating group affiliations, for instance, may prove significant predictors of the vote without our model indicating the process through which such affiliations matter. Specifying the context explicitly enables us to test particular understandings of how and why the context matters.

---

[1] In one sense, variations in these are trivial. Parties may do better in one area than another because the former contains more of their natural supporters. The context becomes interesting when this explanation is no longer sufficient, when the party does better, or worse, than would be expected and thus individuals behave in unexpected ways.

2 How does context matter?

Two quite different mechanisms may generate compositional effects.[2] One is inter-personal communication, the classic 'neighbourhood' effect. A voter may be drawn to the majority viewpoint or party simply as a result of everyday conversations in which the information and evaluations conveyed are biased towards one viewpoint. This appears as a tendency for individuals who might otherwise be expected to vote for party B to vote for party A when the latter is very strong in a district. A second mech-anism is personal experience and observation. Voters may acquire information and make evaluations by looking as well as by talking. Their neighbourhood provides the major experiential source. Again, this may appear as a compositional effect, but rests on quite different foundations. These two mechanisms, although typically associated with compositional differences, may also be responsible for the impact of global effects. The structuring of information, via TV, radio stations, or local newspapers, may generate global effects directly, or indirectly through the flow of personal commu-nication.[3]

Quite a different mechanism is selection bias (see Johnson et al., chapter 5). This is where people from an area behave differently from what would be expected on the basis of individual-level characteristics because such people have selected themselves on the basis of a difference on the dependent variable of interest. If voters choose to live close to other voters of a similar political outlook, contextual effects will mani-fest themselves when we are modelling such outlooks. Arguably these should be seen as spurious, but they certainly appear as contextual effects (Achen and Shively, 1995). The importance of such a mechanism depends on the likelihood of individuals selecting an area because of its partisanship as opposed to cost, the location of family, friends, schools, or jobs. For the most part this seems unlikely, and although choice may be determined by a wider set of political attitudes[4], these can be controlled for in a properly specified model.

3 What can be done

The existence of contextual factors raises a number of issues for research design and analysis.[5] These involve both what should be studied and how that should be done. Should the emphasis be on the effect or the mechanism, what sort of effects are most

---

[2] This is a simplified description. For a broader discussion see, for example, Burbank (1994).

[3] Books and Prysby (1994) p. 258) see local mass media as a third mechanism for contextual effects. It seems to make more sense to see them as a global factor mediated by personal consumption or interper-sonal contact, or both.

[4] 'If there are *any* direct effects of the independent variable or its correlates on geographic location — effects not mediated by the independent variable(s) — then phantom 'contextual' effects will be created to confound analysis in aggregate data' (Achen and Shively, 1995 p. 227 emphasis original).

[5] I mean here analysis in the most general sense. As far as statistical analysis is concerned there is a large literature on what are appropriate models for the multi-level data structures implied by contextual effects. See, for example, Iverson (1990).

important, and how can these best be studied? The most common approach is simply to add more variables to the election study to enable the analyst to capture context, assessing the effect, and at least considering the mechanism. In its simplest manifestation, this entails adding data about localities to the basic data file on individuals, supplementing conventional election study data with census data and other material relating to the smallest possible geographical districts. Voters may also be asked about their locality, providing information on their perceptions of the social and political environment. British election studies, for example, have been doing this in one way or another for some time, and many research questions have been explored using such data. One research theme has been devoted to explain the regional differences in changing support patterns. Some have argued that the effects of certain variables are not constant across all regional contexts. In contrast McAllister and Studlar (1992), echoing the seminal critique of contextual effects by Hauser (1974), argued that regional differences were merely a function of individual-level variations across the country. Controlling for social composition, various political attitudes, constituency profile, and economic evaluations, they demonstrated that little regional variation remained unaccounted for. In essence, the apparent effects could be explained purely by differences in the composition of different areas, across which individual-level variables had constant, not differential, impacts. What remains problematic about this critique is whether contextual effects have been shown to be spurious or merely 'interpreted' in statistical terms. The disappearance of regional differences when controls for political attitudes are introduced, for instance, may be held to demonstrate how and why regions are different, rather than demonstrating that, other things being equal, they are all the same.

The debate continues as others argue that differences between regions are significant, and that there are clear contextual effects on individual-level variables. Pattie and Johnston (1995) use the 1992 British Election Study items on perceptions of the regional economy to test whether regional differences stem from evaluations of local economic conditions. They find some evidence for this, but conclude that 'region still matters' when such variables are taken into account. Either way, their analysis suggests that local differences cannot be explained away even if their source remains uncertain. Pattie and Johnston (1997) argue that 'global' cultural and economic factors are the most likely reasons, and dismiss the argument for 'neighbourhood' communications on several grounds: that differences occur in areas which are too large for such effects to work; that such a model performs badly in explaining short-term changes rather than long-term stability; and the lack of communication about politics within neighbourhoods.

Regions, such as Wales, the South West, and the Midlands, are of course large and often amorphous areas. Some work has also been done on much smaller units, examining constituency and even ward-level effects on voting. Such effects have been identified by, for instance, Heath et al. (1985, pp. 76–78) who demonstrated differences in the propensity of working class voters to support the Conservative party according to the class composition of their ward — a local electoral area. Curtice (1995) also looked at the mechanisms underpinning apparent compositional effects at district level and found no support for the role of interpersonal communication. For the most part, while there has been interesting work done on regional patterns, neighbourhood effects, as well as tactical voting (Evans et al., 1998; cf. Catt, 1996), the importance of locality has been an 'add on' in UK studies. This may easily be justified, at least with respect to compositional effects. Bodman (1983) argued that whatever effects existed were relatively small, and the weight of later analysis to date has not provided grounds for any major reassessment of this conclusion.

A rather different approach is typified in the work of Huckfeldt and Sprague (1995). Their study is a good example of one designed specifically to uncover the process of individual decision-making, and the mechanisms through which context matters. It is an election study, in the sense that it deals with the behaviour of voters in an election, but, like the earliest election studies (e.g. Berelson et al., 1954), it employs a local rather than a national sample. Huckfield and Sprague are interested not in explaining the national decision but in the decision-making processes of voters, the extent to which decisions are contextually determined, and, in particular, the processes underlying this.

Huckfield and Sprague's study took the city of South Bend, Indiana, as the research site. A stratified sampling design was employed, with neighbourhoods (areas of around 2000 inhabitants)[6] selected to reflect a variety of class and ethnic compositions; 1500 individuals were selected randomly within those neighbourhoods. Official information of various kinds was available for those neighbourhoods, which could be used as described above. In addition, Huckfeldt and Sprague interviewed some 900 people with whom voters claimed to discuss important matters, including politics. Thus, the authors had a database which included voters from a variety of local contexts, plus information about the informal network to which voters belonged. Working from the assumption that individual voters are part of a rich variety of social interaction patterns, they use these data to describe those patterns, and to examine the micro-mechanisms of social influence during campaigns and the roles played by parties in exercising social influence. A constant theme is the manner in which local majorities and community norms are perpetuated.

Addressing the issue of whether campaigns matter, and, if so, how, Huckfeldt and Sprague demonstrate how campaigns activate supporters, who, in turn, via their own networks, influence others. Neighbourhood matters. The differences in visible campaign efforts — posters on houses or lawns and bumper stickers — influence how people think their neighbourhood will vote independently of their own orientations and the actual orientations of the neighbourhood. Party identification is affected similarly. Even with individual controls for several factors, neighbourhood party identification exercises a significant impact on an individual's party loyalty. Huckfeldt and Sprague argue that what channels much of this influence is the informal pattern of communications. Voters do not control who they come into contact with, and they are rarely insulated from their environment. Thus, the makeup of their environment will have some effect on their attitudes and behaviour. Vote choice itself is influenced by the vote choice of those who discussed politics with the primary respondents.

---

[6] 'Neighbourhoods are important because they determine proximity and exposure — they serve to structure important elements if involuntary social interaction' (Huckfeldt and Sprague 1995, p. 36).

One important aspect of this study is that context is not described in geographical terms but in terms of communication networks. While neighbourhoods are concrete localities, Huckfeldt and Sprague are also interested in work, churchgoing, and other social networks, each of which can be influential. Environment acts as a 'filter' for political communications (Huckfeldt et al., 1995), but which environment is most important? If the task is to construct a regression model including appropriate individual and contextual variables, and individual/contextual interactions, where should one stop? Books and Prysby (1991) argue it is expedient to confine attention to formal localities, even if other networks may be influential. Reviewing this work, Huckfeldt (1992, p. 091)) demurs, citing 'a whole series of alternative contexts connected to workplaces, churches, tavern, bowling leagues, and so on. Each of these contexts, in turn, serves to establish constraints and opportunities acting on political experience, and hence on the acquisition of political information'. There is little recognition of the value of parsimony in models of voting behaviour constructed on such foundations. All individuals operate in their own unique social context. What we must seek to do is to define the main parameters of these contexts.

While Huckfeldt and Sprague's strategy is reasonable if the goal is to explore the relative importance of different contexts, it has no justification in a full-scale election study unless it can be shown that all of these contexts are necessary components of an acceptable explanatory model. Some comfort for those committed to simple models comes from the apparent size of the sort of effects identified by Huckfeldt and Sprague. While they are often significant, they are generally not large, being one of the many influences. Moreover, discussions between spouses seem to be much more effective than those between other pairs of individuals; and discussions between unrelated individuals are not significant at all (Huckfeldt and Sprague, 1993, Table 9.3).

If full generalisation of Huckfeldt and Sprague's approach to national studies remains, at best, problematic, it is clear that national election studies can pay attention to locality, and even to patterns of political discussion. For instance, MacKuen and Brown (1987) use data from the 1980 American National Election Study to examine neighbourhood and county-level effects on opinion formation and attitude change to illustrate that the exploration of such issues can be done within national election studies, as did Miller's (1956) paper some 30 years earlier. Several national surveys have been carried out which employ some of the same techniques (Huckfeldt et al., 1995). A recent paper using such data on several countries (Beck and Richardson, 1999) finds that political communication is only weakly channelled along partisan lines. While this supports Huckfeldt and Sprague's conclusion about the extent to which people do not control whom they come into contact with (and hence the importance of networks which structure social interaction), one might argue, alternatively, that the uncertainty of contact makes any attempt to measure it increasingly fruitless.

Another strategy for dealing with context is by over-sampling interesting contexts. In a national election study, this would demand some disproportional sampling of certain units (see chapter 6). This is the typical design in comparative studies, where sample size at national level is not proportional to country size. Beck and Richardson's paper uses data from several countries, although this aspect is not central to their conclusions. In other work, the national context has been much more central, notably in European election studies carried out in 1989, 1994 (van der Eijk et al., 1996a), and 1999. In much of this work, as in that of Huckfeldt and Sprague, the focus is more on electoral behaviour than on election outcome, but national samples are used and, more importantly, the design is comparative across countries, which also highlights issues of equivalence.

The European Election Studies (EES) were fielded ostensibly not only to study the behaviour of voters in elections to the European Parliament, but also to study the behaviour of European voters (van der Eijk and Franklin, 1996; van der Eijk et al., 1996a). The European Parliament elections are held almost simultaneously in EU member states. The dominant theoretical tool for understanding electoral behaviour in these contests is that the elections are essentially second-order national elections. That is, there is not one European election but many national ones, and in each national election national circumstances are critical; in particular, the national circumstances relating to national parties and the competition for power within the national political system (Reif and Schmitt, 1980). Aggregate data illustrates some obvious patterns consistent with this view. For instance, government parties tend to perform worse in European Parliament elections than they would in a national election, falling short of their vote share either in the previous or the next national parliamentary election. Furthermore, in elections to the first four directly elected parliaments, their perform- ance is related to the timing of the European Parliament election in the national election cycle (Marsh, 1998). This is but one way in which electoral behaviour may be influ- enced by national context.

The EES study design makes national context central. It does so in several ways. The most important is the sampling strategy. The sample is not a simple random one of European voters but a disproportionate stratified random sample (see Stoker, chapter 6), with normally 1000 respondents from each EU country. Given the huge variation in country size between, at one extreme, Germany and, at the other, Luxembourg, this is very disproportionate.[7] However, it provides the necessary database for identifying national differences in voting behaviour. A sample of the same size designed simply to maximise inference to the European electorate would have far too few individuals to assess the extent to which voters in Ireland, Denmark, or Sweden fitted the European model as well as those in France, The Netherlands, or Finland.

This fact about the study design can be made use of in several ways. First, of course, country context is a coded variable, so various aspects of national circumstances unmeasured by the survey can be added to the data set. These include things such as which parties are in government, or how much time has elapsed since the last elec- tion, or is due to elapse before the next one. Of course, this can be done with a conventional study design, but in the EES the number of cases from each significant context is sufficient to make this worthwhile. A second added element is the ability to tailor questions to the context. It is known, for example, which parties are competing, which issues are salient, and which newspapers are read.

---

[7] In fact, Luxembourg tends to have a smaller sample, as does Northern Ireland, which is treated as a sepa- rate national context from mainland Britain. Flanders and Wallonia are treated as separate sampling units in Belgium.

A more extensive, as well as more intensive, version of the EES is the Comparative Study of Electoral Systems project (CSES).[8] This has sought to construct an extensive database to answer questions about the impact of different electoral institutions on electoral behaviour by placing a small module of appropriate questions in national election study questionnaires. It is a collaborative venture which now encompasses over 50 countries. There are several general themes but a key one is: to what extent, and in what ways, is the impact of the characteristics of individuals on vote choice and satisfaction with democracy contingent upon institutional structures? A few papers have now been written using these data (Blais et al., 1999; Karp and Banducci, 1999; Norris, 1999) and more are in preparation.

Equivalence remains a major problem even with such a design. A novel approach to the problem is that of van der Eijk et al. (1996a) who sought to generate equivalent measures from the very different contextual and cultural environments of the EU member states. In order to examine the impact of religion, for example, on party choice, van der Eijk et al. (1996b) estimate for their measure of party support the value predicted by two measures of religion (a voter's religious denomination and frequency of church attendance). Religion is related in nationally unique ways to parties, due to the different histories of politicisation, different party options, and the different demographies of religious observance. But in a cross-national study they were really interested in how far party preference can be understood from the way in which religion and party are entwined. These predicted values (y-hats) can be thought of as measures of the extent to which religion determines preferences for that party — and the accuracy of these measures is shown by the association between preferences and the y-hats.[9] When the exercise is repeated across parties and countries, this provides a measure of 'predicted religious effect' which is cross-nationally comparable. The correlation between the y-hats (for religion) and party choice then shows the relationship between religion and party choice, allowing for the differences in parties across contexts and the differences in the extent to which religion has been politicised. This technique can be used for many independent variables.

4 Conclusions

This brief review of contextual effects has sought to identify the main types of, and reasons for, contextual effects, and to point to some ways in which the design of election studies can take such effects into account. A few points are worth emphasising here. First, within-nation compositional effects, however interesting, are in the main quite small. This is evident even in the work of those, like Huckfeldt, committed to exploring them. To some degree they may be explained away, as Hauser (1974)

---

[8] See Thomassen et al. (1994) for the original design arguments and the CSES web pages for details of on-going studies: www.umich.edu/~nes/cses.

[9] It should be clear that this does not tell us *why* religion is more important in one country than another. That is a very interesting question, but not one of the objectives of the EES study, and would certainly require a rather different study design if it were to be a central question.

suggested. This, of course, may beg further questions — for example, about the processes earlier in the chain of explanation — but arguably these are the proper focus of studies other than those fundamentally concerned with an election. This implies that the resources in national election studies devoted to capturing them should also be modest, unless there are strong grounds for thinking them to be very significant.

A stronger case may be made for considering 'global' contextual effects. There is a wealth of comparative literature that has pointed out the importance of such factors for electoral behaviour, and the CSES project promises much more. The 'context' of a particular election is an obvious factor (see Curtice, this volume, chapter 1), as are variations in party systems in comparative studies. Media structures, institutions facilitating accountability, and economic performance are all potentially important contextual variables. Some of these may be appropriate factors for consideration at the local level in the national election studies, particularly in less nationalised political systems. Global factors may also be more likely to be fitted into a geographical context, an election district, or constituency, unlike many possible compositional effects.

This ties in with a final point: attention should also be paid to the equivalence of measurement. What is an obvious problem in comparative studies is less widely considered within national studies. As national election studies are increasingly used for time-series analysis (see Erikson, this volume, chapter 7), and as parts of wider comparative studies, these issues will receive more attention. Yet even within a national study, the question of the equivalence across districts of dependent and independent variables may sometimes be problematic.

Acknowledgments

I would like to thank Cees van der Eijk and the anonymous reviewers for their helpful comments but naturally absolve them from any responsibility for the consequences.

References

Achen, C., Shively, W. 1995. Cross-level Inference. University of Chicago Press, Chicago.

Blais, A., Gidengil, E., Nadeau, R., Nevitte, N. 1999. Measuring party identification: Canada, Britain, and the United States. Paper presented at the Annual Meeting of the American Political Science Association.

Beck, P., Richardson, B. 1999. The communication contexts of voting behaviour: a cross-national comparison. Paper presented at the Annual Meeting of the American Political Science Association.

Bodman, A. 1983. The neighbourhood effect: a test of the Butler–Stokes model, British Journal of Political Science 13, pp. 243–249.

Books, J., Prysby, C. 1991. Political Behaviour and the Local Context. Praeger, New York.

Books, J., Prysby, C. 1994. On the future of contextual models of political behaviour. In: Eagles, M. (ed.), Spatial and Contextual Models in Political Research. Taylor and Francis, London.

Berelson, B., Lazarsfeld, P., McPhee, W. 1954. Voting: A Study of Opinion Formation in a Presidential Election. University of Chicago Press, Chicago.

Burbank, M. 1994. How do contextual effects work? Developing a theoretical model. In: Eagles, M. (ed.), Spatial and Contextual Models in Political Research. Taylor and Francis, London.

Catt, H. 1996. Voting Behaviour: A Radical Critique. Leicester University Press, London.

Curtice, J. 1995. Is talking over the garden fence of political import? In: Eagles, M. (ed.), Spatial and Contextual Models in Political Research. Taylor and Francis, London.

van der Eijk, C., Franklin, M. (eds). 1996. Choosing Europe? The European Electorate and National Politics in the Face of Union. University of Michigan Press, Ann Arbor, MI.

van der Eijk, C., Franklin, M., Marsh, M. 1996. What voters tell us about Europe-wide elections; what Europe-wide elections tell us about voters, Electoral Studies 15, pp. 149–166.

van der Eijk, C., Franklin, M., Oppenhuis, E. 1996. The strategic context: party choice. In: van der Eijk, C., Franklin, M. (eds).

Evans, G., Curtice, J., Norris, P. 1998. New Labour, new tactical voting? In: Denver, D., Fisher, J., Cowley, P., Pattie, C. (eds), The 1997 General Election, British Elections and Parties Review 8. Frank Cass, London.

Hauser, R. 1974. Contextual analysis revisited, Sociological Methods and Research 2, pp. 365–376.

Heath, A., Jowell, R., Curtice, J. 1985. How Britain Votes. Pergamon Press, Oxford.

Huckfeldt, R. 1992. Review of books and Prysby's political behaviour and the local context, Journal of Politics 54, pp. 1190–1192.

Huckfeldt, R., Sprague, J. 1993. Citizens, contexts and politics. In: Finifter, A. (ed.), Political Science: The State of the Discipline II. APSA, Washington, DC.

Huckfeldt, R., Beck, P., Dalton, R., Levine, J. 1995. Political environments, cohesive social groups, and the communication of public opinion, American Journal of Political Science 39, pp. 1025–1054.

Huckfeldt, R., Sprague, J. 1995. Citizens, Politics and Social Communication. Cambridge University Press, Cambridge.

Iverson, G. 1990. Contextual Analysis. Sage, London.

Karp, J., Banducci, S. 1999. Electoral rules and voter participation: a cross-national analysis of individual-level behavior. Paper presented at the Annual Meeting of the American Political Science Association.

Lazarsfeld, P., Menzel, H. 1972. On the relation between individual and collective properties. In: Lazarsfeld, P., Pasanella, A. and Rosenberg, M. (eds), Continuities in the Language of Social Research. Free Press, Glencoe.

MacKuen, M., Brown, C. 1987. Political context and attitude change, American Political Science Review 81, pp. 471–490.

McAllister, I., Studlar, D. 1992. Region and voting in Britain: territorial polarisation or artifact? American Journal of Political Science 3, pp. 168–199.

McLean, I. 1973. The problem of proportionate swing, Political Studies 21, pp. 57–63.

Marsh, M. 1998. Testing the second-order election model after four European elections, British Journal of Political Science 28, pp. 591–607.

Miller, W. 1956. One-party politics and the voter, American Political Science Review 50, pp. 707–725.

Norris, P. 1999. Ballots not bullets: testing consociational theories of ethnic conflict, electoral systems and democratization. Paper prepared for the International Conference on Institutional Design, Conflict Management and Democracy in the Late Twentieth Century.

Pattie, C., Johnston, R. 1995. It's not like that around here — region, economic evaluations and voting at the British 1992 General Election, European Journal of Political Research 28, pp. 1–32.

Pattie, C., Johnston, R. 1997. Local economic contexts and changing party allegiance at the 1992 British general election, Party Politics 3, pp. 79–96.

Reif, K., Schmitt, H. 1980. Nine second-order national elections: a conceptual framework for the analysis of European Election results, European Journal of Political Research 8, pp. 3–44.

Thomassen, J., Rosenstone, S., Klingemann, H.-D., Curtice, J. 1994. The Comparative Study of Electoral Systems. Stimulus paper for a conference on The Comparative Study of Electoral Systems. ICORE, Berlin.

Chapter 5

Contextual data and the study of elections and voting behavior: Connecting individuals to environments

M. Johnson, W. Phillips Shively and R.M. Stein

Studies of contextual processes have always involved the possibility that if individuals' aggregation into geographic units is not exogenous to their values on the dependent variable, then what appear to be 'contextual processes' may be solely due to selection effects. We propose a method to test whether observed contextual effects are real or phantom. The integration of individuals in their neighborhoods is measured by response latency on questions about the neighborhood; if contextual effects are based on what happens to people in their neighborhoods (that is, the apparent effects are not solely because of selection effects), they should be more pronounced among those who are most integrated into their neighborhood. An empirical example illustrates the technique. We propose instrumentation by which electoral studies can test for true contextual effects. The availability of this test should encourage greater emphasis in electoral studies on the search for contextual processes.

1 Introduction

The collection and analysis of contextual data has a long and mixed tradition in the study of elections and voting behavior (for reviews, see Huckfeldt and Sprague, 1993; Achen and Shively, 1995; Books and Prysby, 1991). Contextual analysis has enriched political theory by studying the voter as more than an isolated individual making solely individual decisions. The circumstances under which individuals make their decisions, and the varied influences that work on them in their social environments, have come to the fore in contextual analysis.

The Future of Election Studies
ISBN: 0-08-044174-2

Two problems have dogged contextual analysis, however: the proper measurement of context, and the problem of selection bias in aggregation, which can create phantom 'contextual effects' where none truly exist.[1] In this chapter we explore a strategy to improve the conceptualization and measurement of contexts. Further, by bringing the measure of context closer to the individual, the research design we offer provides a test for the problems associated with selection in aggregation. We propose that the effect of context on individuals can be identified with greater certainty by measuring the extent to which individuals are connected to their contexts; that is, by measuring the accessibility of context in decision-making.

2 A definition of context[2]

In its generic form, context refers to the environment in which individuals reside and behave. Contextual analysis asks how these 'environmental properties determine variation in a given behavior of interest' (Sprague, 1982, p. 100). Two common uses of context are popular with social scientists studying elections and voting behavior. The first refers to specific institutional structures, rules, and procedures that formally or informally define relationships among individuals and, in turn, influence individual behavior. We consider this aspect first.

Rules governing the aggregation of votes (by plurality, simple majority, or super-majority), the method of representation (at-large versus single member), and the scope of the franchise (white male versus universal suffrage) have been found to directly influence the outcome of elections and the behavior of individual voters. Consequently, it is common to collect and analyze information on different institutional variables when conducting election studies. Rational choice theory provides a straight-forward explanation for how electoral rules influence the choices of individual voters and outcome of elections: "the outcome resulting from the game depends upon the set of feasible outcomes, individual preference, and the rules which govern the game . . ." (Plott, 1978). Rules are taken to be exogenous to individual behavior; and the level at which we measure institutional rules is determined by the unit and level of analysis at which research is being conducted.[3] Institutional measures of context are readily available and have been routinely included in national election surveys since the 1960s. Our concern in this chapter, however, is with the study of social context and its influence on elections and electoral behavior.

A second conceptualization of context and contextual analysis refers to the social setting in which individuals function: "Contextual theories of politics are built on an assertion of behavioral interdependence: the actions of individual citizens are to be understood as the intersection between individually defined circumstances" (Huckfeldt and Sprague, 1993, p. 281). In this regard, individual behavior is contingent upon the

[1] See Achen and Shively (1995, pp. 230–232).
[2] This section draws heavily upon Sprague (1982) and Huckfeldt and Sprague (1993)
[3] Of course, assuming the exogeneity of rules is quite problematic. Do systems using a proportional representation rule exhibit a more divided party landscape because PR causes a multiplication of parties, for instance; or is it because divided societies find it easier to live with a PR rule than with a plurality rule? For a further discussion of these issues, see Taagepera and Shugart (1989) and Monroe (1995).

environment created by the aggregation of individual traits: "A theory is contextual when variation in some aggregated individual trait (mean income, percent white, etc.) produces variation in an observed individual behavior among individuals who share the aggregate trait" (Huckfeldt and Sprague, 1993, p. 281). Sprague refers to this condition as 'social resonance' as the underlying intuition is 'one of reinforcement of a property possessed by an individual through repeatedly encountering the same property in the environment' (Sprague, 1982, p. 101). A related, but more complex, contextual model is 'behavioral contagion'. Here the observed individual behavior is a function of the observed aggregate behavior. A voter ballots for a Democratic candidate because significant proportions of his neighbors do the same. Underlying contextual explanations of individual behavior, is the process of social interaction among individuals. The product of these social interactions, especially for those individuals strongly imbedded in these social networks, should be an observable correlation between individual attitudes, behavior, and group messages.

Central to contextual analysis is cross-level inference. Substantively, this means "observing individuals at the same time we observe the collective properties of the aggregates within which individuals are embedded" (Huckfeldt and Sprague, 1993, p. 284). In their simplest form, "contextual studies aim to demonstrate that friends' and neighbors' opinions cause one's own opinions" (Achen and Shively, 1995, p. 230). The problems associated with cross-level inferences were popularized by Robinson's (1950) paper on the ecological fallacy associated with behavioral inferences drawn from aggregate data analysis. We do not intend to review the history of cross-level inference. Several volumes, including Achen and Shively (1995) and King (1997), address solutions for the ecological fallacy. The focus of our review is on the use of contextual analysis and explanations for individual level behavior.

3 Pseudo-contextual effects and threats to contextual analysis

A central problem of contextual analysis has been that, because the forces allegedly at work are observable only in aggregates, social context cannot always be taken as exogenous. In fact, it may be that context is almost never fully exogenous. Contextual explanations of individual behavior are valid only if we can establish that the location of individuals in a district, city, or other aggregation unit, is uncorrelated with values on the dependent variable.[4] In the absence of this independence we have a classic selection bias, and cannot establish an independent relationship between context and the individual-level dependent variable. Although they were by no means the first to show this, Achen and Shively (1995) demonstrate the potential of geographic selection to produce phantom, apparently contextual, effects by a simulation in which people choose where to live in a city based on how strongly they support funds for schools. In their simulation, there is no individual-to-individual influence; rather, all

---

[4] More specifically, the partial correlation between area location and the dependent variable, controlling for the individual variable(s), must be zero. That is, there can be no independent effect of the dependent variable on individuals' location in districts.

members of the population have fixed opinions on how much money the schools should get. In the simulation, opinion on this question varies with social class. These individuals then migrate to neighborhoods in the city, based partly on the situation of schools in the neighborhood. As a result, like-minded people tend to live together. Those who favor school spending (for instance) have tended to move into the districts with higher taxes and better schools. Purely as a result of this self-selection into districts, a strong apparently contextual effect emerges: in districts that are 40% middle class, about 20% of middle-class residents support higher school expenditure; in districts that are 70% middle class, about 90% of the middle-class residents support higher school expenditure. Researchers confronted with these data might be tempted to attribute this phenomenon to a contextual effect, despite the fact that *no individual in the simulation exerted any influence over any of her neighbours.*

It is suggested elsewhere (van der Eijk, this volume, chapter 3) that one way of eliminating the endogeneity problem is to measure contextual variables separately from the individual-level variables, and later to connect them to the survey data by means of linkage variables. The purpose of this procedure is to break one of the links between the respondents and their context by avoiding reliance on respondents for information about their contexts. It should be noted, however, that this solution will not eliminate phantom contextual effects due to geographic selection. Geographic selection, when it exists, would be problematic no matter how the characteristics of the neighborhoods were measured. Indeed, they would be more apparent the more accurately neighborhood characteristics were measured.

Obviously, if selection patterns like this are widespread, they cast a pall of doubt over any empirical demonstration of contextual effects. How widespread are these selection patterns? One obvious example of selection bias occurs in research on racial and ethnic tolerance, but the problem is likely to be quite widespread indeed. Achen and Shively (1995, p. 227) point out:

> Similarly, people who like to hunt will tend to cluster together, as will those who like chamber music, those who oppose abortion, those who like to do yard work, and so on. Any of these may correlate with political choices; at one point early in the postwar period, public opinion pollsters in West Germany found that their best single predictor of voting behavior was whether people had little statues of dwarves in their gardens.

It is possible that almost any contextual variable could show apparent effects on voting and other political behavior, whether or not a true contextual effect was present.

Several solutions for the endogeneity effects of selection have been offered. Erbring and Young (1979) operationalize the social context as the scores on the dependent variable of all other individuals with whom the respondent is in contact. Thus, the context effect is measured at the individual level. Of course, identifying the myriad of discussants in each respondent's social network is a daunting task. Moreover, since in their model influence works both ways in each dyad, estimating discussant effects requires structural equation techniques where the number of equations (that is, dyadic interactions) might exceed the number of individuals in the network.[5] Huckfeldt and Sprague's research approaches this measurement problem by identifying the respondent's 'main' discussant and regressing vote choice on the discussant's vote choice, other individual demographic traits, and levels of union membership in the respondent's neighborhood. While this is an important step forward, it still requires a contextual measure — union strength in the neighborhood — that carries the endogeneity problem in its train. So, our dilemma is that, of the various solutions, only Erbring and Young solve the endogeneity problem fully; by reducing context to a set of solely individual-level relationships. In practice, however, their solution is probably unworkable.

It should be possible, nonetheless, to mitigate the problem of endogeneity by deriving from the contextual model purely individual-level relationships that — while they do not express the contextual model directly — are predicted by the model and serve as indirect tracers for the presence of its contextual effects. For instance, if contextual effects are present, we would expect those for whom the context is most relevant and important to exhibit the effects most strongly. This prediction can be tested using a solely individual-level measure, with none of the problems of aggregation and selection bias that make direct examination of the contextual relationships problematic.

In the example above, we would predict that if there were a contextual process of neighbor-to-neighbor influence, then those for whom the neighborhood was an especially relevant context would show stronger contextual effects than others — the 'bowling alone' crowd, who perhaps do not even know their neighbors. That is, we would expect that among those for whom the neighborhood was particularly relevant, the relationship between class and support for school expenditures would vary more strongly with neighborhood composition than it would among those for whom the neighborhood was not a relevant context. In other words, we would predict that the contextual effect would interact with the relevance of the neighborhood. This provides a critical test for the counter-hypothesis that an observed 'contextual' effect is an artifact of selection, because we would have no reason to expect this interaction as an outcome of selection. We leave the measurement of 'relevance of a context' to the next section, where we propose the use of survey question response times as a measurement of the accessibility of context to an individual.[6]

This test, then, allows a check for selection effects when performing contextual analysis. If we find an apparent contextual effect, and the predicted interaction with

---

[5] Achen and Shively (1995, p. 228).

[6] Although we do not explore this here, we speculate also that one might be able to dispense entirely with measurement of the context and still test for the presence of contextual effects. If we knew that a characteristic (class in the example above) was distributed unequally across contexts (neighborhoods in the example), then if there was an individual level relationship between that characteristic and a dependent variable, that relationship should be exaggerated by any contextual effects if they are present. And the relationship should be most exaggerated among those who are most connected to the neighborhood. We could thus predict that if contextual effects (not due to selection) are present, (class and support for school expenditures in the example) they should interact positively with the individual-level relationship of connectedness to the neighborhood. This prediction could be tested without ever measuring the context itself.

relevance of context is present at the individual level, then we can conclude that at least some of the observed contextual effect is due to inter-personal influence within the neighborhood, rather than solely to selection effects. It is no small accomplishment to reject the counter-hypothesis that a proposed contextual effect is an artifact of selection effects.

4 Attitude accessibility and latency measures of contextual influence

Researchers who posit the existence of causal relationships between an individual's environment, her opinions, and her actions often justify their inferences on the basis of vague theoretical linkages between persons and their social worlds. Environment is thought to influence opinions, but few scholars elaborate models of why or how this happens. Kinder (1998, p. 817) observes that, in contextual analysis, "measures are frequently indirect, and explanatory mechanisms are too often left unspecified and untested". Even studies that suggest an explicit mechanism, such as political discussion with social network as the agent of contextual influence (Huckfeldt, 1984), or the role of mass media in communicating messages to social collectives (Price, 1988), rarely expand on the internal individual processes that facilitate this connection. The emphasis is placed on the aggregate or sociological aspect of the linkage puzzle.

We are interested in understanding the extent to which individuals are tied to their environments. Specifically, what is the nature of the context–individual linkage to the person involved? How does it work? MacKuen and Brown (1987, p. 471) point the way: "Citizens form opinions about politics by evaluating information that is filtered through the social environment in which they live". The implication is that social context, or an evaluation of a social context, is embedded as an element in the cognitive structure an actor employs to encode and store information.[7] Thus, a person's perception of his or her context itself becomes an attitudinal construct. What we mean by connection to a context or the accessibility of a context is perhaps more easily understood with this model in mind.

Accessibility is nothing more than the 'readiness with which a stored construct is utilized in information processing' (Higgins and King, 1981, p. 71). The more accessible a mental construct is to a respondent, the more influential it should be in the formation of opinions, and the more effective the context should be in the perception, encoding, and storage of information and attitudes (Fazio, 1995; Higgins and King, 1981). We hypothesize that the increased accessibility of information and attitudes about social context is positively associated with the influence that context has on an individual's decisions and behavior.

Researchers have long maintained that stronger attitudes are more consequential, especially for predicting behavior and policy opinions.[8] The certainty and strength with

[7] See Hastie (1986), Lodge and McGraw (1995), Eagly and Chaiken (1998) for reviews of the information processing literature.
[8] For reviews see Krosnick and Petty (1995) and Abelson (1995).

which an attitude is held, as well as the level of information and centrality of the attitude to one's belief system, are all relevant to demonstrating that attitudes matter for predicting and explaining behavior. Measurement of attitude strength, however, poses a number of problems. Reactivity to questions that inquire about the respondent's commitment to, and the strength of, their attitude responses create serious measurement problems.

Fazio and his colleagues[9] have identified attitude accessibility as a principal indicator of the stability, strength, and predictability of attitudes. Attitude accessibility refers to the likelihood that 'the attitude will be activated from memory automatically when the object is encountered' (Fazio, 1995, p. 248). Here the term 'automatically' is important, because it suggests that the attitude is 'being activated effortlessly and inescapably'. The strength of the attitude object evaluation is hypothesized to be the main determinant of the likelihood that an attitude will be activated from memory when an individual confronts the attitude object.

Attitude accessibility is, therefore, related to Converse's (1964) distinction between attitudes and non-attitudes. In the case of a completely inaccessible attitude, the individual has no apparent a priori evaluation of the attitude object, a condition similar to Converse's definition of a non-attitude. Students of accessibility suggest that when respondents are probed about attitudes that are more meaningful, salient, and stable (that is, more 'real' attitudes), they will respond to questions more quickly. Question response time is a commonly used measure of attitude accessibility. The logic behind this is transparent: "the less cognitive work the individual would have to do to respond to the query. . . . The less time the individual would require" (Fazio, 1995, p. 249).

Laboratory experiments conducted by Fazio et al. (1982, 1986), Fazio and Williams (1986) and Roskos-Ewoldsen and Fazio (1992) have demonstrated the validity and reliability of their response latency methodology and its ability to predict attitude–behavior relationships. A new methodology for response latency measures has been developed for computer assisted telephone interviews (Bassilli, 1993; Bassilli and Fletcher, 1991; Bassilli, 1995). Researchers employ a computer-based 'stop watch' to time the interval between the end of an interviewer's question and a respondent's answer. Although this is an intuitively pleasing measurement technique, the use of response times bears some costs. The collection and interpretation of latencies is far from foolproof. Interviewers may make errors in the use of CATI technology and respondents may, for example, lose interest in the survey instrument, distorting response times. But, 'used appropriately and interpreted judiciously, latency measures can be very informative' (Fazio, 1990, p. 95). In our estimation, the benefits outweigh the costs.[10]

As Bassilli (1995) notes, the response latency methodology for measuring attitude accessibility is unobtrusive, reliable, and a valid predictor of attitude stability and

---

[9] For reviews see Fazio (1995), Fazio and Williams (1986), and Fazio (1990).

[10] Much can be done to improve the use and interpretation of raw response time data. Huckfeldt et al. (1999) and Fazio (1990) outline several strategies to 'clean' latency measures and correct for the baseline response speed among survey participants in statistical analysis. These cleaning procedures are discussed in the analysis below.

associated properties of salience and importance. Recent work by Huckfeldt et al. (1999) has found that partisanship and ideology are more influential among voters who have faster response times to questions about these voting cues, indicating the accessibility of these constructs.

5 Research design and setting

Ennis (1962, p. 181) lamented the lack of data available to scholars interested in contextual questions, particularly the discipline's interest in national surveys:

> ... studies have suffered from a consistent limitation: the voter is cut off from his surroundings, suspended as it were, above the political and social conditions of his community ... The community context of voting has either been randomized, as in the nationwide cross section of voters used in such studies as Campbell (1954), or the effects of community context as a variable have been eliminated by sampling voters from a single community.

Sprague (1982) raises similar concerns about national surveys, noting that national samples pull people out of their contexts. These concerns with the detection of relevant contexts and appropriate variation in the extent of people's interests highlight the need for survey data collected below the national level, but in relatively diverse populations, sampling residents in a variety of communities, neighbourhoods, census tracts, voting precincts, and the like.

We utilize data from a survey of 750 registered voters conducted in Houston, Texas, and the surrounding Harris County during 23–29 September 1999. Our hypotheses are tested with data on past presidential voting and partisan identification. Our contextual measure is the respondent's perception of the partisan make-up of their neighborhood. Specifically, each respondent was asked: "Generally speaking, do you usually think of your neighborhood as Republican, Democratic, or Independent?"[11] In addition, data were collected on respondent partisan identification,[12] and their vote choice in the 1996 presidential election.[13]

Our collection of response times closely follows procedures recommended by Bassilli (1993) and Huckfeldt et al. (1999). Using computer-assisted telephone inter-

---

[11] Respondents were not prompted to assess their neighborhood as having mixed partisan affiliations. Those who responded that their neighborhood was mixed were set to missing in the analysis: 48 respondents out of 617 valid cases (7.8%).

[12] The question for self-reported partisanship was: "Generally speaking, do you usually think of yourself as a Republican, a Democrat, an Independent, or what?" Respondents who indicated no preference of affiliation with another political party were set to missing in the analysis (44 cases, 7.1% of the sample).

[13] For this analysis, we examine only the major vote, with a dependent variable coded 0, indicating a vote for Republican Bob Dole, and 1, indicating a vote for incumbent Democratic President Bill Clinton. Other candidate responses were discarded from the analysis. The only other candidate of note on the ballot was the Reform Party's Ross Perot, who garnered the support of 4.4% of the respondents to this survey.

viewing (CATI) technology, interviewers were instructed to start and stop an internal computer 'stop watch', activated by pressing the space bar on their computer keyboards, to record the time between the end of each question asked and the beginning of a respondent's answer. We use these elapsed response times as a measure of latency. Times were collected for responses to all the questions on the Houston-area survey.[14]

As discussed above, the logic of this measure is that the longer it takes a respondent to answer a question, the less accessible that attitude should be. Latency on a respondent's assessment of the partisanship of their neighbors — a faster response time — should indicate that their context is more important, salient, and accessible, and should exert more influence on their behavior. The key variable in our analysis is the interaction between a respondent's perception of the partisan make up of their neighborhood and the latency of this perception. When this perception is latent, as indicated by a faster response time to the question, context should have a significant effect on reported vote choice. Conversely, when respondents are slow to assess the partisanship of their neighborhood — the context does not come quickly to mind — we expect less of a relationship between context and behavior.

There are two important qualifications to be made about our hypothesized relationship between context and behavior, one methodological and the other substantive. First, as discussed in other research on response times (Fazio, 1990; Bassilli, 1993; Huckfeldt et al., 1999), respondents have different cadences with which they answer questions. Consequently, we need to statistically control for average response times for each respondent. To account for this, we constructed a baseline measure of latency from the responses to factual and demographic questions.[15]

The second qualification concerns the conditions under which we expect to observe the effects of context. Where might we expect to observe this relationship? The claim we have made thus far is that context is more influential when it is more accessible. We also suggest that it will be easier to detect the effects of context when that environment is perceived to have attributes incongruent with the respondent's. Here, the respondent may be subject to conflicting rather than reinforcing messages, cues and information about how to vote, for example.[16]

---

[14] Several steps were taken to 'clean' these latency measures. First, we removed from the analysis cases where the interviewer incorrectly recorded the response time. This represented 17.7% of the sample (133 respondents). We removed cases from the right-hand tail of the distributions of response times by eliminating respondents with time scores more than 3 standard deviations above the mean. Then we logged the raw latency measure and constructed a dummy variable from these cleaned, logged response times. All of our latency measures are coded 0 for response times greater than the median, and 1 for response times lower than the median. The measure is a positive indicator of latency.

[15] The baseline response time measure was constructed by taking the average response time to four questions: respondent education, employment status, length of residence at current address, and whether a respondent owns or rents their home. Scaled, the items have a Chronbach's $\alpha = 0.712$. A factor analysis of the response times for these four questions produced a single factor with an eigenvalue of 2.27, accounting for 56.8% of the variance in this factor. The measure was inserted in the analysis as a dummy variable with 0 indicating a mean response time greater than the median response time and 1 indicating a response time lower than the median.

[16] This condition of information asymmetry plays an important role in other literature on voting behavior (Zaller, 1992, 1996).

Table 1: Response times for persons with congruent and incongruent perceptions about the partisan make-up of their neighborhoods

	Individual partisanship RT[a]	Contextual partisanship RT
Congruent	4.17	4.66
Incongruent	4.34	4.91
	$(t = 1.957, p = 0.051)$	$(t = 2.241, p = 0.025)$

[a] Tabled values indicate the mean of the logged response times (see footnote 14 in the text).

Thus, we expect that Republicans residing in neighborhoods they perceive to be Democratic will be more likely to vote for Democrats when their perception of the partisan make-up of their neighborhood is readily accessible. Moreover, we might expect that the accessibility of one's context will be greater when that context is congruent with a respondent's personal preference. A difference of means test lends support to this intuition. Examining the continuous latency measure, persons who experience an incongruity between their partisanship and the perceived partisan make-up of their neighborhoods were significantly slower in answering questions both about their own partisanship and their context. Moreover, the differences are significant substantively, not just statistically. They look small as shown in Table 1, but what one sees there are logged raw time scores; if the scores are re-transformed back to real time values, congruous respondents are 15–20% faster on these questions than incongruous respondents.

With the caveats outlined above, we selected only respondents with partisan iden-tifications that were incongruent with their perception of the partisanship of their neighborhood.[17] We then estimated a logit model of the 1996 presidential vote with the following independent regressors:

$$\text{Vote Choice} = \alpha + \beta_1 \text{ Self-reported Party Identification}$$
$$+ \beta_2 \text{ Perceived Neighborhood Partisanship (Context)}$$
$$+ \beta_3 \text{ Response time for Context}$$
$$+ \beta_4 \text{ Context} \times \text{Response time for Context}$$
$$+ \beta_5 \text{ Baseline Response time}$$
$$+ \beta_6 \text{ Context} \times \text{Baseline Response time}$$

[17] There are two ways we can conduct this analysis. In the analysis presented in Table 2, we physically partition out the data set into respondents whose party identification is consonant with their perception of their context. However, we also ran the analysis for the full data set utilizing a dummy variable for congru-ence and a series of interaction terms, including a three-way interaction between assessment of context, the response time for that assessment and the congruence dummy. The results of these two analyses are substantively and statistically identical, so we report the less cumbersome model.

Table 2: Logit estimates for 1996 presidential vote choice for respondents living in neighborhoods perceived to have partisan identities at variance with their own[a]

	β	s.e.	Wald
Party ID (self-reported)	3.685**	(0.718)	26.333
Neighborhood partisanship (perceived)	−0.493	(0.744)	0.439
Response time for context	−2.737*	(1.591)	2.959
Context × Response time for context	1.442*	(0.778)	3.434
Baseline response time	−1.296	(1.574)	0.678
Context × Baseline response time	0.302	(0.765)	0.156
Constant	4.769	(2.186)	4.783

[a] **$p < 0.01$; *$p < 0.05$ (one-tailed test); $N = 148$; Naglekerke $R^2 = 0.70$; percent predicted correctly = 88.4; dependent variable, 1996 Presidential Vote Choice: 1, Democrat Bill Clinton; 0, Republican Bob Dole

The results of this analysis, shown in Table 2, lend support to our hypotheses about the influence of context on behavior and the importance of the accessibility of that context. The model predicts 88.39 of the cases correctly. More importantly, however, the key independent variable, the interaction of contextual assessment and the response time associated with this variable, is signed in the hypothesized direction and is statistically significant.

In Table 3 we report the estimated probabilities of voting for the Democrat, President Clinton, in a variety of different scenarios involving personal partisanship, perception of context, and latency of that contextual assessment. Perhaps the obvious place to start is to note that Democrats are almost impervious to context in choosing to vote for a popular President of their party. The Independents and Republicans are more interesting, however. A Republican living in a Democratic neighborhood and keenly aware of his surroundings is more than twice as likely to vote for Clinton as a Republican in what he perceives as an Independent neighborhood. Being aware of context to the extent that the neighborhood make-up comes to mind more quickly makes a Republican four times more likely to vote for Clinton than Republicans who are 'disconnected' from their Democratic neighborhoods (0.28 compared to 0.07).

The Independents seem swayed by their neighborhood make-up as well, provided they are aware of it. Independents in Democratic neighborhoods are almost as likely to vote for Clinton as Democrats themselves. However, being aware of a mass of Republican neighbors reduces the likelihood that an Independent would vote for the incumbent President by almost one third (0.69 compared to 0.94).

Table 3: Probability of voting for Clinton by personal partisanship, context, and response time

Respondent	Context	Fast RT	Slow RT
Democrat	Independent	0.996	0.995
	Republican	0.989	0.997
Independent	Democrat	0.94	0.76
	Republican	0.69	0.89[a]
Republican	Democrat	0.28	0.07
	Independent	0.13	0.11

[a] Most typical case, given data frequencies.

6 Discussion

We believe the main contributions of this chapter are its proposal of the interaction test for selection effects, and the latency measure as a superior measure of people's connection to their contexts. The example we have provided demonstrates the feasibility and potential benefit of these techniques. These benefits would often apply even when using methods advocated elsewhere (van der Eijk, this volume, chapter 3) for linking to the core election study contextual data acquired by other means, thereby avoiding reliance on respondents for information about their context.

We realize, of course, that the example cited involves familiar problems of endogeneity, especially between personal party identification and the vote, but also between perceived partisan make-up of the neighborhood and the vote. Nonetheless, using the latency technique explored in this example:

1. We can definitively rule out the counter-hypothesis that the observed contextual effect is due to selection. The statistically significant interaction between context and its accessibility assures us of this.
2. Whatever other problems of endogeneity are present in the estimates, the latency measure used in the test for selection is clearly exogenous to the vote.
3. The latency measure for connectedness gives us an unusually tight, non-reactive measure of the key variable in the test.

Beyond the methodological advantages of the interaction test, though, we are also struck by the theoretic possibilities of the interaction with connectedness. One interpretation of Table 3, and the one we at first intended, is that it shows definitively that the contextual effect is not an artifact of selection. We are also impressed, however, with the richer understanding of the contextual effect provided by the results in the table. A subset of the population is identified there that does almost all of the heavy lifting in the contextual process. It should be possible to develop interesting models, related to theories of 'social capital', that specify who will be connected to their neighborhoods, and therefore among whom contextual effects will occur.

The interaction prediction may also offer us something beyond the up-or-down test for selection effects. If we are in a position to make one additional assumption, the interaction will also allow us to compare the impacts of an individual's varying contexts. The assumption here is: to use the interaction as a check on a single context, we had to assume (a) that the two non-context variables (class and school support, in the simulation) were correlated, and (b) that the density of the independent non-context variable (class) varied by contextual unit (neighborhoods). Both of these are straightforward assumptions, since both can be checked empirically. If both are true, then we expect the interaction to have a independent effect on support for spending if there is interpersonal influence within the contextual units. If we can further assume that the relationships described in (a) and (b) are of approximately equal strength for each of two or more contexts (neighborhood and workplace, for instance), then any difference in the strength of the interactions with the two contexts must be proportional to the strength of the interpersonal influences in the two contexts. With this assumption we can compare the impact of various contexts. It also appears likely to us, though we have not worked it out here, that one could develop corrections for any observed differences either in the individual-level correlations of assumption (a), or the cross-context variances of assumption (b), so that one would not even have to make an assumption of equality but could rather correct for differences.

What are the implications of all this for the design of election studies? First, the solution we propose to the problem of selection-based artifacts should encourage election studies to raise their sights a bit, and emphasize the search for contextual processes more than they have in the past. Our solution removes a pesky counter-hypothesis that has always been present for contextual studies. Secondly, our solution requires some simple additional instrumentation and measurement, such as questions about contexts, with latency measured on those questions. And thirdly, and perhaps most importantly, this is not just a matter of new instrumentation. The approach we have proposed enriches election studies theoretically in two ways. By making the measurement of contextual models more feasible, it will help to overcome the tendency of national samples to commingle incomparable circumstances. A working-class voter in a West Virginia coal town is different from a working-class voter in La Jolla. It also enriches contextual models, by introducing a new factor that mediates contextual effects: voters' connections to their contexts.

References

Abelson, R. 1995. Attitude extremity. In: Petty, R., Krosnick, J. (eds), Attitude Strength: Antecedents and Consequences. Erlbaum (Lawrence), Mahwah, NJ.

Achen, C., Shively, W. 1995. Cross-Level Inference. University of Chicago Press, Chicago.

Bassilli, J., Fletcher, J. 1991. Response–time measurement in survey research: a method for CATI and a new look at nonattitudes, Public Opinion Quarterly 55, pp. 329–344.

Bassilli, J. 1993. Response latency versus certainty as indexes of strength of voting intentions in a CATI survey, Public Opinion Quarterly 57, pp. 54–61.

Books, J., Prysby, C. 1991. Political Behaviour and the Local Context. Praeger, New York.

Converse, P. 1964. The nature of belief systems in mass publics. In: Apter, D. (ed.), Ideology and Discontent. Free Press, New York.

Eagly, A., Chaiken, N. 1998. Attitudes. In: Gilbert, D., Fiske, S., Lindzey, G. (eds), The Handbook of Social Psychology, 4th ed. McGraw-Hill, Boston.

Ennis, P.,1962. The contextual dimension in voting. In: McPhee, W., Glaser, W. (eds), Public Opinion and Congressional Elections. Free Press, Glencoe.

Erbring, L., Young, A. 1979. Individuals and social structure: contextual effects as endogenous feedback, Sociological Methods and Research 7, pp. 396–430.

Fazio, R. 1990. A practical guided to the use of response latency in social psychological research. In: Hendrick, C., Clark, M. (eds), Research Methods in Personality and Social Psychology. Sage, Newbury Park, CA.

Fazio, R. 1995. Attitudes as object–evaluation associations: determinants, consequences and correlates of attitude accessibility. In: Petty, R., Krosnick, J. (eds).

Fazio, R., Williams, C. 1986. Attitude accessibility as a moderator of the attitude–perception and attitude–behavior relationship: an investigation of the 1984 Presidential Election, Journal of Personality and Social Psychology 51, pp. 505–514.

Higgins, E., King, G. 1981. Accessibility of social constructs: information-processing and consequences of individual and contextual variation. In: Kantor, N., Kihlstrom, J. (eds), Personality, Cognition and Social Interaction. Erlbaum (Lawrence), Hillsdale, NJ.

Huckfeldt, R. 1984. Political loyalties and social class ties: the mechanisms of contextual influence, American Journal of Political Science 78, pp. 399–417.

Huckfeldt, R., Sprague, J. 1993. Citizens, contexts and politics. In: Finifter, A. (ed.), Political Science: The State of the Discipline II. APSA, Washington, DC.

Huckfeldt, R., Levine, J., Morgan, W., Sprague, J. 1999. Accessibility and the political utility of partisan and ideological orientations, American Journal of Political Science 43, pp. 888–991.

Kinder, D. 1998. Opinion and action in the realm of politics. In: Gilbert, D., Fiske, S., Lindzey, G. (eds), The Handbook of Social Psychology, 4th ed. McGraw-Hill, Boston.

King, G. 1997. A Solution to the Ecological Inference Problem: Reconstructing Individual Behavior from Aggregate Data. Princeton University Press, Princeton, NJ.

Krosnick, J., Petty, R. 1995. Attitude strength: an overview. In: Petty, R., Krosnick, J. (eds).

MacKuen, M., Brown, C. 1987. Political context and attitude change, American Political Science Review 81, pp. 471–490.

Monroe, B. 1995. Fully proportional representation, American Political Science Review 89, pp. 925–940.

Plott, C. 1978. Rawls' theory of justice: an impossibility result. In: Gottinger, H., Leinfeller, W. (eds), Decision Theory and Social Ethics, Issues in Social Choice. Reidel, Dordrecht.

Price, V. 1988. On the public aspects of opinion: linking levels of analysis in public opinion research, Communication Research 15, pp. 659–679.

Robinson, W.S. 1950. Ecological correlations and the behavior of individuals, American Sociological Review 15, pp. 351–367.

Sprague, J. 1982. Is there a micro-theory consistent with contextual analysis? In: Ostrom, E. (ed.), The Nature of Political Inquiry. Sage, Beverley Hills, CA.

Taagepera, R., Shugart, M. 1989. Seats and Votes: The Effects and Determinants of Electoral Systems. Yale University Press, New Haven.

Zaller, J. 1992. The Nature and Origins of Mass Opinion. Cambridge University Press, Cambridge.

Chapter 6

Designing multi-level studies:
Sampling voters and electoral contexts

Laura Stoker and Jake Bowers

Every two years in the US, 435 congressional elections take place that scholars study using data from the National Election Studies (NES) survey of the American electorate. With a focus on sampling, this chapter explores two issues: (1) How best to design a national election study if the aim is to understand voting behavior within and across subnational contexts; and (2) How, by comparison, the existing NES surveys have been designed. Although our arguments specifically address how one should sample individuals and congressional districts in the US, our conclusions apply to any situation where one is sampling micro-level units nested within diverse and influential macro-level contexts.

1 Introduction

Data from national election studies are often used to study voting behavior in subnational electoral districts. In the United States, the National Election Studies (NES) surveys the American electorate every two years, collecting data relevant to explaining election outcomes at the national (presidential) and subnational (congressional) level. Although national survey data are valuable for studying each type of election, the fact that congressional elections are inherently subnational events has implications for survey design. In any given election year, 435 different contests take place across the country, in districts with varying characteristics, with varying pairs of candidates running varying election campaigns. Hence, the questions we address in this chapter arise: How should one design a national election study in order to best understand these diverse subnational contests? And, how, by comparison, have the American National Election Studies been designed?

These are large questions, and, if left unfocused, larger than we can confront in this chapter. We focus, therefore, on one crucial aspect of the design of a national survey:

the sample design. Although sampling considerations are important to the design of any survey, they are particularly important in the kind of case we have at hand — where individuals from all across the nation are surveyed concerning the particular elections taking place within the districts in which they reside. In order to analyze these elections fruitfully, scholars must link micro-level survey data to macro-level data on attributes of the districts, the candidates, and the campaigns. As we will demonstrate, the effectiveness of the resulting analysis depends, to an important extent, on how the survey sample is designed.

In what follows we develop our arguments with respect to the problem of sampling citizens within and across congressional districts in the United States. The sampling issues we confront, however, are much more general than this. They arise any time that one is sampling micro-level units nested within diverse and influential macro-level contexts. They arise, for example, for researchers designing survey research on voting in US presidential elections, in that presidential campaigns are waged very differently across the 50 US states (Shaw, 1999a,b). If that state-by-state variation influences how voters make their choices, then researchers must confront how to sample voters within and across states. In this case, as with the case of congressional electoral research that we address in detail, below, sampling designs constrain what one will be able to learn. We first elaborate this point through example, by considering two contrasting survey designs.

2 Two contrasting designs

Imagine a design where 3000 eligible voters are selected at random within a single congressional district (CD), which, itself, is selected at random from within the 435 congressional districts in the US. With these data, we could study how various individual-level explanatory variables affect a dependent variable like vote choice in this election, although we could not draw conclusions from such findings about congressional elections in general. More importantly, we could not study how district, candidate, or campaign characteristics influence how citizens vote, since the study design generates no variation on such variables. For the same reason, we could not study how CD-level characteristics interact with individual-level characteristics in influencing the vote. As a consequence, our model of the vote will be incomplete, and hence inadequate for explaining the election outcome even within the congressional district we studied. In this design, any effect of CD-level variables is operating in a wholly unobserved fashion. Even with data on 3000 eligible voters, we could not fully explain why people voted, why they voted the way they did, or why candidate A ended up beating candidate B.[1]

---

[1] To illustrate, imagine that our sampled CD involves a highly contested race with a Democratic incumbent in a district where voters are no more Democratic than Republican in their party identification. Let's say that the Democrat wins by a narrow margin in part because of the effect of incumbency — i.e., because voters are more likely to cast their votes for an incumbent than a non-incumbent, ceteris paribus. We cannot estimate this effect, since we only observe one race, and hence our explanation of the vote will be incomplete. Still, since there is no variance on this or any other CD-level variable in our study, our

By contrast, imagine a design in which 100 congressional districts are first sampled at random, and then within each CD 30 eligible voters are randomly selected.[2] Like the first design, we could use the sample of 3000 respondents to evaluate the effects of individual-level characteristics like partisan identification. Since this design builds in variation at the CD-level, we could also study how district, campaign, and candidate characteristics influence the vote (assuming we gather the requisite data at the CD-level). For the same reason, we could study the interaction of CD- and individual-level explanatory variables, asking, for example, whether the effect of party identification depends upon the nature of the campaign. Since respondents are sampled at random within districts and the number per district is relatively large ($n = 30$), we could also aggregate responses within districts to generate contextual independent variables (e.g., "climate of opinion" variables), or could link the aggregated survey findings to data on members of Congress, as did Miller and Stokes (1963) in their study of representation. We could even draw district-level conclusions about the behavior of voters or about election outcomes, although the within-district n of 30 is limiting in this respect. However, since both districts and respondents are sampled at random, we could pursue the same kind of exercise for particular district types. For example, we could demonstrate the extent to which the outcome of open-seat contests hinged on candidate quality as opposed to the partisanship of the district's voters, employing the "Level Importance" technique described by Achen (1982).[3] Since the CDs are sampled at random within the nation, we could draw further conclusions from the data about the overall pattern of congressional election results in the nation as a whole.

These two designs differ in the number of CDs sampled (which we will refer to as "J") and the number of respondents per district (n). The first involves a simple random sample ($n = 3000$, within one CD), whereas the second involves a two-stage, cluster sample; first a sample of CDs (clusters) is selected ($J = 100$), and then individuals are chosen within CDs ($n = 30$). Both designs produce an overall sample (N) of 3000 eligible voters. Neither design involves stratification.

Stratification in the first design would involve sorting the population of eligible voters into categories on one or more stratifying variables before sampling. Within each stratum, respondents would be sampled in proportion to their population

---

estimates of the effects of individual-level variables like party identification are not biased; they are simply not generalizable. For example, the effect of party identification in this district might be weaker than the effect of party identification in races with open seats, and we would not know it.

[2] This is a two-stage cluster sample design. Assuming that each CD has the same number of eligible voters, it generates an equal probability sample of eligible voters in the US.

[3] Sampling at random within a given CD ensures that sample findings can be generalized to the population of eligible voters within that CD. Sampling CDs at random ensures that the sample findings concerning open-seat CDs can be generalized to the population of open-seat CDs. Taken together, this means that the whole set of findings can be generalized to the population of eligible voters living within open-seat CDs. If we had random sampling within CDs but a purposive sample of open-seat CDs, we could only generalize results to the population of eligible voters within the sampled CDs. If we had random sampling of CDs but a purposive sample of eligible voters within CDs, then, strictly speaking, we would not be able to generalize any findings concerning individuals at all.

frequency if one was striving to achieve an equal probability design. This procedure would ensure that the sample percentage of respondents within a stratum equaled the population percentage, and would increase the power[4] of statistical tests involving dependent variables that were correlated with the stratifying variable(s) (Kish, 1965; Judd et al., 1991). Stratifying also enables one to over-sample within strata — to sample disproportionately so as to increase the representation of a group that otherwise would be represented in the sample in small numbers. In the second design, one could repeat such a procedure at each sampling stage — stratifying the population of CDs before selecting 100 of them at the first stage, and stratifying eligible voters within CDs before selecting 30 of them (within each CD) at the second stage. In important ways that we describe later, stratification at the macro-level can be one of the most crucial aspects of the sample design.

In general, and as these examples have suggested, our ability to use national survey data to understand congressional elections depends on how both districts and individuals are sampled within the study. In order to explicate this point further, and to arrive at general guidelines for sample design, we must consider how the data on individuals and on districts are gathered and analyzed.

3 Multi-level data and analysis

As illustrated by our examples as well as past research (e.g., Jacobson, 1997; Brown and Woods, 1992; McPhee and Glaser, 1962), studies of congressional elections are likely to require data on eligible voters, the congressional districts, the campaigns run in those districts, and the candidates contesting the election. This means that the analysis will be based on data characterizing both micro- and macro-level units, integrated into one multi-level dataset. The multi-level structure of the data creates special problems for conventional data analysis.

Below, we briefly discuss the roles played by micro- and macro-level variables in analyses of voting behavior in congressional elections. We then describe different ways of analyzing the integrated, multi-level data: (1) Aggregating all data to the macro-level, (2) treating all data as if it were gathered at the micro-level, and (3) analyzing the micro- and macro-level data simultaneously while also taking into account which data are gathered on which units — i.e., analyzing the data through multi-level modeling. This sets up our subsequent discussion of sample design and statistical efficiency, which assumes that the data will be analyzed through multi-level modeling techniques.

Survey data provide individual-level information on the dependent variable — turnout, vote choice, information about the candidates, and the like. Survey data also provide information on individual characteristics that operate as independent variables, like partisan identification, group characteristics, and issue positions. And survey data provide information on individual characteristics that either mediate or moderate the

---

[4] The *power* of a test refers to the probability that one will reject the null hypothesis when the null hypothesis is false (specifically, when a particular alternative hypothesis is true).

effects of contextual characteristics on outcomes. For example, a respondent's level of political awareness may influence how he or she responds to the messages of the campaign (Zaller, 1992).

Information on congressional district-level characteristics may be drawn from many sources. Census data, official government records, campaign documents, and mass media sources all contain relevant data. Even survey responses, if aggregated to the CD-level, can provide useful data on candidates or campaigns. One could, for example, use the within-district mean placement of a candidate on a liberal-conservative scale as an index of the candidate's ideology (although for incumbents, of course, other measures of this are readily available, such as indices based on votes cast in Congress). Such a procedure treats survey respondents as informants.[5]

The effects of CD-level variables can be thought of in two ways. First, the attributes of districts, candidates, or campaigns can influence vote choices and electoral outcomes. This influence might be either direct, or indirect — i.e., mediated by other CD-level or individual-level characteristics. Second, they can identify contexts which influence how other variables (individual- or CD-level) influence the vote and election outcome. In other words, they can identify contexts across which the explanatory model varies.[6]

There are different ways to represent the relationships between CD-level variables (as independent) and individual-level variables (as both independent and dependent). One way would be to aggregate the individual-level responses to the CD-level, by averaging across individuals within each district, and then to regress an aggregated dependent variable on relevant CD-level variables and on other aggregated individual-level variables. A simple version of this model is depicted below:

$$\bar{Y}_j = \beta_0 + \beta_1 \bar{X}_j + \beta_2 Z_j + E_j \tag{1}$$

In Eq. (1), $\bar{Y}_j$ is the mean of the individual-level dependent variable within each CD, $\bar{X}_j$ is the mean of a relevant individual-level variable within each CD, and Z_j is an attribute of each district, measured at the district level (i.e., not using survey data). In such a regression, one would be able to say something about how, say, mean turnout levels vary depending on whether or not an incumbent is running. One problem with this method is that there is no guarantee that the relationship found using aggregated individual-level variables will be the same as the relationship found when using the

---

[5] This requires that respondents be randomly sampled within CDs, and for a reliable measure, that the within-district n be relatively large.

[6] If one expects the explanatory model to vary across CDs, then one would build interactions into the model. When those interactions involve an individual-level variable in addition to a CD-level variable they are usually called "cross-level interactions," a term we employ below. Cross-level interactions can be used to represent how attributes of districts shape the influence exerted by some individual-level independent variable (e.g., the notion that in an open-seat contest party identification has more effect on the vote than it has in races involving an incumbent), but can also be used to represent how attributes of individuals shape the influence exerted by some district-level independent variable (e.g., the notion that politically unsophisticated voters are more likely to be affected by negative campaigning than politically sophisticated voters). See Fisher (1988) for an excellent discussion of how the same interaction term can be used to estimate coefficients from very different models.

disaggregated individual-level variables. This is the cross-level inference problem (Achen and Shively, 1995). Relatedly, this model is incapable of representing cross-level interactions, where the effects of micro-level variables vary across macro-level contexts, or vice-versa. Another problem is that, since the typical survey includes many more individuals than districts, the degrees of freedom available for hypothesis testing are often drastically reduced via such aggregation. If the survey were using the second hypothetical design we described above, this aggregate regression would have 100 degrees of freedom, despite the availability of information about 3000 individuals.

Alternatively, one might be tempted to model all of the data at the individual level, pretending, in effect, that we have 3000 observations at the CD-level rather than the true number, 100 (again, alluding to the second design example we presented above). Eq. (2) presents such a model. In this case, we've added a subscript of i to the CD-level variable Z.

$$Y_{ij} = \beta_0 + \beta_1 X_{ij} + \beta_2 Z_{ij} + E_{ij} \tag{2}$$

One problem with this method of modeling the data is that we do not have $N = J \times n$ (number of districts $\times$ number of individuals per district) independent values of Z or of X. Rather, we only observe J independent values of Z, and somewhere between J and N independent values of X. OLS, in this case, would not estimate the correct standard errors.

The number of independent observations obtained in a multi-level design is called the "effective N." In a simple two-stage design like we described in our earlier example, the effective N of macro-level units is J, the number of such units randomly sampled at the first stage.[7] The effective N of micro-level units is more complicated. Because individuals are nested within districts, the values that individual-level variables take on are not likely to be independent within districts. Put another way, we would expect a sample of individuals chosen at random within a district to be more similar to each other than a sample of individuals chosen at random from within the population at large. The most common way to gauge this homogeneity is to summarize it using a statistic known as "rho", the "intraclass correlation coefficient" (ρ).[8] The coefficient ρ ranges from 0 to 1, where $\rho = 0$ corresponds to the case where there is no tendency for individuals nested within macro-level units to be similar to one another, and $\rho = 1$ corresponds to the case where all individuals nested within macro-

---

[7] If a multi-stage sample design is used where district selection occurs at a later stage, CDs will be clustered within higher-level units and thus the effective N of CDs will be less than the total number represented in the sample. Similarly, as long as the first stage involves sampling areas that contain more than one CD, then even if the CD is not a sampling unit at later stages the effective N of CDs will be less than the number of CDs that fall into the sample. As we describe later, this is true of the sample designs NES has used, with the exceptions of the 1978 and 1980 studies. To estimate the effective N in such cases, one would follow a procedure comparable to the one used for estimating the effective N of micro-level units, which we describe next.

[8] Kish (1965, p. 161) introduced this statistic and called it "roh." Most other authors have depicted "rho" by the Greek letter ρ, which is the symbol Kish assigned to this statistic when using it in mathematical formulas. Kish chose "roh" because it is an acronym for "rate of homogeneity."

level units are identical to one another.[9] Kish (1965) used this measure of homogeneity within clusters to calculate the effective N of observations for a given individual-level variable, as depicted below (for the equal cluster size case).

$$\text{effective } N = \frac{N}{1 + (n - 1)\rho} = \frac{Jn}{1 + (n - 1)\rho} \tag{4}$$

Eq. (4) shows that, as the homogeneity within clusters (ρ) increases, then the effective N decreases.[10] Further, when holding the total sample size (N) constant, as the cluster size (n) increases, then the effective N also decreases. Since $N = J \times n$, what this means is that as n increases and J decreases — i.e., when the degree of clustering in the design increases — the effective N of micro-level units decreases.

Despite the fact that we can identify the effective N for each of the variables in any given model, the fact that the effective Ns vary across the variables still poses a problem for OLS.[11] The most appropriate model for estimating effects with nested data is the hierarchical or multi-level model. The multi-level model was developed to represent how the behavior of individuals is influenced by their own (micro-level) characteristics as well as the characteristics of the macro-level contexts in which they are nested (CDs, in our case). It enables one to simultaneously estimate the effects of micro-level variables, macro-level variables, and interaction variables, including cross-level interactions, all while taking into account the multi-level nature of the data. In Appendix A, we provide a very brief description of the model. Jones and Steenbergen (1997) provide a very useful overview, illustrating their discussion with examples from political science. Further information can be found in Bryk and Raudenbush (1992), Goldstein (1999), Kreft and De Leeuw (1998), Longford (1993), Pinheiro and Bates (2000), and Snijders and Bosker (1999).

For our purposes, what is important is how various sample design decisions influence statistical efficiency and the power of hypothesis tests when multi-level models are estimated. We take up this issue next.

---

[9] Eq. (3) shows one way to depict the formula for ρ.

$$\rho = \frac{\text{variance between macro-units}}{\text{total variance}} = \frac{\tau^2}{\tau^2 + \sigma^2}.$$

In this formula, τ^2 represents the between-group variance, and σ^2 represents the within-group variance. As this formula suggests, ρ indicates the proportion of the total variance in some variable that is attributable to the macro-level unit. There are numerous methods of estimating ρ. Later in this chapter we use the so-called "ANOVA method" where

$$\hat{\rho} = \frac{(F - 1)J/n}{1 + (F - 1)J/n}$$

(Snijders and Bosker, 1999).

[10] When $\rho = 0$ the effective N is simply N, and when $\rho = 1$ (i.e., all individuals nested within CDs take on the same value) the effective N is J.

[11] OLS is no longer BLUE. What is more, OLS yields biased coefficient estimates if the model estimated involves cross-level interactions (see, for example, Kreft and De Leeuw, 1998, especially Chap. 2).

4 Sample design and efficiency in the estimation of macro-level effects

4.1 Number of CDs (J) and respondents per CD (n)

As our previous discussion has implied, all other things held constant, statistical efficiency in estimating macro-level effects is enhanced by increasing the number of macro-level units — in our case, CDs. This is simply a matter of the effective N of macro-level units. In any analysis involving CD-level explanatory variables, the degrees of freedom available for estimating CD-level effects is determined by taking into account the number of CDs, rather than the number of individuals, that fall into the sample. Hence, the efficiency of statistical estimates (and the power of hypothesis tests) is strongly influenced by the number of CDs sampled.

> A relevant general remark is that the sample size at the highest level is usually the most restrictive element in the design. For example, a two-level design with 10 groups, i.e. a macro-level sample size of 10, is at least as uncomfortable as a single-level design with a sample size of 10. Requirements on the sample size at the highest level, for a hierarchical linear model with q explanatory variables at this level, are at least as stringent as requirements on the sample size in a single level design with q explanatory variables (Snijders and Bosker, 1999, p. 140).

At the same time, when one is estimating multi-level models, then both the number of macro-level units (J) and the number of micro-level units nested within them (n), and, hence, the total number of micro-level units (N), affects the efficiency of one's estimates, as does ρ (Kreft and De Leeuw, 1998; Mok, 1995; Snijders and Bosker, 1999).[12] To see this, consider Fig. 1, which uses an algorithm developed by Raudenbush (1997) to show how the power of statistical tests concerning the effects of CD-level variables is influenced by J, n, and ρ.[13]

In this simulation, we stipulate a very simple model, in which one macro-level variable is seen as affecting a micro-level dependent variable. We assume that the true effect, gauged in terms of a standardized regression coefficient, is 0.1.[14] The two panels show how increasing J and n increase the power of a hypothesis test concerning the

[12] The estimators of the coefficients in multi-level models are consistent, but not unbiased. As Mok (1995) has demonstrated, increasing J also diminishes the degree of bias in the coefficient estimates. ". . . consistent with advice given in the classical literature on cluster sampling designs, if resources were available for a sample size n, comprising J schools with I students from each school, then less bias and more efficiency would be expected from sample designs involving more schools (large J), and fewer students per schools (small I) than sample designs involving fewer schools (small J), and more students per school (large I)" (Mok, 1995, p. 6).

[13] Professor Raudenbush sent us the SAS code to implement his algorithm, and we modified it for use in Splus.

[14] The program actually requires us to stipulate an "effect size". We stipulated an effect size of 0.2, which corresponds to a standardized regression (correlation) coefficient of 0.1 (Snijders and Bosker, 1999, p. 147).

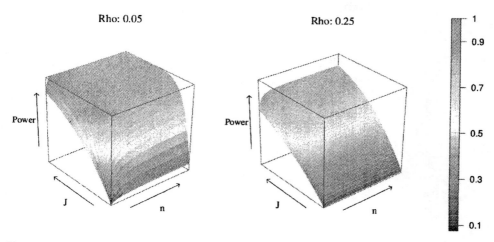

Note: α = .05, effect size = .2, 4 < J < 200, 2 < n < 200.

Fig. 1: Power of tests for macro-level effects.

effect of the macro-level variable. The left panel portrays the case where $\rho = 0.05$ (i.e. the case where individuals are not very homogeneous within districts) and the right panel portrays the case where $\rho = 0.25$ (i.e. the case where individuals are quite homogeneous within districts).[15] Thus, in this simulation, we are allowing three aspects of the design to vary: the number of macro-units (J), the number of micro-units per macro-unit (n), and the amount of homogeneity among micro-units that are nested within macro-level units (ρ). The results in Fig. 1 show that ρ plays an important role in determining the power of tests concerning the macro-level variable; the higher the ρ, the lower the power. Further, increasing both J and n — and, hence, N — also increases power. More importantly, however, power is much more dramatically enhanced by increasing J than by increasing n.[16]

To further illustrate this tradeoff, we also used a simulation to estimate the standard errors associated with coefficients in a more complex multi-level model. The model called for one micro-level dependent variable to be regressed on (a) one micro-level independent variable, (b) two CD-level independent variables, and (c) two cross-level interactions — i.e., the interactions between each CD-level variable and the micro-level independent variable. For example, one might think of this model as regressing a summary index of knowledge about the candidates on the respondent's level of

[15] Estimated values of ρ calculated using NES data are typically in the 0.05 to 0.3 range. See below, Table 6.
[16] As Fig. 1 also shows, the effect on power (in testing for macro-level effects) of increasing the within-district sample size, n, depends on whether ρ is small or large. If ρ is small (0.05 in the simulation), then increasing the n is somewhat helpful. If ρ is large (0.25 in the simulation), then increasing the n is not helpful. Similarly, a high ρ limits the improvement in power produced by increasing J.

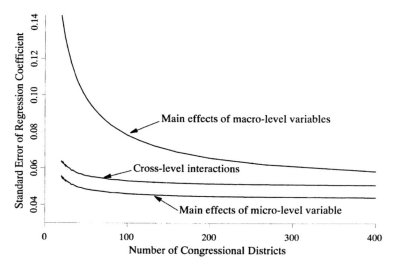

Note: N is held constant in this simulation, so that as the number of congressional districts increases (J), the within-district n decreases. See text for further details.

Fig. 2: Simulated standard errors of micro-level, macro-level,
and cross-level effect estimates.

political awareness, whether or not the election involved an open-seat, whether or not the race was competitive, and the interaction between these CD-level characteristics and the respondent's political awareness level.

This simulation holds the total number of micro-level cases (N) constant, while varying J and n. Hence, as J is increased, n is necessarily decreased, and vice-versa. Fig. 2 shows how the relative sizes of J and n affect the standard errors of the independent variables.[17] In this figure, the x-axis shows the number of congressional

---

[17] We used the program PINT (Power in Two-Level Designs) developed by Tom Snijders and Roel Bosker (Snijders and Bosker, 1993). We defined the macro-level variables as dichotomous (each scored 0 and 1), with means of 0.5 and variances of 0.25, and as uncorrelated with each other. We defined both independent and dependent micro-level variables as standardized (mean 0 and variance 1), and set the correlation between the macro-level and micro-level explanatory variables to 0. We set $N = 800$, the variance of the residuals at the micro-level to 0.8, and the variance/covariance matrix of the random coefficients (intercept and slope) to

$$\begin{bmatrix} 0.09 & -0.01 \\ -0.01 & 0.0075 \end{bmatrix}.$$

Varying these specifications does not alter general conclusions about the tradeoff between J and n as depicted in Fig. 2, but it does matter to the details. In particular, as the variation across electoral contexts in the slope and intercept of the individual-level independent variable increases (i.e., as the main diagonals of the the matrix above increase), increasing J at the expense of n becomes even more desirable.

districts (J), leaving the number of cases sampled within each district (n) implicit. As J increases, however, n is decreasing. As Fig. 2 shows, increasing J has an enormous effect on the size of the standard errors associated with the macro-level variables. Yet, in this simulation, and as a general matter, the gains (in terms of smaller standard errors) diminish as J increases. The standard errors of the micro-level variables, and of the cross-level interactions, also decrease as J increases, but much less dramatically. This pattern reflects how the effective Ns are changing. For the macro-level variables, the effective N is J. For the micro-level variables and cross-level interactions, the effective N is changing as the clustering (as indexed by n, given a fixed N) in the sample decreases.

The idea that particular characteristics of an electoral context shape how individuals make their voting decisions often seems married to an intuition that one should sample a very large number of individuals within particular electoral contexts. As we have seen, however, this is generally not an optimal design strategy. It is much more advantageous to the analyst if J is increased at the expense of n.

If one were especially interested in generalizing about a particular election, then it would, of course, make sense to draw a large and representative sample within the electoral district. That is why, for example, in order to facilitate the study of US Presidential elections, the NES strives to draw a large and nationally representative sample of eligible voters in the US.[18] But scholars of congressional elections are not typically interested in explaining the vote in a particular district, nor are they likely to believe that the relevant model of the vote (or of other dependent variables) takes a different form in each of the 435 CDs in the US. Rather, they are likely to believe that the model varies in systematic and explicit ways depending on the "type" of CD — whether, for example, it involves an open seat or whether the race is highly contested. As such, what is important for analysis is that the total number of individuals falling into each type of CD is not unduly small.[19] Having a large sample size within each CD of a given type is not necessary — nor, as we have suggested, is it generally desirable.

4.2 Variances of, and intercorrelations among, CD-level variables

Efficiency in the estimation of causal parameters is also a function of the variance of the explanatory variables as well as the degree of intercorrelation between them (or the linear dependency among a set of three or more). In particular, statistical efficiency in the estimation of CD-level effects is enhanced when the variance on CD-level variables is maximized and the intercorrelation between them is minimized.

---

[18] Even so, such a design is limited in that it lacks variation on explanatory variables that only vary across nations, just as a large-scale study of one congressional district is limited by the absence of variation in explanatory variables that distinguish districts, as we suggested earlier. The Comparative Study of Electoral Systems project (CSES), of which the NES is a part, is a response to this kind of limitation.
[19] We illustrate this point via simulation in the next section.

These outcomes can be accomplished through stratification in the sampling procedure used to generate survey respondents. In a multi-stage sample design, the probability that any one individual falls into the sample is the product of the probability of selection at each stage. Thus, one can sample disproportionately within strata at the first stage, so as to produce a desired distribution of macro-level units on the stratifying variable, and then compensate at the second stage if one desires an equal probability sample at the micro-level. If, for example, a certain type of CD has a higher probability of selection into the sample than would be warranted by its prevalence in the population, then one would sample individuals within such a CD at a lower rate to compensate.

Both of these points can be clarified through the use of an example. Our example identifies two macro-level stratifying variables, both treated as dichotomous: whether or not the race involves an open seat (*Open*), and whether or not the race is competitive (*Competitive*). Although the general point illustrated by this example does not depend on the particular stratifying variables we have chosen, it is worth briefly addressing why we selected them nonetheless. There are two reasons.

First, they illustrate a general stratification principle: Select stratifying variables that one expects to be important to explaining key dependent variables. The gains from stratification, in terms of statistical efficiency, are a function of the extent to which the stratifying variable is related to the dependent variable in question, whether causally or spuriously (Kish, 1965). Research on congressional elections suggests that incumbency and competitiveness — and variables correlated with these — are important to understanding many phenomena of interest.[20] Stratification is helpful whether or not one samples macro-level units within strata in proportion to their population frequency, and whether or not one eventually seeks an equal probability sample of micro-level units. Yet, as we will show, stratifying on key macro-level variables also enables one to employ disproportionate sampling so as to enhance statistical efficiency in estimating macro-level effects.[21]

The second reason is practicality. We have data on these variables for congressional districts in the US from 1948 to 1998. Later, we generate simulations and present analyses that take advantage of this fact. Further, we have chosen variables easily represented as dichotomies so as to keep the example simple. Thus, we avoided other variables, such as the partisan balance in the district, that might be strong candidates for a stratification scheme.

---

[20] The variable *Competitive* is meant to be an indicator of how closely contested the race is, and hence an indicator of campaign intensity (Westlye, 1991). Below we gauge competitiveness by using information on the electoral margin of victory. Since this kind of information is only available after the election is over, it is not plausible to think of this as information that one could rely upon to make stratification decisions. Margin of victory will, however, be correlated with other CD-level characteristics, like the partisan balance in the district, that one should be able to measure in advance of the election.

[21] If one samples proportionately within strata one can ensure that the percentage of sample units with a given attribute equals the percentage of population units with that attribute. This is an important benefit when random departures from such a result, which are to be expected without stratification, can seriously hamper the analysis. We consider this benefit of stratification in a later section. In this section we focus on the gains from disproportionate stratified sampling.

Table 1: Population

	Uncompetitive	Competitive
Incumbent	5,000,000 individuals 500 CDs @10,000 each	1,000,000 individuals 100 CDs @10,000 each
Open-seat	1,000,000 individuals 100 CDs @10,000 each	1,000,000 individuals 100 CDs @10,000 each

Table 2: Sample design A, equal probability sample at each stage

	Uncompetitive	Competitive
Incumbent	50 CDs $n = 10$ $N = 500$	10 CDs $n = 10$ $N = 100$
Open-seat	10 CDs $n = 10$ $N = 100$	10 CDs $n = 10$ $N = 100$

Suppose, then, that the population distribution of CDs and eligible voters across the four cells defined by these two stratifying variables is as given in Table 1. (We have used unrealistic numbers here — with a total of 8 million people scattered across 800 CDs — to keep things simple.) In design A, the population is stratified by the two macro-level variables, *Open* and *Competitive*, CDs are sampled within strata in proportion to their frequency in the population, and then an equal number of individuals is chosen at random within each CD so as to generate an equal probability sample of individuals. This is shown in Table 2. In design B, the population is again stratified by the two CD-level variables, but now CDs are sampled disproportionately in order to create an equal number of CDs in each of the four strata — i.e., a balanced design at the CD-level. Then, an unequal number of individuals is chosen at random within each CD so as to generate an equal probability sample of individuals. This design is shown in Table 3.

Both designs generate equal probability, representative samples of individuals, but they differ in the sample of CDs that is drawn and the pattern of clustering within CDs. In design A, only 20 of the 80 sampled CDs (25%) involve open-seat races, and only 20 (25%) are classified as competitive; taken together, only 10 sampled CDs (13%) involve competitive, open-seat races. In design B, by contrast, the distribution of CDs is balanced on each of the stratifying variables, so that each of the four cells contains 20 CDs (25%). Thinking only of the CD-level aspect of the design, in design

Table 3: Sample design B, balanced at stage 1, equal probability at stage 2

	Uncompetitive	**Competitive**
Incumbent	20 CDs $n = 25$ $N = 500$	20 CDs $n = 5$ $N = 100$
Open-seat	20 CDs $n = 5$ $N = 100$	20 CDs $n = 5$ $N = 100$

A the two stratifying variables have limited variances (0.1875 in each case) and a moderate positive correlation (0.33). In design B, the two stratifying variables have maximum variances (0.25 in each case) and zero intercorrelation.

If all individual-level data were aggregated, so the analysis was performed at the CD-level (i.e., our sample size in each design is 80), and we simply regressed some aggregated Y variable on *Open* and *Competitive*, design B would be superior in that the two variables are uncorrelated and each have maximum variance, and hence the standard errors associated with estimates of their effects would be smaller in design B than in design A.[22] At the same time, the number of individuals per CD is constant ($n = 10$) in design A but varies in design B ($n = 5$ or 25). This means that design B introduces heteroskedasticity — the mean of an aggregated Y variable would be estimated with varying reliability across the CDs (Hanushek and Jackson, 1977, Chap. 6), and GLS rather than OLS must be used to estimate the model. More importantly, this type of analysis throws away information, as we suggested before, and would only be appropriate if one were interested in cause and effect relationships at the CD-level, whereas most analysts studying subnational elections are interested in explaining individual-level phenomena — or at least first explaining individual-level phenomena and then using those findings to draw implications at the CD- or national-level. This focus requires an analysis which retains individuals as the unit of analysis.

If we work with the data at the individual level, and think of the simplest possible analysis — regressing an individual-level Y on the two contextual variables using OLS — then the two designs are equivalent with respect to a number of things that will influence the estimated standard errors: (1) the number of individuals ($N = 800$), (2) the variances of *Open* and *Competitive* (calculated with the individual-level data), and (3) the correlation between *Open* and *Competitive* (calculated with the individual-level data). In such an analysis, the macro-level variables are treated as attributes of individuals, such that all survey respondents living within, say, a district with an open-

---

[22] In a trivariate model, the standard error of each slope coefficient is a function of the variance in the stochastic term, the sample size, the variance in the independent variable, and the correlation between the pair of independent variables (Hanushek and Jackson, 1977). The standard error diminishes as the variance in X increases and as the correlation between the independent variables diminishes (approaches zero).

seat race, would all be assigned the same value on *Open*. As far as OLS is concerned, there is no difference between these macro-level and other, micro-level variables. Hence, if we were estimating a simple regression model with OLS — which, as we argued earlier, is not advisable — the features distinguishing design A and B would not produce differences in their expected standard errors.

This is useful to notice, we think, but the much more important point concerns how the designs affect statistical efficiency when more appropriate models are estimated — multi-level models which recognize that individuals are nested within macro-level units.

One difference between the designs that is taken into account in multi-level modeling involves the effective N that each provides, which varies because of the different clustering entailed in each design. If we assume the intracluster correlation coefficient, ρ, is 0.2, we obtain the effective Ns for each design that are depicted in Table 4.[23] This analysis suggests that design A is better in terms of the overall effective N, but that design B increases the effective N in the strata that are sparsely populated, and produces something close to parity in the effective sample size across the four cells.[24]

Overall, then, design A is advantaged by its larger effective N, but design B is advantaged in that it maximizes variance in the macro-level variables and minimizes their intercorrelation. As this simple example demonstrates, whether designing a sample that is balanced at the CD-level improves the efficiency of one's estimates depends upon whether the efficiency gain in terms of greater variance in the macro-level variables and lower correlation between them outweighs the efficiency loss incurred by the smaller effective sample size.

To illustrate this tradeoff further, and to add more specificity, we draw on the results of simulations similar to the ones we described earlier, where we generated standard errors associated with the coefficients of a multi-level model that included one micro-level explanatory variable (*Political Awareness*), two macro-level

Table 4: Effective sample size

Actual N = 800		Design A		Design B	
		Effective N = 287		Effective N = 254	
500	100	179	36	86	56
100	100	36	36	56	56

[23] Actually, ρ is likely to be variable across these cells, not constant at 0.2, but we set that complication aside.
[24] By increasing the effective N in the sparsely populated cells — e.g., the open seat CDs in our example — design B facilitates subgroup analysis. There are effectively 112 individual-level cases in open seat districts in design B compared to 72 in design A.

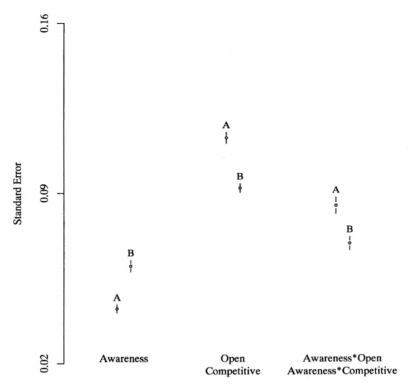

Fig. 3: Simulated standard errors for design A versus design B.

explanatory variables (*Open* and *Competitive*), and the two cross-level interactions. Here, our simulations build in the characteristics of the data implied by design A and design B.[25] Fig. 3 shows the results. As would be expected, the standard errors on *Knowledge* and the cross-level interactions tend to be higher under design B than design A. This reflects design B's smaller effective N. But design B yields more precise estimates of the effects of the macro-level variables. In this case, the benefit from using design B is more substantial than the loss, although the advantage is not overwhelming.

[25] Scholars have given close attention to power in two-level designs characterized by equal cluster sizes, but have not given any attention to designs, like our design B, characterized by unequal cluster sizes. Thus, while programs like PINT will estimate standard errors in designs with equal cluster sizes, they do not recognize the possibility of unequal cluster sizes. Hence, we developed our own simulations, using the lme package in Splus. For design A, $N = 800$, $J = 80$, $n = 10$, *Open* and *Competitive* each have means of 0.25, variances of 0.1875 and are correlated at 0.33. For design B, $N = 800$, $J = 80$, the ns are either 5 or 25, and *Open* and *Competitive* have means of 0.5, maximum variances (0.25) and zero intercorrelation.

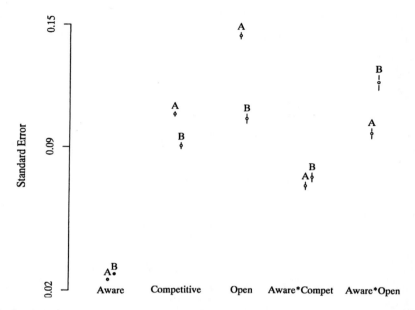

Note: Entries depict the standard errors obtained under designs A and B across 1000 simulations. The dots mark the median SE obtained, while the lines indicate 5th and 95th percentiles. See the text for further details.

Fig. 4: Simulated standard errors for design A versus design B: "realistic" parameter values.

Fig. 4 shows how the standard errors vary across the two designs when the distributions of *Open* and *Competitive* are even more skewed, as is typically the case — with 7% of the races involving open-seats and 13% of the races competitive — and when N and J are set at values more typical of NES studies (1800 cases distributed across 120 CDs).[26] When the population distribution of CD-level characteristics is highly skewed, a sampling plan like design A, which simply reproduces that skewed distribution in the sample, can leave analysts with little power for studying CD-level

All other parameters were set to the values given in footnote 17. For each design, we ran 1000 simulations to generate our standard error estimates. The programs which generated the results in Figs. 3 and 4, can be found at http://socrates.berkeley.edu/~stoker/sampledesign.html. We are grateful to José Pinheiro for helping us with the lme code.

[26] For design A, $n = 15$ (1800/120). For design B, the average $n = 15$, though the cluster sizes vary across cells of the stratification matrix (from a minimum of 2 to a maximum of 50). For design A, the variance of *Open* is 0.062, the variance of *Competitive* is 0.116, and their intercorrelation is 0.29. Design B again assumes maximum variance in *Open* and *Competitive* (0.25) and no intercorrelation. Other parameters were set to the values given in footnote 17.

[27] Since the dependent variables are standardized in these simulations, this means that a true effect size of 1/4 standard deviation would not be discernable.

effects. For example, the estimated standard error on *Open* is almost 0.15, which means that a regression coefficient of magnitude 0.25 would fail to achieve statistical significance at conventional levels.[27] Design B, which balances the sample distribution of each CD-level variable, substantially enhances power in this respect. That enhanced power, however, does not come without cost. One pays some price in terms of the efficiency with which micro-level and cross-level effects are estimated.

Although a sample design that is balanced at the macro-level — like design B — can yield more statistical power than one that is not, statistical efficiency is still hampered by one constraint that is common to both designs: the production of an equal probability sample of individuals. This is most easily illustrated by considering the "realistic" version of design B. The constraints built into that design — that $N = 1800$, $J = 120$, the two macro-level variables be uncorrelated and of maximum variance (i.e., that 30 CDs from each stratum are chosen), and the design produce an equal probability sample of micro-level units — together imply that the sample has dramatically different cluster sizes (n) across the CDs falling into the four cells of the stratifying table. In the open/competitive cell, we have very few respondents per CD (60 total respondents across 30 CDs, for an n of 2), but in the incumbent/non-competitive cell, we have many respondents per CD (1500 total respondents across 30 CDs, for an n of 50). Greater efficiency gains could obviously be made if one did not insist on drawing an equal probability sample at the micro-level. One could then select fewer respondents within the incumbent/non-competitive CDs, which would reduce the average cluster size (n), and then increase the overall number of CDs sampled (J). One might also increase the n of respondents selected in open-seat and competitive districts so as to facilitate subgroup analysis.[28]

In sum, sampling so as to produce greater balance in the distribution of macro-level units across the stratifying variables — and thus, maximizing their variances and minimizing their intercorrelation — can substantially enhance statistical power in estimating macro-level effects. This is particularly the case when the stratifying variables identify relatively rare attributes — like the presence of an open seat, or existence of a highly competitive congressional race. One can achieve even greater gains in efficiency if the design need not produce an equal-probability sample at the individual level (which tends to produce large, inefficient clusters); resources that otherwise must be devoted to increasing n can instead be directed toward increasing J.

5 Sample design and the NES

Although the sample design that the NES has employed over the years has varied, it has typically involved a multi-stage procedure like the one described below for 1988.

---

[28] Simulations comparing design A (equal probability at both stages) and design B (balanced at the macro-level) with a design that is balanced at both levels demonstrate that the latter is far superior in terms of statistical efficiency in estimating both macro-level effects and cross-level interaction effects. See http://socrates.berkeley.edu/~stoker/sampledesign.html.

The 1988 NES is based on a multi-stage area probability sample selected from the survey research center's (SRC) [1980] national sample design. Identification of the 1988 NES sample respondents was conducted using a four stage sampling process — a primary stage sampling of US standard metropolitan statistical areas (SMSAs) and counties, followed by a second stage sampling of area segments, a third stage sampling of housing units within sampled area segments and concluding with the random selection of a single respondent from selected housing units (Miller, 1988).

From the 1988 sampling design emerged 45 1st-stage geographic areas, of which 11 entered at the first stage with a probability of 1 (all large cities), and 34 entered with probability proportionate to their population size. A total of 2040 individuals living in 135 congressional districts responded to the 1988 NES survey, an average of about 15 individuals per district. CDs were partially nested within primary sampling units, so that the effective N of CDs is in the 105–109 range.[29]

Table 5 provides summary information about the sampling design of the NES for each year that congressional district data were gathered since 1956 (a total of 21 years).[30] The only time that the NES departed from its basic area probability sampling design was in 1978 and 1980, when the NES employed a multi-stage procedure that used the CD as the 1st-stage sampling unit. In 1978, 108 CDs were selected at the first stage (J), and roughly 25 individuals per CD (n) were selected in later stages. CDs were first stratified on the basis of a combination of variables that included geographic region, state, urbanization, and recent voting behavior. The individuals sampled within CDs were clustered within lower units, so that the effective N within the districts is substantially lower than 25, on average. As such, the within-district findings cannot be generalized to the CD as a whole.

5.1 *J, n, and* ρ

Fig. 5 contains boxplots that depict the number of respondents per congressional district (n), and list the number of CDs (J), across the NES studies from 1956 to 1998.

[29] Calculating the effective N requires taking into account the degree of clustering in the sample design and the intraclass correlation for any given variable of interest. We estimated the intraclass correlation (ρ) for two variables, one characterizing the race as open or as involving an incumbent (*Open*), and one characterizing the margin of victory (*Margin*). The analysis examined the degree to which CDs were clustered within primary sampling units (i.e., what percentage of the total variation in the two variables was between-PSU variation as opposed to within-PSU variation). For *Open* the $\hat{\rho}$ was 0.14 and for *Margin* the $\hat{\rho}$ was 0.12, and the n was, on average, 3. This translates into an effective N of 105 and 109, respectively. In this analysis and in others that follow we relied upon data on US congressional districts over the 1948–1998 period. We started with machine-readable data put together by Gary King, which covered the 1948–1990 period (ICPSR #6311). We extended the dataset through 1998 using data provided to us by Jennifer Steen. We also linked these data to the NES survey data over the period, allowing us to characterize the CDs sampled by the NES and to identify how they differed from the population of CDs. In such analyses, we excluded CDs from Hawaii and Alaska since those states are excluded from the NES sampling frame.
[30] Additional information about the NES study designs is available at http://www.umich.edu/~nes.

Table 5: NES sample designs since 1956

Year	N of CDs	N of respondents	Sample design summary[a]
1956	145	1762	1950 SRC Sampling Frame 12 sr+54 nsr = 66 PSUs
1958	141	1450	1950 SRC Sampling Frame 12 sr+54 nsr = 66 PSUs
1960	141	1181	1950 SRC Sampling Frame 12 sr+54 nsr = 66 PSUs
1964	138	1571	1960 SRC Sampling Frame 12 sr+62 nsr = 74 PSUs
1966	133	1291	1960 SRC Sampling Frame 12 sr+62 nsr = 74 PSUs
1968	144	1557	1960 SRC Sampling Frame 12 sr+62 nsr = 74 PSUs
1970	155	1507	1960 SRC Sampling Frame 12 sr+62 nsr = 74 PSUs
1972	164	2705	1970 SRC Sampling Frame 12 sr+62 nsr = 74 PSUs
1974	155	1575	1970 SRC Sampling Frame 12 sr+62 nsr = 74 PSUs
1976	162	2248	1970 SRC Sampling Frame 12 sr+62 nsr = 74 PSUs
1978	108	2304	108 CD PSUs
1980	113	1614	108 CD PSUs (1978 Frame)
1982	168	1418	1970 SRC Sampling Frame 12 sr+62 nsr = 74 PSUs
1984	134	2257	1980 SRC Sampling Frame 16 sr+68 nsr = 84 PSUs (11+34 = 45 used)
1986	180	2176	1980 SRC Sampling Frame 16 sr+68 nsr = 84 PSUs (16+45 = 61 used)
1988	135	2040	1980 SRC Sampling Frame 16 sr+68 nsr = 84 PSUs (11+34 = 45 used)
1990	121	1980	1980 SRC Sampling Frame 16 sr+68 nsr = 84 PSUs (11+34 = 45 used)
1992	181	2485	1980 SRC Sampling Frame 16 sr+68 nsr = 84 PSUs (16+45 = 61 used)
1994	190	1795	1980 SRC Sampling Frame 16 sr+68 nsr = 84 PSUs (16+45 = 61 used)
1996	246	1714	1990 SRC Sampling Frame 28 sr+80 nsr = 108 PSUs (18+36 = 44 used)
1998	128	1281	1990 SRC Sampling Frame 28 sr+80 nsr = 108 PSUs (18+36 = 44 used)

[a] In the "Sample design summary" column, we first list the year identifying the SRC sampling frame, and then the number of primary sampling units (PSUs) chosen at the first stage of the sample design. The abbreviation "sr" refers to self-representing (probability of selection = 1), while "nsr" refers to non-self representing. When we identify the number used in parentheses, this means that only a subset of the available PSUs were used in the particular study. A number of studies involved both cross and panel respondents. Only in 1996 did this involve panel respondents who were selected from a different sampling frame (1980) than were the cross-section respondents (1990), and hence from a different collection of PSUs. This is why the number of CDs is so high in 1996.

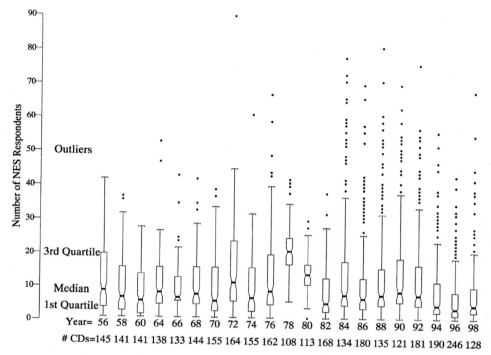

Fig. 5: The number of NES respondents per congressional district, 1956–1998.

The number of CDs varies over time from a low of 108 (in 1978) to a high of 246 (in 1996), with an average of 150. Most of the over-time variation in the number of CDs falling into the sample is a function of how many units were selected at the 1st stage of the multi-stage design (the number of primary sampling units, or PSUs; see Table 5). The unusually high number of CDs in 1996 — 246 — occurred because the study included respondents drawn from both the 1990 PSUs and the 1980 PSUs.[31] The number of PSUs represented in the NES data, therefore, was larger in 1996 than in any other NES study over the period.

The within-district sample sizes ranged from a low of 1 to a high of 90. Except for 1978 and 1980, in each year the distribution of cluster sizes tended to be skewed to the left, with a long right tail. Thus the median *n* tends to be in the range of 6–10, while the means are often substantially larger. Because urban areas fall into the typical

---

[31] Every ten years, after the decennial census, the University of Michigan Survey Research Center redesigns its sampling frame and selects a new set of PSUs. Hence, NES samples are typically drawn from one set of PSUs for four to five election studies, and then when the sampling frame is redesigned, drawn from a new set of PSUs (see Table 5). In the 1996 NES, the panel respondents had originally been selected in 1992 from the 1980 SRC sampling frame, while the fresh cross-section respondents were drawn from the 1990 SRC sampling frame.

NES sample with a high probability at the first stage, most of the CDs with a small *n* are urban and most with a large *n* are rural. In other words, NES respondents are more clustered in rural, than in urban CDs.[32]

It is ironic that the smallest *J* (108) and the largest average *n* (25) over the time series occurs in 1978, the year NES first used the CD as a primary sampling unit in an effort to advance scholars' ability to study congressional elections. Although there are reasons to seek a large within-district *n*, as we have suggested — e.g., if one seeks to generalize to a particular district; to produce within-district "climate of opinion" estimates; to use respondents as informants about the district, candidates or campaigns; or to generate reliable aggregate district opinion measures for use in studies of representation — all of these purposes require a large *effective N* of respondents within districts. As mentioned previously, because of the degree of within-district clustering in the 1978 sample design, this condition is not met. In any event, a large sample of congressional districts still remains very important, in that it substantially affects one's ability to draw conclusions from the data about both the micro- and the macro-level dynamics at work. One could argue, then, that the 1978 design would have been enhanced by increasing *J* at the expense of *n*.

As we pointed out earlier, the effective *N* in a cluster design is a function of ρ (rho) as well as *J* and *n*. For micro-level variables, ρ indicates the extent to which respondents are similar to one another within macro-level units. Table 6 shows typical values of $\hat{\rho}$ for an illustrative set of NES variables, based on treating respondents as nested within congressional districts. As would be expected, the $\hat{\rho}$ values are largest when the variables concern CD-specific stimuli. Notice, for example, that the $\hat{\rho}$ is higher for *Incumbent Approval* than for *Congress Approval*. That is, the within-district similarity is higher when respondents are asked about their own district's incumbent than when they are asked about Congress.[33] Notice also that the values of $\hat{\rho}$ are substantially higher for two specific variables in the set: Vote Choice, and *Incumbent's Perceived Ideology* (average $\hat{\rho}$ values of 0.275 and 0.213, respectively). What such high values of $\hat{\rho}$ reflect is the explanatory importance of CD-level variables. There is more homogeneity within districts on variables like *Vote Choice* and *Incumbent's Perceived Ideology* than on the others in the table; correspondingly, more of the total variation in these two variables is between-district variation.

These high values of $\hat{\rho}$ convey two points simultaneously. First, they remind us, vividly, that CD-level variables are likely to be very important to explaining why

---

[32] Since the 1st stage of the sampling procedure is only redesigned every decade, following the decennial census, there is a very substantial departure from independence in the sampling of CDs and individuals over time. This issue is discussed and illustrated in Appendix B.

[33] When one is gathering data on respondents' judgments and choices concerning the candidates in their own districts but striving to analyze the full national sample of respondents, one must construct variables that render the judgments and choices of respondents across districts comparable. This means, for example, recording the respondent's vote choice as a vote for the Democrat or the Republican, even though there is a different pair of Democratic and Republican candidates involved in each district. The ρs will tend to be higher for such variables than for variables where common questions were asked of all respondents concerning common stimuli (e.g., evaluations of Congress or of the President); the variance across districts (relative to within) will tend to be higher because the stimulus itself is varying across the districts.

Table 6: Homogeneity among NES respondents within Congressional districts: intraclass correlation coefficients ($\hat{\rho}$)[a]

	Party identification	Vote turnout	Vote choice	Congress approval	Incumbent approval	Candidate recall	Candidate salience	Incumbent thermometer	Incumbent's ideology
Mean $\hat{\rho}$	0.105	0.066	0.275	0.014	0.067	0.102	0.117	0.076	0.213
Minimum $\hat{\rho}$	0.074	0.024	0.111	0.000	0.004	0.063	0.051	0.032	0.122
Maximum $\hat{\rho}$	0.158	0.134	0.495	0.032	0.125	0.207	0.235	0.144	0.293

[a] Entries are summaries (mean, minimum, maximum) of the estimated intraclass correlation coefficient ($\hat{\rho}$) for the variable named in the column across the 21 election studies. $\hat{\rho}$ is calculated based on the decomposition of the total sums of squares for Y (the column variable) into two components: the variation within CDs and the variation between CDs. $\hat{\rho}$ is essentially a ratio of the between-CD variation to the total variation.

voters make the choices they do. Understanding variation in the vote requires understanding how the attributes of candidates, campaigns, and district contexts enter in.
Second, they imply that when the design clusters a relatively large number of respondents into a relatively small number of congressional districts, then the effective
micro-level N relevant to analyses of the vote will be substantially diminished. In 1988,
for example, while the total N was 2040, the effective N given a $\hat{\rho}$ of 0.275 was about
1/5 of that — 420.[34] No design modification will influence the fact that, as long as
CD-level variables are influential, then individuals who are nested within CDs will
tend toward homogeneity. The only response one can make is to try and exploit the
features of the design that are under one's control. With ρ reaching magnitudes of 0.2
and even up to 0.5 (see Table 6), the imperative to do so is even stronger. In short,
these findings underscore the importance of trying to build more power into one's
sample design — by increasing J at the expense of n, and by employing stratification
strategically.

5.2 Using CD as a sampling unit — or not

Most of our earlier discussion has focused on how to design a sample under the
assumption that one would use the congressional district as a 1st-stage sampling unit.
Yet, with the exception of 1978 and 1980, this has not been the NES practice. There
are two important implications that follow from this.

First, if the CD is not a sampling unit, one cannot exert the same kind of control
over those aspects of the research design that we have emphasized — J, n, and the
characteristics of the CDs sampled (stratification). One can still exert some control, of
course, by, for example, increasing the number of PSUs sampled (and hence the
number of CDs) and by stratifying PSUs on attributes likely to be correlated with variables important to understanding congressional elections (which is probably not
urban/rural). Consider the 1996 NES study, which turned out to have a relatively strong
design for the analysis of congressional elections. Because the NES in 1996 reinter-
viewed some respondents originally selected in 1992 using the 1980 SRC sampling
frame, while also interviewing a fresh cross-section of respondents drawn from the
1990 SRC sampling frame, the number of CDs was unusually large and the average
n was unusually small. This was probably an unforeseen, but nevertheless fortuitous,
side-effect of a design settled upon for reasons that have nothing to do with studying
congressional elections. In any event, in terms of the control that can be exerted over
the design, one is far better off using the CD as the sampling unit.[35]

---

[34] In calculating this figure we used the average *Vote Choice* $\hat{\rho}$ of 0.275, the N of 2040, the average n of
15, and the equation for effective N shown earlier [Eq. (4)]. Even this low estimate of the effective N is
probably too large, in that it assumes that the CDs are chosen at random (i.e., that the effective N of CDs
is J). But CDs were partially nested within PSUs in 1988.

[35] It is conceivable that one would field a large enough study to gather survey data on individuals within
all 435 districts in the US. Then, the CD would not be a sampling unit; instead, the sample design would
involve stratification by CD.

The second issue concerns generalization. The NES studies have been designed to generate a representative sample of eligible voters but not a representative sample of congressional districts (except, as noted above, in 1978 and 1980). If the CD is not used as a basis of sampling, then CDs fall into the sample for reasons that are not entirely foreseeable, or at least fall into the sample with no well-defined probability.[36] Since we do not have an equal probability sample of CDs there is no reason to expect the NES sample of CDs to look just like the population. In fact, for example, the NES has tended to overrepresent CDs with Democratic incumbents or where Democrats have tended to win by large margins. Correspondingly, the NES has tended to underrepresent CDs with Republican incumbents or large Republican margins of victory. This is demonstrated in Fig. 6.[37]

Without random selection at the CD stage one cannot generalize sample findings about districts to the population of CDs, just as one cannot generalize from a non-probability sample of individuals to a larger population of individuals. In other words, there is no reason to believe that findings based on the CDs that fall into the NES

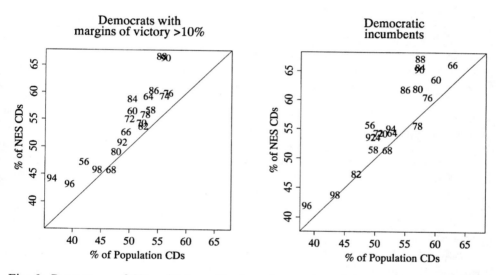

Fig. 6: Percentage of CDs with large Democratic margins of victory, and percentage of CDs with Democratic incumbents — population percentages versus NES percentages.

[36] In fact, the probability of selection for any given CD could, in principle, be estimated, using information about the probability of selection, and population size, of PSUs and lower-level sampling units. This would not be an easy task — and to our knowledge, it has never been attempted — but if these probabilities were calculated then sampling weights could be devised to remedy the problems concerning generalizability we address here.

[37] We emphasize: This does not mean that the NES sample of respondents fails to represent the population from which it is drawn. Except in 1978 and 1980, the NES studies have not been designed to generate a representative sample of CDs, but only to generate a representative sample of eligible voters in the continental United States (excluding Alaska and Hawaii).

sample would be similar to what one would observe if analyzing the population of CDs as a whole. With a design like the NES, one can only make generalizable statements about individuals, and even then one must avoid statements which sneak in the assumption that the NES sample of CDs is representative. For example, one would be on shaky ground concluding that "Men and women reacted differently to the female congressional candidates running in 1998" if such a conclusion emerged from an analysis of the NES data. There is no particular reason to believe that this same relationship would be observed in an analysis of how voters reacted to the full set of female congressional candidates vying for office across the nation.

5.3 Sampling CDs with rare attributes — or not

When sampling rare events, one is more likely to undersample them than to oversample them, especially if the number of independent draws is small. With a dichotomous variable, where one outcome is rare (e.g., competitive race) and the other outcome is common (uncompetitive race), this is given by the asymmetry of the binomial distribution. If, for example, 5% of the races in the population are competitive, then it is likely that less than 5% of one's sampled CDs will be competitive. This is one reason why stratification is a useful procedure. If the population were first stratified on the basis of the competitive/uncompetitive variable, then any random deviations from the 5%/95% breakdown in the sample could be avoided. One could, for example, ensure that exactly five competitive CDs fell into one's sample of 100 CDs.

In the case of the NES, the number of independent draws is sufficiently small so as to make this a potential problem, at least with respect to sampling relatively rare events (e.g., CDs with competitive, open-seat races). That number — i.e., the effective N of CDs — is no more than the actual number of CDs that falls into the NES sample, and can be substantially lower than that, given the multi-stage clustered sample design that the NES employs (though it will be no smaller than the number of primary sampling units drawn at the first stage of the sample). As mentioned earlier, in 1988, for example, 135 CDs fell into the NES study, but the effective N was in the range of 105 to 109. Fig. 7 shows that, across the 21 election studies we are examining, the NES sample did tend to produce fewer CDs with competitive, open-seat races than were present in the population. This pattern is consistent with the argument we reviewed above, although it is also possible that it is caused by some other aspect of the multi-stage sample design.

The fact that we are vulnerable to undersampling CDs with rare traits is not inconsequential, but the much more serious problem is that, even without such accidents of chance — i.e., even if our sample percentage exactly equaled the population percentage — we end up with a sample with very, very few micro- and macro-level cases with the attribute in question. The worst year for the NES in this respect was 1988, where only 22 respondents came from a district with a competitive, open-seat race (1.1% of the total sample), and all of these respondents came from one district (see Table 7). By contrast, 1776 (90.1%) of the 1988 NES respondents, from 121 districts, faced

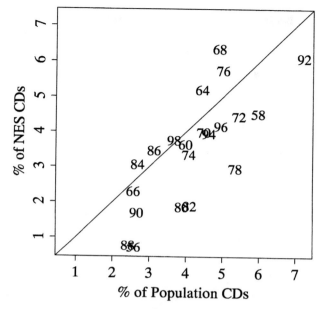

Fig. 7: Percentage of CDs with open-seat and competitive races — population percentages versus NES percentages.

uncompetitive races involving an incumbent. In one of the better years, 1994, the NES sample included 111 respondents (6.7%) from seven districts in the competitive/open category, and 1254 respondents (75.2%) from 138 districts in the uncompetitive/incumbent category.

What this means is that the variance in CD-level explanatory variables like *Open* and *Competitive* is typically, and in years like 1988, extremely limited. With so few CD-level cases in three of the four cells of the table obtained by crossing *Open* and *Competitive*, statistical efficiency is seriously diminished. And, if one seeks to elaborate the model by adding additional CD-level variables or by building interactions among them, serious problems involving multicollinearity are likely to arise.

One response in this circumstance, as we suggested earlier, is to alter the sample design by sampling so as to ensure balance in the number of CDs with crucial attributes (our "design B", Table 3). This would essentially even out the CD percentages in Table 7 and generate more statistical power for estimating CD-level effects. This, however, may not be a bold enough step. If the sample design remains an equal probability sample at the individual-level, the alteration just described would leave the percentage of respondents falling into the various CD categories in Table 7 unchanged. Do we really want upwards of 75% — and as high as 90% — of the NES respondents to reside in districts where there is essentially no race?

Table 7: Congressional districts in the NES: distribution of CDs and respondents[a]

Year		Incumbent not competitive	Incumbent competitive	Open-seat not competitive	Open-seat competitive
56	NES CDs	76.1	17.6	5.6	0.7
	NES Rs	76.2	18.2	4.2	1.4
58	NES CDs	66.2	20.3	9.0	4.5
	NES Rs	56.9	30.3	9.1	3.6
60	NES CDs	78.3	14.5	3.6	3.6
	NES Rs	69.9	21.4	5.5	3.1
64	NES CDs	71.1	16.3	7.4	5.2
	NES Rs	66.4	21.9	6.8	4.8
66	NES CDs	78.6	12.2	6.9	2.3
	NES Rs	80.3	11.3	7.2	1.2
68	NES CDs	78.2	9.2	6.3	6.3
	NES Rs	78.0	11.9	4.0	6.1
70	NES CDs	81.5	7.9	6.6	4.0
	NES Rs	84.5	8.2	5.0	2.3
72	NES CDs	75.9	8.9	10.8	4.4
	NES Rs	78.0	7.0	9.0	6.0
74	NES CDs	70.7	16.0	10.0	3.3
	NES Rs	66.8	19.5	7.4	6.2
76	NES CDs	80.3	5.7	8.3	5.7
	NES Rs	78.0	6.4	11.7	3.9
78	NES CDs	80.4	6.9	9.8	2.9
	NES Rs	80.0	7.3	9.2	3.5
80	NES CDs	83.3	11.1	3.7	1.9
	NES Rs	82.4	11.2	4.9	1.5
82	NES CDs	69.4	13.8	15.0	1.9
	NES Rs	71.4	15.0	10.4	3.2
84	NES CDs	83.2	7.6	6.1	3.1
	NES Rs	80.6	10.2	8.5	0.7
86	NES CDs	86.2	4.6	5.7	3.4
	NES Rs	88.4	5.2	4.9	1.4
88	NES CDs	91.7	2.3	5.3	0.8
	NES Rs	90.1	1.2	7.6	1.1
90	NES CDs	88.2	5.0	5.0	1.7
	NES Rs	87.8	3.0	4.6	4.7
92	NES CDs	68.0	13.3	12.7	6.1
	NES Rs	67.4	12.4	15.7	4.5
94	NES CDs	77.5	11.8	6.7	3.9
	NES Rs	75.2	10.0	8.2	6.7
96	NES CDs	75.9	12.9	7.1	4.1
	NES Rs	77.8	12.9	5.5	3.7
98	NES CDs	83.2	9.3	3.7	3.7
	NES Rs	76.8	11.4	1.6	10.2

[a] Cell entries contain %s, describing the distribution of NES cases across the four category CD-level variable identified in the top row. The % of NES CDs is the % of CDs in the NES sample (i.e., represented by at least one NES respondent) with the named characteristic. The % of Rs is the % of respondents falling into the named type of CD.

6 Conclusion

Our advice about how to design a study of congressional elections challenges both conventional wisdom and current practice. If congressional elections are predominantly local affairs, where what is happening in local contexts is critical to understanding the election outcome, then despite intuition to the contrary, we should be designing national surveys that sample relatively few individuals within relatively many CDs. We should also exert control over which CDs fall into our sample, by using CD as a sampling unit and stratifying by important explanatory variables. These stratifying variables are likely to be political, not geographic. Stratification will ensure that our sample contains sufficient variation on key macro-level explanatory variables, enhancing the value of the data to analysts. Even further gains in statistical efficiency can be made by undertaking a national survey that does not generate an equal probability sample of eligible voters (though it should, of course, sample eligible voters with known probability so that sampling weights can be devised and applied). This means oversampling individuals within districts that have rare traits, undersampling in other districts to avoid the inefficiencies of large clusters, and directing resources toward extending the overall CD sample size.

To illustrate and defend these arguments, we have relied on examples, simulations, and data analysis. In this process, we have been quite critical of the NES multi-stage cluster sample design. What we have not discussed is that the NES' use of this design reflects cost considerations that flow from the NES commitment to in-person interviewing, which, itself is based on a commitment to data quality. It is simply too costly (in terms of expense) to conduct in-person interviews with a widely dispersed sample of respondents, and too costly (in terms of data quality) to abandon the in-person sampling frame and interview format. Throughout this chapter we have not considered the practical difficulties associated with implementing various sample designs, nor situated our advice about sampling within a broader research design framework. But, of course, it makes no sense to encourage researchers to pursue sampling strategies that are too expensive to execute or would compromise data quality. Similarly, while stratification on political variables is desirable from a theoretical standpoint, one needs stratifying variables for which data on population units can be collected, with relative ease, well in advance of the fieldwork. When designing any sample, such considerations must be balanced alongside the kinds of statistical considerations that we have emphasized.

Thus, we think of our advice as opening or reopening, not closing, the discussion about how to design surveys of congressional elections. At the same time, although we have mentioned "congressional" 53 times, "district" 115 times and "NES" 116 times so far, this chapter has not just been about designing research focused on congressional elections in the United States. Our arguments are applicable to any research problem involving multiple levels of analysis. The most obvious extension is to research focused on subnational elections in other countries. But multi-level problems are many and varied. Researchers studying political institutions examine bureaucrats nested within bureaucracies and legislators nested within legislatures. Political communications researchers gather data on newspaper articles nested within newspapers and advertisements nested within campaigns. In each of these cases and others, researchers must decide how to trade J for n, how to stratify, and must grapple with ρ. We hope that this discussion, while focused on the study of congressional elections in the US, sheds light on the design issues scholars facing other multi-level problems must confront.

Acknowledgements

In preparing this chapter, we benefited from helpful conversations with Charles Franklin, Don Green, Jim Lepkowski, Sam Lucas, Richard Gonzales, José Pinheiro, Stephen Raudenbush, Tom Snijders, and Charles Stein. Ben Highton, Mark Franklin, Tom Piazza, and Chris Wlezien gave us helpful comments on an earlier draft. The Institute of Governmental Studies and the Survey Research Center at UC-Berkeley provided valuable research support. Our analysis uses the program PINT (Power in Two-Level Designs) developed by Tom Snijders and Roel Bosker, available at http://stat.gamma.rug.nl/snijders/. We are also grateful to Stephen Raudenbush for providing us with a beta-version of Optimal Design, and the associated algorithm for calculating power in multi-level designs, and to Liu Xiaofeng for helping us with that transaction. Finally, we thank Jennifer Steen for providing us with machine-readable data on US congressional districts from 1992 to 1998, and Pat Luevano of the NES staff for helping us sort out various discrepancies between the district-level data and the NES data. We alone retain responsibility for any errors of fact or interpretation.

Appendix A: The multi-level model

The multi-level model was developed to represent how the behavior of individuals is influenced by their own (individual-level) characteristics as well as the characteristics of the contexts in which they are nested (CDs, in our case). Below, we illustrate the model for the case in which there are two district-level explanatory variables and one individual-level explanatory variable. Interested readers should consult Bryk and Raudenbush (1992), Goldstein (1999), Jones and Steenbergen (1997), Kreft and De Leeuw (1998), and Snijders and Bosker (1999) for further details.

$$y_{ij} = \beta_{0j} + \beta_{1j} x_{ij} + e_{ij} \tag{A1}$$

$$\beta_{0j} = \gamma_{00} + \gamma_{01} z_{1j} + \gamma_{02} z_{2j} + u_{0j} \tag{A2}$$

$$\beta_{1j} = \gamma_{10} + \gamma_{11} z_{1j} + \gamma_{12} z_{2j} + u_{1j} \tag{A3}$$

Combining the previous three equations, we have:

$$y_{ij} = \gamma_{00} + \gamma_{01} z_{1j} + \gamma_{02} z_{2j} + u_{0j} + (x_{ij})(\gamma_{10} + \gamma_{11} z_{1j} + \gamma_{12} z_{2j} + u_{1j}) + e_{ij} \tag{A4}$$

$$= \gamma_{00} + \gamma_{01} z_{1j} + \gamma_{02} z_{2j} + \gamma_{10} x_{ij} + \gamma_{11} z_{1j} x_{ij} + \gamma_{12} z_{2j} x_{ij} + (u_{0j} + u_{1j} x_{ij} + e_{ij}), \tag{A5}$$

where $j = 1 \ldots J$ and $i = 1 \ldots n_j$.

Eq. (A1) specifies the relationship at the micro level (where x_{ij} is the individual-level independent variable). Eqs (A2) and (A3) specify the relationship between the coefficients of the micro-level equation and the macro-level variables. Finally, Eqs (A4) and (A5) combine the previous equations into a single equation. With this model, one can evaluate the extent to which a macro-level variable (z_{1j} or z_{2j}) directly influences the dependent variable. At the same time, the micro-level regression coefficients β, are allowed to vary across macro-level units. That is, each macro-level unit (j) is allowed to have its own intercept (β_{0j}) and slope (β_{1j}). The mean of the distributions of these intercepts and slopes is summarized by the γ terms found in Eq. (A5). The term γ_{00} is the overall mean of y_{ij}; γ_{01} and γ_{02} indicate the (average) direct effects of the macro-level variables on y_{ij}; γ_{10} indicates the (average) direct effect of the micro-level variable; γ_{11} and γ_{12} indicate the (average) effect of the cross-level interactions.

In Eq. (A5) the terms from Eq. (A4) have been reordered to put all of the error terms at the end, in parentheses. Notice that this error component includes a term that refers to the micro-level independent variable. The existence of this term is taken into account in multi-level model estimation, but would not be taken into account if one simply tried to estimate the effect of micro-level, macro-level, and cross-level interaction variables with OLS (hence, resulting in bias with OLS estimation). This error component also includes terms (u_{0j} and u_{1j}) that refer to the variance in the macro-level intercepts and slopes, respectively. And, it contains the micro-level disturbance (e_{ij}). Either Maximum Likelihood or Generalized Least Squares is necessary to efficiently estimate the model (Snijders and Bosker, 1999, pp. 56–57).

Appendix B: Non-independence across time in the NES sample of CDs

The first stage of the NES sampling procedure, involving the selection of PSUs, is revised every ten years, in the wake of the decennial census. Because of this, once a CD falls into the sample it tends to stay there for study after study, until the next census is taken and the NES sampling frame is revised. In other words, there is a substantial departure from independence in the sampling of CDs (and individuals) over time. The extent of this departure is illustrated in Fig. 8. Along the X-axis is the number of times that a CD fell into the NES sample over the 21 election studies between 1956 and 1998 where CD information is available from NES. The height of the bars represents the proportion of CDs falling into each category along the X-axis. Thus, for example, the first bar shows that 14.8% of the CDs were never represented in any NES sample over the period, while the last bar shows that .6% were represented 20 out of 21 times. The area under the illustrated density curve indicates the expected percentages under an assumption of independence of the draws.[38] The contrast is stark.

This figure can be viewed as illustrative, but no more, in that it builds in a problematic assumption — namely, that the identity of a given CD is unchanging over the

---

[38] The figure depicts the binomial density with P set to .35, since on average over the period the NES sample included 35% of the population of CDs.

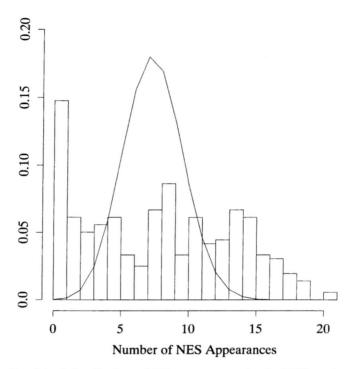

Number of NES Appearances

Fig. 8: Empirical distribution of CD appearances in the NES, and expected distribution under an assumption of independence in the draws.

entire time span. In developing this figure, we first threw out all CDs that did not "endure" over the 1956–1998 period. Some were created after 1956, as a function of redistricting, and some that once existed later disappeared, again because of redistricting. By our count, a total of 512 CDs were in existence for at least one election over the 32 years; 359 were in existence for the entire period. This assumes, however, that any district which retained its unique identifying number over time was actually the same unit at each point in time. This, however, is clearly wrong. Minnesota District 2, for example, may have completely been transformed in its boundaries, perhaps several times, over the period. The over-time dependence in the sample of CDs, illustrated in Fig. 8, only becomes an issue for research that analyzes CD-level data over time. Yet such research cannot even be begun without solving the seemingly intractable "unit change" problem just described.

References

Achen, C.H. 1982. Interpreting and Using Regression. Sage, Newbury Park, CA.
Achen, C.H., Shively, W.P. 1995. Cross-Level Inference. University of Chicago Press, Chicago.

Brown, R.D., Woods, J.A. 1992. Toward a model of congressional elections, Journal of Politics 53(2), pp. 454–473.

Bryk, A.S., Raudenbush, S.W. 1992. Hierarchical Linear Models. Sage, Newbury Park, CA.

Fisher, G.A. 1988. Problems in the use and interpretation of product variables, In: Long, J.S. (ed.), Common Problems, Proper Solutions: Avoiding Error in Quantitative Research. Sage, Newbury Park, CA.

Goldstein, H. 1999. Multilevel Statistical Models. Arnold, London. Internet Edition, available at http://www.arnoldpublishers.com/support/goldstein.htm.

Hanushek, E.A., Jackson, J.E. 1977. Statistical Methods for Social Scientists. Academic Press, San Diego, CA.

Jacobson, G.C. 1997. The Politics of Congressional Elections, 4th ed. Longman, London.

Jones, B.S., Steenbergen, M.R. 1997. Modeling multilevel data structures. Paper prepared for the 14th annual meeting of the Political Methodology Society, Columbus OH, July 25.

Judd, C.M., Smith, E.R., Kidder, L.H. 1991. Research Methods in Social Relations, 6th ed. Harcourt Brace Jovanovich, New York.

Kish, L. 1965. Survey Sampling. Wiley, New York.

Kreft, I., De Leeuw, J. 1998. Introducing Multilevel Modeling. Sage, London.

Longford, N.T. 1993. Random Coefficient Models. Clarendon Press, Oxford.

McPhee, W.N., Glaser, W.A. 1962. Public Opinion and Congressional Elections. Free Press, New York.

Miller, W.E. 1988. Codebook: American National Election Studies: 1988 Pre-Post Study. University of Michigan: Center for Political Studies, Michigan.

Miller, W.E., Stokes, D.E. 1963. Onstituency influence in congress, American Political Science Review 57, pp. 45–56.

Mok, M. 1995. Sample size requirements for 2-level designs in educational research. Unpublished manuscript.

Pinheiro, J.C., Bates, D.M. 2000. Mixed-Effects Models in S and S-PLUS. Springer, New York

Raudenbush, S.W. 1997. Statistical analysis and optimal design for cluster randomized trials, Psychological Methods 2(2), pp. 173–185.

Shaw, D.R. 1999. The effect of TV ads and candidate appearances on statewide presidential votes, 1988–96, American Political Science Review 93(2), pp. 345–361.

Shaw, D.R. 1999. The methods behind the madness: presidential electoral college strategies, 1988–1996, Journal of Politics 61(4), pp. 893–913.

Snijders, T., Bosker, R. 1993. Standard errors and sample sizes for two-level research, Journal of Educational Statistics 18(3), pp. 237–259.

Snijders, T., Bosker, R. 1999. Multilevel Modeling: An Introduction to Basic and Advanced Multilevel Modeling. Sage, London.

Westlye, M.C. 1991. Senate Elections and Campaign Intensity. Johns Hopkins University Press, Baltimore, MD.

Zaller, J.R. 1992. The Nature and Origins of Mass Opinion. Cambridge University Press, New York.

Chapter 7

National election studies and macro analysis

R.S. Erikson

This chapter discusses the contribution of the American National Election Studies (ANES) data to the understanding of macro-level election analysis. It reviews the theory of the micro–macro connection and presents two brief examples where ANES data are used to explain macro-level variation in election outcomes. It argues that the ANES — indeed, most election studies — as currently constituted are quite useful for the purposes of explaining election outcomes. However, with proper attention to the requirements of such explanations, they can be made more useful still.

1 Introduction

Studies of voting and elections take place at both the micro- and the macro-level. Micro-level explanations account for individual vote decisions, such as 'why did some people vote for x while others voted for y?'. Macro-level explanations account for aggregate election outcomes, such as 'why did x win the election and by that particular margin of victory?'. Each has an important place in the study of electoral politics, and each is compatible with the other in the sense that macro-level explanations must derive — in theory — from micro-level behavior.

As national election studies provide data about individual voters, they primarily serve the interests of micro-level analysts. In theory if not in practice, national election studies also provide information for macro-level explanation. The most obvious way is when sample means from surveys (e.g. mean party identification) serve as independent variables predicting election outcomes. More importantly, national election studies allow for close attention to the micro–macro connection, to reveal how micro-level processes translate into macro-level electoral change. With care, national election studies allow estimates not only of why people vote the way they do but also why each election turns out the way it does.

The Future of Election Studies
Copyright © 2002 by Elsevier Science Ltd.
All rights of reproduction in any form reserved.
ISBN: 0-08-044174-2

This chapter addresses the contribution — in theory and practice — of the American National Election Studies (ANES) to the macro-level analysis of election outcomes in the United States. A brief historical context is presented Section 2. Section 3 addresses the theory of how the micro-level analysis of survey respondents informs macro-level understanding, with two illustrations of macro-level explanation built from the foundations of the ANES. Section 4 recalls Donald Stokes' (1966) six-component model of election outcomes, first unveiled in 1966. In Section 5, I attempt to account for the recent presidential elections in terms of ideological proximity and party identification, using ANES data. The chapter concludes with a brief discussion of potential changes in national election studies to enhance macro-level understanding.

2 Historical context

The explanation of national election outcomes has always been an implicit goal of the 'Michigan' national election studies. The authors of *The American Voter* (Campbell et al., 1960) posed a central question: why did Republican Dwight Eisenhower win the presidential elections of 1952 and 1956? Their answer was that despite the Democratic edge in party identification, Ike won because he was likeable.

The same authors and their intellectual progeny studied subsequent elections with similar implicit questions specific to the particular contests. For the 1960 election, they asked: was Kennedy helped more than hurt by his Catholicism (Converse, 1966; Converse et al., 1966)? For 1964 they asked: was Johnson's landslide victory due to Goldwater's perceived extremism (Converse et al., 1965)? And for 1968 and 1972, they asked, among other questions: what was the role of the War in Vietnam (Converse et al., 1969; Miller et al., 1976)?

Although of interest to their contemporaries, from today's vantage point these studies provide, at best, impressionistic accounts of past elections. By the 1980s, American political scientists largely stopped trying to explain specific election outcomes. At least with their 'political scientist' hats in place, they rarely ventured answers to such questions as to why Ronald Reagan, or later Bill Clinton, got elected or re-elected, or exactly why Bush beat Dukakis. Despite their obvious topical appeal, these questions have a case study feel to them and are not easily answered in a vacuum. The one recent election to provoke a mild outburst of interest in specific electoral explanation was the 1994 mid-term election in which the Republicans gained control of the Congress after a 40-year drought. There the question was not so much why the Republicans did so well in this particular instance but whether it meant the arrival of the long-awaited permanent realignment of American electoral politics (Abramowitz and Saunders, 1998).

In recent decades, the analysis of election outcomes has shifted from the collection of case studies to the analysis of time-series data. These studies emphasize the role of economic indicators (especially) together with auxiliary indicators of government popularity (Erikson and Wlezien, 1996; Campbell and Garand, 2000). We learn from these studies that election results strongly follow the economy, with good times leading to the electoral success of the incumbent party. Having a popular president helps, too, even apart from the economy.

Perhaps regrettably, contemporary macro-level models have become largely divorced from the ANES and the study of micro-level data. If macro-level models imply a particular micro-level model as their foundation, it might seem to be the model of the apolitical voter who puts a finger to the wind to see how the economic winds are blowing, and from this, and more intangible candidate likeability factors, chooses a candidate. From micro-level studies, we know this to be a deficient model of the individual voter. People evaluate parties and candidates based on issues or ideology, and, above all, on the standing decision that is their party identification. Do these variables have no role in American electoral politics? Could it not be the case that elections are won or lost based on which candidate best follows the moderating directives of Downs's (1957) *Economic Theory of Democracy*? And what about changing party identification? For instance, could we explain the Democratic Party's dominance of the congressional elections and the displacement by a Republican majority in 1994 by, first, the Democratic edge in party identification, and then the diminution, if not extinction, of this Democratic edge by the mid-1990s?

The resolution of these seeming contradictions is complex. However, the simple answer is that variables which are important at the micro-level are not necessarily the same variables that are important at the macro-level. Although party identification and ideology account for individual votes, their ability to account for macro-level electoral change is limited by their seeming constancy. For instance, the authors of *The American Voter* never thought to explain election outcomes by a changing partisanship of the electorate (except on realignment) because they thought that partisanship rarely changed (except, again, on realignment).

3 Theory: the micro–macro connection

Just as some variables are important at the micro-level but fairly constant at the macro-level, other variables may be relatively unimportant at explaining individual votes but still important at the macro-level. Economic perceptions provide an example. All voters are influenced to some degree — perhaps very slight — by the common signal of the national economy. Variations in the economy from election year to election year would leave but a trace effect with individual voters, yet the movement would be unidirectional toward or against the incumbent party, and by an amount calibrated by the degree of economic success or failure.[1]

It is a cliché to say that a macro-level phenomenon represents the aggregate composition of micro-level phenomena. Applied to voting data, the composition equation takes the general form:

$$V_{it} = \alpha_t + \sum_{j=1}^{k} \beta_{jt} X_{ijt} + u_{it} \tag{1}$$

---

[1] This position is consistent with Kramer's (1983) argument about the limits of understanding economic effects using individual-level perceptual data. One learns more about economic effects from studying economic aggregate data than from studying varying perceptions of survey respondents regarding the common signal of the cross-sectional national economy.

where V_{it} is the vote margin for a specific party, which we designate to be the Republicans (or the propensity to vote for that party, using probit), accounted for as a function of k independent (X) variables plus a time-varying election specific para-meter, α_t. Time is subscripted here since we presume the equation spans multiple elections. The β parameters are subscripted by time to signify that they can be allowed to vary by time.

It helps to calibrate the X's by measuring them as deviations from their zero points, where zero is scored as the point that represents partisan neutrality ('Independent' or 'moderate'). With natural zero points for the Xs, we test whether the X's successfully account for the election outcome. We see this by converting the micro-level equation, Eq. (1), into its corresponding macro-level equation, Eq. (2). In Eq. (2), the units are now mean scores for each election year:

$$\bar{V}_t = \alpha_t + \sum_{j=1}^{k} \beta_{jt} \bar{X}_{jt} \tag{2}$$

where the mean u_i for each year t dissipates to zero as errors cancel out. In Eq. (2), the α_t parameter represents the expected vote when the Xs are neutral. If α_t is 0.5 (with OLS, or zero with probit), the Xs perfectly account for the aggregate vote's departure from the benchmark of an even 50–50 split. Higher values of α_t signify that additional unobserved variables push the net vote more Republican than the X's do by themselves. Lower values signify the comparable Democratic push by unobserved variables.[2]

Because the variances of the variables are different at the micro-level (Eq. (1)) and macro-level (Eq. (2)), independent variables can be relatively 'important' at the macro-level but not at the micro-level, and vice versa.[3] At the micro-level, the important independent variables have large 'within-year' variances. At the macro-level, the im-portant independent variables have large 'between-year' variances.

Suppose we model Eq. (1) by applying probit or OLS to the survey data from multiple national election studies in different years.[4] Special attention should be given to the intercept, or α_t term, for year effects. Year effects would be represented by a set of year dummy variables. Their coefficients would suggest importance at the macro-level because all the variance of these dummies would be between years rather than within years. At the same time, the goal would be to make these year effects go away, as they become subsumed by other variables. When year effects disappear, one has successfully identified the micro-level processes that account for the macro-level differences. We will see that this can be an illusive goal.

---

[2] While all this is neat and tidy, we should be aware of the complication of contextual effects: that the composition of others' individual attributes can affect individual decisions. For example, the commonly shared perceptions of a robust economy could affect voting decisions independent of individuals reacting to their individual perceptions of the economy. Or the ideological extremism of a candidate could affect the candidate's attractiveness independently of people responding to their personal ideological proximity to the candidate.

[3] By importance, we mean in the sense of 'beta' coefficients or explained variance (not always the same thing). The more variance in the independent variable, the greater will be its beta coefficient and the amount of variance it can explain.

[4] Or, by analogy, multiple national election studies for similar time points but different countries.

4 The Stokes six-components model

In 1966, Donald Stokes published a six-components model of presidential elections, 1952–1964. Stokes began with a micro-level analysis to account for vote decisions as a function of the responses to open-ended party and candidate evaluations. These were coded according to the frequency and valence of open-ended responses about party and candidate likes and dislikes, along six specific attitude dimensions. Stokes then translated the micro-level equations into macro-level effects based on the mean levels of the six components and the changing estimates of the parameters, following the logic discussed above in relation to Eqs. (1) and (2). Stokes validated that the six components did indeed approximately account for the actual vote margins in the four elections in the sense that the projected vote was close to 50–50 when the X's were neutral.

This analysis had several noteworthy features. First, it was performed using regression rather than probit, which allowed the accounting to proceed by the direct summing of vote components into the vote margin. Second, the modeling assumed separate β coefficients for each year, so that a dimension can rise or fall in aggregate importance based both on the mean response and the dimension's salience. Third, the modeling was unique in its reliance solely on open-ended responses for the generation of independent variables.

Stokes' six-component model has been updated several times (Popkin et al., 1976; Kagay and Caldeira, 1979; Asher, 1984; Gapoian and Hackett, 1986), although with little fanfare. Table 1 updates the Stokes analysis through 1992, thanks to the compilation by Wattier (n.d.). Included in Table 1 is the illustration of the construction of the six components, using the 1992 election as the example.

As Stokes was the first to note, the components that move the most are the personal characteristics for the Democratic and Republican candidates. Note for instance the positive (pro-Republican) effect of Eisenhower in 1952 and 1956, and the negative effect of Goldwater in 1964. The lesson would appear to be that one cannot predict an election outcome until one knows the candidates and how the voters react to them. Left unanswered is why certain candidates are popular or unpopular.

The major test of the completeness of the six-components model is how closely it predicts the *aggregate* vote of the ANES survey samples. For most elections, the predicted vote and the actual are quite close, but there are exceptions — the most notable being 1984. For that election, the Stokes model predicts that, based on the six components, the average voter preferred Mondale to Reagan. Evidently, the source of Reagan's victory was embedded in the equation intercept and not in the six components themselves. Thus, the lesson of applying the Stokes model to 1984 is that, for that election, the inventory of independent variables explaining the election outcome was quite incomplete.

This discrepancy in 1984 highlights an interesting use of the six-components model specifically and accounting for macro-effects with micro models in general. As first noted by Gapoian and Hackett (1986), people seemed to vote for Reagan for reasons that they did not divulge in their open-ended responses. Reagan's legendary personal appeal was not evident in the open-ended responses, and thus perhaps not the

Table 1: Net partisan advantage of six partisan attitudes 1952–1992

	1952	1956	1960	1964	1968	1972	1976	1980	1984	1988	1992
Partisan component											
Attitudes toward Democrat	-1.2	0.2	-2.0	-4.0	0.9	4.3	-0.1	-0.4	1.3	0.2	-0.8
Attitudes toward Republican	4.4	7.6	5.7	-2.6	1.6	4.0	2.2	-0.5	1.5	0.8	0.7
Group-related attitudes	-4.3	-5.5	-4.0	-2.6	-3.6	-4.6	-4.5	-4.5	-5.6	-6.2	-4.3
Domestic policy attitudes	-1.3	-0.9	-0.5	-2.4	1.1	1.4	-0.7	3.1	1.5	1.2	-5.0
Foreign policy attitudes	3.3	2.5	1.8	-0.3	1.0	3.2	0.4	2.8	-0.3	0.6	0.1
Party management attitudes	5.4	1.2	1.2	-0.3	1.5	0.0	0.2	0.6	0.5	1.1	0.5
Percent Republican vote											
Partisan components prediction (a)	56.3	55.1	52.2	37.8	52.5	58.3	47.5	51.1	48.9	47.7	41.2
NES sample reported vote (b)	58.1	59.6	50.3	32.5	53.8	64.3	49.3	56.3	58.2	52.4	41.6
Difference (b) − (a)	+1.8	+4.5	-1.9	-5.3	+1.3	+7.0	+1.8	+5.3	+9.3	+5.7	+0.4
Actual national vote	55.4	57.8	49.9	38.6	50.4	61.8	48.9	55.3	59.2	53.9	46.5

Two candidate component results 1992

Partisan attitude	Beta (β)	Mean ($\bar{X}$)	Net partisan advantage ($\beta \times \bar{X}$)
Attitudes toward Clinton	-0.085	0.093	-0.008
Attitudes toward Bush	0.065	0.113	0.007
Group-related attitudes	0.050	-0.861	-0.043
Domestic policy attitudes	0.045	-10.116	-0.050
Foreign policy attitudes	0.052	0.017	0.001
Party management attitudes	0.051	0.105	0.005

Source: Wattier, n.d.

explanation for his victory. But neither were the standard foreign policy and domestic policy dimensions. Judging by their verbalized open-ended responses, the electorate had more reasons to vote for Mondale than Reagan. What was the source of the silent vote for Reagan? Erikson (1989) attempted to answer this question by adding additional survey items to the six components for 1984. The answer was a combination of positive evaluations about the economy plus conservative racial attitudes. With these variables added to the model along with the six original components, the equation predicts a solid Reagan victory.

The validity of the Stokes model depends on whether the reasons for peoples' votes are captured adequately by open-ended responses. The 1984 mis-prediction is reason for caution. One perspective on the 1984 case is that the open-ended responses gave little hint of President Reagan's supposed personal popularity. Either Reagan was not particularly popular, but winning on more mysterious issues (such as race or the economy), or Reagan was indeed popular but people muffled their expression of this view in the open-ended responses.

Note that I have not extended the Stokes model to incorporate 1996. Among the ANES's 1996 respondents, Dole received, on balance, more favorable commentary than Clinton. It is implausible that Dole was seen more favorable in terms of personal attributes that included competence and leadership ability. Inspection of the data shows that Dole voters vented their frustration by verbalizing an exceptionally high number of negative comments about Clinton's 'character', thus distorting the data. At least in some instances — 1984 and 1996 — open-ended comments provide a cheap mechanism for survey respondents supporting of the losing side to express an exaggerated version of their opposition to the likely winner. The result is that the open-ended likes and dislikes about candidate personal attributes are contaminated as a measure of aggregate voter sentiment about the candidates.

5 Partisanship, ideological proximity and the vote

For a second illustration of the macro–micro connection using ANES data, I attempt to explain presidential election results 1972–1996 as a function of partisanship and ideological proximity, two prominent variables in the micro-analysis of the vote. The independent variables are chosen because party identification and ideological proximity are major predictors of individual voting. Here I ask: how well do over-time variations in partisanship and ideological proximity account for the aggregate election results for the ANES samples? This brief analysis is limited to the seven elections, 1972–1996, because 1972 was the first presidential election in which the ANES asked respondents to place themselves and the candidates on a 7-point liberal–conservative scale.

Partisanship is measured using the usual 7-point party identification scale founded by *The American Voter* (Campbell et al., 1960), re-scaled to range from -3 to $+3$ with 'pure Independents' set at zero. Ideological proximity is measured only for those 'sophisticated' voters who both hold an ideological preference and correctly view the Republican candidate to be to the right of the Democrat. For voters who correctly place the candidates, I measure their relative proximity on a scale from left of the Democrat to right of the Republican.[5]

Scores for 'sophisticated' respondents are as follows, based on how they place themselves on the left–right scale relative to the two candidates:

1. -3 = self left of both candidates;
2. -2 = self exactly at Democrats' placement;
3. -1 = self in between the candidates, closer to the Democrat;
4. 0   = self midway between candidates;
5. $+1$ = self in between the candidates, closer to the Republican;
6. $+2$ = self exactly at Republicans' placement;
7. $+3$ = self right of both candidates.

Because the respondents are divided into sophisticated and unsophisticated groups, I calculated separate equations for each. Sophisticated votes are predicted as a function of partisanship, ideological proximity, plus a set of year dummies. Unsophisticated votes are predicted from the same variables except for ideological proximity. Unlike Stokes, I presume that the parameters for the partisanship and ideological proximity effects are constant across all years. Also unlike Stokes, I use a probit equation instead of regression.

The two individual-level equations are shown in Table 2. Partisanship and ideological proximity, of course, are both highly significant with similar coefficients. Also the partisanship coefficients for the two groups are similar. For the most part, so too are the year dummy coefficients. Clearly, partisanship and ideology matter for individual voters.

In Table 3, the regressions are translated into net effects for the different years. The ideological proximity effects are interesting. They show that the Republicans were advantaged ideologically in 1972, 1976, and 1988, but not in the other years. For instance, in 1984, Reagan repelled slightly more voters than he attracted on ideological grounds. Meanwhile, the partisan effects are quite neutral for the sophisticated voters. But unsophisticated voters give a decidedly partisan edge to the Democrats.

If it were the case that partisanship and ideological proximity accounted for macro-level election results, the year effects would be zero. But they are not zero. At best, ideological proximity and partisanship account for 33% of the between-elections variance in the behavior of the sophisticated, while partisanship accounts for 67% of the variance for the unsophisticated.[6] The remainder is due to otherwise unaccounted for

---

[5] This scale is not the respondent's relative difference in absolute proximity to the Democratic and the Republican candidate. Rather it corresponds to the difference between the relative quadratic utility losses when the two candidates are fixed at their relatively liberal and conservative positions. The idea is that a person is more likely to vote Democratic, for instance, when she is to the left of both candidates than when she is at exactly the Democrat's position. See Rosenstone (1983) for a discussion.

[6] These estimates are based on OLS regressions of the two-party vote on the prediction from partisanship and proximity for sophisticated voters and partisanship for unsophisticated voters. The estimated contributions of partisanship and ideology are lower if the standard is the ratio of predicted and observed variances. The discrepancy is due to year effects correlating with partisanship and ideology effects. One

Table 2: Predicting vote decisions (via Probit) from partisanship, ideological proximity, and political sophistication (standard errors in parentheses)

Dependent variable = Republican vote	All cases	Ideologically sophisticated	Ideologically unsophisticated
Party identification	0.465 (0.011)	0.475 (0.15)	0.439 (0.016)
Ideological proximity	0.383 (0.015)	0.381 (0.015)	–
Year effects			
1972	0.623	0.621	0.608
1976	0.095	0.191	−0.002
1980	0.558	0.573	0.574
1984	0.546	0.622	0.514
1988	0.128	0.198	0.023
1992	−0.119	−0.050	−0.245
1996	−0.264	−0.107	−0.723
Pseudo R^2	0.692	0.743	0.520
N	(7308)	(4741)	(2567)

'year effects'. We conclude that, for both sophisticated and unsophisticated voters, much of the variance of the vote was due to these unexplained year effects. Republicans used to win presidential elections (until Clinton) in large part due to factors that went beyond partisanship and ideological proximity. Or at least that is what this initial foray would tell us.

We have seen that partisanship and ideological proximity are of some importance when explaining election results. Yet we observe that their possible impact on election outcomes is far less marked than their strong impact at the micro-level. Our exercise validates that much of the variation in election outcomes is due to variables that are not taken into account by the measurement of party identification and ideological proximity.

We also see that the Republicans perform better than they 'should' in presidential elections. First, we see that the Republicans won four out of five presidential elections from an electorate that identified more with the Democratic Party. Second, we also see that they won without a decisive edge in terms of ideological proximity. This underscores the mystery of electoral explanation. Republicans have done well in the

interpretation is that ideological proximity and party identification may have a contextual effect on the vote, as represented by year effects. In other words, the party advantaged by the fundamentals of partisanship and ideological proximity may gain a positive reputation generally, over and above the contribution of individual effects of these variables. With but seven cases (elections) any such conclusion must be speculative.

Table 3: Accounting for aggregate vote propensity (in sample) from sample characteristics and residual year effects (note: any combination of effects can be read as a number of standard deviation units, where the corresponding cumulative normal distribution equals the expected percent voting Republican)

	1972	1976	1980	1984	1988	1992	1996
Sophisticated							
Party identification	$0.475 \times$ 0.033 = 0.015	$0.475 \times$ −0.008 = −0.004	$0.475 \times$ 0.099 = 0.046	$0.475 \times$ 0.084 = 0.039	$0.475 \times$ 0.307 = 0.143	0.475 $\times$−0.155 = − 0.072	$0.475 \times$ 0.188 = 0.087
Ideological proximity	$0.381 \times$ 0.670 = 0.257	$0.381 \times$ 0.364 = 0.139	$0.381 \times$ −0.091 = −0.035	$0.381 \times$ −0.016 = −0.006	$0.381 \times$ 0.309 = 0.118	$0.381 \times$ −0.104 = − 0.140	$0.381 \times$ −0.261 = −0.100
Party + ideology	0.273	0.135	0.011	0.033	0.281	−0.212	−0.013
Year effect	0.623	0.094	0.558	0.546	0.128	−0.119	−0.264
Total	0.896	0.129	0.569	0.579	0.409	−0.332	−0.277
Percentage of voters sophisticated	62	58	48	68	66	72	77
Unsophisticated							
Party identification	$0.439 \times$ −0.519 = −0.228	$0.439 \times$ −0.611 = −0.268	$0.439 \times$ −0.668 = −0.293	$0.439 \times$ −0.602 = −0.264	$0.439 \times$ −0.829 = −0.363	$0.439 \times$ −0.880 = −0.386	$0.439 \times$ −1.415 = −0.621
Year effect	0.608	−0.001	0.474	0.412	0.023	−0.245	−0.704
Total	−0.388	−0.269	0.181	0.148	−0.340	−0.631	−1.325
Percentage of voters unsophisticated	38	42	52	32	34	28	23

presidential elections for reasons that we summarize only as the effects of dummy variables for the election years.

6 Conclusions

The study of electoral politics in the United States has seen a certain disconnection between the micro-level and macro-level of analysis. Yet in theory, the connection is perfect. To know everything there is to know about individual-level voting should tell us everything there is to know about elections in the aggregate.

To make clear the micro–macro connection, independent variables ideally are measured with neutral zero points. For the United States, party identification can be re-scaled so that pure Independents are scored as zero. Relative ideological proximity has a natural zero point: a tie between the candidates. Responses to open-ended questions such as the ANES' likes–dislikes questions have a natural zero point of neutrality between the candidates. If seemingly neutral voters depart systematically from 50–50 in their choices, we conclude that one candidate was favored by variables omitted in the analysis. We learn from our examples that more often than not in the United States, it is the Republican candidate who is favored by unmeasured variables.

Potentially, the resources of the ANES can bridge the connection between macro- and micro-level analyses of the US electorate. With modern technology and with data readily available from the Interuniversity Consortium for Political and Social Research, today one can access *all* the data from the Michigan/ANES surveys collected over half a century with virtually the same ease as accessing the data set from a single election study. With multiple surveys over several years, one can address the goal of explaining the vote sufficiently to make irrelevant the use of dummy variables to represent the otherwise unexplained effects of specific years. Ideally, macro-level outcomes are explained by (weighted) macro-level election-year means of the relevant micro-level variables.

This is easier said than done. In the simple analyses explored here, the year effects survive, exposing our ignorance. Further research could see an increase in the number of theoretically relevant variables for the multivariate explanation of election outcomes. And, to aid the task, we can import year-specific macro-level variables (such as national economic indicators) to explain micro-level vote decisions, thus enhancing the understanding of the macro–micro connection.[7]

What innovations could be made in the ANES — and other national election studies — to improve understanding of the macro–micro connection? The objective, of course, is the availability over time of data that is both useful and uniform across election years. Since a wealth of uniformly measured variables already exists for multiple election studies, one imperative is simply to maintain the historical time series. A corollary is the necessity of pursuing useful innovations in ANES data collection; and when useful

---

[7] As an example, Markus (1988) explains the vote in different election years as a function of both micro-level and macro-level economic variables. When using macro-level variables to explain micro-level phenomena, care must be taken not to misattribute the source of between-election variation.

innovations are found, to maintain the items in future election studies for the benefit of future time series. And finally, when explaining the results of even single elections, it helps to have variables with obvious neutral points. When seemingly neutral voters (based on the independent variables) are more likely to choose one candidate rather than the other, we know that explanation of the election outcome is incomplete.

References

Abramowitz, A., Saunders, K.L. 1998. Ideological Realignment in the U.S. Electorate, Journal of Politics 60, pp. 643–652.

Asher, H. 1984. Presidential Elections and American Politics. Dorsey, Homewood, IL.

Campbell, A., Converse, P.E., Miller, W.E., Stokes, D.E. 1960. The American Voter. Wiley, New York.

Campbell, J.E., Garand, J.C. (eds), 2000. Before the Vote: Forecasting American National Elections. Sage, Thousand Oaks, CA.

Converse, P.E. 1966. Religion and politics: the 1960 election. In: Campbell, A., Converse, P.E., Miller, W.E., Stokes, D.E. (eds), Elections and the Political Order. Wiley, New York.

Converse, P.E., Campbell, A., Miller, W.E., Stokes, D.E. 1966. Stability and change in 1960: a reinstating election. In: Campbell, A., Converse, P.E., Miller, W.E., Stokes, D.E. (eds), Elections and the Political Order. Wiley, New York.

Converse, P.E., Clausen, A.R., Miller, W.E. 1965. Electoral myth and reality: the 1964 election, American Political Science Review 59, pp. 322–335.

Converse, P.E., Miller, W.E., Rusk, J.G., Wolfe, A.C. 1969. Continuity and change in American politics: parties and issues in the 1968 election, American Political Science Review 63, pp. 1083–1105.

Downs, A. 1957. An Economic Theory of Democracy. Harper and Row, New York.

Erikson, R.S. 1989. Ronald Reagan and the 'Michigan' model of the vote. Paper presented to the American Political Science Association Convention.

Erikson, R.S., Wlezien, C. 1996. Of time and presidential election forecasts, Political Science and Politics 29, pp. 37–39.

Gapoian, D., Hackett, D. 1986. Why the jackasses can't win. Paper presented to the American Political Science Association Convention.

Kagay, M., Caldeira, G.A. 1979. A reformed electorate? At least a changed electorate. In: Crotty, W. (ed.), Paths to Political Reform., D.C. Heath, Lexington, MA.

Kramer, G. 1983. Ecological fallacy revisited: aggregate- vs. individual-level findings on economics and elections, and sociotropic voting, American Political Science Review 77, pp. 92–111.

Markus, G.B. 1988. The impact of personal and national economic conditions on the Presidential vote: a pooled cross-sectional analysis, American Journal of Political Science 32, pp. 137–154.

Miller, A.S., Miller, W.E., Raines, A.S., Brown, T.A. 1976. A majority party in disarray: party polarization in the 1972 election, American Political Science Review 70, pp. 753–778.

Popkin, S., Gorman, J.W., Phillips, C., Smith, J.A. 1976. What have you done for me lately? Toward an investment theory of voting, American Political Science Review 70, pp. 779–805.

Rosenstone, S.J. 1983. Forecasting Presidential Elections. Yale University Press, New Haven.

Stokes, D.E. 1966. Some dynamic elements of contests for the Presidency, American Political Science Review 60, pp. 19–28.

Wattier, M. n.d. Components Analysis, 1952–92. Mimeo.

Chapter 8

The rolling cross-section design

Richard Johnston and Henry E. Brady

This chapter describes the 'rolling cross-section', a design well-adapted to telephone surveys and to capturing real-time effects in campaigns. In one sense, the design is just a standard cross-section, but the day on which a respondent is interviewed is chosen randomly. As a result, analysis of longitudinal factors is possible with only modest controls. The design necessitates an estimation strategy that distinguishes time-series from cross-sectional effects. We outline alternative strategies and show that the design is especially powerful if it is wedded to a post-election panel wave. We also show how graphical analysis enhances its power. Illustrative examples are drawn from the 1993 Canadian Election Study. We compare the design to some obvious alternatives and argue that, for reasons of cost and simplicity, any national election study based on telephone interviewing is best conducted this way.

The 'rolling cross-section' (RCS) is a design that facilitates detailed exploration of campaign dynamics. Its essence is to take a one-shot cross-section and distribute interviewing in a controlled way over time. Properly done, the date on which a respondent is interviewed is as much a product of random selection as the initial inclusion of that respondent in the sample. Because observations are temporally distributed yet closely spaced, the design moves survey research close to true causal inference. It enables links to debates, news coverage, and campaign advertising, as well as identification of the social and psychological mechanisms that mediate the potential impact from external forces.

The first RCS was an adjunct to the 1984 US National Election Study (ANES); the second was the 1987–88 US 'super Tuesday' primary study.[1] The design's coming of age, however, was the 1988 Canadian Election Study (CES). This study and its successors in 1992–3 and 1997, have been intensely mined for their dynamic properties, and

---

[1] The 1984 data were aired in Brady and Johnston (1987) and Bartels (1987, 1988). The 1988 Super Tuesday data, however, seem to lie fallow.

[2] See, in particular, Johnston et al. (1992, 1994, 1996) and Nevitte et al. (2000).

---

campaign effects have become, arguably, the CES's abiding theme.[2] The Canadian example was followed in the 1996 New Zealand Election Study,[3] in the 1998 ANES pilot study, and the massive 'Year 2000' study at the Annenberg School for Communication, University of Pennsylvania.[4]

New forms of data demand new forms of analysis. Parameters appear that hitherto were not identifiable. RCS data require — and also repay — intense graphical treatment. Indeed, informal, nonparametric, visual analysis is often necessary prior to formal, statistical effort. This chapter illustrates these propositions by showing how vote intentions evolve over a campaign, by presenting alternative statistical models to help explain vote dynamics, and by showing how graphical analysis helps to resolve the remaining explanatory uncertainties. First, however, what *is* a rolling cross-section?

1 Basic elements of the design

In itself, conducting a telephone survey as a rolling cross-section is unremarkable. All polls with stretched-out fieldwork harbor temporal heterogeneity. If these properties are acknowledged, it is mainly as a problem, because those interviewed later usually differ in important ways from those interviewed earlier. For the 1988 Canadian team, the conceptual breakthrough was to see the need for protracted sample clearance not as a problem, but as an opportunity. By being self-conscious about release and clearance of the sample, we could convert temporal heterogeneity into an object of study.

A rolling cross-section design using a telephone survey requires, first, a body of telephone numbers sufficiently large to yield a target number of interviews. This body is then broken up into *replicates*. In the CES case, one replicate is generated for each day of projected interviewing.[5] Each replicate is a miniature of the total, in that assignment to a replicate is essentially random, just as initial selection for the total sample is random. The CES goes into the field within days of the start of the election campaign, but, in principle, fieldwork can start at any time.

Although each day has its replicate, the replicate itself is not the proper unit for representing campaign time. This would imply that all numbers in a given replicate remain open for contact by interviewers on one day only. This is obviously bad survey practice, as only the easiest to reach would be contacted. Fig. 1(A) profiles the lag, for the 1993 Canadian data, between the release of a telephone number to sample and actual completion of an interview at that number. From the typical replicate, almost half the interviews are ultimately completed on the day of release. Another one-sixth are completed the next day, one-twelfth, the day after that, and so on. The median lag is 1 day and the mean lag is 2.1 days. Five-sixths of the interviews that will ever be completed from a replicate are completed in 5 days, including the release day. The

---

[3] See Vowles et al. (1998), especially ch. 5 (Johnston) and ch. 8 (Miller).

[4] Co-investigators on the Year 2000 Study are Johnston and Kathleen Hall Jamieson. The first publication based on this study is Hagen et al. (2000).

[5] Nothing requires that only one replicate is issued per day. The Annenberg Year 2000 study, for instance, varied the overall intensity and the geographic focus of fieldwork according to the year's electoral rhythms. The RCS response rate model differs subtly from other designs, as shown below.

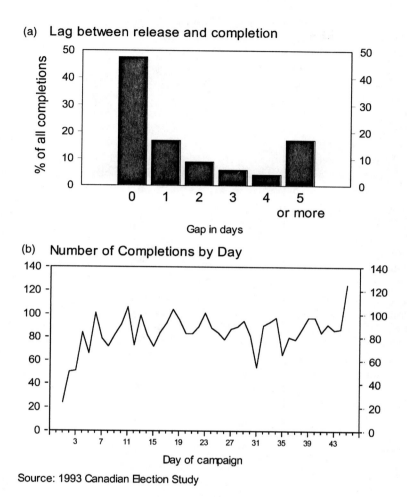

(a) Lag between release and completion

Source: 1993 Canadian Election Study

Fig. 1: Distribution of interviews.

remaining one-sixth is distributed thinly over succeeding days, and virtually all are completed inside 2 weeks.

The distribution of completed interviews by fieldwork day in the 1993 study is shown in Fig. 1(B). Days 1–3 are qualitatively different from all that follow, in that there were fewer than 50 completions. By day 4, completions clear 80 per day, roughly the daily average from then on. It is at this point that the day of interview becomes, effectively, a random event. Only at the very end does anything beyond stochastic error appear. The last day's take exceeds 120, over one-third greater than usual. This reflects prospective respondents' realization that there is no tomorrow; an interview cannot be scheduled for another day.

Critically, no intensification of effort occurs in this period, and the integrity of the design requires that there be no such intensification. Otherwise, the date of interview would not be a random event (and, frankly, it is not at the beginning and not quite on the last day). This does mean, however, that the overall response rate for an RCS will be lower than for a less time-conscious design. Stable clearance effort necessarily implies that late replicates will not be exhausted as completely as earlier ones. Total completions do not flag, as Fig. 1(B) makes clear, but only because earlier replicates are finally seeing their tardy members cleared. Completions from late replicates begin to drop with 2 weeks to go, as we would expect from discussion, above, of Fig. 1(A). In the second last week, the drop is very gradual, from a daily completion rate in the mid-80s to one in the mid-70s. In the last week, the drop is precipitate, to the 60s and then below 50 on the last day. Had we been able to continue clearing replicates after election day, the response rate could have been about three percentage points higher. Had we released telephone numbers to sample as quickly as house capacity allowed and begun aggressive clearance early, we might have gained still more respondents. But then we would not have had a rolling cross-section.

What do we get when we get a rolling cross-section? Fig. 2(A) shows how a dynamic analysis might start. It tracks one of the critical quantities of the 1993 campaign: the share of vote intentions accruing to the governing Conservative Party.[6] The jagged line is the daily share and the smooth line is the 7-day moving average of that share. Early on, the Conservative share is in the mid-30s, very close to the share (not presented) for its chief rival, the Liberal Party. Between fieldwork days 11 and 13, according to the moving average tracking, the Conservative Party share dropped nearly ten points, and by day 15 there could be no doubt that the party had lost at least that much.

The daily tracking is, of course, highly variable day to day, but it hints that this collapse required only 2 days. It plunged a party then in power into a fight for its very life. Subsequent events admit contrary readings. On one reading, the balance of the campaign is just the gradual playing out of the initial shock. On another, that shock plays out within days, such that the Conservative share now oscillates at a new equilibrium, in the mid-20s. Only after day 34 does the share take its final dive, also of 10 points.[7]

2   Estimating longitudinal effects

Clearly, something happened early in the campaign to update voters' beliefs about the Conservative Party. Something else might have happened late in the campaign, but this is more contestable. How do we represent the effect of updated beliefs?

---

[6] Quebec respondents are excluded, as campaign dynamics in that province were weaker and subtly different from elsewhere. In the typical day, Quebec dwellers constituted about 25% of the total sample, so the daily readings in Fig. 2 rest on just over 60 respondents.

[7] We lean to the second reading. Between days 15 and 34, virtually no trend is visible. The eye may be led to see one, but that, we submit, is a visual trick played by the last 10 days. A sign test on the middle 20 days yields as many positives as negatives on consecutive days. After day 34 virtually every pair of days yields a negative change. The drop over this 10-day period is roughly 10 points, half the total slide.

Quebec Respondents Excluded

(a)   Conservative Share of Vote Intentions

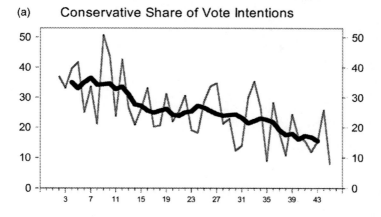

(b)   Leader Rating and Vote Intention

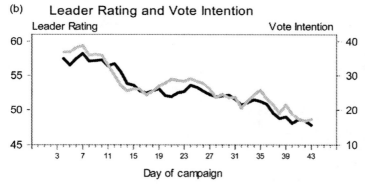

Day of campaign

Smoothing by 7-day centred moving average
Source: 1993 Canadian Election Study

Fig. 2: Conservative vote, Conservative leader. Quebec respondents excluded.

Assume for the sake of argument that we have only one relevant belief, be it about an issue, a leader, or a strategic contingency. Consider, then, some belief B_{it} at time t for person i.[8] For the effect of B_{it} on Y_{it} to be related to the campaign proper, the pre-campaign likelihood of voting for the party must be controlled. The simplest way to do this is with the following conditional change model:

$$Y_{it} = \alpha_1 + \beta_1 B_{it} + \delta_1 Y_{it}^0 + \varepsilon_{it} \tag{1}$$

[8] Of course, no person interviewed at one time within the campaign is interviewed at another such time. For notational simplicity, we assume an equal number of respondents I for each time period t. Fig. 1 indicates that this is not quite true, but that it is almost true for all but the very first and the very last days.

where Y_{it}^0 is the likelihood of person i who is eventually interviewed at time t voting for the party at the beginning of the campaign ($t = 0$).[9] The coefficient β_1 represents the impact of B_{it}. Eq. (1) is essentially the standard model in the campaign-effects literature (Finkel, 1993, p. 6; 1995, pp. 6–7), and it implies that the likelihood at time t of person i voting for the leader is a function of the likelihood at the beginning of the campaign plus the effect of the current belief B_{it}.

The likelihood of voting for the party based upon the person's belief B_{it}^0 at $t = 0$, before the campaign, is:

$$Y_{it}^0 = \alpha_0 + \beta_0 B_{it}^0 + \varepsilon_{it}^0. \tag{2}$$

Substituting Eq. (2) into Eq. (1) and collecting terms yields the following:

$$
\begin{aligned}
Y_{it} &= \alpha_1 + \beta_1 B_{it} + \delta_1(\alpha_0 + \beta_0 B_{it}^0 + \varepsilon_{it}^0) + \varepsilon_{it} \\
&= (\alpha_1 + \delta_1\alpha_0) + \beta_1 B_{it} + \delta_1\beta_0 B_{it}^0 + (\delta_1\varepsilon_{it}^0 + \varepsilon_{it}),
\end{aligned}
\tag{3}
$$

where the coefficient of interest is β_1. We can simplify this by writing:

$$Y_{it} = \alpha_2 + \beta_1 B_{it} + \delta_2 B_{it}^0 + \psi_{it} \tag{4}$$

where, obviously:

$$\alpha_2 = (\alpha_1 + \delta_1\alpha_0); \quad \delta_2 = \delta_1\beta_0 \quad \text{and} \quad \psi_{it} = (\delta_1\varepsilon_{it}^0 + \varepsilon_{it}).$$

If B_{it}^0 is the person's initial belief, and if B_{it} is the belief at the time of interview, then the coefficient β_1 on B_{it} seems like a reasonable definition of a campaign effect. We can then estimate campaign effects by regressing vote intention at t on beliefs at t as well as on beliefs at the beginning of the campaign.

This brings us to an obvious problem. In the Canadian studies, as in the other RCS samples drawn so far, the RCS wave is itself the first one; there is no pre-campaign baseline. It is not even clear that we want one, given that a pre-campaign interview primes respondents in ways that make the campaign wave unrepresentative. Be that as it may, this leaves us lacking direct evidence for B_{it}^0. It does not suffice just to enter B_{it} into an estimation of Y_{it}, as doing so would confound longitudinal with cross-sectional impact because of the correlation between B_{it} and the omitted B_{it}^0. As a general proposition, there is no way to assess the impact of omitting B_{it}^0 because there is no reason to assume any particular covariance between time-series and cross-section. This is a point made forcefully by Kramer (1983), and it applies not just to campaign

---

[9] The subscript t represents the cross-section in which the respondent is interviewed and i is that respondent's identifier within the cross-section. If the variable is measured at the RCS interview, then we do not add a superscript (hence Y_{it} and not Y_{it}^t), but if it is measured at another time, say, in a pre-election baseline, then we add the superscript for time, in this example, Y_{it}^0.

studies such as the CES but also to any analysis that employs the same measures in repeated samples. Just as Kramer's problem has been addressed elsewhere (Markus, 1988), so it can be in the RCS design.

This requires us to consider other starting places for estimation. One place to look is *after* election day, if the design includes a post-election wave. The other place is inside the RCS itself, especially if post-election information is not available.

If key measures from the campaign-wave RCS are repeated post-election, then B_{it}^{T+1} is observed. If we allow ourselves a strong assumption about how beliefs change, we can substitute B_{it}^{T+1} for B_{it}^0. Let us assume that B_{it} changes as follows:

$$B_{it} = B_{it}^0 + D_t, \tag{5}$$

where B_{it}^0 is the cross-sectional state of belief at time zero and D_t is the time-series variation.[10] This assumes that today's belief equals that at the beginning of the campaign plus some time-series effect that is common across all people. Everyone's opinion, then, is affected by the same amount, D_t, at each time period t.[11] We wish to estimate Eq. (4), and it can be estimated if we have values for B_{it} and B_{it}^0. We observe B_{it}, but what can we use for B_{it}^0? If Eq. (5) is correct, then B_{it}^{T+1}, a person's belief after the end of the campaign as reported on the post-election interview, will be:

$$B_{it}^{T+1} = B_{it}^0 + D_{T+1}, \tag{6}$$

so that B_{it}^{T+1} differs from B_{it}^0 only in the constant D_{T+1} and it will be perfectly correlated with B_{it}^0. Consequently, we can substitute B_{it}^{T+1} into Eq. (4) to represent B_{it}^0 and the only change in (4) will be in the intercept $\alpha*_2 = \alpha_2 - \delta_2 D_{T+1}$:

$$Y_{it} = \alpha_2^* + \beta_1 B_{it} + \delta_2 B_{it}^{T+1} + \psi_{it}. \tag{7}$$

In reality, B_{it}^{T+1} and B_{it}^0 will not be perfectly correlated. We can imagine some obvious possibilities: changes that are random, uncorrelated with initial beliefs, as suggested by the literatures on non-attitudes and on measurement error; or change that is systematic, but correlated with original beliefs, as in opinion crystallization. These take us beyond the scope of this chapter. We note, however, that where such change occurs — and thus Eq. (5) is unwarranted — then B_{it}^0 is just as inadequate as a starting point as B_{it}^{T+1}.

The fact still remains that all variance in the post-election measure B_{it}^{T+1} is, for our purposes, cross-sectional: the election is over and the furor has died immediately; clearance of the post-election sample is relatively rapid; and initiation of contact is orthogonal to the date of pre-election interview. Thus, the post-election reading is a reasonable starting point for separating cross-sectional from longitudinal effects. When taken together, Eqs. (4) and (7) show that the coefficient (β_1) on the RCS wave

---

[10] Note: D stands for 'diachronic', meaning variation over time.

[11] This assumption is not warranted by the facts but it is a useful starting point, and space does not permit further consideration here. Brady and Johnston (1996) discuss the consequences of relaxing it.

measure (B_{it}) indicates the campaign effect, while the coefficient (δ_2) on the post-election measure of belief (B_{it}^{T+1}) measures the residual impact of the baseline belief. The rest of the impact is in β_1, and so the full cross-sectional effect is indicated by $(\beta_1 + \delta_2)$.[12]

Post-election indicators are not always ready to hand. Neither the 1984 nor the 1988 US RCS has a post-election wave, and not even in the CES is every serious campaign-period factor measured twice. Commonly, then, we are forced to condition on day-to-day information. An obvious starting point is to average across the B_{it} in each daily sample:

$$B_t^* = \sum_{i=1,I} \frac{B_{it}}{I},$$
(8)

to get a quantity to represent the time-series effect and to use $(B_{it} - B_t^*)$ to represent the cross-sectional effect B_{it}^0. To see that these indicators will do the trick, go back to the logic in Eq. (5). Assume first, for mathematical simplicity, that the population mean of B_{it}^0 is set to zero, so that we can scale B_{it}.[13] Then if Eq. (5) is true we can take averages on both sides over each daily sample to get:

$$B_t^* = \sum_{i=1,I} \frac{B_{it}}{I} = \sum_{i=1,I} \frac{B_{it}^0}{I} + \sum_{i=1,I} \frac{D_t}{I} = D_t,$$
(9)

where we have assumed that the sample mean of B_{it}^0 is zero because the population mean is zero. (That is, we assume that the sample quantity B_t^* is a good approximation of D_t, which will be true for large daily samples.) With this result, we can rearrange Eq. (5) to get an expression for B_{it}^0 in terms of observable quantities:

$$B_{it}^0 = B_{it} - D_t = B_{it} - B_t^*.$$
(10)

If we have large daily samples, then B_t^* should be close to the true D_t and the estimate of B_{it}^0 in Eq. (10) should be close to the actual B_{it}^0. Hence, we can regress Y_{it} on B_{it} and on $(B_{it} - B_t^*)$ from (10). This procedure should yield a consistent estimator of campaign effects. To see this, go back again to Eq. (4) and substitute $(B_{it} - B_t^*)$ for B_{it}^0:

$$Y_{it} = \alpha_2 + \beta_1 B_{it} + \delta_2(B_{it} - B_t^*) + \psi_{it}.$$
(11)

Coefficients have the same interpretation as in Eq. (7).

In principle, this is a very attractive strategy. The key phrase in the foregoing, however, is 'large daily sample'. The statistical consistency that made the estimator so attractive accrues as the size of the daily samples increases without limit. Two

[12] An intuitive statement of these relationships can be found in Johnston et al. (1992). A somewhat formal elaboration can be found in Brady and Johnston (1996), where we weaken the assumptions in Eq. (5).
[13] This is a harmless assumption that, operationally, only requires that we calculate the mean, B_0^* of the B_{it}^0 and subtract this quantity from all B_{it} including B_{it}^0. This amounts, then, to setting B_0^* to zero.

related consequences of small daily samples occur to us. First, the sampling variance associated with 80+ completions per day introduces extra error into Eq. (8) as an indicator of the true daily mean. This presents us with a classic errors-in-variables problem, which could bias δ_2 towards zero and, possibly, β_1 in the other direction. Second, to the extent that B_t^* is mismeasured, variation in B_{it} will leak into $(B_{it} - B_t^*)$, such that the two will be collinear, inflating standard errors on both β_1 and δ_2.

3 An example

Table 1 gives a practical example, by showing the impact of leader ratings on 1993 Conservative vote intention, estimated each way. Coefficients are extracted from a larger estimation, which also includes policy and expectations variables.[14] The alternative setups provide highly similar estimations of total time-series plus cross-sectional effect, but the daily-mean version assigns more of the total to the time series. Note also that the daily-mean time-series coefficients, although large, are unstable. We suspect this reflects the artifacts just discussed. For all that, however, the alternatives provide broadly similar readings. Our sense is that the pre–post design dominates the

Table 1: The impact of leader ratings on Conservative vote[a]

	Conditioning on:	
Leader	**Individual info — post**	**Daily mean**
Conservative		
β_1	0.95*** (0.06)	1.05*** (0.27)
δ_2	0.17** (0.06)	−0.08 (0.27)
Liberal		
β_1	−0.60*** (0.06)	−0.76* (0.38)
δ_2	−0.25*** (0.07)	0.09 (0.38)
Reform		
β_1	−0.43*** (0.06)	−0.71** (0.23)
δ_2	−0.02 (0.06)	0.30 (0.24)
R^2-adj	0.37	0.30
SEE	0.36	0.37
N	1501	1984

[a] Estimation by OLS. Standard errors in parentheses. *$p < 0.05$; **$p < 0.01$; ***$p < 0.001$.

[14] Leader ratings are 100-point thermometer scales compressed to the 0–1 interval. A complete description of the variables can be found in Brady and Johnston (1996). Note, however, that the estimation here varies in some particulars from the one reported there.

daily-mean design. However, if conditioning on post-election information is not possible, daily-mean estimates should not lead us far astray, especially if daily samples are large. For 1993, both treatments suggest that judgments on Kim Campbell, the Conservative leader, powerfully influenced her party's chances.

But did leader judgments, in fact, have this effect? Fig. 2(B) confirms that her ratings fell over the campaign, but perhaps she just fell along with her party, and judgments on her were as much consequence as cause. It is true that other key factors are controlled in Table 1, but controls do not dispose of the causal issue.

This is where visual analysis comes back into play, as judicious manipulation of graphs helps address the issue of causal priority. If re-evaluation of Kim Campbell was critical to, say, the early precipitate drop in Conservative vote intentions, then that re-evaluation had better precede, not follow, the vote shift. Fig. 2(B) attempted to sort out temporal priority. The visual challenge was to get the vertical scale of vote intention and leader evaluation into the same range, so that the temporal priority could be established by horizontal comparison. This was accomplished by:

- assigning leader evaluation to one *Y*-axis and vote intention to the other; and
- setting the vertical range separately on each axis. Mean leader ratings span larger values but a shorter range than percentages of vote intention.

With this done, Fig. 2(B), page 127, makes a strong prima facie case that re-evaluation of Campbell was indeed critical to the Conservatives' sharp drop. It also makes clear that, thereafter, she ceased to play an independent dynamic role. Her ratings dropped further, but not with any obvious temporal lead over her party.

4 Discussion

There is no compelling reason *not* to conduct an RCS where fieldwork is temporally dispersed in the pre-election period, as it almost always is. Any campaign period is bound to make response vary over time, even if the campaign only demarcates the run-up to a deadline. Shifts can be very rapid, so almost any survey fieldwork is vulnerable to this heterogeneity. We argue that the RCS is the most effective design for dealing with the problem. Indeed the design converts the problem into an opportunity.

As a design to capture campaign effects, does the RCS dominate a panel? We have already admitted that the repeated-measures design is the canonical way to begin thinking about the problem. Moreover, where the same individuals are measured twice, sampling error is not an issue for estimating net change even as individual trajectories can be captured. Thus, especially where the interval is short, panels have an obvious appeal. This theoretical appeal, however, is very hard to realise in practice. In most electoral contexts the obvious time spans are too long for panels to permit fine-grained causal attribution and for easy maintenance of the panel itself. Repeated panels might permit somewhat fine-grained coverage, but at considerable expense. Moreover, any panel wave other than the very first one is no longer a cross-section and thus is no longer representative of the electorate in the conventional sense, as panel mortality bends later waves away from being demographically representative. No less important, respondents are altered by the earlier interview, and so identification of the campaign's intrinsic dynamic effect is problematic. These considerations also tell against mounting a pre-campaign, conventional cross-section and then drawing out the second, panel wave as a kind of campaign RCS. Besides, a stable second-wave clearance strategy — so critical to making inference with the RCS easy — is almost unimaginable.[15]

At the same time, an RCS is next to impossible to construct after the fact. Commercial polls are now ubiquitous, at least in the US, and it is tempting to use them to reconstruct the dynamics of the campaign. For earlier campaigns, we have no choice but to assemble the data this way. Variation from survey house to house in sample frame, screening, weighting, and question wording is remarkable, however, such that house effects are likely to contribute as much error variance as sampling itself.[16] In addition, commercial data are rarely available at the individual level.

The implication seems clear. If one is to be in the field for a large part of a campaign period, thought and effort should be given to controlling the release and clearance of the sample, so as to make the data collection sensitive, with minimal controls, to events in real time. Obviously, the larger the overall sample, the more sensitive can be samples gathered within temporal subdivisions. For many operations, only a small conceptual leap is required to grasp that the effective size of the overall sample may already be quite large. Commercial operations that publish 'tracking polls' are already accumulating massive total samples. Even commercial companies that publish, say, weekly cross-sections would do better to see the separate weekly studies as part of a consolidated design spanning the whole period of interest, and then to control sampling from start to finish. In an ideal world, the academic community should have the resources to do this for itself. But with a modest raising of self-consciousness, commercial polls can also create an enduring research legacy, even as they enhance the short-run proprietary value of their data.

The RCS as we describe it presupposes interviewing by telephone.[17] In-home interviewing makes controlled release and clearance of a sample all but impossible. Only if the pace of events is sufficiently slow that the time scale is conceived in weeks rather than days could the design be wedded to a face-to-face survey. That said, the estimation strategy we outline is not peculiar to the RCS. Although it was necessitated by our self-conscious attention to processes operating in real time, its logic is general to *any* analysis that involves survey data collected at different times. What distinguishes the RCS from such merged files is not temporal heterogeneity as such, which may be present in both situations, but the fact that the heterogeneity in the RCS can involve days so closely spaced that clearance from a sample released on one of the days may not have been properly completed before the next relevant day arrives. It is the interleaving of sample replicates, day by day, that distinguishes the design.

---

[15] This discussion does not preclude a stand-alone cross-sectional survey to establish a pre-election baseline, as long as it is understood that that baseline would permit only aggregate comparisons with the later RCS. And the earlier fieldwork starts relative to election day, the more can early interviews in the RCS itself serve as an aggregate baseline.

[16] See Erikson and Wlezien (1999). The discussion on p. 171 is particularly relevant.

[17] It is conceivable that an RCS could be conducted over the Internet.

If the design opens up new possibilities for analysis, its full exploitation requires new estimators and new ways of thinking. Once in the RCS framework, estimation should take the obvious step beyond the assumptions underlying dynamic analysis with panels. Although we find it useful to start by conceiving of RCS estimation as if it were a panel in which the second wave is released gradually rather than at one shot, we shy away from recommending a pre-campaign baseline wave. However, we must look for a baseline somewhere. One compelling strategy is to find it in a post-campaign wave.[18] We argue that a later wave is probably no worse a representation of the baseline than a pre-campaign wave would have been. Sometimes not even a post-campaign wave is available, and so we also need tools for extracting a notional baseline from inside the RCS proper.

Perhaps the biggest change forced on us by the RCS is to take visual presentation seriously, not just as an expository device but as an original research tool. RCS data commonly do not begin to speak until they are arrayed visually, with the daily noise of sampling smoothed away. Of course, pictures can mislead as readily as inform. But in tandem with formalized, parametric techniques, they supply evidence which is no less powerful for being circumstantial.

Acknowledgements

Data for this chapter are drawn from the 1992–93 Canadian Referendum and Election Study, for which Johnston was principal investigator and Brady was a co-investigator. Other co-investigators were André Blais, Elisabeth Gidengil, and Neil Nevitte. The study was supported by the Social Sciences and Humanities Research Council of Canada and by the investigators' universities. Fieldwork was conducted by the Institute for Social Research, York University, under the direction of David Northrup. We thank Mark Franklin, Chris Wlezien, and Charles Franklin for comments on earlier drafts. None of the foregoing are responsible for any errors of analysis or interpretation.

References

Bartels, L.M. 1987. Candidate choice and the dynamics of the presidential nominating process. American Journal of Political Science 31, 1–30.

Bartels, L.M. 1988. Presidential Primaries and the Dynamics of Public Choice. Princeton University Press, Princeton.

Brady, H.E., Johnston, R. 1987. What's the primary message: horse race or issue journalism? In: Orren, G.R., Polsby, N.W. (eds). Media and Momentum: the New Hampshire Primary and Nomination Politics. Chatham House, Chatham, NJ.

Brady, H.E., Johnston, R. 1996. Statistical methods for analyzing rolling cross-sections with examples from the 1988 and 1993 Canadian Election Studies. Paper presented at the 1996 Annual Meeting of the Midwest Political Science Association.

---

[18] To serve as a baseline in the strict sense we intend here, the post-election wave must be a panel. Where resources permit, it is also useful to collect a fresh cross-section after the election, but the uses of the latter lie elsewhere than as a baseline for the estimations discussed earlier in this chapter.

Erikson, R.S., Wlezien, C. 1999. Presidential polls as a time series: the case of 1996. Public Opinion Quarterly 63, 163–177.

Finkel, S. 1993. Reexamining the 'minimal effects' model in recent Presidential campaigns. Journal of Politics 55, 1–21.

Finkel, S. 1995. Causal analysis with panel data. In: Sage university papers series. Quantitative Applications in the Social Sciences, 07-105. Sage Publications, Thousand Oaks, CA.

Hagen, M.G., Johnston, R., Jamieson, K.H., Dutwin, D., Kenski, K. 2000. Dynamics of the 2000 Republican primaries. Annals of the American Association for Political and Social Sciences 572, 33–49.

Johnston, R., Blais, A., Brady, H.E., Crête, J. 1992. Letting the People Decide: Dynamics of a Canadian Election. McGill-Queen's University Press, Montreal.

Johnston, R., Blais, A., Brady, H.E., Gidengil, E., Nevitte, N. 1994. The collapse of a party system? The 1993 Canadian General Election. Paper presented to the 1994 Annual Meeting of the American Political Science Association.

Johnston, R., Blais, A., Gidengil, E., Nevitte, N. 1996. The Challenge of Direct Democracy: The 1992 Canadian Referendum. McGill-Queen's University Press, Montreal.

Kramer, G. 1983. Ecological fallacy revisited: aggregate- vs. individual-level findings on economics and elections, and sociotropic voting. American Political Science Review 77, 92–111.

Markus, G.B. 1988. The impact of personal and national economic conditions on the presidential vote: a pooled cross-sectional analysis. American Journal of Political Science 32, 137–154.

Nevitte, N., Blais, A., Gidengil, E., Nadeau, R. 2000. Unsteady State: The 1997 Canadian Federal Election. Oxford University Press, Don Mills, Ontario.

Vowles, J., Aimer, P., Banducci, S., Karp, J. (ed.) 1998. Voters' Victory? New Zealand's First Election under Proportional Representation. Auckland University Press, Auckland.

Chapter 9

The statistical power of election studies to detect media exposure effects in political campaigns

John Zaller

This chapter analyzes the power of national election studies to detect the effects of exposure to political communication on vote choice in US presidential elections. In particular, it examines the power of surveys (with *N*s from 500 to 5000) to detect exposure effects of different sizes (3, 5, 10 percentage points in aggregate) and shapes (linear, exponential, non-monotonic). The results indicate that most surveys — and many other political science data sets — have less power than most scholars appear to think. For example, the chapter finds a case in which a plausible 'wrong' model that involves no exposure effect is more likely to be supported by standard data sets than a 'correct' model that involves an exposure term, despite the fact that a large exposure effect is present in the population from which the data have been sampled. The chapter, which includes a tour of issues in power analysis, concludes by advocating increased sensitivity to this problem by those who create and those who consume survey data.

1 Introduction

The proper size of national election surveys — how many cases are needed to answer the questions under study — has not been the subject of much analytical effort. In recent elections, the *grand dame* of election surveys, the American National Election Studies, has tapped roughly 1800 respondents in its pre-election wave. Some national election studies have gone as low as 1000 respondents and several European election studies now routinely survey 3000 to 5000 persons. In the current election cycle, the Annenberg School for Communication is setting a record for academic campaign studies by conducting some 100,000 interviews. But one searches in vain for analytical justification of these choices. In the United States at least, scholars seem to decide the size of election studies by holding a finger to the wind and asking how much funding agencies are willing to spend.[1]

The scholars who analyze these surveys do no better. To judge from most published work, whatever survey they are analyzing is plenty big enough to answer the question they are asking. If they get a null result, the normal assumption is that the hypothesis under investigation is weak or wrong.[2] This state of affairs is odd. It is as if astronomers built telescopes and set out looking for new celestial objects without first calculating what can be seen through a telescope of a given resolution. The primary suggestion of this chapter is, therefore, that both those who create and those who consume election studies should be more self-conscious about what their measuring instrument can accomplish. In technical jargon, they should engage in statistical power analysis.

Unfortunately, power analysis in the domain of electoral research, and probably other non-experimental domains, is not straightforward. To show how it can be done, this chapter reports an extended analysis of statistical power for one important research problem: media exposure effects in US presidential election campaigns. For reasons that will become apparent, the chapter relies on simulation rather than closed-form analysis. It reports a series of Monte Carlo experiments to determine the statistical power of campaign surveys of given size to determine whether persons who are more heavily exposed to the mass media are more likely to register the effects of political communication in their vote decisions. The method is to create a 'campaign exposure effect' in realistically simulated data and determine how frequently statistical analysis can recover evidence of such effects in data sets of different sizes.

The results of the study indicate that the vast majority of election studies lack the statistical power to detect exposure effects for the three, five, or perhaps 10 point shifts in vote choice that are the biggest that may be reasonably expected to occur. Even a study with as many as 100,000 interviews could, depending on how it deploys resources around particular campaign events, have difficulty pinning down important communication effects of the size and nature that are likely to occur. To be sure, this finding applies only to a single research problem. Other problems have other data needs and existing election studies are no doubt sufficient for many of them. Yet the results of this study show that the power of surveys to answer important questions cannot be taken for granted simply because the sample is of conventional size.

Accordingly, this chapter has two aims. The first is to suggest what a serious justification for the proper size of a national election study might look like. The hope is that, once such a justification has been more fully developed, it will persuade funding agencies of the need for larger surveys for at least some kinds of problems. The second is to show how to determine what can and cannot be reliably accomplished with existing data sets. The hope here is that scholars who turn up null or trace findings for effects 'that just have to be there' may hereafter accompany their null reports with statements of the power of their data and their model to detect the effects they expected to find.

---

[1] This statement is based on experience of two terms on the Board of Overseers of the National Election Studies and occasional consultation to other surveys.
[2] I do not exclude myself from this generalization.

Although the chapter focuses on the problem of detecting exposure effects in campaign surveys, the need for attention to power analysis is not notably less acute in comparative politics, international relations, or other branches of American politics. In the course of preparing this report, I was surprised to discover that even some experimentalists have only passing familiarity with power analysis. Thus, the exercise reported in this chapter may have wide significance.

2 Analysis vs. simulation

In principle, one could analyze the power of a survey to detect communication effects by formal analysis or by simulation. In the analytical mode, one uses a statistical formula to determine the probability that a survey of given size can detect an effect of given size. In simulation, one generates artificial data sets that embody particular effects, and then tests how often the simulated effects can be recovered in data analysis.

Suppose, for example, that one wants to know the standard error of a simple random survey whose sample mean was $p = 0.40$ and whose size was $n = 1000$. To solve this problem by simulation, one would obtain a coin known to come up heads 40% of the time — or, more likely, the computer equivalent thereof — and flip it over and over in sets of 1000 tosses each. Each sample proportion p from each set of 1000 tosses would be close to the coin's true value of 0.40, but there would be small variation in the ps from one sample of tosses to another. Taking the standard deviation of the ps in these samples would be a perfectly valid method of estimating the standard error of an actual random survey with sample $p = 0.4$ and $n = 1000$. In practice, of course, one would never estimate the standard error of a poll by simulation, since a simple analytical formula exists to do the job much more easily. But simulation could do the job to an arbitrarily high level of precision.

In this study, I opt for simulation. Formulae exist to calculate the sample size needed to test relationships between variables in regression analysis (Cohen, 1988; King et al., 1997, p. 213), but they have important limitations. They do not formally incorporate the effects of measurement error, nor do they accommodate the residual error that arises when, as in American voting studies, the dependent variable is a dichotomy. Hsieh et al. (1998) present a power formula for logit models, but it is limited to cases in which the independent variable is either dichotomous or normal. Since, as we shall see, the independent variables that one must use in the study of communication effects have markedly non-normal distributions, this formula has little value in the present context.[3] Excellent programs exist for doing power calculations for many types of problems, but they are based on existing formulae and so share their limitations (e.g. NCSC, 2000[4]). Thus, simulation is the best available tool for assessing the power of surveys to detect the effect of media exposure on vote choice.

---

[3] In the analyses below, the variable of interest will be the interaction between a 0–1 variable (for pre- and post-campaign events) and a skewed media exposure variable. The distribution of this interaction variable resembles no standard distribution.

[4] The program is available for downloading at http://www.icw.com/ncss/pass.html.

3 Issues in simulation

The paramount issue in simulation is creating data that match relevant characteristics of actual data. In the matter of flipping coins to simulate random sampling of 0–1 outcomes, this is easy to accomplish: using a computer to flip coins is reasonably close to how random surveys are done in practice and perfectly equivalent to how random surveys are supposed to be done. (Insofar as actual survey sampling departs from purely random sampling, the analytical calculation of SEs will be just as far off from the truth as the coin-flipping simulation.)

By contrast, in simulating a campaign effect in an election survey, there are numerous ways in which simulated data might fail to resemble real data. I survey these danger points in detail shortly. But first, the bare-bones of how I went about the simulations reported here.

1. *Specify an interesting and plausible campaign effect.* In the 1992 fall campaign, for example, Ross Perot lost about five percentage points in the polls after the media heaped scornful coverage on him for his statement that he had temporarily quit the race in July from fear that Republicans would sabotage his daughter's wedding. As other evidence shows, sometimes people are influenced by political communication in proportion to their level of exposure to it. It is therefore plausible to posit for analysis the following general campaign effect: News coverage of a candidate gaff causes a five-point drop in the polls for the candidate, and the amount of the fall-off is a linear function of self-reported degree of exposure to the news.
2. *Generate artificial but realistic sets of public opinion data that embody the campaign effect chosen for study.* The data sets must resemble actual opinion data in the elementary sense that they consist of hundreds or perhaps thousands of cases, where cases are understood as 'individuals' with scores on variables such as partisanship, media exposure, vote choice, and time of interview (i.e. before or after the event that is supposed to have caused a campaign effect). The simulated data are sufficiently realistic that a naïve analyst could mistake them for actual survey data. Further, the simulated data are constructed such that, as in actual survey data, individuals' partisanship and demographics explain most of the variance in vote choice, but that some other variable of interest, such as media exposure, explains a small amount of variance in the vote after the occurrence of the campaign event; that is, enough variance so that, as in the Perot example, aggregate exposure to news in the data set as a whole creates a five-point dip in candidate support. Thus, people heavily exposed to the news might undergo a 10 percentage point drop, those with low exposure no drop at all, so yielding an aggregate drop of five percentage points. Finally, the data are constructed so as to include random measurement error, multicolinearity among independent variables, and other features of actual survey data.
3. *Using hundreds of artificial datasets of given size, determine how often an appropriate regression model yields statistically significant evidence of the specified campaign effect.* In the Perot example, we might specify a regression in which

support for Perot (coded 0–1) is the dependent variable and 'media exposure X time of interview' (an interaction term) is one of the independent variables. 'Time of interview' would be coded as 0 before the campaign gaff and 1 afterwards; 'media exposure' would be a self-report of attention to the mass media. The coefficient on 'media exposure X time of interview' would then indicate whether, as would be expected, media exposure has more effect on support for Perot after the gaff than before. Due to sampling variability, the regression would not always turn up a statistically significant coefficient for 'media exposure X time of interview', but it would do so more often when samples were larger. The question is: How large must samples be in order for an appropriate regression model reliably to capture a campaign effect that is actually in the data (along with sampling and other forms of random error)?

4 Simulating campaign data

The key to doing a valid simulation of this kind is creating data that match all relevant characteristics of actual data. But what characteristics are relevant? And how do we determine numerical values for these characteristics?

These issues are taken up in this section. First, I survey literature on campaign effects and specify the particular effects to be analyzed in the power simulations. The idea is to make the campaign effects simulated — that is, the dependent variable in the simulations — comparable to campaign effects that typically occur in the real world. Second, arguing from statistical theory, I develop the general characteristics of the independent variables that must be matched in the simulation. For example, I show that it is necessary in power simulation to match the variance of one's simulated independent variable to the variance of the independent variable one would use in a real world study. Finally, National Election Study data are used to determine the particular numerical values of these general characteristics (e.g. the variance that the simulated media exposure scale must have). Once these steps are completed, the simulation, data analysis, and presentation of results go quickly and easily

4.1 Specifying the campaign effects to be studied

Campaign effects come in many shapes and sizes. In this study, I simulate cases in which an important campaign event occurs at a discrete point in the campaign, and in which individuals are affected in relation to their degree of media exposure. Admittedly, many other kinds of campaign effects can occur. Two particularly important ones are priming effects that cause a shift in mean support for one of the candidates, and lagged effects that develop gradually over a period of days rather than all at once. Moreover, the different types may blend into one another; for example, a priming effect that develops over time among those most heavily exposed to the news. This initial foray into simulation of campaign effects is limited to relatively straightforward exposure effects of the kind indicated. Also, the knotty question of the persistence of campaign effects is avoided.[5]

There are two independent dimensions to exposure effects. One is magnitude: what percentage of the public is affected? The other is shape or incidence: which people at which levels of media exposure are affected? I deal with each in turn.

A good compendium of the magnitude of recent campaign effects — none of which is linked to individual differences in exposure to campaign stimuli — is found in Holbrook (1996). The most reliable effect in presidential campaigns is the 'convention bounce' — the gain a candidate picks up in the aftermath of a nominating convention. According to Holbrook's survey of data from 1984 to 1992, the mean convention bounce was 6.5 percentage points with an SD of 3.75 (his table 4.1). Examining data for the period 1952 to 1992, Shaw (1999) found a mean effect of 7.4 points with an SD of 3.3. From my calculations, convention bounces in 1996 and 2000 were probably at the long-term average.

Presidential debates are another predictable campaign effect, but generally a smaller one. According to Holbrook, the mean of the six presidential debates from 1984 to 1992 was 2.2 percentage points with a SD of 1.3. The most a Democrat or Republican gained was 3.5 percentage points, but Ross Perot in 1992 may have gained close to 5 points in one of the debates (Holbrook, 1996, table 5.4).[6] Shaw finds that the immediate effect of debates averages a little less than 2 percentage points, but that the effect tends to grow over time. Again, there are no links to campaign exposure.

In their outstanding study of the 1988 Canadian election, Johnston et al. (1992) argue that one of the candidate debates was the pivot of the entire election, generating a 10 point bounce for one party, priming attitudes toward a key issue, and setting the agenda for the rest of the campaign. These authors link campaign effects to a measure of campaign exposure, but there is no test of the statistical significance of the exposure effect and little emphasis on the finding. Although the reason for underplaying exposure effects in a study of campaign dynamics is not made explicit, it seems obvious enough: lack of power. How much do authors want to say about an effect that, however important, may not be statistically significant at conventional levels?

Dramatic media stories also sometimes occur, though not at predictable times. By Shaw's (Shaw, 1999) coding, candidates and the media co-operate to create an average of about one major candidate 'blunder' per election, with the blunder rate increasing over time. An example is Ronald Reagan's declaration in August 1980 that the country was in 'depression'. Perot's remark about his daughter's wedding would also meet Shaw's coding criteria. Shaw finds that blunders cost candidates an average of 6.3 percentage points.

---

[5] Shaw (1999) finds that the effects of conventions and debates tend to persist or increase over time, but that the effects of gaffes tend to spike and disappear. However, there is likely to be a fair amount of heterogeneity within the categories of Shaw's analysis, so that the best generalization is probably 'sometimes campaign effects persist and sometimes they don't'.

[6] However, Holbrook (1996) (fig. 5.3) makes it appear dubious that debates were wholly responsible for these gains. From tracking poll data I have analyzed, Perot's average gain was 1.2 points per debate (Hunt and Zaller, 1995).

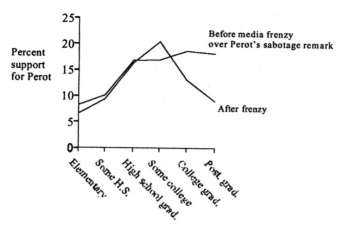

Fig. 1: Education and responsiveness to Perot campaign story.
Source: *ABC News–Washington Post* tracking polls.

In light of these data, the magnitudes I examine are mean shifts in the vote of 3%, 5%, and 10%. Campaign effects much bigger than this are unusual; effects much smaller turn out to be too small to detect associations with exposure except under unusual circumstances. The values chosen correspond to something like a big presidential debate effect, a typical blunder, and a large convention bounce, respectively.

Turning to the shape of campaign exposure effects, the three most obvious possibilities are that those most exposed to the mass media may be most affected; that those most exposed to the media could be least affected; and that people at middle levels of media exposure could be the most affected. For purposes of power calculations, the first and third of these possibilities can be regarded as identical linear effects (with opposite signs). Another important possibility is the 'elite exposure effect', in which a campaign event affects no one in the bottom half of the attentive public, and affects people in the upper half of the attentiveness spectrum in proportion to their level of media exposure. This effect is an *elite* effect because it affects only the upper part of the electorate, and an *exposure* effect because it is proportional to exposure.

Fig. 1 presents an example of an elite exposure effect. The figure shows public opinion just before and just after the media frenzy over Perot's statement about his daughter's wedding. If we accept education as a proxy for media exposure, we see that the pattern conforms to the conditions of the elite exposure effect: no change among persons moderate-to-low on exposure, and changes that are linear with respect to exposure among the rest. (Direct measures of media exposure are unavailable in this data set.)

Fig. 2 shows the shape and magnitude of the particular exposure effects I have just described. A few comments are in order. First of all, note that there is a linear positive relationship between exposure and support for Candidate A in the baseline condition in all panels in Fig. 2. This reflects the fact that this zero-order relationship exists in actual data. In my simulation, as in the actual data, the correlation is spurious

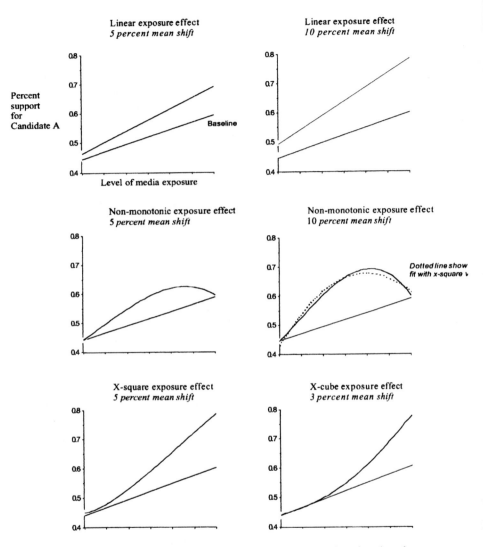

Fig. 2: The size and shape of campaign effects to be simulated.

and has no direct effect on the vote once controls are imposed. But it is nonetheless important, for reasons explained below, to incorporate the correlation into the simulations, as shown in Fig. 2.

In the data analysis section of this chapter, I use a series of logit models to recover the campaign effects built into the simulations. The first of these models, shown below, will be used to recover linear exposure effects of the kind shown in the top panels of Fig. 1:

$$\text{Vote}_i = b_0 + b_1\text{Exposure}_i + b_2\text{Time}_i + b_3\text{Exposure}_i \times \text{Time}_i + b_4 X_{i4} \ldots b_k X_{ik} \tag{1}$$

Exposure in this equation is an individual-level variable standing for level of exposure to the mass media. The specification and construction of this variable are described at length in the next section. The time variable is a dichotomy, taking the value of 0 before the campaign event and 1 afterwards. Vote is also a dichotomous variable, taking the value 1 if the individual supports Candidate A and 0 otherwise. The variables X_4 to X_k are control variables, as described in the next section. The form of the statistical model is the same as used to create the campaign effect in the simulation. Given all this, the test of statistical power will be how often a statistically significant b_3 coefficient can be recovered when this model is run on the simulated data.

The following logit model is used for the non-monotonic effects:

$$\text{Vote}_i = b_0 + b_1\text{Exposure}_i + b_2\text{Time}_i + b_3\text{Exposure}_i \times \text{Time}_i +$$
$$b_4\text{Exposure}_i^2 + b_5\text{Exposure}_i^2 \times \text{Time}_i + b_6 X_{4i} \ldots \tag{2}$$

The coefficient of critical interest here is b_5, since this is the coefficient that determines the downturn in persuasion at high levels of media exposure. Unless this coefficient is both negative and achieves statistical significance, there is no clear detection of a non-monotonic effect.

This model, I must emphasize, is similar but not identical to the model used to create the campaign effect in the simulation. The difference is that, in simulating the campaign effect, a media-cubed variable rather than a media-squared variable is used because it was, as I found, necessary to achieve the shape I think I see in real data. Yet, I used the media-squared variable to test for the campaign effect because this is what I believe researchers would typically use to test for non-monotonicity.[7] Note that the panel depicting the 10% non-monotonic effect in Fig. 2 has a solid and a dotted line. The solid line shows the actual data, as created from an equation with an x-cubed term; the dotted line shows a fit with an x-squared term. This is discussed further below.

The models used to test for the elite exposure effect are the same as actually used to simulate the effects. For the 5% and 3% effects, the models are, respectively:

$$\text{Vote}_i = b_0 + b_1\text{Exposure}_i^2 + b_2\text{Time}_i + b_3\text{Exposure}_i^2 \times \text{Time}_i + b_4 X_{4i} \ldots \tag{3}$$

$$\text{Vote}_i = b_0 + b_1\text{Exposure}_i^3 + b_2\text{Time}_i + b_3\text{Exposure}_i^3 \times \text{Time}_i + b_4 X_{4i} \ldots \tag{4}$$

The reason for using the media-cubed term in the 3% model is that otherwise the sort of elite effect I was trying to simulate could not be achieved. In particular, I could not mimic the pattern in Fig. 1 without cubing the media variable.[8] In the analysis that

---

[7] More complicated models, such as those used in Zaller (1992), are beyond what can be analyzed in this paper.

[8] I omitted first order exposure terms from these models because I happened to know that they did not belong in the 'true model'. Including them would have led to multicollinearity and hence reduced statistical power. Although it is unusual to use second and third order terms without lower order ones, it is not any different, in principle, from using log transformations without lower order terms.

follows, the ability of a simple linear model to capture these two media effects is also tested, since I think that many analysts would, in this situation, prefer a conventional linear model to an apparently ad hoc x-square or x-cube model. The reason for not testing 10% variants of the elite exposure models is that they would require unrealistically high levels of opinion change among the most attentive.

A final point that may seem technical but is substantively pregnant is that for the two linear models in the upper panels of Fig. 1, support for Candidate A is higher at T_1 at every level of exposure, even when exposure is at zero. Thus, the y-intercept is slightly positive rather than, as might have been expected, zero. The slightly positive intercept captures the idea that a few people who have zero media exposure may nonetheless respond to campaign events, presumably because they discuss politics with people who have higher levels of media exposure (Huckfeldt and Sprague, 1995).

This specification effectively reduces *campaign effects* of 5% and 10% to *media exposure effects* of roughly 4% and 8%, with the rest of the campaign effect occurring by word-of-mouth and getting absorbed by the intercept. This, in turn, makes it harder to recover statistically significant exposure effects. This feature of the simulations seems clearly realistic, but its effect on power should be kept in mind.

It also needs to be kept in mind that the tests for the non-monotonic and elite exposure effects do not include 'discussion effects' (i.e. a slightly positive intercept). Keep in mind, too, that I attempt to recover linear effects with the 'correct' model but use a slightly mis-specified model for the non-monotonic effects. There are reasons for these choices. The discussion effects would be more likely to occur for a linear effect than for an elite effect which, as conceptualized, does not penetrate to the lowest strata of society. The same goes for non-monotonic exposure effects, which are often defined by the idea that the persuasive message does not penetrate all strata of society (Converse, 1962). Further, researchers are more likely to use the 'correct' model when analyzing a linear effect than when analyzing a non-monotonic effect.

5 Matching simulated to actual data

Having specified the campaign effects to be analyzed, I now turn to the question of how to embed these effects in simulated data sets that match actual data sets in 'relevant respects'. What are relevant here are any characteristics of actual data that affect statistical power. Therefore, the discussion is organized in terms of threats to statistical power.

Since power increases as standard errors decrease, the discussion begins with the formula for the standard error (SE) of an OLS regression coefficient. By analyzing this formula, we can determine several of the most important threats to power.

The formula for the SE of the coefficient for variable X in a multiple regression having k independent variables and n cases may be written in standard notation as:

$$SE_{\text{slope of } X} = \left[\frac{\sum_{i}^{n} \frac{e_i^2}{(n - k - 1)}}{(1 - R_{\text{aux}}^2)\,(n \times \text{Var}(X))} \right]^{1/2}$$

   This formula needs translating into words and its implications for power analysis need to be shown. There are four points here, each keyed to a particular part of the formula.

- *More cases make for smaller standard errors.* The intuition here is that more cases mean more information and hence less uncertainty (i.e. smaller SEs) about the coefficient. As regards the formula, note that the denominator includes n, so that as n increases, the SE decreases (all else being equal).
- *Increasing the range or 'spread out-ness' of the X-variable makes for smaller standard errors.* The intuition here is best conveyed by example: we can more precisely estimate the impact of education on income from a sample in which educational attainment varies from first grade to Ph.D. than from a sample in which education varies from high school graduate to college graduate. As regards the formula, if the values of the X-variable are spread out over a large range (rather than bunched together in the middle of a range), the variance of X will be greater, which will increase the size of the denominator, thereby decreasing the standard error.
- *Less residual (or unexplained) variation makes for smaller standard errors.* The intuition is that one can more precisely tell what is going on in a data set when the random noise in it is low. As regards the formula, the numerator in the formula is the variance of the residuals of the regression. If, all else being equal, the variance of the residuals is lower, the numerator of the above fraction will also be lower, thereby reducing the SE of the coefficient and increasing statistical power.
   As is well-known, smaller residuals also make for a higher r-square. Thus we can also say that higher r-squares make for smaller standard errors and more statistical power. (The r-square referred to in the previous sentence is not the r-square appearing in the formula; that r-square is discussed under the next bullet.)
- *Multicollinearity reduces statistical power.* Multicollinearity is defined as the correlation between a given X-variable and the other independent variables. As is widely known, a high level of multicollinearity causes higher standard errors and hence lower levels of statistical power. The intuition is that a high correlation among the independent variables makes it hard to tell which are important and which are not, which is then reflected in large standard errors. In the formula, multicollinearity is measured by the r-square of an auxiliary regression in which the X-variable of interest is regressed on all other independent variables in the main regression. The higher the r-square, the greater the multicollinearity. Since the formula for the SE contains the term $(1 - R^2_{aux})$ in the denominator, high multicollinearity increases the SE, which in turn reduces statistical power.

   Multicollinearity is an especially serious problem in the detection of campaign exposure effects, for the following reason. As modeled at the individual level, campaign effects typically involve a campaign-induced change in the effect of key independent variables on vote choice. Such changes are naturally modeled in terms of interactions. For example, if one effect of a campaign is to prime a certain variable, such as media exposure, so increasing its impact on vote choice, the effect of that variable is appropriately modeled as an interaction with time. The particular campaign effects described in the previous section also involve interaction terms, as noted.

To estimate interactions between one variable and another, one must normally include each variable twice — once for its direct effect and once for its interactive effect. These two variables will be at least moderately correlated, which creates the problem of multicollinearity. Models to capture non-monotonic effects are doubly cursed: terms for exposure and exposure-squared, plus the interaction of time with each. Thus, the exposure variable may appear four times in the model (see Eq. (2) above).

Interaction effects are not the only source of multicollinearity. Consider the priming effect documented by Johnston et al. in the 1988 Canadian election (Johnston et al., 1992). The candidate debate, news coverage, and advertising all function to prime the effect on vote choice of attitudes toward a Free Trade Agreement (FTA). But trade policy had been the subject of partisan contention for some time and so was likely to be correlated with party affiliation and other attitudes, thereby presenting an issue of multicollinearity. This sort of problem is common, in that many political attitudes — on party, race, abortion, defense spending, government services — are likely to be at least moderately correlated with one another. Therefore, it is important to build into the simulations an appropriate amount of multicollinearity.

The latter three bullets are of the greatest importance for simulation. If the variance of the X-variable, the size of the residuals, and the degree of multicollinearity (as measured by an auxiliary r-square) determine statistical power, then our simulated data must match actual data on each of these characteristics.

A final theoretical issue is measurement error. No term for measurement error appears in the formula for the SE. This is because the standard SE formula assumes that all variables have been measured without error. But measurement error is nonetheless universally important in survey work, causing biased coefficient estimates and reduced statistical power. Hence, building into simulations an appropriate form of measurement error is necessary to assure the validity of the simulations.

5.1 Determining the empirical values for variables in the simulation

In the previous section we saw that simulated data must match actual data in particular ways. The next step is to determine the empirical values that must be matched. Given, for example, that simulated data must have the same amount of measurement error as actual data, we must determine how much measurement error exists in actual data — and, in particular, how much measurement error exists in the media exposure scales typically used in studies of campaign effects. For each of the characteristics on which our simulated data must match actual data, we must determine what actual election study data are like.

5.2 The exposure variable

The central variable in this analysis, media exposure, is also the most challenging to simulate in a credible manner. The 1996 ANES study offers several possibilities for

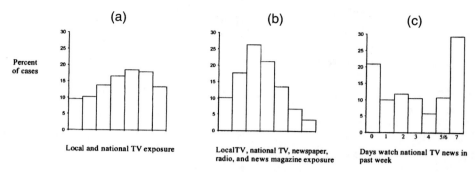

Fig. 3: Three commonly used media exposure variables: (a) local and national TV exposure (four items, alpha reliability = 0.79, SD = 1.85, mean = 4.32, correlation with information, $r = 0.20$, $n = 1711$); (b) local TV, national TV, newspaper, radio and news magazine exposure (10 items, alpha reliability = 0.73, SD = 1.47, mean = 3.41, correlation with information, $r = 0.43$, $n = 1525$); (c) days on which national TV news had been viewed in past week (one item, test–retest reliability = 0.58 (1997 Pilot, $n = 545$), SD = 2.73, mean = 3.56, correlation with information, $r = 0.17$, $n = 1712$). Note: the TV exposure scale is based on items v0242 to v0245. The omnibus measure adds items v0246, v0248 and v1333 to v1336. The scales were built from a principal components factor analysis and recoded to seven-point scales with intervals of equal width.

Source: 1996 NES study.

measuring it, but none is ideal, and scholars have achieved no consensus on which is best. The lack of agreement is not for want of effort. The literature is full of conflicting advice and argument on how to 'measure media exposure correctly'. Meanwhile, different measures have different variances, reliabilities, and auxiliary correlations with other variables, each of which affects the power of statistical analyses in which the media variable is used. In these circumstances, there is no avoiding a review of the terrain. I shall keep this review both empirical and tightly tethered to the options available in the data at hand.[9]

Fig. 3 gives three examples of media scales that can be built from the 1996 ANES study. In the left-hand panel is the distribution for a four-item additive scale based on number of days watching local news, days watching national TV news, amount of attention to campaign stories on local TV, and amount of attention to campaign stories on national TV. These items make a coherent and focused scale with an alpha reliability of 0.79, but the scale correlates poorly with a 13-item measure of political information ($r = 0.20$). Although some scholars disagree with me, I find it difficult to

[9] I have argued elsewhere that political information is the best available measure of media exposure (Zaller, 1990; Price and Zaller, 1993). However, I do not see how simulation could shed any light on that issue and so ignore it in this paper. Information scales tend to have reliabilities equal to or lower than good media exposure scales, but to perform better in many kinds of tests.

take seriously a measure of news exposure that has so weak an association with what ought to be the effect of news exposure.

A longer and more general measure of media exposure is shown in panel (b) of Fig. 3. It includes two items each on national TV, local TV, newspapers, radio, and magazines, for a total of 10 items. All of the items from the previous scale are also in this one. The alpha reliability is lower (0.73), but its correlation with information is somewhat better ($r = 0.43$).

These results suggest one problem in measuring media exposure. The reason the longer scale has a lower reliability is that few people attend to all media, preferring to specialize in just one or two. This leads to lower inter-item correlations and thereby lower alpha. The usual prescription in this circumstance is to use the shorter and more coherent scale. Yet, when a big campaign story occurs, it is generally covered in all media, and the analyst then wants to measure exposure to all media. A narrowly focused media scale does not achieve this. Nor, typically, is it feasible to use a series of scales, one for each medium, since this mires the analysis in multicollinearity. These considerations favor the longer, omnibus scale. So also does the fact that the longer scale has better external validation in the form of a higher correlation with political information.

Another difficulty is suggested by the right-hand panel of Fig. 3, which shows how often Americans claim to watch the national TV news. As can be seen, about 30% claim to watch every day of the week. In a country of about 200 million adults, this translates into about 60 million viewers per night. Yet, according to Nielsen ratings, the combined daily audience for the networks plus CNN is around 20 million. And this is only part of the story. By also taking into account the people who claim to watch the news only one to six nights a week, we reach the startling conclusion that about half the respondents to NES surveys — and, by extension, half the adult population of the country — watch the national news on any given night.[10] This comes to about 100 million adults, or about five times as many as actually watch, according to Nielsen's more careful methods. This sort of overstatement is common in survey reports of media exposure. For example, a 1989 survey found that about 10% of respondents claimed to read the Wall Street Journal. This comes to 20 million readers, although the paper's circulation is around two million. Among the supposed readers, a few claimed to read it six or seven days a week, even though the paper is published only on five days a week.[11]

What might be the effect of such rampant overstatement on the ability of a measure of media exposure to detect campaign effects? A standard result of econometric theory is that systematic overstatement of scores on an X variable does not bias coefficients (though it does bias the intercept). But systematic overstatement of X *in combination with* truncation of the high end of the X variable is another matter. When this occurs,

---

[10] Some respondents may have misunderstood the question, thinking that they saw national news on their local TV news program. A later question, however, permits correction for this misunderstanding. When respondents were asked which national news program they watched, some said they did not watch any. Filtering out these respondents yields an estimate that 48% of respondents watch a national news program on any given night; without the filter, the estimate is 51%.

[11] Actually, 2 of 48, or 4.2%, but even so the anecdote is too good to pass up (ANES Pilot Study, 1998).

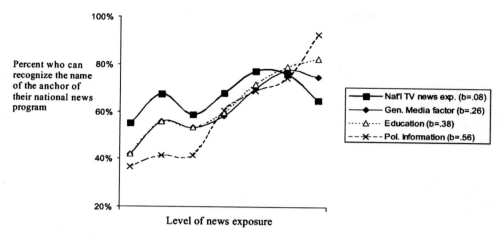

Fig. 4: How four measures of news exposure affect learning the names of network anchors. A typical question was: 'We're interested in how much people learn about television news personalities. Take Tom Brokaw. Do you happen to know which network he works for . . . is it CBS, CNNorwich? . . . Peter Jennings? . . . Dan Rather? . . . Bernard Shaw?' Note: Bs in key are unstandardized slopes from OLS regressions in which each independent variable has been scaled to a 1–7 range.
Source: 1996 National Election Study.

people whose true scores are low to middle on the X variable can overstate their media exposure, but people whose true scores are at the top cannot. This leads to a bunching up of dissimilar types in the top scale category, which fills up with a mix of middle-range people who are exaggerating and high-end people who are unable to exaggerate. The expected effect is attenuation of the discriminating power of the scale at the high end. A probable example of such attenuation is shown in Fig. 4.

Fig. 4 shows the percentage of respondents who can identify the anchor of the TV network news programs they most often watch. For example, if a respondent said he watched the NBC *Nightly News*, he was asked which network Tom Brokaw worked for. People who said they never watched the network news, or were unsure which they watched, are excluded from the analysis.[12] Fig. 4 shows how four measures of news exposure affect 'knowing your own anchor'.

By far the worst exposure measure is the item that ought to perform best: namely, asking how many days in a week the respondent watches the national news. This item is only weakly correlated with the ability to recognize the anchor of one's news show, and the people at the highest level of self-reported exposure are hardly more likely to get the right answer than people with the lowest exposure level. Thus, when TV news exposure and TV news exposure-squared are used in a logit model to predict anchor

[12] Respondents were asked about the anchors for the three networks plus CNN, but I analyze only responses to the question about each person's own most watched program.

recognition, the term for exposure-squared is statistically significant at $p = 0.003$ (two-tailed).[13] A plausible explanation for this odd pattern is that a high proportion of the people at the highest level of self-report are exaggerators, and therefore fail to show the expected effect of high exposure.

Fig. 4 also shows comparable results for three other measures. The broader measure of general news exposure has 10 items, three of which are questions about 'how many days in the past week' and probably suffer from some degree of over-report. This general measure also shows some non-monotonicity, though less than the TV exposure item alone.[14] Meanwhile, two measures that do not suffer from over-report bias — education and an information scale based on objective tests — show much stronger relationships with recognition of the name of one's news anchor.

Over-report bias, which no doubt varies across respondents and items, does not reduce calculated estimates of scale reliability. On the contrary, it tends to enhance apparent reliability. As long as survey respondents exaggerate with some degree of consistency from one exposure item to the next and one survey to the next, over-report bias cuts randomness and thereby enhances estimates of reliability. Over-report bias can thus hide the damage it does behind exaggerated reliability estimates.

From the ANES data, then, there seem to be two kinds of media exposure scales: broad or omnibus scales that have a low mean level of news exposure and exhibit no clear evidence of exaggeration; and more narrowly focused scales that have a higher mean and do exhibit evidence of exaggeration. In the simulations that follow, I focus primarily on the broad type of exposure scale, for three reasons. First, it is what many, perhaps most, researchers use when testing for exposure effects. Second, as explained above, good reasons exist for preferring the broader scale despite the apparently higher reliability statistics of more focused scales. Third, some survey respondents appear to exaggerate much more than others;[15] the simulation of a narrowly focused scale could accommodate this inter-personal difference, but it would require stronger assumptions than could be readily justified. Later I simulate an exaggerated exposure scale, but the exaggeration will be based on the simplistic assumption that everyone exaggerates to the same degree, and I will not rely heavily on this scale for any of the main conclusions of the study.

Let me, then, begin by simulating a media exposure scale. The first step is to assume a specific distribution of true media exposure scores. The one I have assumed is shown on the left of Fig. 5. This distribution is not meant to recapitulate what gets measured in surveys, but, rather, to depict what exposure scores would look like if they could be observed independently of the random and systematic error that plagues survey measurements.

Although the assumed true-score distribution is partly guesswork, it is not unconstrained guesswork. Its most notable feature is a sparsely populated right tail. This reflects the assumption that I am simulating true scores on an omnibus scale — a scale

---

[13] When exposure and exposure-squared are used to predict anchor recognition, the term for exposure-squared is statistically significant at $p = 0.008$ (two-tailed).

[14] In a logit like the one above, the exposure-squared term has a two-sided p-value of 0.08.

[15] As shown above, many people exaggerate their exposure to network news; yet, at the same time, Fig. 1 also shows a large fraction of people who cannot be exaggerating (on the upside) because they say they never watch.

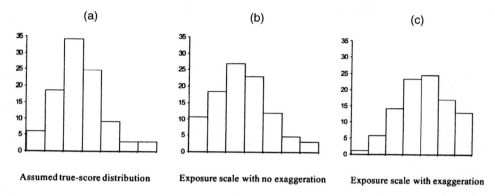

Fig. 5: Simulated media exposure scales: (a) SD = 1.32, mean = 3.34; (b) true-score reliability = 0.70; SD = 1.53, mean = 3.37; (c) true-score reliability = 0.66; SD = 1.47, mean = 4.70.

that covers everything from TV to newspapers to radio to magazines, and that therefore gives respondents more opportunities to claim media use than any but a handful could honestly take.[16] In a scale intended to measure the gamut of media behaviors, the true score distribution *should* have a sparsely populated right tail. Moreover, I chose a true-score distribution that can, by the addition of random measurement error, be transformed into an 'observed-score' distribution having properties similar to the ANES omnibus exposure scale shown earlier. This observed-score distribution is shown as the middle distribution in Fig. 3. As can be seen, the mean, standard deviation, reliability, and general shape of this distribution are similar to those of the ANES omnibus exposure scale in Fig. 1. The observed-score distribution in Fig. 3 — or, rather, the individual scores contributing to it — will be the primary media exposure variable in the simulations that follow.

The method for creating the observed-score distribution was trial and error. Working on an Excel spreadsheet, true-score distributions of various shapes were created, with more or less randomness being added experimentally,[17] until I had a true score distribution that could be transformed into an observed score distribution that closely resembled the ANES observed score distribution. The properties of the two simulated distributions are consequential for all that follows. The true-score distribution specifies

[16] Questions that might be used to create a scale with a comparably under-populated left tail — e.g. 'How many years has it been since you read a campaign story in a newspaper' — are not very often asked. Thus we are less likely to observe a sparsely populated left tail on an actual multi-item scale than a sparsely populated right one.

[17] Excel has a command for generating random numbers on a flat 0–1 interval. To create random measurement error, I added two of such random numbers, subtracted 1 (to center the sum on zero), and multiplied by 2.05. This yielded an error distribution with a range of −2.05 to +2.05, and SD = 0.84, and a roughly normal shape (except for fatter tails). A draw from this distribution was added to each individual's true media score in order to create an error-laden observed media score. The result was an observed score distribution having properties similar to NES observed scores, as explained.

the *X*-variance that, as shown earlier, affects statistical power. Thus, the assumption that true scores are bunched and skewed rather than spread out and symmetrical makes a difference. The amount of measurement error in the observed-score distribution also affects statistical power. If a scale with more variance, or less measurement error, had been chosen, it would generate higher estimates of statistical power than the ones reported below. Hence, the justification given for the assumptions made in simulating true scores and observed scores needs to be carefully pondered.

Finally, the distribution in the right part of Fig. 3 shows the scores that result when both over-reporting and random measurement error are added to the initial true-score distribution. The measurement error is the same as for the previous scale; over-reporting is a constant 1.5 scale units for each person on a seven-point scale. Limited use is made of this scale in the simulations that follow.[18]

Before going further, my use of the term 'reliability' needs to be clarified, as it is deployed in two different ways in the research literature. The most common usage is that of Carmines and Zeller (1979) (pp. 11–13): '*reliability* concerns the extent to which an experiment, test, or any measuring procedure yields the same results on repeated trials'. They distinguish reliability from validity, which is the extent to which a measure "measures what it purports to measure". They add: "just because a measure is quite reliable, this does not mean that it is also relatively valid". Thus, over-reporting of media exposure could, in their senses of the terms, make a media exposure variable more reliable but less valid. Lord and Novick's (Lord and Novick, 1968) classic treatment offers a different conception of reliability: "The reliability of a test is defined as the squared correlation, ρ_{XT}^2, between observed score and true score" (p. 61). In this usage, the distinction between reliability and validity does not exist.

In this study, reliability is used in Lord and Novick's true-score sense rather than the repeated trials sense of Carmines and Zeller. Since my simulation generates both true scores and observed scores but no repeated measures, it is easy to use the *r*-square between them as the measure of reliability.[19] The true-score concept also seems more natural in cases, as in my simulations, in which there is no validity concern. Note, however, that the alpha reliability estimates calculated from ANES data embody the repeated-trials approach and carry no implications whatsoever about validity. Thus, if — as is likely — the ANES data suffer from over-reporting and other validity problems, an alpha reliability of 0.80 from actual data could be lower than a true-score reliability of 0.70 from simulated data in which there is no validity concern. Indeed, I assume that, if true-score reliabilities could be calculated for the ANES data, they would be as low or lower than the true-score reliabilities used in the simulations.[20]

---

[18] Note that it is possible, through a careful choice of error structure, to transform the true-score distribution in Fig. 3 into a scale having virtually the same mean, variance, and reliability as the four-item ANES TV exposure scale in Fig. 1. But I concluded that, as indicated above, the assumptions necessary to do so are unavoidably arbitrary. Therefore, the analysis is confined to the simpler over-report scale discussed in the text.

[19] The simulation does not generate a measure based on repeated trials, but could readily be made to do so if there were reason.

[20] Alpha reliabilities are lower-bound estimates of reliability in the repeated-trials sense and would be higher if item difficulties vary, which they certainly do, especially in the general ANES exposure scale in

In sum, I simulated a primary media exposure scale that is based on a plausible distribution of underlying true scores, and that has observable characteristics quite similar to those of the media exposure scale many researchers would build from the 1996 ANES survey. The most important parameters of the simulated scale are its true-score variance (as fixed by its distribution) and its true-score reliability. Just two parameters of the simulation now remain to be fixed: the amount of residual variance in the vote equation used to test for media effects, and the amount of multicollinearity. Happily, neither presents much challenge.

5.3 Overall r-square of model

As explained earlier, the probability of obtaining a statistically significant coefficient for a given X variable is higher, all else being equal, if other X variables are present in the model to hold down random error and drive up the overall r-square of the regression. For this reason, researchers are normally happy to load up their regression models with co-variates, provided only that multicollinearity does not become an issue. In the context of presidential vote models, there may be 10, 20, or even more co-variates.

Yet, the last handful of variables typically explain little additional variance and may even reduce the adjusted r-square. The bulk of the heavy-lifting in presidential vote models is done by party identification, along with a few others. Table 1 gives results for a series of logit models used to predict the two-party vote in the 1996 ANES study. For each of the 12 models, vote choice is the dependent variable, but the independent variables vary as indicated. For example, in model 1, party identification is the only independent variable; but in model 2, a set of standard independent variables is included, such as ideology and race, but party is not included. Each model involves a somewhat different configuration of the variables researchers might use.

As the table shows, party identification alone can generate a pseudo r-square of 0.55 and correctly predict 88% of the cases. When standard co-variates such as issue positions and demographics are added, as in models 3 and 4, these figures rise to 66% and 91%. This level of fit for a dichotomous dependent variable ought to be high enough for anyone, but it is not unusual for analysts to add evaluations of the candidates on such traits as competence and compassion, and emotional reactions to the candidates on such dimensions as fear and pride. Occasionally one sees candidate-feeling thermometers as independent variables. The addition of these variables to presidential vote models raises the pseudo r-square close to 0.80 and the percent of correctly predicted cases to about 95%. Higher values can be seen in some published articles.

Yet, as regards the detection of campaign effects, the models that achieve the highest r-squares come at a cost. The trait, emotion, and thermometer variables are so powerful, and so proximate to vote choice that they absorb the impact of other variables. Thus, when the trait and emotion variables are added to the model that

Fig. 1. Even so, I suspect on the basis of much experience with the sort of data shown in Fig. 2 that the true-score reliabilities of the scales used in the simulations are higher than those of actual data. However, not all researchers may have this view.

Table 1: Fit statistics for alternative models of the 1996 two-party presidential vote[a]

Model	Pseudo r-square	Percent of cases correctly predicted
1. Five-point party ID scale only	0.55	88.3
2. Standard covariates only[b]	0.50	84.5
3. Five-point party ID Standard covariates	0.66	91.0
4. Dem. and Rep. Party ID dummies Standard covariates	0.65	90.6
5. Five-point party ID Standard covariates Traits battery	0.76	93.9
6. Five-point party ID Standard covariates Emotions battery	0.75	93.8
7. Five-point party ID Standard covariates Candidate thermometer difference	0.79	94.2
8. Five-point party ID Standard covariates Traits battery Emotions battery Candidate thermometer difference	0.80	94.5
9. Five-point party ID Traits battery Emotions battery Candidate thermometer difference	0.78	94.8
10. Five-point party ID		
11. Traits battery Emotions battery	0.75	93.9
12. Five-point party ID Candidate thermometer difference	0.77	94.0

No. of cases = 1034

[a] The table reports summary statistics for each of 12 logit models. In each, major party vote in the 1996 is the dependent variable, but the independent variables are different across tests. Source: 1996 National Election Study.
[b] The standard covariates are self-described ideology; short scales on government spending and moral tolerance; one-item scales on national economic conditions, abortion, aid to blacks, government services, defense spending, job guarantees; respondent's race, age and gender.

previously contained only party ID and the standard co-variates, the r-square goes up but the coefficients for party and the other standard co-variates go down. For the coefficients that are statistically significant in the initial model, the mean reduction in size is 36%. When thermometer scores are added along with traits and emotions, the overall reduction in size of previously significant coefficients is 46%.[21] If candidate evaluations were short-term causes of party identification, political ideology, and other standard covariates, this would not be a problem. However, it is more likely that candidate evaluations are the effect rather than cause of these variables and hence absorb variance that 'belongs' to them.

The same can no doubt happen in the case of campaign effects. If exposure to a debate or news story makes citizens more likely to vote for a candidate, it might positively affect trait judgments, emotional reactions, and thermometer scores, and these variables might then absorb the media effect. This danger would be especially great if media exposure were measured with more error than the other variables, as it may well be. The problem can occur in any sort of model, but is especially likely to occur when summary variables, like trait evaluations or emotional reactions, are included in a vote model.

In view of these considerations, the analysis focuses on models having r-squares of 0.65.[22] Models with higher r-squares would show greater power to detect media effects, but since I cannot credibly simulate how candidate evaluation variables might absorb the effect of media exposure, the results would not be interpretable.

5.4 Multicollinearity

If the variables used to predict vote choice in Table 1 are instead used to predict scores on the ANES omnibus media exposure scale in Fig. 3, the r-squares are about 0.14. The zero-order correlations between these media scales and vote choice are about 0.10. Therefore, relationships of these magnitudes are built into the simulated data.

The most important source of multicollinearity in the simulations, however, comes from use of interaction terms, as explained earlier. If, for example, the auxiliary r-square for the interaction term in Eq. (1) is calculated from simulated data, it is about 0.85. For the non-monotonic models, it is around 0.98. These are not values built into the simulation, but are values that have 'fallen out' of the data set as constructed to the specifications described above.[23]

---

[21] A useful point of reference: when party ID was added to a model that previously contained only the standard co-variates, the average reduction of coefficients that had been statistically significant in the initial model was 18%. Reductions were greatest for ideology (50%) and cuts in government services (59%).

[22] See Appendix A for discussion of the error term used to achieve this r-square.

[23] These r-squares are also comparable to what are obtained in actual ANES data when a 10-item media exposure variable is interacted with an arbitrary 0–1 variable and made the dependent variable of an auxiliary regression in which media exposure, the 0–1 variable, and other 'ideology' variables are used as independent variables.

6 Results

We have now developed specific empirical values for all of the general data characteristics that, as the earlier analysis indicated, affect statistical power in models of campaign effects. These are: the variance of true-score media exposure (as fixed by its assumed distribution) and the reliability of this scale; the residual variance in standard vote models, as measured by r-square; and the degree of multicollinearity between our key independent variable, media exposure, and other independent variables. We have also determined the size and shape of the particular campaign effects that may occur in US presidential elections. We can therefore proceed with the simulation.

The essence of simulation is to create serial data sets in order to test how often particular relationships appear. I created data sets of a given sample size that embody one of the campaign effects described above and that meet all the data constraints described in the previous section. Then a logit regression was run for each data set in order to find out how often — over many such data sets — a statistically significant coefficient for the campaign effect embedded in the data could be recovered. I report two cutoffs for statistical significance: 0.05 for two-tailed and 0.10 for one-tailed. The particular models and coefficients of prime interest are those described above in the section on campaign effects. (For more details on the simulations, see Appendix A.)

The simulations were structured so that half the individuals were interviewed prior to the campaign event and half afterwards, thus maximizing statistical power. Thus, if the N of a simulation is 2000, it means there are 1000 interviews in a baseline condition and 1000 in the period following the media event. Note that the Ns required to achieve a given level of power do not necessarily refer to the total size of the study, but refer to the cases available for a particular test. Typically, the available N is smaller, perhaps greatly smaller, than total N. Thus if, for example, one were testing the impact of exposure to a presidential debate in an ANES survey of 2000 respondents, probably not all 2000 cases could be used in the test. Rather, one would probably compare opinion in the week or so before the debate with opinion in the week afterwards. Given the ANES design, this might involve, at most, 500 respondents from the total sample of 2000.

The results of the simulations are shown in Fig. 6. The panels are arranged to correspond to the layout of Fig. 2, which showed the shape and size of the campaign effects under study.

The most general finding in Fig. 6 is that detection of exposure effects is likely to be unreliable unless the effects are both large and captured in a large survey. Surveys, or subsets of surveys, having fewer than about 2000 cases may be unreliable for detecting almost any sort of likely exposure effect; even surveys of 3000 could easily fail to detect politically important effects.

To take an example: The 2000 Democratic convention produced a 7.3% bounce for Al Gore,[24] which, in political terms, was a huge shift in vote preference. But if researchers had interviewed 1000 people in independent samples before and after the

---

[24] This is the average Gore gain in six polls reported by Adam Clymer in 'In Postconvention Polls, Gore Bounces Just Ahead of Bush', *New York Times*, 22 August 2000, p. A18.

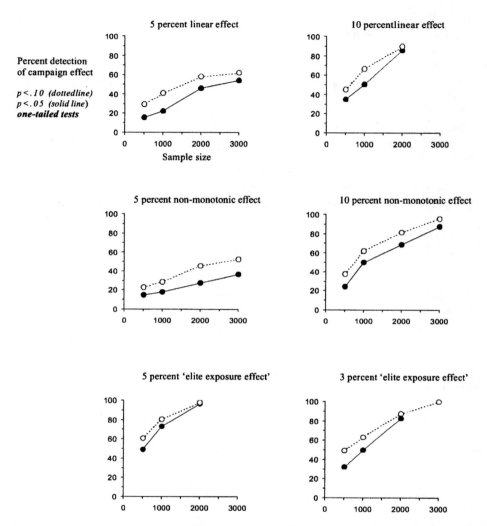

Fig. 6: Detection rates for campaign effects of given size and shape. Note: size and shape of campaign effects are as given in Fig. 2 and accompanying text. Each point in each graph is based on at least 50 trials at a given sample size, and the vast majority are based on 100–200 trials.

convention, for a total of 2000 respondents, and if the bounce was non-monotonic with respect to media exposure, the chance of detecting it at the 0.05 level (one-tailed) would be about 45%.[25] And this assumes a media exposure scale comparable in reliability to the 10-item scale carried in the 1996 ANES.

[25] This result has been interpolated from the 5% and 10% non-monotonic sub-panels of Fig. 6 below.

But this may be overly blunt and pessimistic. A more differentiated summary of the findings in Fig. 6 may be offered as follows:

- Some large campaign effects — linear exposure effects of about 10%, which is the size of a large convention bounce — can be reliably captured in election surveys of 2000 respondents. Elite exposure effects of 5% can also be reliably captured with 2000 respondents, and can be fairly reliably captured with only 1000 respondents.
- Linear and non-monotonic campaign effects of normal size — a five-point shift, which is equivalent to a gaffe or large debate bounce — cannot be reliably captured in any reasonably sized election survey. A separate series of runs, not shown in Fig. 6, shows that with 5000 respondents, a 5% non-monotonic effect can be detected at the 0.05 level with only about 50% reliability.
- The big surprise of the simulations is the relatively high level of detectability of what I call 'the elite exposure effect'. A 3% elite exposure effect is more detectable than a 5% linear or non-monotonic effect, and nearly as detectable as a 10% linear effect. (Recall that linear exposure effects, as I have tried realistically to define them, include a 'discussion effect' that is independent of individual media exposure.)[26]

One feature of these simulations is that I nearly always used a particular model to create an effect and then tried to recover the effect with that same model. But the question arises: what if, as is essentially always the case, scholars are unsure what the right model is — that is, what model has generated the campaign effect they are trying to detect? And what if they use a 'wrong' model — a model that seems plausible but is not the one actually at work? As one always knows the 'right' model when doing simulations, it is possible to address this question.

Let us begin with the non-monotonic exposure model. As explained earlier, I used a slightly 'wrong' model in attempting to recover the non-monotonic exposure effect. I created the effect with a function that uses media exposure and media exposure-cubed, but attempted to recover it with a model using media exposure and media exposure-squared. I did this because I surmised that, although scholars might perhaps try a model with media exposure-cubed in it, they would be reluctant to report an x-cubed effect for fear that it would raise the spectre of ad hoc data mining and overfitting.

But how serious is this problem? In the case of the non-monotonic exposure model, it is not serious at all. In a set of 100 trials of sample $n = 1000$ and a 10% effect, the media-squared term in the model was significant 44 times at the 0.05 level. For the same 100 samples, a media-cubed term in the model was significant 45 times. A similar test was carried out for the cubed version of the elite exposure model. Here the results suggest a possible advantage to the unconventional models. In 100 trials on samples of 2000, the correct media-cubed interaction term captured the campaign effect 76% of the time, compared with 77% for a media-squared interaction term and 66% for a linear media interaction term.

---

[26] I did not expect the elite exposure effect to be so detectable when it was selected for study. It was chosen because, from various data I have examined, it seems to be relatively common, as in Fig. 1. However I now suspect that I had this sense because this kind of effect is so easy to capture in surveys. Non-monotonic effects of 5% could occur just as often and remain invisible most of the time.

More simulations are needed to pin down this result. But on the assumption that it holds, the question arises: why does having the 'correct' model not make more difference in these cases? The answer, I suspect, is measurement error on the media exposure variable. Degradation of the independent variable takes the edge off — or flattens — its relationship with the dependent variable, so that a 'wrong' linear or square term works almost as well as the 'correct' cubed term. This, however, is only speculation.

Given the low power of most surveys to detect non-monotonic effects when they occur, a related question arises: if researchers test the 'correct' non-monotonic model but fail to find support for it, what do they do next? The answer, in many cases, is that they revert to a less complicated model. But the results of doing so may often give a misleading impression. When a 5% non-monotonic effect has occurred, the chances of getting support for Eq. (2) are only 18% for a sample of 500 and 28% for a sample of 1000. But a model that drops the media exposure variables and uses time as the sole campaign variable gets significant coefficients for time with 62% and 88% frequency, respectively. This is despite the fact that time ought to have no effect apart from its interaction with media exposure (see Fig. 2).

Researchers who fail to find support for the model they expected to hold, but do find support for a simpler and perhaps less likely model, will normally report results for the model that 'worked', perhaps mentioning in passing that the expected model failed to work. What else can they really do? Actually, there is something. Researchers who obtain null results for their expected model could, and probably should, attempt to assess the statistical power of their test. They should ask: 'what are my chances of finding statistically significant support for my expected model, given the amount and reliability of data that I have to work with?'. I return to this in my concluding remarks.

One final set of results. I noted earlier that many media exposure scales are afflicted by exaggerated statements of usage. I tested the effect of such over-reporting by simulating a media exposure scale with the same true score and random error variance as my primary scale, but with a 1.5 point across-the-board over-reporting added to true scores on a seven-point scale. Persons who scored at the top of the true exposure scale without the over-reporting could not go over the top, but were held down to the top category.

From the test runs, it appeared that over-reporting did not undermine power to detect either linear effects (where power was low to begin with) or elite exposure effects (where tests were not very sensitive to model form either). However, it did appear that over-reporting had an important effect on tests of the non-monotonic model. For a sample of 1000 and an effect size of 10%, power was reduced from 50% with the primary media scale to 27% with the scale containing over-reporting. When the sample size was raised to 3000, the effect of over-reporting was to reduce power from 88% to 51%. These tests were based on 100 trials per cell.

7 Concluding comments

In opening an article in the American Political Science Review, Larry Bartels (1993) (p. 267) wrote:

The state of research on media effects is one of the most notable embar-
rassments of modern social science. The pervasiveness of the mass
media and their virtual monopoly over the presentation of many kinds
of information must suggest to reasonable observers that what these
media say and how they say it has enormous social and political consequences. Nevertheless, the scholarly literature has been much better at
refuting, qualifying, and circumscribing the thesis of media impact than
at supporting it.

Bartels' attributes this state of affairs in part to scholarly 'carelessness' about the
consequences of measurement error and in part to 'limitations of research design'. The
limitation I have sought to bring into sharp relief in this chapter is an aspect of research
design: the size of surveys. When the data available to test models of exposure effects
have three times more power for supporting 'wrong' models that have no media variables than for 'correct' models that do, it cannot be good for communication studies.
One must wonder, in particular, how many of the null findings that pervade the study
of mass communication are actually cases in which the truth (if it could be known) is
a 5% non-monotonic effect that cannot be detected in any reasonably sized sample, so
registers in the data as a null effect for campaign exposure. It is hard even to make a
plausible guess about how often this might happen.

What, then, is to be done? The easy answer is that funding agencies should give
scholars more money to do bigger studies. With the kinds of analyses reported in this
chapter, scholars can write grant proposals that make a more persuasive case for big
surveys than has been made in the past, and funding agencies will respond by opening
their checkbooks. Or perhaps not. Although I think scholars who design surveys should
devote more attention to power than they typically do — that is, close to none — I
doubt that simply dropping a power analysis or two into a grant proposal will have a
dramatic impact on support. For one thing, the need for cases must always be judged
in light of particular purposes. If, as suggested by my analysis, some important communication effects cannot be reliably detected even with 5000 cases, funding agencies
might insist that scholars give up the Holy Grail of explaining the effects of media
exposure and focus instead on more realistic goals. Moreover, no case for bigger
surveys is likely to be persuasive if it is confined to grant proposals and to 'methods'
papers like this one. It will be persuasive only when a large fraction of the scholarly
community internalizes the lessons of methodological critiques concerning power,
measurement error, modeling sophistication, and other matters, and demonstrates
by the collective weight of what is published that we really are at the limits of what
we can accomplish with studies of conventional size. We are a long way from this
situation.

It would also seem that the scholars who consume surveys should make more use
of power analysis in their studies, especially in studies which turn up null or trace
effects. That is, they should estimate the probability of rejecting the null hypothesis
with respect to the particular size of effect they expect, given the model they are using,
the characteristics of the variables in it, and the amount of data they have. The first to
profit from such analysis would be the scholars themselves, who will presumably find

it easier to publish null findings if they can show that their analysis has been sufficiently powerful to detect a real effect if one existed.

Most researchers, however, behave as if they are intuitive believers in what
Kahneman and Tversky have called 'the law of small numbers'. If an effect is real, it
will show up in the data at hand, even if the data are rather limited. Scholars who take
this attitude might profit from pondering Fig. 7, which gives a fuller view of a typical
Monte Carlo experiment than has been shown above. In repeated attempts to recover
a 10% non-monotonic effect from samples of 1000, I succeeded at the 0.01 (one-tailed)
level 22% of the time and at the 0.05 level for an additional 22% of the time. Yet I
also failed to make a weak 0.25 (one-tailed) cutoff 16% of the time and failed to make
even a 0.40 cutoff 14% of the time. Further, in the 50 trials on which these figures are
based, I got sign reversals on the critical 'time X media squared' term on five occasions, or 10% of cases.

As we have seen, 10% is a big campaign effect and 1000 cases is a reasonably
typical sample size. Researchers often deal with smaller effects and smaller samples
or sub-samples. It would be interesting to know how many of the studies that have
fed the 'minimal effects' orthodoxy of the past five decades had the power to detect
medium or large effects if such effects had been present.

For scholars who sometimes behave — whether as designers or consumers of
surveys — as if they are intuitive believers in the law of small numbers, the message
of this study is that power issues need more attention than they have customarily
received. Even so, the incorporation of power analysis into substantive research reports
cannot be expected to happen quickly. Indeed, if the researchers have to undertake as
much work as was necessary to produce this chapter, it may take a very long time. A
priority for future studies of mass communications should, therefore, be to figure out
how to accomplish power analysis more efficiently.

For certain purposes in communication studies, and in political science more generally, the formulae set out in Jacob Cohen's *Statistical Power Analysis in the Behavioral
Sciences* (Cohen, 1988) would give accurate forecasts of power. These formulae and

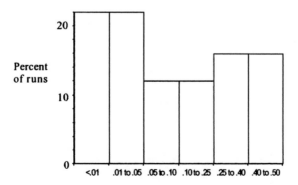

Fig. 7: Distribution of one-tailed *p*-values for tests of 10% non-monotonic effect in
samples of 1000 ($N = 50$ trials).

more have been incorporated into highly accessible computer programs, such as PASS2000 (NCSC, 2000), which should be used much more frequently in behavioral research. There is, however, a significant impediment to the routine use of power formulae in communication studies and elsewhere: figuring out expected effect sizes and translating them into increments of r-square, as required for input into power formulae for regression models. It would be hard to get such values without going through most of the steps reported in this study.[27] Suppose, for example, that my Eq. (1) were a simple OLS model, for which analytical calculations can be made. How would a researcher specify, a priori, the expected increment in r-square (net of multicollinearity) from the b_3 coefficient, so that the power of a given data set to capture it could be calculated? Only by simulation, I suspect. And simulation, as this chapter shows, is a cumbersome undertaking. If scholars must do simulations to determine the inputs to power formulae, it may be a long time before power analysis is used as routinely as it should be.

Even if effect size were easy to specify and power calculations extremely easy to carry out, scholars might still be slow to adopt power analysis. In other scientific domains in which power analysis is, in fact, much easier to do, it has still made only limited headway. For example, it is quite easy to use power analysis to determine how many subjects are necessary to observe a mean difference of given size in an experimental study with a dichotomous treatment variable. Yet in experimental studies from medicine to psychology, such calculations have been slow to become routine. For example, a study in the 1994 *Journal of the American Medical Association* (Moher and Wells, 1994) calculated the power of 102 randomized experimental trials of new drugs or treatments that had turned up null results. It turned out that only 16% of these studies, all of which had been published in top journals, had the power to reliably detect a 25% experimental effect on their dependent variable, and only 36% could reliably detect a 50% experimental effect.

There are, to be sure, signs of progress. Yet, after reviewing them in the preface to the second edition of his power analysis textbook, Cohen (1988) (p. xiv) commented:

> It is clear that power analysis has not had the impact on behavioral research that I (and other right-thinking methodologists) had expected [when he published the first textbook on power analysis in 1969]. But we are convinced that it is just a matter of time.

Those of us who have designed studies intended to measure communication effects, as well as those of us who have used the data generated by these studies, have been among the laggards in taking power issues seriously. It would behove us, as laborers in a sub-field full of minimal and null effects, to get to the vanguard.

---

[27] The actual inputs to power formulae are r-square with and without the test variable(s) in the model. No direct value for multicollinearity is used; however, the difference in r-square is strongly affected by the degree of multicollinearity between the test variable and other X variables in the model. Hence, multicollinearity must be taken into account when calculating the difference in r-square. When multicollinearity is high, it may be hard to get a large increment in the r-square even when the effect of the test variable on Y is large.

Acknowledgements

The idea for this chapter originated at a conference on *The Future of Election Studies* at the University of Houston in March 1999. However, I would never have written it had Chris Wlezien not made me. I thank Gary King for much advice (although he has not read the paper). I also thank Kathy Bawn, Kathy Cramer Walsh, Roland Strum, an anonymous reviewer, and especially Jim DeNardo for helpful comments in this chapter, but stress that I alone am responsible for any errors it may still contain.

Appendix A

A.1 Description of the data simulation

Each of several thousand 'individuals' on a spreadsheet was assigned a fixed value on a 'true media exposure scale'. The values on this scale ran from 1 to 7 and have the distribution shown in Fig. 3. Each individual was also assigned a 'measurement error' value, which, when added to their true media score, generated a new 'observed media' score. Each individual was also given a time score of 0 or 1 to indicate whether they had been interviewed before or after the media event. This yielded four columns of variables: time, true media exposure, measurement error, and observed media exposure (as sum of two previous columns).

Next, each individual was assigned two 'ideology' scores, each of which was a separate variable. These scores were based on random numbers on a uniform 0–1 interval. To the first ideology score was added a fraction of each person's observed media score, where the fraction was chosen by trial-and-error to induce the necessary amount of multicollinearity with observed media exposure in the final vote equation. The two ideology scores were then combined, along with an additional dose of random error, to create a 'presidential preference' scale. The amount of this random error was chosen to produce the desired overall r-square for the vote equation, 0.65. The form of the random error was a uniform distribution.[28]

The presidential preference variable was a continuous scale designed to simulate individuals' underlying preferences for the two candidates. It ran from about -2 to $+2$, with a mean of 0 and an SD of 0.8. At this point, three more columns of variables had been added to the spreadsheet. The preference scale was later converted to a 0–1 vote variable and then discarded. In view of this, I see no reason in statistical theory that the underlying presidential preference scale must match aspects of real data. Yet prudence suggests that its distribution not stray too far from actual data. For this

---

[28] The conventional assumption would be normal errors. However, normal errors are at least as unlikely as uniform errors. A sensitivity test, with errors formed as the sum of two uniform distributions, produced a very normal-looking (though not quite actually normal) distribution. It turned out that it made no difference: for a 10% linear effect on samples of 1000, detection at the 0.05 level over 250 trials was 48% for uniform errors and 50.8% for the second error structure.

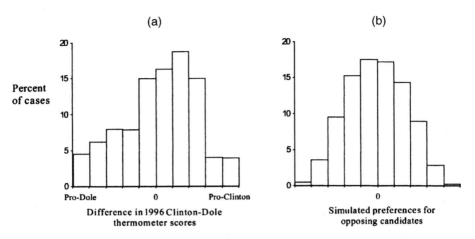

Fig. 8: Actual and assumed distribution of voter preferences: (a) SD = 2.25 when
scores are recoded to the 11-point scale shown above; (b) SD = 1.78.

Source: 1996 NES study.

reason, Fig. 8 was created to compare its distribution with that of the feeling thermometer difference scores of the two candidates in the 1996 election. Despite the
pro-Clinton skew of the 1996 data, the shapes of the two distributions are roughly
similar. When both scales were coded to a common 11-point range, their SDs are
reasonably similar, as the figure shows.

Before the preference scale was recoded to 0–1 and discarded, it was 'shocked' to
create a campaign effect. For individuals who are 0 on time, there was no shock. But
everyone who scored 1 on time has their continuous preference score adjusted to be
somewhat more favorable to Candidate A. The amount of the adjustment was in relation to true media exposure scores, but the particulars of the adjustment depended on
the shape and size of the media impact to be created. For example, if the aim was to
create a non-monotonic campaign effect, people with middle range true media exposure received the biggest shocks. Note the use of true media scores to create the shocks:
candidate preferences were adjusted on the basis of true media exposure, but I later
attempted to recover the media effect with error-laden observed media scores. This
was an obviously realistic feature of the simulation.

For candidates who were extremely pro- or anti-Candidate A to begin with, the
shock made no difference, because they did not cross the threshold between the two
candidates. But for persons whose preferences were initially just below the threshold
of support for Candidate A, the shock might have made a difference. The size of the
shock was chosen to create the desired amount of aggregate change — a 3%, 5%, or
10% shift towards Candidate A. Finally, the candidate preference scale was converted
to a 0–1 variable, indicating a vote for Candidate A or his opponent. This vote variable was then used as the dependent variable in the analysis.

New randomness terms were added at several points in each new data set: the assignment of scores on the two 'ideology' variables, the assignment of measurement error, and the assignment of a random term to the continuous candidate preference scale. In each of the many artificial data sets created, individuals' observed scores changed but basic relationships in the data remained, in expectation, the same.[29]

The Excel spreadsheet used to create the 10% linear effect is available on my web page as 'powersheet' at www.sscnet.ucla.edu/polisci/faculty/zaller/.

A.2 Accuracy of the simulations

To check the accuracy of my general approach, I did power simulations for cases for which power formula could also be used. That is, I did the regression equivalent of (1) simulating the SE of a survey of $p = 0.4$ and $N = 1000$ through computer-generated coin-tosses; and (2) compared the result to the SE as calculated by the standard formula. The simulations in general were in accord with the results obtained from the standard regression formula. I also confirmed that my statistical program, STATA, produced standard errors for coefficients that were generally consistent with the SD of coefficients obtained from repeated trials. By generally consistent I mean that sets of simulations were within 5–10% of expected values, and that the results did not seem, on visual inspection, to be consistently above or below expectation.

References

Bartels, L. 1993. Messages received: the political impact of media exposure, American Political Science Review 87, pp. 267–286.

Carmines, E. 1979. Zeller Reliability Analysis. Sage, Thousand Oaks, CA.

Cohen, J. 1988. Statistical Power Analysis in the Behavioral Sciences. Erlbaum, Hillsdale, NJ.

Converse, P.E. 1962. Information flow and the stability of partisan attitudes, Public Opinion Quarterly 26, pp. 578–599.

Holbrook, T. 1996. Do Campaigns Matter? Sage, Thousand Oaks, CA.

Hsieh, F.Y., Block, D.A., Larsen, M.D. 1998. A simple method of sample size calculation for linear and logistic regression, Statistics in Medicine 17, pp. 1623–1634.

Huckfeldt, R., Sprague, J. 1995. Citizens, Politics, and Social Communication: Information and Influence in an Election Campaign. Cambridge University Press, Cambridge.

Hunt, M., Zaller, J. 1995. The rise and fall of candidate Perot: the outsider vs. the system, Political Communication 12, pp. 97–123.

Johnston, R., Blais, A., Brady, H.E., Crête, J. 1992. Letting the People Decide: Dynamics of a Canadian Election. McGill-Queen's University Press, Montreal and Kingston.

King, G., Keohane, R., Verba, S. 1997. Designing Social Inquiry. Princeton University Press, Princeton, NJ.

---

[29] In a classical Monte Carlo experiment, the ideology scores also would have been fixed from trial to trial rather than, as here, drawn fresh in every simulation. I doubt this feature will make any difference, given the relatively large ns of the experiments. The media exposure variable is fixed X, except for measurement error, which is freshly drawn for each simulation.

Lord, F., Novick, M. 1968. Statistical Theories of Mental Test Scores. Addison-Wesley, Reading, MA.

Moher, D., Wells, G. 1994. Statistical power, sample size, and their reporting in randomized controlled trials, Journal of the American Medical Association 272, pp. 122–124.

Price, V., Zaller, J. 1993. Who gets the news? Alternative measures of news reception and their implications for research, Public Opinion Quarterly 57, pp. 133–164.

Shaw, D. 1999. A study of presidential campaign event effects from 1952 to 1992, Journal of Politics 61, pp. 387–422.

Zaller, J. 1990. Political awareness, elite opinion leadership, and the mass survey response, Social Cognition 8, pp. 125–153.

Zaller, J. 1992. The Nature and Origins of Mass Opinion. Cambridge University Press, Cambridge.

Chapter 10

Reinventing election studies

Mark Franklin and Christopher Wlezien

> In this chapter, we summarize some of the main findings and implications of the contributions to this symposium, and draw our own conclusions about the likely future of election studies.

Electoral research is at a time of flux. As the chapters in this Symposium have shown, the traditional monolithic survey-based research project, designed to study voting behavior at a particular election (chapter 2), is seen by many to be approaching the end of its useful life. Change is being forced on those of us who do electoral research; forced by the imperatives of our evolving research questions, and by individuals who see the opportunity for change in the dominant paradigm. There have always been those who have opposed the monolithic election study, but the evolving nature of the substantive questions on the agenda of electoral research have given such individuals new arguments and new allies. Of course, these new arguments are only possible because of huge advances in our knowledge. We stand 'on the shoulders of giants', and we have the benefit of the longer view that this vantage point gives us. In this concluding chapter we survey the developments that have changed the intellectual climate within which election studies are conducted, and the opportunities that these changes present for future electoral research — opportunities which, in our view, utterly trump any arguments against the continuation of election studies.

The first thing that has changed is the relative balance of the objectives in election studies, from a focus on one election as a locus for research to a focus on adding to the series of election studies currently in existence. Instead of providing two or three thousand cases for a stand-alone analysis of voting behavior at one election, a new study is increasingly seen as adding one case to a time-series of electoral data for a particular country or countries (chapter 1). This shift was inevitable as election studies accumulated. A time-series provides a means to analyze change, and it is the changing balance of electoral forces and the way in which elections effectuate changes in government personnel and policies that has come to be the overriding concern of those who study them. When a series was only a few elections long, the ability to use the series to study change was very limited, although some nevertheless made the most of it (e.g. Stokes, 1966). As the series lengthens, so the analytic tools that can be brought to bear become increasingly sophisticated and the payoff in time-serial leverage of each additional case comes increasingly to rival in importance the payoff to be gained from the analysis of individual voting behavior at that election. This should continue to be true at least for the foreseeable future.

In the United States, a time-series of presidential election studies now spans the second half of the 20th century. Linked studies have been conducted at each presidential election starting with that in 1952, covering 13 elections in all. In Germany and Sweden the time-series of national election studies approaches the same length as in the United States. In Britain and several other countries the total number of elections studied now stands at 10 or 11. Ten to thirteen cases is still a small N for time-series analysis, but it is verging on the number that permits simple models to be tested.[1] And over the next decade we will acquire the capacity to study pooled time-series of 12 or more cases for ever-increasing numbers of countries. This has obvious benefits: for one, it increases the power of our statistical tests. Some of the potential of such pooled time-series already has been shown in the analysis of Eurobarometer data which extends back to the early 1970s for nine countries and which, while not explicitly linked to the occurrence of national elections, permits scholars to extract surveys conducted within three months of each election in each country. From these surveys nine series of 'quasi-election studies' can be constructed, permitting pooled time-series analyses with Ns of 30 cases or more. Some such studies are in progress, although none, to our knowledge, has yet been published. An early exercise in pooling national election studies can be found in Franklin et al. (1992), which achieved an effective N of 39 cases by pooling between one and three election studies (or quasi-election studies) from 16 countries. The ability to view elections in time-series perspective provides one of the major themes of the chapters in this Symposium.

Mention of Eurobarometer data suggests a second major change in the intellectual climate within which election studies are conducted. The first election studies were also among the first studies of public opinion using nationwide probability samples. So all scholars interested in public opinion research were forced to use these data. There were no other data available for this purpose. Over the past 50 years, however, there has been a proliferation of academic studies of public opinion. In particular, the General Social Survey (GSS) conducted by the National Opinion Research Center at the University of Chicago since 1970, and copied in several other countries, provides an alternative means for studying the nature and dynamics of public opinion, and a means more suited to studying certain types of change which are hard to capture in surveys conducted only every four years or so (see Wlezien, 1995). GSS-type surveys

---

[1] Witness the literature on election prediction and forecasting (Wlezien and Erikson, 1996; Campbell and Garand, 2000).

are generally conducted annually, which also means that a useful time-series becomes available much more quickly than with election studies. Already the American GSS contains the best part of 30 annual cases. The Eurobarometer, which until recently was conducted twice a year, accumulated even faster and now comprises close to 50 studies.

The changes in focus from static to dynamic, and from election studies as the only barometer of public opinion to election studies as one of several alternative barometers, are by no means the only changes affecting the intellectual climate of electoral research. Just as important as the ability to view electoral decisions in temporal perspective has been the increasing ability to view electoral decisions within the specific context in which they occur. Several of the chapters in this Symposium have focussed on the way in which contextual information can be linked to survey data to provide powerful tools that cannot be supplied by survey data alone. Marsh's contribution (chapter 4) stresses the fact that, unless we take context into account, many of our models of voting behavior can be badly mis-specified. The linkage to contextual information can occur within national surveys, with respondents from different parts of a country being supplied with additional variables that define the unique contexts within which they are embedded. Contextual information can also be added to survey data by virtue of the temporal location of each survey in a series of election studies. In this way the characteristics of the electoral context can be employed to study effects that would have been constant within any one election study. In addition, the increasing availability of comparable studies from different countries enables researchers to link the information pertaining to each voter in their study to information about the political system in which that voter resides. Such linkages have turned out to have a powerful effect on the nature of electoral decisions — bringing the state back in by coding differences in institutional structures, and bringing parties and party systems back in by coding differences in party structures. This type of linkage (cross-temporal as well as cross-national) also promises to permit direct estimation of the effects of economic conditions and other macro-level variables. Until now, these kinds of variables have generally been employed in survey research only to the extent that respondents have perceptions of these conditions that could meaningfully be measured and used as independent variables — van der Eijk (chapter 3) stressed the limitations of this approach.

These multiple windows onto the political world have opened two related but different possibilities. First, they have made it possible for us to triangulate from one study to another by making use of the fact that different scholars have approached the same theoretical issues in different ways. They have asked different questions, or the same questions at different times, or in different places, giving us the possibility of adding a perspective akin to binocular vision. Second, they have made it possible for scholars to link their surveys in ways that were discussed by van der Eijk (chapter 3) and will be discussed further below. Both of these strategies require co-ordination between studies, a point to which we return.

These exciting new opportunities have brought with them daunting new problems. The first problem that needs to be clearly recognized is the loss of primacy. Election studies are no longer the only (and to many scholars no longer the primary) means for studying public opinion. For this reason, many in the scholarly community wish to economize on scarce resources by drastically curtailing, if not eliminating, expenditure on these studies. This threat has been present for years and in some countries has prevented a viable series of national election studies from being established, eliminating many of the opportunities for elaborating the electoral research enterprise outlined above and detailed in this symposium. It seems to us that the only defense against this attack on election studies is for these studies to embrace the changes that the new intellectual climate has made possible. Other research designs that compete with election studies for scarce funding will certainly embrace these changes. If election studies do not change, they are likely to be eliminated. The choice is as stark as that.

Some of the opportunities for change and some of the means for taking advantage of these opportunities have been the subjects of chapter in this symposium. No doubt many other opportunities exist, and many other means for taking advantage of the opportunities than those explored here. The objective of these chapters — like the objective of the initiating conference — was not to come up with definitive proposals in each and every case, but simply to begin a dialog that would explore some of the opportunities available.

The most important of the opportunities, at least as seen through the eyes of contributors to this volume, is the opportunity to confront and perhaps even tame the endogeneity problem. This problem, which Cees van der Eijk considers in this book, is essentially one of acquiring information about the world that is independent of voters' own assessments. If we treat voters as experts and ask them about the policies of the parties they choose between, or about the economic circumstances they experience, then we risk the answers being contaminated by the political orientation of our 'expert' witnesses. When we then use those answers as independent variables in a study of political orientations, our analysis is flawed because of circularity.

Even if we have access to wholly external information about the locality in which individuals reside, Johnson et al. (chapter 5) have shown that we can be mistaken in thinking that this information is exogenous (if individuals could have chosen their place of abode, giving rise to selection effects). That chapter suggests a possible solution to the problem of selection effects. But it is important to note (as pointed out in the introduction to that chapter) that these effects only operate in relation to contexts that people could realistically select between. Even with the extent of contemporary international migration, proportionately few individuals get to choose the institutional setting within which they live, yielding some robustness against selection effects in the case of contexts derived from different countries (chapter 4). And no respondent to a normal survey gets to choose the time at which they are surveyed. Contextual variables that vary over time would seemingly be free from selection effects (chapters 7 and 8), although of course they are instead subject to compositional effects — demographic shifts linked to generational replacement, population growth, and other processes that change the composition of the population under study. This topic is not specifically covered in any of the chapters contributed to this symposium, but compositional effects of this kind (the words are sometimes used with a different meaning) are important potential contaminants that need to be taken into account in any cross-temporal research endeavor,[2] except perhaps one using a rolling cross-section design that spans only a very short period.[3]

A second set of problems, related particularly to cross-level linkages — problems of achieving adequate numbers of cases at the higher level of aggregation — are discussed in the paper by Stoker and Bowers (chapter 6). These problems are, of course, also pertinent to data collection efforts that straddle different national contexts (chapter 4).[4]

There is no such thing as a free lunch. All attempts to link data from one study with data from another are fraught with difficulty, whether the linkage be cross-level, over time, or between different samples drawn at the same point in time and at the same level of analysis. Nevertheless, linking data from different levels, different times, and different samples offers promise of addressing many of the contemporary problems facing election studies. Links to different levels and different times will yield the gain of large numbers of variables additional to those specifically asked about in election surveys (and variables which are, incidentally, largely free from endogeneity problems). Links to different samples will allow election studies to focus not only on the vote and allied concepts, which are then available for linking to more specialized surveys, but also to focus with the power of those specialized surveys on such topics as economic voting, social–psychological theories of voting, campaign or media effects, and so on. Moreover, the survey strategies of these studies can be optimally designed for their primary purposes, often economizing on sample size in order to be able to afford to measure more variables even while the core election study can maximize its sample size because it has sloughed off so much of its customary weight. Increased sample size is what is needed most (see chapter 9) to address a fundamental problem shared by most election studies: the lack of power to detect communication effects even of large magnitude, such as those that happen during political campaigns. But increased sample size would be prohibitively expensive for the traditional monolithic election study. Linking a massive core election study with a massive study of campaign effects would not, however, be out of the question. Other linked studies could be much smaller.

By defining individuals in terms of characteristics relevant to different research concerns we provide all the specificity that is needed for social science survey-based research. Survey researchers are not interested in specific individuals, only in classes of individuals. So nothing is lost by linking datasets provided the classes of individuals of interest to different research enterprises are adequately identified. This does not mean that linking datasets is straightforward. There is a linkage problem, as touched on by van der Eijk (chapter 3). One needs to incorporate into the data from an election study a large number of linkage variables; variables whose sole

---

[2] See Franklin and Ladner (1995) for an example of the way in which compositional effects have bedeviled our understanding of an historical event.

[3] But in that case, instead one has the problem of chance differences in composition between a number of relatively small samples (see chapter 2).

[4] It is interesting to note that a procedure advocated by Stoker and Bowers, of sampling different numbers of individuals in different contexts, is the solution forced upon early EES and CSES studies by the very enterprise of acquiring data across national contexts.

purpose is to delineate as accurately as possible, and in as much detail as possible, the characteristics of each voter that define the ways in which that voter would be expected to differ from other voters on the basis of the different theories that might be brought to bear by researchers with different substantive concerns. To link with sociological studies, we need variables specifying social location; to link with media studies, we need variables specifying media consumption; to link with psychological studies, we need variables relating to psychological profile; and so on. Temporal and multi-level linkages might appear more straightforward, and certainly it is true that a date is a date and a place is a place. But dates do not always define the relevant position of individuals in a developing temporal context;[5] and the aggregate-level context of relevance to a particular research design might not be geographic (see chapter 4).

Indeed, it might be thought that the linkage variables needed in order to make an election study truly useful to all its potential users would rival in number the variables that would have been needed in a traditional study that tried to be all things to all social scientists. But this is not so. For one thing, very many of the linkages that might be of interest are geographically based. Many contextual variables are supposed to have their effect because of geographic proximity; and geographic location is easily coded with as great an accuracy as privacy laws permit. For another thing, many of the interests of social scientists in different sub-fields can be met by using identical linkage variables: the standard demographic variables of occupation, education, age, income, religion and union membership go a long way, in conjunction with geographic and temporal information, towards determining the media market in which respondents find themselves, as well as the social stratum and social–psychological profile that is likely to be theirs.

Election studies will certainly have to provide linkage variables beyond geographic location and standard demographics, and sub-fields with particular linkage needs will have to make those needs known to the directors of national election studies. But even quite coarse categories can prove adequate for achieving quite complex linkages[6] and it will often prove possible for researchers in one sub-field to make productive use of linkage variables originally intended for quite different purposes. Generally, the required degree of specificity needed for linkage to a new sub-field, once standard demographic and geographic identifiers are in place, should be achievable by the addition of only a handful of variables instead of the literally dozens needed to do justice to the research questions specific to that sub-field. The very fact that different social sciences, and different sub-fields within those social sciences, all deal with human beings (and to a large extent borrow from each other their understanding of what constitutes a human being) ensures that the number of ways in which a person can be characterized is not limitless.

Nevertheless, in our view, election studies should abandon any attempt to be all things to all social scientists. Instead, they should focus on only two things: providing

---

[5] For an example, see Franklin et al. (1992, chap. 19).
[6] See Franklin (1991) for an example that involved linking two waves of the 1989 European Election Study (two waves that constituted independent samples), using only standard demographic variables to create a 'quasi-panel' study.

adequate linkage variables for use by other specialists, and providing the best possible characterization of the nature and concomitants of the voting act (chapter 3). This change of focus should enable political scientists who study elections to direct their substantive attention to what they know best and leave to others the implementation of research designs specific to other sub-fields. It should also permit the directors of election studies proper to give more attention to sampling strategies for adequately representing groups and contexts of relevance to the largest possible variety of research questions (see chapters 3, 4 and 6).[7]

Specialization of this kind should yield the same sort of comparative advantage for election studies as it does in other areas of social and economic life. Indeed, the productivity of social scientists employing election studies in their work may well be much increased as a consequence. Reinvented in this way, election studies will have a future that seems to us to be very bright.

As mentioned in the preface to this volume, many of the innovations outlined by our contributors have already made their way (or are currently making their way) into contemporary election studies. The 'probability to vote' questions are already employed in a large and growing number of election studies. Focussing on the core business of election studies has already happened in the European Election Studies and the Comparative Study of Electoral Systems project because it has proved impossible to field more than a minimum number of questions in identical terms across any large number of countries. For other reasons, Johnston and Brady's rolling cross-section design was used in the Annenberg study of voter preferences during the 2000 presidential election campaign, and Stoker and Bowers' multi-level design has been incorporated into the American National Election Study itself. So the future development of election studies is already in progress along lines outlined in the chapters included in this book. It is well known that predicting the future is difficult but, in the wake of these developments in the design of election studies, prediction is a breeze. The future, it appears, is already here.

Acknowledgements

We thank Cees van der Eijk and two anonymous reviewers for helpful comments on earlier drafts of this manuscript.

---

[7] The biggest risk associated with such a development seems to us to be the possibility that particular aspects of the electoral situation (for example, perceptions by voters of the policy positions taken by parties and candidates) will be neglected in particular elections if they are no longer embedded in the 'core' study. For this reason, certain questions (such as those measuring the salience of particular issues to individual voters) may need to be included in these 'reinvented' election studies in the interest of maintaining the long-term time-series, and for fear that they would not otherwise be measured at all. We foresee considerable disagreement about which variables should be contained in the core; but, even on generous assumptions about what needs to be included in a time-series of election data, the result should still be a much more parsimonious (and cheaper) election study than is currently the norm.

Bibliography

Campbell, J.E., Garand, J.C. 2000. Before the Vote: Forecasting American National Elections. Sage, Thousand Oaks, CA.

Franklin, M.N. 1991. Getting out the vote: social structure and the mobilization of partisanship in the 1989 European Elections, European Journal of Political Research 19, pp. 129–148.

Franklin, M.N., Ladner, M. 1995. The undoing of Winston Churchill: mobilization and conversion in the 1945 realignment of British voters, British Journal of Political Science 25, pp. 429–452.

Franklin, M., Mackie, T., Valen, H., Bean, C., Borre, O., Clarke, H., Dimitras, P. 1992. Electoral Change. Cambridge University Press, Cambridge, UK.

Stokes, D.E. 1966. Some dynamic elements of contests for the Presidency, American Political Science Review 60, pp. 19–28.

Wlezien, C. 1995. The public as thermostat: dynamics of preferences for spending, American Journal of Political Science 39, pp. 981–1000.

Wlezien, C., Erikson, R.S. 1996. Temporal horizons and Presidential election forecasts, American Politics Quarterly 24, pp. 492–505.

"Is there a security

Elizabeth looked at Bra—
executives have a key
you doing?"

"Taking the kiss I really wanted.

The last time he'd kissed her it had been earth-shaking, and even though she was prepared, there was an initial shock that sent waves of sensation down her body. She shut her eyes, but that only intensified the feel of his mouth on hers. He put his hands on her waist and pulled her closer. For once she just forgot everything and gave in....

His hands caressed her back and then slid lower. He drew her into his body and groaned deep in his throat.

Finally, she felt the rough exhalation of his breath against the side of her cheek as he pulled his mouth from hers.

She opened her eyes and looked up into the dark green gaze of the only man she'd never been able to fit into the "just friends" category. From the moment they'd met, she'd wanted more—that made him dangerous.

Danger at eighteen looked different at thirty, and she knew he still wasn't a safe option, but she couldn't walk away. This time, she would take what she wanted.

Blaze

Dear Reader,

Happy holidays! I hope you are ready for my new series, Holiday Heat. I had so much fun writing about these couples and can't wait for you to read their stories.

Elizabeth Anders is focused and driven. She has always put her career first, except for one night when she watched her younger sister getting married and felt a little sorry for herself and what she was missing out on. Her best friend, Bradley, was only too happy to give her a shoulder to lean on, a kiss and a promise that if they were both still single at thirty, they'd hook up and give a relationship a chance.

To be honest, Elizabeth never expected she'd still be single by then or that she'd start having red-hot fantasies about her best friend. Suddenly she's thirty, and the idea of bringing those fantasies to life is more than she can resist. But she's not sure she wants more than just hot nights in Bradley's bed.... Still, it's almost Thanksgiving, and she's thinking a lot about what truly matters in life, and the way she feels in Bradley's arms makes her think he might be the one.

Thanksgiving has always been my favorite holiday. I think I love it so much because everyone gets together and there's no pressure to buy gifts. Though I do love Christmas, too. It's just that at Thanksgiving I really have a chance to take time to remember all the things I'm grateful for—like my readers!

Happy Thanksgiving!

Katherine

Katherine Garbera

—

In Too Close

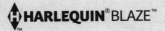

HARLEQUIN® BLAZE™

Recycling programs
for this product may
not exist in your area.

ISBN-13: 978-0-373-79826-1

In Too Close

Printed in U.S.A.

ABOUT THE AUTHOR

Katherine Garbera is a *USA TODAY* bestselling author of more than fifty books and has always believed in happy endings. She lives in England with her husband, children and their pampered pet, Godiva. Visit Katherine on the web at www.katherinegarbera.com, or catch up with her on Facebook and Twitter.

Books by Katherine Garbera

HARLEQUIN BLAZE
732—ONE MORE KISS
741—SIZZLE

HARLEQUIN DESIRE
2079—REUNITED...WITH CHILD+
2102—THE REBEL TYCOON RETURNS
2160—READY FOR HER CLOSE-UP~
2177—A CASE OF KISS AND TELL~
2196—CALLING ALL THE SHOTS~
2249—HIS INSTANT HEIR^^
2286—BOUND BY A CHILD^^
2331—FOR HER SON'S SAKE^^

SILHOUETTE DESIRE
1845—THE GREEK TYCOON'S SECRET HEIR**
1851—THE WEALTHY FRENCHMAN'S PROPOSITION**
1858—THE SPANISH ARISTOCRAT'S WOMAN**
1888—BABY BUSINESS
1927—THE MORETTI HEIR^
1935—THE MORETTI SEDUCTION^
1943—THE MORETTI ARRANGEMENT^
1952—TAMING THE TEXAS TYCOON
1999—MASTERS OF FORTUNE@
2007—SCANDALIZING THE CEO@
2014—HIS ROYAL PRIZE@
2068—TAMING THE VIP PLAYBOY+
2074—SEDUCING HIS OPPOSITION+

**Sons of Privilege
^Moretti's Legacy
@The Devonshire Heirs
+Miami Nights
~Matchmakers, Inc.
^^Baby Business

Other titles by this author available in ebook format.

When I think of all the blessings in my life, it's easy for me to be grateful. I'm thankful for my wonderful husband, who renewed my faith in love, my children, who remind me every day that being a mom is truly the most rewarding thing a woman can be, and my parents, who showed me by example that family should always come first.

A special thank you to Laura Barth for all of her editing on this book. It was fun working on this series with you!

Also thanks to Eve Gaddy, who FaceTime chatted with me whenever I hit a snag.

1

CANDLELIGHT FLICKERED IN Elizabeth Anders's office, reflecting off the lacquer finish on her Louis Sue Parisian art-deco desk. The stone floor was cold under her feet and she glanced down to see that she'd inadvertently slipped off her Jimmy Choo shoes. Suddenly a shiver raced down her spine. She felt as if someone else was in the room but couldn't see anyone. There was no sense of menace... more a heightened anticipation. She knew the person in the shadows.

Bradley Hunt.

Her best friend, the man she kept at arm's length but secretly lusted after. She held him at bay because her goals were too important to get tangled up in sex. And he was a playboy, someone who worked hard but played even harder. Not the kind of man she could ever be interested in, but...

He liked to play at being relaxed and easygoing and he wore his thick brown hair collar length like a corporate raider and always had a day's worth of stubble on his jaw. He seemed casual but he was just as intense as she was when it came to business. The main difference was that she worked for an exclusive luxury hotel chain and he worked for himself.

He revealed himself and her breath caught as her eyes moved over his rippling muscles and lean six-pack abs. He arched one arrogant dark brown eyebrow at her as he flexed his pectorals. Then he strode toward her.

She groaned as a wave of pleasure swept through her and she knew that no matter how much she might say they were just friends she craved more. She'd wanted him from their first meeting at his frat house when he'd been shirtless on that warm, sunny day and had offered to help her move into her dorm.

Now, as his arms wrapped around her and he drew her closer into his embrace, all those old feelings came flooding back. His mouth was hot, his tongue talented as he used his kisses to melt away the last of her resistance. She knew better than to give in to passion, but for once she wanted to forget all of that and experience everything he had to offer.

Bradley's hazel eyes were half closed and a dark flush spread across his cheeks as his lips continued their slow, sensual descent. His breath was warm and each exhalation brushed against her neck as he nibbled at the length of it. Shivers of delight pulsed through her and she squirmed, trying to get nearer to him, but he refused to let her close the gap. Only the heat of their bodies touched and, of course, his mouth on her skin.

His hands hovered just over her chest. Their eyes met as she glanced up to see why he wasn't caressing her. His gaze on her body was intense as he slowly traced just one finger over the exposed flesh.

"Are you sure?" he asked, his voice deep and husky. It was a tone she'd only heard from him one time before.

The last thing she wanted to do at this moment was debate the wisdom of this. She took his hand and guided it to her breast. He moaned her name on a long, guttural sigh as his hand encompassed her entire breast and squeezed it gently. "Lift your shirt," he said, the command in his voice mirrored in the intensity of his stare.

His hands were already there. First, just that sensuous rubbing over the globes of her breasts, and then cupping them as his fingers moved in ever-narrowing circles while he touched then tweaked her nipples. She squirmed and shivered as she felt a pulse of heat between her legs.

She parted them and leaned back as his hand drifted down to her stomach and then settled on top of her feminine mound.

Bzzz! Bzzz!

Elizabeth jerked awake and sat up to find her own hand between her legs and her cell phone vibrating on the nightstand. She sighed. Of course she'd have a hot sex dream about Bradley Hunt. It made sense. One kiss five years ago had ignited a flame inside of her that had never been extinguished.

She glanced over at the phone and saw Bradley's smiling face on the screen. It was a selfie he'd sent to her. The man had an ego as large as the Wasatch Range that surrounded Park City.

Groaning, she reached for the phone. At first she'd thought she conjured him up with her erotic dream, but then cold, hard reality hit her. She'd left a message for him earlier so he was simply calling her back. "Do you know what time it is?" she asked by way of greeting. The clock said 2:00 a.m. Her pulse was still racing. She wanted to be calm and collected but so wasn't. Something about Bradley always got her riled up.

"Sorry, I'm in London. I can't ever remember the difference between GMT and Mountain time."

"Seven hours, lame-o," she said. "You run a multimillion-dollar sport outfitter and travel all over the world opening retail stores and yet can't tell time.... How do you do it?"

"I can tell time, Lizzie, just not time zones. Anyway, I wanted to be the first to congratulate you on your promotion, and I knew our friends would wait until the hour was decent."

"But not my bad-boy best friend," she said, trying not to sigh. A part of her had hoped he'd called because he remembered their friends-with-benefits pact, but clearly that wasn't the case.

"I like being first," he replied.

That wasn't news to her. When they'd first met, he turned getting good grades into a competition and she'd risen to the challenge. She hated to lose. Had to bite her lip and smile politely when she did, and in Bradley she'd found a fellow competitor who always wanted to win. If things had been different... She thought of her torrid dream and the one scorching kiss they'd shared five years ago.

"Did you fall back to sleep?" he asked, breaking into her thoughts.

"No, of course not," she said.

"Then, what's up, Lizzie?"

"How many times do I have to tell you not to call me Lizzie?" She was stalling for time. How was she going to bring up something that had been said so long ago? Something he'd more than likely forgotten but that she'd kept tucked away in the back of her mind as a kind of insurance policy.

"An infinite number, but I like it," he said. "Lizzie suits you."

"My boss wouldn't agree," she retorted.

Lars Usten, former Olympian and owner of the very exclusive Lars Usten Lodge and Spa luxury hotel chain, never called her anything but Elizabeth.

"He doesn't know the real woman."

"And you think *you* do?" she asked. She doubted that Bradley had ever really paid any attention to anything other than himself. He was fun, flirty and way too self-absorbed, or so she'd always thought.

"I know I do," he said.

"Cocky and arrogant, as always," she said. "Okay, hot-shot. Prove it."

"I know that you're an executive now, so you've met your business goals. I know that you're going to be thirty on December 31. And I know that we made a bargain with each other that if we were both still single at thirty…"

He let the words trail off and she lay in her bed, sheets twisted around her hips, shaking her head that he'd beaten her to it. She wanted to be mad but could only laugh. This was one time when she was glad he had won. His ability to always rise to any challenge was one of the things she'd always liked about him.

"I wasn't sure you remembered," she admitted.

"How could I forget?" he asked. "I've had a thing for you for years, but you've always kept your distance."

"It was hard to tell you wanted me through all the women surrounding you," she quipped.

He laughed. "Touché. So, you still want to give it a try?"

He was so blasé about it that she wondered if there was something she was missing. She'd spent her entire adult life focused and contained so that she wouldn't do anything stupid like she had when she was twenty. Now, ten years later, she'd accomplished everything she'd always wanted to.

She had it all…except for a lover.

And playboy jokester Bradley…well, he turned her on like no one else, and unless she'd missed something, he could be hers. She wanted him in her life temporarily to sooth that sexual ache that was keeping her up at night. It wasn't surprising, given his virile nature and how demonstrative he was all the time, but over the years she'd always felt a little ping of excitement in her stomach whenever he called her or walked into a room.

"Do *you?*" she asked, throwing the ball back into his court.

"I brought it up. Do I really have to be the one to say yes first?"

"Yes," Elizabeth said. She needed to be very careful about how she handled this because she wanted to keep their friendship intact. He was one of her longest relationships, and he got her in ways others didn't. Maybe he wasn't as self-absorbed as she'd always wanted to believe. Her girlfriends all teased her about being too intense, but not him. She guessed it was because she was always busy and distracted with work. Plus, as her female friends started getting married and having kids, she'd stepped back. That whole thing—husbands, kids, settled life—it wasn't her.

"Okay, fine, I want to try dating and see if our friendship can be more." He paused. "And if not, it will finally put to rest that nagging question."

"What nagging question?" she asked, trying to play it cool. Bradley and this affair thing were like a business deal. But in her heart she knew it was more.

"Was that kiss a fluke or is there real sexual attraction between us?" he asked.

"Oh, I think it was real," she said. "As real as you can get."

BRADLEY HUNT LEANED farther back in his seat in the departure lounge at London's Heathrow airport. Cradling his smartphone in his hand, he pictured Elizabeth with her long blond hair falling around her shoulders, her blue-green eyes sleepy, maybe even drifting shut, and wearing some sort of pajamas that covered her from her neck to her toes. She was that buttoned-up, but there had always been something more lingering beneath the surface. She needed a lover to awaken her and remind her she was young.

Hiding in the depths of her beautiful eyes he occasionally caught a fleeting glimpse of fire and passion. And he'd wanted to unlock it, but she'd shut him down each and every time.

Starting when they'd first met…

They'd originally crossed paths when she'd stopped in front of his frat house on her moving-in day at the University of Texas at Austin and asked for directions. She'd been so damned cute with her ponytail and large horn-rimmed glasses that he'd been unable to resist making a pass. And, being Elizabeth, she'd turned him down flat.

He'd taken that rejection as a challenge and the game between the two of them had started. A game she'd done her best to simply ignore until that kiss five years ago that had culminated in a sweet, slightly inebriated bargain.

Back then, on that one unforgettable night, it had seemed as if he was finally going to get a chance to see if the attraction between them was genuine, but in the end… she'd been too vulnerable. He intended to win and have her in his bed, but not because she was feeling lonely and any man would do.

He'd have felt like a cad if he'd gone through with seducing her when she was clearly so not herself. The Elizabeth he wanted to make love with was feisty and confident. Not scared of ending up alone. She was *this* woman. At her prime. Youngest general manager in the Lars Usten Corporation. He was very proud of her and had never wanted her more.

But with Elizabeth, just as with any competitor, he couldn't let her see it. He'd built his business from the ground up with hard work. One client at a time. Which was why he had to keep her guessing about how he felt and what he really wanted. She liked the challenge as much as he did. "What makes you think the attraction is real?" he finally asked, breaking the silence.

"Because you wouldn't still be sniffing around if it wasn't."

He laughed despite himself. "So true. And *you* wouldn't be talking on the phone with me in the middle of the night unless you wanted...me."

"I'm not going to deny it," she said. "I have thought of that kiss at Marina's wedding more than once."

Seeing her younger sister married five years ago, coming on the heels of a bad breakup, had shaken Elizabeth. It hadn't taken a rocket scientist to understand it. He'd glimpsed beneath the outer facade of his best friend and something had changed inside him at that moment.

"I still can't eat chocolate cake without remembering the way it tasted on your lips," he admitted.

"Me, either," she said softly. "So, are you—we—really doing this?"

"Doing what?" he drawled, unable to resist teasing her.

She cleared her throat. "You know...are we going to try the friends-with-benefits thing?"

"Yes. I want to," he confessed, totally serious now. "You have your career on track and my business is going steady. There's nothing stopping us."

She took a deep breath. "This is just sex, right? You know I'm still not interested in anything long-term."

"Yes." *For now.* Bradley knew he wouldn't be satisfied until he had everything that Elizabeth had to offer. Until she was his, body and soul. But for the time being, friends with benefits worked for him.

He heard the rustle of sheets as she rolled over. Feeling an all-too-familiar throbbing, he straightened his legs to make room for his erection as he pictured her topless, wearing only a pair of sheer black panties....

His imagination took over. If he were with her right now, he would take both of her wrists in one of his hands and hold them behind her back so that her breasts were thrust forward. He'd move in closer to caress her but wouldn't touch her until she was calling his name, begging for more.

"Bradley?"

He shook himself and thrust his hand through his hair as he realized he needed to get her into bed...and the sooner the better so he could stop fantasizing about her.

"I suggest dinner, once you've had a chance to recover from the jet lag. Do you think in two days time would be okay?"

"Yes."

"We can talk about the details of our arrangement then," she told him.

"Lizzie, do you really have arrangements with the men you sleep with?" he asked harshly. "I'm not another corporate entity that you are trying to merge with."

"I know that, really, I do. But I'm not sure how to approach this without keeping it more in business terms. I don't want—"

"To get hurt, the way you were when Ken left you," he said.

She didn't say anything and he wondered if he'd gone too far, but the truth was, they weren't like other couples that were starting a relationship. They knew each other's pasts and closely guarded secrets. In a way, Bradley thought it might make things easier. Yet she was still a mystery from his point of view. And he was dying to know how they'd be in bed.

And if they were half as good as that long-ago kiss and his red-hot fantasies, then he figured they'd have a rocking good time together.

"Exactly. But you haven't been exactly shy around women, Bradley. You've broken a few hearts."

"Not as often as you make it sound. I tend to date women who know the score," he said. It was true that he was careful to make sure he didn't date women looking for marriage and long term. There was only one woman he wanted to try a real relationship with, and that was Elizabeth.

"See? You're just proving my point. Who knows what you think the score is?" she asked. "I don't want to be roadkill on your journey."

"That's horrible. I've never left any roadkill, despite what any woman might have told you. In general, the ladies tend to give up on me when they realize that I'm exactly what I said I was and they can't change me."

"What makes you think I won't try to change you?" she asked.

"You already know me, Lizzie, and I know you. We both like to win. I'm not laboring under any misconception that you are going to ever put a man before your job, and you know that I need to be free to do my thing at work and at play."

"But you'd be faithful to me?" she asked. "Cheating is…well, cheating. I'm not interested in being part of your rotating harem."

There it was, he thought. That hint of vulnerability left behind from that bastard Ken who'd thought that Elizabeth really was the same hard woman in real life as she was in the boardroom. That she'd be able to understand he needed variety in the bedroom. Bradley had made sure that Ken regretted two-timing her.

"Of course. I might like women, but you know once I commit I don't play around."

"I do know that. You even broke up with Samantha just so you could kiss me at Marina's wedding."

He'd forgotten about that. Samantha and he hadn't been that serious, so their split hadn't been much of an issue, and he'd wanted Elizabeth in that instant with such fierceness....

"Okay, I think we're getting a bit off topic here. So... dinner in a couple of nights? Shall I pick you up at your place or at the lodge?"

"The lodge. I will have to be on call," she said. Once again, he heard the rustling of her sheets as she moved on the bed, and he groaned as he imagined her naked.

"Of course."

"And Bradley...?"

"Yes?" he asked coyly. He had to play this right. If he sounded too anxious she'd back away. Elizabeth had always been wary of him.

"I don't want to lose this," she whispered.

"What?"

"Our friendship. You're the only one who calls me after midnight. Who competes full-out with me and doesn't hate it when I win. You make me feel like it's okay to be me," she said. "If we sleep with each other, that could change."

"We'll just have to do our best to make sure it doesn't change. I'll always want to wake you after midnight."

"Really?" she asked, her voice soft and husky, so different from how she was during the regular business day.

"Yes. That's the time when the line between reality and fantasy are blurred, and attraction and wanting are at their strongest. I can't imagine that would change just because we were sleeping next to each other. Do you?"

"I guess not."

"Have a little faith, Elizabeth—we're both intelligent and we both know what we want. We're not going to hurt each other. We're going to give each other pleasure and more friendship."

"You sound so confident," she said.

"I am. Trust me."

He had waited such a long time for Elizabeth, and he knew that she liked to set up rules and barriers between them. But he wasn't a man to take no for an answer.

This time he was coming for her and nothing—not even Elizabeth—was going to stand in his way.

She sighed. "Well, then, I guess I'll see you soon, Bradley."

"You most definitely will, Lizzie."

2

A LIGHT DUSTING of fresh snow covered the employee parking lot of the Lars Usten Lodge as Elizabeth pulled her SUV into the spot labeled General Manager.

The Lars Usten Lodge/Spa ski resort was the idea of Lars Usten, a two-time gold-medal alpine skier. The runs on the Wasatch Range were used by the U.S. Olympic ski team for practice and training, and although the runs still prohibited snowboarders, they enjoyed a steady stream of lodgers year round.

She hopped out of her SUV and pulled her thick red wool coat tighter to ward off the cold. Then she glanced surreptitiously around before she took out her iPhone and photographed the sign with her name on it.

General Manager, Elizabeth Anders.

Oh, my God. Now it seemed real. Seeing her name on the plaque made her want to do the Snoopy dance of joy, but she was an adult.

"Want me to take your photo next to the sign?"

She glanced over at Lindsey Collins, a former Olympic alpine skier and currently one of the ski instructors at the Lars Usten Lodge, who was standing there with a bemused smile on her face.

Lindsey had wide Nordic features and brown eyes. She was taller than Elizabeth, at five feet ten inches, and wore a thick ski headband in her hair to hold her shoulder-length blond locks off her face. If not for a career-ending accident at the Winter Olympics in Sochi, she'd be up on the mountain training right now.

"You saw?" Elizabeth asked a bit sheepishly.

"Yeah, but I thought it was cute. And you have worked damned hard to get here…so, do you want a photo next to the sign?"

"Yes," Elizabeth replied. She already had a picture frame on her dresser ready for the photo that would be a reminder—or a touchstone, rather—to keep her on track as she worked every day at her job.

She'd even dressed the part in a swanky black dress that she'd paired with her mother's pearls and her father's big gold watch. She wouldn't be where she was today without her parents.

"Go on, then," Lindsey said.

Elizabeth walked over to the sign and turned to look back at the camera. Inside she might feel like grinning, but her expression for the photo was serious and intent. "Got it. You want to join me for breakfast?" Lindsey asked.

"Yes, I'd love to. But first I want to touch base with the night manager and make sure everything is on track. So… thirty minutes?"

"Perfect. I want to check the ski valet and make sure that Thompson Holmes's skis arrived."

"I was going to ask you about that," Elizabeth said. Thompson Holmes was a Hollywood director but also an avid outdoorsman. He loved the lodge and they kept one of their private cabins on standby for him since he often called at the last minute.

"We can discuss over breakfast," Lindsey replied. "My treat."

"Why?" Elizabeth asked. Over the last few months, as Lindsey had adjusted to being one of the ski instructors, the two women had become friends. They often had breakfast together, but each always paid her own way.

"To celebrate. It's my way of saying congratulations on your promotion."

"Oh, well, thanks," Elizabeth said. "It's not that big a deal."

"Yes, it is. I'm proud of you," Lindsey added before turning and walking away. Elizabeth drew her coat a little closer around herself as she walked toward the lodge and her office. It was situated with all of the executive offices, on the second floor, behind a massive stone atrium wall with a fireplace in it. When she moved into her new one she'd have a view of the Wasatch Range.

The view wasn't what she'd worked so hard for, but she'd definitely enjoy it.

As she entered the lodge she was greeted by the doorman, Henry, who'd been trained at some of the finest hotels in Europe. Lars only hired the very best to staff his lodge. The moment she walked inside everyone began offering congratulations and she took the time to greet them all by name.

She'd learned from Lars that little gestures like that meant the difference between good and great. Good didn't lead, but great could.

Elizabeth walked over to her desk and shook her head as she remembered her lurid dream about Bradley last night. She tossed her designer tote onto her dark-stained walnut sideboard and skimmed the room with her eyes, half expecting him to be waiting in the corner. But that was just wishful thinking, and this was real. She was the general manager of the Lars Usten Lodge. It was a big deal. She wished her father were here for her to call. He would have been so proud of her for getting this promotion.

He'd been a middle manager and traveled a lot when she and her sister were little. His dream had been to see them both succeed and be happy. Elizabeth had always been his little shadow.

She paused for a moment, letting the heels of her shiny black pumps sink into her bespoke geometrically designed Persian rug, before she sat down behind her desk. Knowing she had a busy day ahead of her, she took out her laptop and powered it up, then switched on her Tiffany lamp and got to work. Barely ten minutes later she heard a knock. She glanced up from the memo she was typing and invited the person to enter. It was her boss, Lars.

She stood up, wiped her hands on her skirt and walked around her desk to greet the chairman of the board. He was sixty-five but showed little sign of slowing down. Lars had once been a champion giant-slalom skier and still started every day with some sort of outdoor activity, which probably accounted for his good health.

"Good morning, Elizabeth," the silver-haired gentleman said. "Are you ready for the morning report?"

"Morning, Lars," she said, holding her hand out to him and following his ritual of the European air kiss to each cheek before returning to sit behind her desk. Her computer screen flashed a message and she saw that the morning report had just arrived in her mailbox.

This was the second time that Jerry had been late in filing the report and she jotted a quick note to have a discussion with him. She'd worked with him in her former position as well, and knew that his lateness was becoming a habit.

She skimmed the email and started to discuss it with

her boss. When she finished he leaned back in the art-deco guest chair, crossing one leg over the other.

"Very good. I can see you have this all under control. I think I will move our meetings to weekly instead of daily."

"Okay. I will have Paula make the adjustments to our calendars," Elizabeth said calmly, but inside she was doing the a victory dance. It had taken five long years, but finally she thought she had gained Lars's trust.

He nodded and then stood up and walked over to the floor-to-ceiling plate-glass windows. Elizabeth hesitated for a second before going to join him.

"I want to warn you, Elizabeth, that this job is not without its drawbacks. You have worked hard to get here but you haven't reached the final destination. You will still have to work hard—harder even than before—and there is a lot that you will find yourself sacrificing."

"I'm aware of that," she said.

"If at any time you find that you no longer wish to make that sacrifice, let me know."

"That's not going to happen," Elizabeth reassured him.

"You might find yourself feeling differently," he said. "I've always put the lodge first."

"I do, as well," she said. "This job is the most important thing in my life."

"I have noticed, but you do run the risk of ending up just like me."

"Great," she said. "I want to be successful."

"But you might also wind up alone. It's not for everyone," he said. "Just think about it."

She nodded, and he said his goodbyes and left. She thought about her midnight call from Bradley and their dinner plans for tomorrow. She didn't know if it was wise to tempt fate and make their friendship into something more, but she also knew she wasn't going to back down.

Having it all seemed like a challenge but she was more than up to the task, she reassured herself. Really, she was.

HER PHONE RANG a little after midnight, just as she shut off the *Late Show* and was preparing to go to sleep.

"Still struggling with the time zones?"

"Yes, but not in the way you mean. I'm wide-awake, even though it's the middle of the night. Too much time in the U.K."

"What were you doing there, by the way?" she asked. "Forgot to ask the other night."

"We just got a new contract. But that's not why I called. We can talk business any time. The middle of the night… that's our time for fantasy."

"Fantasy? I thought you were a real man," she teased. "Did I make you up?"

She got out of bed and walked quickly to the wall switch to turn off the overhead light before going back to bed. She lay in the middle of the queen-size mattress, plumped the pillows up behind her and settled down to talk to Bradley.

A long time ago she'd given up the illusion that any man would be sharing her bed regularly. She thought part of it was due to the fact that she didn't want to have to compromise on any of the things she wanted. But the other part…well, she didn't want to risk falling in love and acting stupid again.

"Oh, I'm real enough. I didn't think you'd appreciate a midnight visit, so I called instead."

"This is getting to be a habit," she said. "I guess you're safely back in Utah?"

"I am. Landed earlier today. Crashed for a few hours and then tried calling you around dinner time."

"I had my phone on silent. I was in an executive meeting," she said. "So, to what do I owe the pleasure of this late-night call? Is it to discuss our benefits?"

"*Benefits*. That's such a fun word. What do you think they should look like?"

"You shirtless, waiting on me hand and foot," she said. *Keep it light.* She wanted him in her bed, too. She wanted someone she could share her fears with. This new job, the one she'd hoped was the pinnacle of her career, suddenly felt like another summit she still had to climb.

"Ah, I see. A glorified cabana boy."

"Sort of. It's a shame you didn't just return from someplace sunny."

"I'm naturally pretty tanned. I don't think you'll be disappointed," he murmured.

She didn't think so, either, but his ego was big enough without her stroking it. Though stroking him was what she wanted. She hated to admit it, but the truth was she was ready for sex. And a lot of it. Yet, by the same token, she didn't want to let this stray into anything other than their regular friendship.

She sighed. *End this now before it turns into another regret.*

"What's wrong, Lizzie?" he asked softly.

Guess she shouldn't be surprised that he'd noticed her sudden trepidation. After all, they'd always been pretty in tune with each other. And even though she kind of wished he wasn't *quite* so observant right now, it was probably better to just get this all out in the open.

"Well, if you must know…we haven't had sex yet and this is getting complicated."

"Only if you let it," he said.

Her friend always knew the right thing to say to calm her down and make her believe things would get better. He was the reason they'd made this bargain. She would have been happy for a one-night hookup at Marina's wedding and a lifetime of loneliness, but Bradley had teased her with the thought that she could have more.

"I hope it's that easy."

"Of course it is," he said.

"You—"

"Me and you," he said. "That's what this is about. We know what we want."

"We do?" she asked. She wasn't as brazen about that now as she had been last night. But then, he hadn't just woken her from a steamy dream that had left her hot for him.

Reality had intruded big-time today and she was confused. That was it. She didn't know what she wanted anymore. It wasn't as straightforward as it had been the day before.

"Lizzie?"

"Yes."

"I want you."

His voice was deep and husky as it vibrated in her ear, and it sent shivers of desire down her spine.

"How do you want me?"

"Lying next to me. Curled up close so that I can lean over you," he said.

"I'd like that. I've been thinking about that one kiss… wanting to know if it was the atmosphere and the champagne that made you taste so good, made it feel so right."

"I can promise it wasn't just that. It was you and me."

You and me. He kept linking them together as though they belonged with each other. "You know this is just sex."

"It's friendship plus."

She laughed. "Plus?"

"Yes, we're still buddies, but now we get all the good stuff. Don't forget we were friends first."

"I'm not. I just need to be very careful that you don't expect more. Like I said last night, I'm not ready for more than…" She couldn't bring herself to say *more than sex*. That would make it seem as if she was using him.

"Late-night rendezvous."

"Yes."

"We're good," he said. "And tomorrow at dinner I will put your doubts about our kiss to rest."

"They aren't doubts," she said.

"What are they?"

Longing. It was the hope that his kisses were just as hot and magical as she remembered, because she wanted Bradley to live up to all the fantasies she'd given him a starring role in.

"Never mind."

"I'll see you tomorrow," he said.

"Good night, Bradley."

"Sweet dreams."

BRADLEY WALKED INTO his offices above Fresh Sno in Park City and tossed his leather duffel bag onto the big, over-stuffed couch in the corner. The office area was a large loft above the retail store, and its open floor plan allotted lots of cubicle space for all his staff. Right now it was fairly empty.

"Cult of Personality" was blaring from the speakers, and his assistant, Tia, stood next to her desk flirting with Carter Shaw, world number-one half-pipe snowboarder and all-around lothario.

Tia was tall, curvy and had thick, brown dreadlocks that hung to the middle of her back. She wore an insanely short denim miniskirt over a pair of mustard-yellow tights and combat boots. She had on a thick Irish wool sweater that Bradley had brought her back after his last trip to the U.K.

Fresh Sno had won a bid to supply skis and boards to a chain of indoor winter sports centers in England, Scotland and Wales, and he'd racked up quite a few frequent-flyer miles traveling overseas these past few months.

"I thought I was paying you to work," he said.

"Believe it or not, boss man, I am working," Tia replied, turning around to face him. "Carter is here with a business proposition."

"I think that's not the *only* proposition he had in mind," Bradley remarked.

The snowboarder threw up his hands. "Hey, a boy can dream, can't he?"

"Indeed. I need coffee, but then we can talk in the conference room at the end of the hall."

"No problem," Carter said, stepping away to check his cell phone. "Take your time."

Carter was an Olympic gold medalist and had the sort of bad-boy reputation that the public adored. He was leading the lobby to have all of the resorts in Park City open all their ski runs up to snowboarding, and having the Thunderbolt Energy Games stop in Park City had certainly helped his cause.

As a retailer who sold a lot of snowboards, Bradley was backing the boarders. The only downside was that it caused some friction between himself and Elizabeth. Most of the luxury resorts preferred to keep to the status quo. Another way that Elizabeth was making herself old before her time.

Bradley didn't enjoy being at odds with her. It reminded him that he came from a different world than she did. And he didn't like it.

"Anything pressing?" he asked Tia as he escorted Carter out and stopped by her desk.

"No. But a package arrived for you from Tiffany's." She gave him a wry look. "Are you dating someone new?"

"None of your biz," Bradley said, as he went to the coffee machine in the corner and made himself a double espresso. It was going to be a long day. But his reward was dinner and an evening with Elizabeth. He'd been in a state of semi-arousal ever since he'd called her two nights ago.

Elizabeth. That one kiss had been way too long ago. A part of him wondered if he'd imagined how good it had been. Her taste had been so unique and so right. He'd kissed other women since then but they'd all left him wanting.

"Not that its any of your business, nosy," Bradley said, "but it's for Elizabeth. She's just been promoted to the general manager of the Lars Usten Lodge."

Carter whistled. "Impressive. That place is first class all the way. They still aren't as boarder friendly as I'd like them to be, though."

"Actually, it is now. I have a contract to provide all equipment for ski rental there." Holding his cup of steaming espresso in one hand and his briefcase in the other, Bradley led the way to the conference room. "But I think you are here to discuss something else."

"Yes, I am. I want to put together a group of exhibition events similar to the Thunderbolt Energy Games and I need some sponsors to do it," Carter told him. "I'd like Fresh Sno to be a major participant."

"Would we do it here in Park City?" Bradley asked as the two of them entered the conference room and took a seat at a long, narrow table. Already he was weighing the pros and cons. He liked community events but his company wasn't big enough to give too much to charity without it affecting the bottom line. "Why would we need to do another Thunderbolt Energy Games thing?"

"I want to combine it with kids who aren't already at the top, the ones who haven't been exposed to good equipment and teachers. Part of it is to use my reputation to give back to the community that nurtured me."

"I like it," Bradley said, the wheels already turning in his head. "I bet we can get some of the resorts in the area to kick in as venues. What do you think?"

"Great idea. I grew up here and I know how hard it can be to get your start if you don't have money. I want the kids who are out there using secondhand boards and skis to have a place to compete and maybe win some new gear. I want to make things easier—"

"I get it," Bradley acknowledged with a smile. "Give them the shot that you wish someone had given you."

"Exactly, dude. I know that I could convince my Thunderbolt Energy Drink sponsor to stop here on their tour but I want some events that aren't part of that."

"So are you thinking this would run concurrently?" Bradley asked. "I don't know how that would work."

"Actually, I'd rather it was a separate event. Use the publicity from the Thunderbolt Energy Games to generate some word of mouth for our Park City games. Or Fresh Sno…I don't know what else we could call it."

"How about Fresh Faces?" Bradley suggested. "I'll ask my marketing guru to get on it."

"I'm going to be traveling the next two weeks but then will be back in Park City the week before Thanksgiving. My mom would kill me if I missed the holiday."

"Moms are like that," Bradley said, because he knew that was what was expected.

"Yeah, but mine's the best, so I don't mind it."

"We can meet that week and I'll let you know what I've come up with. When are you thinking of having this event? I believe that the Thunderbolt Energy Games are going to be in town in January."

"They are, so I was thinking next November. That gives us a year to talk it up and to get everything lined up."

"Okay. Just keep in mind that I'm not making any promises yet. I'll bring this to my team meeting this afternoon and see who wants to get involved."

"Awesome." Carter gave him a high five. "I think I'm going to like working with you, man."

"Would you consider an endorsement deal, too?" Bradley asked. "We could link it with your desire to help the local kids. Maybe get some of Park City Recreation's best and brightest to do the ads with you."

"Yes, I will. Of course, my agent will have to be involved so shoot me over an email with the deets and I'll have him get on it," Carter said, pulling out a business card and handing it over.

Bradley suspected the snowboard/surfer dude thing was just a persona that Carter wore when he was working a deal. But he didn't comment on it. He was used to dealing with people like that. He'd figure Carter out as he had figured out Elizabeth, and once he knew what made the other guy tick, he'd know the best way to move forward.

Elizabeth did the same thing—acted as though she was a tough-as-nails executive when inside she was a woman waiting to be coaxed out of her shell. And he was just the man to do it.

3

ELIZABETH SPENT MOST of the day in meetings. But really her mind was on Bradley. Her friend "plus." She hadn't been able to get that notion out of her head all day, and she was practically counting the minutes until she saw him again.

She stood above the lobby, which was decked out in fall garlands with the signs of harvest all around. It seemed homey—if home was a big mansion with lots of luxury. She remembered the modest ranch-style home she'd grown up in and acknowledged to herself that Thanksgiving looked a lot different this year.

The scent of spiced pumpkin cookies wafted in the air from the bakery down the hall that led out to the ski area. She felt a sense of pride and accomplishment. Suddenly, she heard raised voices at the front desk and realized that Thompson Holmes was demanding something.

She rubbed the back of her neck. He was demanding and not a very nice man. He might be able to make people weep with his blockbuster movies but in real life he was an ass. But it was her job to keep him happy so he'd tell his friends about the resort. A big part of their clientele was Hollywood A-listers.

Her cell phone rang and she glanced down at Bradley's face before answering the call.

"I can't believe you're calling me at a decent hour," she quipped. She kept one eye on the front desk where her manager seemed to be getting Thompson to calm down.

"The hour is always decent when you're on the phone, Lizzie. I'm calling to see if we can bump our dinner to 8:30."

She felt a twinge of disappointment. They'd been friends for years; she was ready for the benefits to kick in. Maybe he had cold feet after their call last night.

"Sure. We don't have to have dinner. You can come by my place later, instead."

"We're having dinner," he said. "I was hoping to add a meeting to your calendar today to discuss an opportunity that Carter Shaw brought me. Our dinner is about you and me. I don't want to talk business then."

She ignored the fact that he'd just made her feel warm and tingly inside. Sex was all she wanted from Bradley, but the truth was he'd always made her feel good. Even when they were competing against each other and he beat her.

"I'd love to discuss this," she said. She needed a community project on the calendar for next year. "But Carter can be...difficult. My board of directors is still a little peeved from the way he pushed for snowboarders. Should I get our ski pro to join us?"

She was already thinking where in her schedule she could fit the meeting in and get Lindsey to join them. That way, she'd ensure it was more business and less date. The more she'd contemplated their friends-with-benefits arrangement today, the more important it seemed to make certain they didn't fall into a relationship. It would just complicate things.

"It's up to you, but at this phase, probably just you and I

would be fine to discuss this idea. I'm talking to the GMs at all the area resorts."

"Okay. So is it something exciting? Give me some details so I can start—"

"So eager. Are you always this impatient?" he asked, a teasing lilt to his voice.

"I just don't like surprises," she said. "Forewarned is forearmed and all that."

"We're not going to battle," he reminded her.

Yet it felt like that at times. Letting her guard down with Bradley would be a mistake. She already liked him way too much.

"I just like having all the facts."

"Fair enough. He wants to do a charity-type winter-sports event in Park City next November. I'm going to donate gear to give to underprivileged kids and I was hoping you could donate the facilities."

She thought about the logistics of what he was asking. "I'm going to have to run some numbers. Let's meet in my office at seven and then we can head down to dinner at the Gastrophile West after."

"Okay, I'll see you then," Bradley said. "But you should know I'm putting the timer on and when it's time for dinner, I'm ending our meeting."

"Fine. I'm not all about business, you know," she reminded him. His words echoed those that she'd heard from her family and friends over the years. In fact, whenever she went home for the weekend, her mom confiscated her cell phone the moment she arrived. "If you're going to have an attitude we can skip the dinner."

"We're not skipping anything. I wasn't giving you a hard time, Lizzie. I just want to make sure that we have enough time to celebrate. What you've accomplished is huge and you deserve at least one dinner where the focus is on you."

She smiled to herself, but felt a shiver of unease go down her spine. "I don't need the spotlight on me."

"Maybe I want it there," he said, his voice dropping to that husky, seductive octave that he'd used in the middle of the night.

"We don't always get we want, Bradley. You should know that by now," she said.

"That might be true for some people, but I'm very determined where you are concerned."

"And what have you determined?" she asked, a bit breathlessly.

He didn't answer right away and she wasn't sure if he was doing that to bide his time or to make her jittery, but the effect was the latter.

This dinner was starting to sound like one of the most dangerous things she'd ever agreed to. A night with Bradley could shake her to her moorings, and she'd always known that, but she'd felt sort of safe because she wanted something from him.

"Bradley?"

"I'm determined to have you, Elizabeth Anders, and I'm not going to let your job, or any other excuse you can find, stand between us. Don't deny you're having second thoughts. I could tell by the way you ended the call last night."

"You're not as clever as you think. I'm not backing away. Just anxious to get to the plus part of this friendship."

He laughed, the sound booming through the phone and making her shiver with sensual awareness. "I love it when you surprise me, Lizzie girl."

She wasn't sure what to say to that. But she knew she'd done something to throw him off his guard. He only called her Lizzie when he was trying to feel her out and figure out what move to make next.

"If I did it all the time it wouldn't be special," she said.

"Right again," he replied under his breath.

She caught hers and waited to see if he'd say anything else, but instead there was only silence. Thompson was shaking the hand of the front-desk manager but Elizabeth still wanted to speak with him and make sure he was taken care of. Doing her job gave her an excuse to escape from Bradley...and all those tumultuous feelings he roused in her. "Look, I'm needed in the lobby, so I'll talk to you later."

THE LARS USTEN LODGE was steeped in American Western tradition and money—two things that hadn't been in play during Bradley's childhood. His dad had been a bull rider who had spent one night with Bradley's mother before moving on. Bradley had never known his old man. He'd given up on that dream when he'd turned ten.

There were still times when the longing to know his father still niggled in the back of his mind, but most days he was content with where he was in the world. He'd carved a successful life for himself and felt a sense of confidence that he wasn't out of his league here. He could afford to stay and play at the exclusive resort if he chose to.

He handed the keys to his classic '69 Chevy Camaro to the valet. He put his shoulders back and walked into the resort with the confidence of a man who'd made his own way in the world. It wasn't lost on him that ten years ago he'd have had to pretend to fit in here, but today he really did.

The staff was friendly and efficient. The lobby spotless and welcoming. He didn't know how much influence Elizabeth had over the look and feel of the resort, but in his mind he saw her little touches everywhere—the art-deco-inspired paintings on the walls, the attention to detail that she brought to everything she did. She'd been working as the assistant general manager before her promotion. And he knew Lars had given her a lot of extra responsibilities.

He shook his head, knowing what he really needed was a kick in the ass. If he had any chance of convincing Elizabeth to be more than his lover, he had to play it cool.

He knew that. But he'd wanted her for so long. Admired her for her hard work, but at the same time also resented the way she was able to compartmentalize everyone and everything in her life. And he was done abiding by her rules. He was changing the play now and determined to win, no matter what the cost.

"Welcome to the Lars Usten Lodge. May I help you?" the concierge—Theo, according to his nametag—asked when Bradley stepped up to the hospitality desk.

"I'm here to see Ms. Anders."

"Do you have an appointment, sir?"

"I do. Bradley Hunt."

"Please have a seat and I'll let her know you're here," Theo said, gesturing to the overstuffed guest chairs.

Bradley walked over to the lobby area but didn't sit down. He was too restless and that worried him. When he felt like this he acted impulsively, and he needed to be calculated and cool.

At times likes this he wished he'd known his father. Was this reckless feeling coursing through him right now something that he'd gotten from those genes? His mom certainly hadn't done many impulsive things after that one-night stand that had netted her a child.

"Bradley."

He turned as Elizabeth walked over to him. She smiled as she saw him, but it was her public smile—the one he knew she used on guests and acquaintances—and that irked him because he wanted her to be happy to see him. Not fake happy.

But then he forgot his irritation as he watched her move. She wore ridiculously high heels, which canted her hips forward and made them sway with each step she took. For a woman so determined to be businesslike, there was something very feminine about the way she dressed and the way she carried herself.

He'd never been able to ignore it and over the years— wait, he didn't have to ignore it now. He closed the gap between the two of them and leaned in for a kiss.

Her eyes widened as she realized what he was doing and she gave him a hard stare before tipping her head back and kissing him full on the mouth. It wasn't meant to be a true embrace but more one-upmanship on her part...yet, for some reason, he didn't care.

Her lips were soft and warm under his. The scent of mint washed over him as he pressed his mouth against hers and encircled her waist with his hands, drawing her close for just a moment before stepping back.

"It's good to see you," he murmured.

"I'm guessing you've picked up some European habits while travelling."

"Uh, I don't know how to break this to you, Lizzie, but no one greets each other like that unless they are very good friends."

She watched him with that rock-steady gaze of hers, and for just a second he saw some wild emotion flash in her eyes. He wondered what she hid. She was always so buttoned up, so careful and cautious in everything she did. And he'd normally put it down to the fact that she was focused on work, but now he sensed it might be something else.

"We've always been friends, Bradley."

"And I see no reason why anything that happens between us now will change that. Our lives are too entwined."

"That they are. If you're ready to discuss business, then let's head up to my office."

"I'm definitely ready to be alone with you," he said, letting his voice drop to a gravelly tone.

Lizzie didn't respond. Instead, she led the way past Theo, who pretended not to notice them, to the private elevator behind the counter.

"I'm not sure what that was about," she said the moment the doors closed.

"It was about me making sure that you know I'm not just some guy you have a meeting with. We're beyond that, and from our conversation two nights ago, I thought you'd agreed with me."

She nibbled on her lower lip and shook her head. "Of course I do. But I need you to understand I can't be gossiped about here. I'm their boss and the employees need to always remember that."

"In that case, I apologize," he said, reaching around her to hit the stop button. "Is there a security camera watching us?"

"No. Only the executives have a key to use this elevator." Her eyes darted toward him nervously. "Why? What are you doing?"

"Taking the kiss I really wanted."

ELIZABETH BRACED HERSELF for the touch of Bradley's mouth against hers. The last time he'd kissed her…it had been earthshaking, and even though she was prepared, there was that initial shock that sent waves of feeling down her body.

She shut her eyes but that only intensified the sensation of his mouth on hers. He put his hands on her waist, drawing her closer to him, and for once she just forgot about everything but the here and now.

She tilted her head to the side to get a better angle, thrust her tongue deep into his mouth and savored the taste of him. This was her reward, she thought. Justifying to herself…taking what she'd longed for.

His hands caressed her back and then slid lower. He cupped her buttocks and drew her into his body. His hips rocked against hers and he groaned deep in his throat.

She smiled inside, where she'd been alone and cold for the longest time, and then tangled her hands in his thick brown hair and drew him even closer to her. She felt the rough exhalation of his breath against the side of her cheek as she pulled her mouth from his.

She opened her eyes and looked up into the dark green gaze of the one man she'd never been able to really categorize as "just a friend." From the first moment they'd met, she had wanted more, which made him extremely dangerous.

And danger at age thirty looked much different than at eighteen, so although she knew in her heart that he still wasn't the safe option, she wasn't walking away this time. She couldn't spend the rest of her life living in a sort of shadow state, never really taking what she wanted.

"I guess I'm not the only one who wanted that kiss," he said, keeping his grip on her waist.

She reached up and touched his lower lip, rubbing her finger back and forth against it while she tried to think of a comeback. It was hard to speak when everything in her body was focused on how good Bradley felt and how she never wanted to leave his arms.

He pressed his hips against her and arched one eyebrow.

"You always did need your ego stroked," she said at last.

"Honey, that's not my ego."

"I know exactly what it is," she murmured, reaching between their bodies to rub his cock through his pants. He groaned and his hands tightened on her a split second before his mouth came down again.

This time there was no illusion of who was doing the claiming. Bradley was staking his, and she enjoyed every second of it. He lifted her off her feet and held her securely to him as his lips devoured hers.

Elizabeth relinquished everything, stopped thinking, stopped worrying and stopped wishing this was something that she could control. And she acknowledged, for perhaps the first time in a really long time, that she wasn't in control of anything.

Gripping Bradley's shoulders, she held on to him as sensations swept over her, and felt herself let go. Really letting go had been a long time coming, and suddenly she couldn't stop.

She lifted her leg and wrapped it around his hips, rubbing the center of her body over the ridge of his cock, and he shuddered in her arms. Then he pulled his mouth from hers, whispering dark words of sexual need against her skin as he nibbled at her neck, and his hands slid lower to cup her buttocks and draw her into fuller contact with him.

With her nails into his shoulders she sought his mouth again as he rocked his hips against hers. The world started spinning around her. Feeling the cold surface of the elevator car against her back and Bradley pressed along her front, she trailed her hands down his back until she felt the barrier of his belt then reached lower and grabbed his butt. Trembling with desire, she squeezed his rock-hard cheeks and drew herself against him.

He sucked her lower lip between his teeth and nibbled at her mouth for a second.

"Are you okay in the elevator?" The voice startled them both.

Bradley pulled back but didn't let her go.

"Hell," he muttered, putting his forehead against hers and holding her for another minute.

"Hello?" the voice said again.

"How do I respond?" Bradley whispered

Elizabeth felt waves of regret wash over her. She knew better than to start this kind of thing at work. "Let me."

She walked to the intercom and pressed the button. "We're fine. Sorry, we were arguing a point."

She hit the button for the elevator to resume movement and turned to look at Bradley, who gave her a rueful smile. "Arguing a point? Who won?"

"Me," she said.

"How do you figure, Lizzie?"

"I wasn't sure if our last kiss was just a fluke," she replied. "But now I know it wasn't." Inside, she did feel as if it was a victory of sorts, because now she knew what she wanted from Bradley.

"Well, I could have told you that from the start," he chided. "I knew from the first moment our lips met that it was more than a coincidence."

"Don't go bragging," she said.

The elevator doors opened and she started to walk away, but his voice followed her down the hall to her office.

"Why not? I like the way you stroke my…ego."

She shook her head as she entered her office and walked behind her desk. She wanted to pretend she was still in charge, both here in the office and in life, but she had a feeling that one trip in the elevator had changed things.

A part of her didn't regret it, but another part of her

was afraid of the way that Bradley made it so easy for her to forget herself and her own rules. Something she knew was incredibly dangerous.

$$4$$

BRADLEY TOOK HIS TIME settling into the swanky guest chair that didn't look as if it could support the weight of anyone who wasn't a supermodel but was surprisingly sturdy. He loosely crossed one leg over the other, resting his foot on his knee, trying to get comfortable with an erection.

He did envy Elizabeth her ability to switch off so easily. It was only when he noticed the slight flush to her skin that he recognized she wasn't as immune to him as she liked to pretend. Something he intended to use to his advantage.

"Business first?" he asked.

"Of course, that is why we're meeting," she said. She pushed a button and the top of her desk opened to reveal a compartment. She took a pen and hotel notepad from it and drew them toward her.

Everything about this room and about the woman herself was feminine, from the way she held herself to the things she surrounded herself with. It was that dichotomy that had caught his attention. She looked girly and soft, but she had a core of solid steel and she was anything but meek.

"So, Carter Shaw wants to do a charity event," she said without preamble. "He's got a huge fan base. Unfortunately, I think having him involved will hurt the chances of making it a success. He's an agitator and very controversial. I think we'd need to have someone who could keep him in line."

"I agree. But he is sincere about this. He wants to get at least the date and the venue picked before the Thunderbolt Energy Games come here in January so he can promote it."

"It is a good idea, but what's in it for him?" she asked. "I'm trying to figure out his angle."

"Believe it or not, I think his heart is in the right place this time," he said. "Carter mentioned he got lucky but most sports were expensive, and snowboarding and skiing even more so when you factored in gear and lift tickets. I think his ultimate aim is to get skis and snowboards into these kids' hands."

She jotted down a few notes and then looked up at him with that clear blue-green gaze of hers. "Why not just give it to them?"

"I think he wants them to work for it. And I agree. I'm not a fan of just giving away gear. But if the kids compete and actually work to earn it, then I'd give them the keys to my shop."

She nodded and nibbled on her lower lip as she made a few notes on her notepad. "Okay. I agree. What do you need from the lodge?"

"I think a venue for the event, but maybe some gratis time on the slopes for those who already know how to ski or snowboard leading up to the event and some lessons for those who want to try it out before the competition."

"We're talking about staff hours. How many lessons?" she asked. He noticed that she didn't commit to anything at all, just kept fishing for information. He already respected her for the job she did, but now, seeing the inner workings of how she managed he was very impressed.

She had changed a lot from the girl she'd been in college, but it occurred to him there was still a lot about Elizabeth he didn't know. He looked forward to peeling away more of her layers and getting up close and personal with the beautiful, confident woman she'd grown into.

"At this point I don't know how many lessons we're looking at. That's the kind of thing we have to hammer out. I was thinking we need a steering committee made up of different players." He paused. "I'm still waiting on my staff to find out who is interested in helping out and will volunteer their time. Tim is an okay skier so he can handle lessons, but he's more recreational than top-ranked amateur."

"I'll run this by my board. I want to take some time to go over our charity work for the coming year. I might try to combine this with something else so we can get more exposure. Maybe we can work with the local recreation center to get the kids lessons before the event."

"I like that idea. Should we meet again in a week or so?"

"Yes," she said, pulling out her smartphone. "I have some time on Thursday...."

He checked his calendar and noticed that he was supposed to call Penny—one of their college friends and Elizabeth's best friend. She was a party planner by profession and had volunteered to coordinate the party. But Bradley still needed to get the details of their celebration party for Elizabeth sorted out. He still had to get a list of local friends to her. "I can do it in the afternoon."

"I've only got thirty minutes but that should be enough time." She smiled. "Thanks for bringing this to the lodge. I'd like to take the lead on this for a Park City venue before you take it to another area ski lodge."

He locked eyes with her and gave her a smoldering look. "Lizzie, I always think of you first."

"That's flattering," she said, looking adorably flustered. "But if you screw up and call me Lizzie in front of anyone, I'm going to get very angry with you."

"Really? What does *really angry* Lizzie look like?"

"You don't want to know."

He laughed. "Dinner?"

"Yes, let's head down to the restaurant. We just hired a top-notch new head chef. Anthony Cruzel." Her lovely face lit up with pride. "We're the only restaurant in Park City doing traditional French cuisine with that Creole spin. I think you're going to be impressed."

"I'm not much of a foodie," he confessed. "I'm more interested in you."

She shifted in her chair and suddenly became focused on her notepad. Was it the fact that he'd stopped talking business and started getting intimate that rattled her?

"Me, too," she said at last.

He was surprised she'd admitted it. She usually—wait, scratch that—there wasn't anything *usual* about them now. They were charting a new path and he had to stop thinking of this as a game. There could be no winners in a competition between lovers. Hadn't he already found that out in the years he'd spent waiting for Elizabeth to make time for him in her life?

"I never thought you'd say that out loud."

"It'd be stupid to deny it after the way I kissed you in the elevator."

"Yes, about that kiss…"

"Friends plus, right?" she said, flashing a very wide smile that he suspected she wanted him to believe was genuine but appeared a little forced and nervous. "We can talk about that after dinner," she said.

"Why?"

Lizzie gave him a saucy look. "Because you don't always get to be in charge."

"And you do?"

"Yes," she said, standing up and leading the way out of her office. "The sooner you realize that, the better."

USTEN'S GASTROPHILE WEST, the five-star restaurant located in the Lars Usten Lodge, re-created the atmosphere of old New Orleans. A large mural that depicted Bourbon Street and the Gastrophile restaurant there covered one wall. There were big trees, with lanterns and lights hanging from the branches, and an indoor water feature made to resemble a river ran around the perimeter of the dining area.

The hostess greeted Elizabeth and led them to a waiting pirogue—a traditional Cajun fishing boat. They were seated in the boat and a uniformed staff member using a pole piloted it to the back of the restaurant and the dock there.

"Welcome to Gastrophile West, ya'll. My name is Etienne and I'll be your server tonight." The waiter had deeply tanned skin, dark curly hair and an accent that was as thick as the humidity in the South. He smiled at Elizabeth as he led the way to their table, which was nestled at the foot of a big old oak tree.

As they were seated, it was easy to forget they were in Utah. Frankly, Bradley was impressed by the new restaurant, which wasn't surprising. Much like Elizabeth.

Etienne took their drink orders, went over the specials of the evening and left them to look over the menu.

"Nice place," Bradley murmured.

"I'm glad you like it. We just reopened last month and so far the response has been great."

"Was this your idea?"

"No, but I hired the people who came up with it," she

said. "I think the success of the renovation of this restaurant and my hiring of Lindsey Collins as our resident ski pro influenced the board's decision to promote me."

"I'm sure that was just the icing on the cake. They know what a gem they have in you," Bradley said.

"A gem?" She arched both eyebrows at him, making him aware of how blue her eyes were tonight. "Are you mocking me?"

"I wouldn't dare. You're too intense in this environment. And you are a very hard worker," he said. "As evidenced by how often you check your phone. Do you think you could put it away for a little while?"

She hesitated, her hand hovering over her cell before she put it in her pocket. "I don't like being out of touch. I'm in charge, and if anything goes wrong—"

"They know you're in here dining, Elizabeth. And I'm sure you will agree that even you are allowed to have a meal uninterrupted," he reminded her.

Taking her hand in his, he turned it over and stroked his finger along her palm. She pulled her hand back and placed both of them in her lap. It amused him in a way, but it also told him that no matter what she said, they had a long way to go before she was going to be comfortable being friends with benefits.

Damn. They were talking too much about it and prolonging the inevitable. He should have taken her in the elevator. Perhaps then she'd be able to relax. "If we're going to be lovers, I should be able to touch you."

"Sorry. You make me nervous," she admitted. "I don't like feeling out of control."

"Too bad," he said with a cocky grin. "You do like other parts of me."

She wrinkled her nose at him. "Don't let it go to your head."

"Oh, I won't," he said. "You have a way of reminding me of my place in your, uh, friend zone." He'd wanted to see how she'd react. Agreeing to be more than just friends was one thing, but even after that smoking-hot kiss in the elevator she'd backed away. She was sending him mixed signals and he needed to be very sure before they moved forward that he was what she wanted.

He'd been waiting in the wings for too long to risk anything else.

"We're not in that zone any more. We're changing," she said, taking a sip of her water.

"Are we?"

"Yes, of course. I mean, after today...well, I think that proved we are definitely in a different place. Friends with..."

"Benefits," he said, with a grin.

She reached over and tentatively stroked her fingers over the back of his hand. "One of the things I admire about you is your tenacity."

"I'm not afraid to go after what I want."

"You've never been one of those guys to take the easy path," she agreed quietly, almost more to herself. "You're so different than the other men I know."

"In what way, Elizabeth?" he asked huskily.

She leaned back in her chair. He noticed she reached into her purse for her phone and then shook herself as if she realized what she as doing.

She licked her lips and he saw her swallow before she nodded slowly and then folded her arms on the table and leaned forward.

"You make me dangerous," she said. "I'm acting in a way that I wouldn't with any other man. But you have always called to the wildness inside me."

"Why not let it out?" he asked. He'd always sensed

that there was more to her than the studious competitor. Normally, brainy girls weren't his type, but from the first moment he'd met Elizabeth she'd inspired scorching-hot dreams.

Now that he was sitting across from her, asking him if he wanted more, he was afraid to admit he did. Afraid to let her see just how much he wanted her, because if she started to let him in and then pushed him away, as she had a million times before, he knew it would hurt.

And then he would have to walk away for good.

THIS WASN'T GOING the way she'd planned it in her head. She didn't want to talk about the way he made her feel or the fact that she even had a wild side. But then nothing with Bradley ever went according to plan. He was mercurial, which explained why she'd tried so hard to keep him at arm's length, even though it was hard for her and she struggled with that a lot.

"I'm not like you, Bradley. I can't just let loose. Control is the only way I can be safe," she said. When she'd been twenty she'd gone a little crazy. Bradley had graduated and she'd felt as though she'd missed out on being young and she had been so afraid that life was passing her by.

She'd started drinking a little too much, to let off steam, and had started an ill-advised affair with someone older. And it had lead to a lot of problems. Problems that she'd had to reach out to her parents to solve.

And they'd helped. They had always been there for her, and that time was no different. She'd promised them no more of that kind of behavior and had kept her word... until now.

She felt the wildness coursing through veins. That feeling that she was going to do something crazy again. Well, crazy for her. An affair with the one man she'd wanted for the longest time. The one man who made her feel like she was more than the cautious girl she'd always had to be.

The one man who was looking at her as if he was waiting for a response.

"What?"

He quirked a brow. "Where did you go?"

"To the past. I don't want to talk anymore. We should just keep on pretending this is a booty call."

He looked at her as though she'd gone mad.

"It would be easier to keep our roles as friends and lovers separate that way."

"Um...no," he said.

This was going to be tricky. Luckily, their waiter came back to take their order. "I'll start with the gator fritters, Etienne, and then have the prime rib as a main," she said, turning her attention to the waiter and off the man annoying her. She took a sip of her mint julep and tried to let it soothe her, but it wasn't working.

Bradley placed his order and leaned back in his chair as Etienne walked away. He crossed his arms over his chest, which drew the fabric taut against his muscles and made her remember very clearly how he'd lifted her off her feet with ease in the elevator.

"So, where were we?" he asked.

She shrugged. But her body tightened and her heart hammered so loudly she was surprised he couldn't hear it.

He leaned forward and rested his elbows on the table, looking over at her with that intense green gaze of his. "I'm sorry. I just needed to know that you were sincere and not looking to blow off some sexual steam now that you've accomplished your business goal."

Except that was exactly what she wanted to do. "Um... that *is* what you proposed. Friends plus, remember?"

"I already regret saying that."

"Why?"

"After years of keeping your distance, now you're willing to try something very intimate with me...." A muscle ticked in his jaw. "You're not the only one who's entitled to be cautious."

She took another sip of her drink, trying to bide her time and assess if he was telling her the truth. But Bradley had never lied to her. It was one of the things she really liked about him.

He took her hand in his and rubbed his thumb over the back of her knuckles. His gesture was soothing and arousing at the same time and when she met his gaze again, he gave her a half smile, the kind that always made her shiver inside.

"I have wanted you since that first moment we met in college, but you didn't want that from me so I was happy to let you set the tone of our relationship." There was a long pause. "But that's all changed now," he said.

"Okay. So, what now?"

"I guess we figure out what each of us thought we were agreeing to," he said.

"Sex," she said. "I'm only interested in keeping this casual, Bradley. I don't have the time for a relationship." She cleared her throat. "I think I'm saying the wrong things. Does this make you want to run for the hills?"

"It should," he said. "If any other woman but you said this..."

"That's B.S.," she retorted. "You have been dancing through life since the moment I met you. It's the only reason I feel safe going into this with you. Other men see me as this girl-next-door type. The kind of woman who wants all the trimmings.

"But not my badass best friend who likes to keep things light."

He gave her a cocky grin, one she was very familiar with seeing on his face. "Can't argue with that."

The fact of the matter was that if this didn't work out with Bradley she'd more than likely spend the rest of her life with her vibrator. She didn't know how to manage a man and her career, and this no-strings-attached thing was the only chance she had of true intimacy with a man. Well, the only chance she was willing to take.

If Bradley seriously wanted more, she would have to turn him down, because they were friends and the last thing she wanted was for him to be hurt by her. She met his dark green gaze and held it steadily, trying to read some sort of emotion in his eyes, but he had his guard up.

She had hers up as well, which was part of the problem if this was going to be anything but a booty call. Someone was going to have to open up. She wanted it to be her. In her mind she saw herself dropping her guard, but in reality it was a little too scary.

5

THEY ENDED UP talking about movies and books throughout dinner. But she couldn't really relax. She knew she wanted more from Bradley. The sexual desire he'd awakened earlier was winding her up, and she felt that same tight knot of anticipation in her gut as Bradley tried to keep the conversation going.

After dinner, they got their coats for a walk along the lodge's scenic trail. She avoided going through the lobby because right now she needed her focus to stay on Bradley. For the first time in a while she wanted a chance at something that was just for her. When they stepped outside they found a light snow was falling.

"I love snow early in the season," she murmured.

"Me, too," he said, joining his hand with hers and leading her toward the head of the trail. "When I was a kid I didn't like it so much."

"Why not? It always seemed magical to me as a child," she said. "My dad was often home for the day because of travel delays and complications and he'd build a snow fort for my sisters and me."

The memory of it was nice. Her dad had traveled a lot

and she'd missed him when he'd been gone. But November snow always reminded her of him.

"My recollections aren't that much fun," he said quietly. "Snow is cold. And heavy at times, and like you said, that meant not going to work, which meant not getting paid, which meant…"

How different they were. She wanted to hug Bradley when she thought of his past and how he'd struggled, but because he was just stating facts, she felt it might make him uncomfortable. "I'm sorry."

"Don't be. It made me who I am today," he said gruffly. "And I love that your dad made a snow fort for you. I know you didn't have that much time with him."

She looked over at him. Normally on a first date, there was lot of getting to know the other person, but she and Bradley had known each other for a long time. A part of her wondered if her idea for a relationship with him had come too late. Was she kidding herself when she thought she could change the dynamic of it? She leaned closer, trying to feel him out, but it was hard to read his expression in the dim glow of the lamps that were placed at intervals around the path.

"You know I always think of you as a smart-ass?" she asked at last, deciding that it was probably better to lighten up the mood.

"Do you?" he asked.

She nodded.

"I guess it's not sexy to talk about our pasts."

"We said we'd keep it light," she reminded him. She could see something in his eyes that reminded her of impatience. And she knew that, more than the fact that they knew a lot about each other, he wouldn't let her hide behind the little verbal games she usually liked to play.

"Can't deny that I can be a joker," he said with that arrogant grin of his. "So, tell me…what magic did you think the snow held?"

All kinds of magic, but tonight, standing here next to him, walking in the bitter chill…she wondered if that little girl's dreams even existed inside of her anymore. When she thought of that time and thought of telling him about it, she felt…well, silly.

"Never mind."

He stopped and turned his intense gaze on her. "Not 'never mind.' If we are going to do this, then I want to know every bit of you."

"I don't like every bit of me," she admitted. The little girl who believed in magic had been weak and made dumb mistakes. And she hoped she was nothing like that anymore.

"Tell me, Lizzie. Let me see the parts you don't think measure up."

"Why?" she asked. Why would he want to know that?

"Because I haven't seen anything about you that I don't like. Not yet."

She sighed. "It's silly and childish."

"Let me be the judge of that," he said.

Glancing out across the darkened landscape with the snow falling softly through the light provided by the lamps on the table, she found it easy to talk. "I thought there was a snow queen who was waiting for me to come outside and be in her court. I used to make Marina act as my lady-in-waiting and follow me around in the snow as we searched for her."

"And she did that?" he asked softly.

"You forget I was her big sister and she didn't like making me mad," Elizabeth said with a snort. "Actually, I was mean when we were little. I don't know why. I've apologized since then."

"Kids are just built that way," he said. "There are some guys I see in Boulder and do business with who were jerks when we were in school."

"Were you bullied?" she asked.

"Nah, one of the positives to working from a young age is I was always strong. Kids sometimes said mean things about my secondhand clothes or me not having a dad. Stuff like that. I tried not to let it bother me, but it was difficult."

She stopped walking, forcing him to do the same, wrapped both her arms around him and hugged him tightly to her. He just stood there in her embrace and she knew he was hurting as he remembered his past. When she stepped back, he gave her a questioning look.

"That was for the little boy inside you who didn't have a dad to build a fort with," she said before starting to walk again.

"The man I am today would like a different kind of embrace," he drawled.

"You haven't earned it yet."

His lips twitched with amusement. "I have to earn it?"

"Hell, yeah. Nothing worth having comes easily, Bradley."

"*Easy* is one word I'd never apply to you," he said.

She stopped walking and Bradley kept on for a few more steps, but she was barely paying attention. Instead, she thought about all the times some man had said the same thing to her. She didn't think she was difficult, but somehow she always came across that way.

"Sorry," she said.

"For what?"

"Being difficult. Being me," she said at last. "I can't change that."

He walked back to her and cupped her face with his hands, tipping her head back until she was staring up into his eyes. He leaned in close as the snowflakes fell on her face and on his hair, and she felt a tinge of that magic she'd always wanted to find as a child out in the snow.

"Never apologize for being yourself, Elizabeth," he said, and then he kissed her. It was a chilly evening, but the warmth of his body surrounded her, heating her from the inside out. And for the first time ever, she felt as though she was okay just the way she was. She knew it was Bradley making her feel that way, but for right now that was all that mattered. His kiss tasted of the coffee they'd drunk at the end of their meal and of something else, something more subtle.

He pulled back and looked down at her. She knew that she needed to say something but was afraid to open her mouth lest she reveal the truth of what she felt at this moment. And that was that Bradley scared her to death and she had the feeling that bringing up their bargain, asking him to sleep with her, was a huge mistake.

Because even though she'd thought she could handle the emotions that went along with it, she realized now she couldn't. That they were stronger than she'd thought they could be, and that might be more than she could handle now or any time in the future.

But he didn't say anything, either, only wrapped his arm around her waist and led her farther away from the lights of the lodge to a small bench nestled under some trees with snow-laden branches. A small fire burned in the fire pit that was on the patio, providing light and warmth.

"I just want to sit here for a few minutes and not talk of the past or the future…just enjoy this moment before everything changes between us."

She nodded and gestured for him to sit down while she went over to the stone wall that lined the path and lifted the large capstone on top of it, reaching in to pull out a heavy blanket. Then she brought it back over to the bench and sat down next to Bradley, draping the blanket over their legs as the snow fell silently around them. He held her with one arm, making her feel as if, at this moment, anything was possible.

When he drew her head down to his shoulder she rested it there and let herself forget about everything except the fact that for the first time, when she looked into her own future, she wanted him somehow to be a part of it.

HE WRAPPED HIS ARM around her and she snuggled closer, enjoying this moment with him.

They were secluded here, alone, and she wanted something that she'd long fantasized about but never had the time for. She wanted to kiss her almost-lover in the snow and forget that the world existed.

She turned to him and their foreheads bumped together as he'd done the same thing.

"Ouch."

She gave a nervous laugh.

He looked into her eyes. They were so close she saw his pupils dilate as she stroked his thigh under the blanket.

"What are you up to, Lizzie?"

"Benefits," she said. "We both know it's what we want."

"Here? Now?" he asked.

He was right—the chance of being discovered out here in the open was pretty high. "I've always followed the rules and tonight you make me want to break a few."

"I'm not saying no, but you work here. I just don't—"

She kissed him before he made her want to leave and hide. She wanted to be the like the couples who came here for romantic getaways. She craved Bradley's arms around her. And his body pressed up against hers. But he didn't take much convincing. He opened his mouth and she felt the warmth of his breath brush over her face and then the touch of his tongue. He pulled his head back and traced the seam of her lips before his met hers.

She felt the desire that had been lying dormant inside of her start to stir to life, awakening all her senses. Her breasts felt fuller, heavier, and her eyes closed as she let everything disappear but the feel of his fingers as he caressed her under the blanket. He rubbed one hand down her spine and brought her more fully against him.

She angled her head and opened her mouth so that the kiss deepened. She kneaded his thigh and then moved her hand higher until she could stroke the length of his erection through the fabric of his pants. He was hot and hard, just as she'd imagined he would be. She wanted more. He shifted his legs and she reached down between them, continuing to stroke him up and down.

She fumbled for the zipper of his pants and reached inside, struggling a little to find the opening in his boxers, until she felt the warm, hard length of him.

He groaned and tore his mouth from hers. Stared into her eyes with such intense need that she felt powerful and totally in control. He fisted his hand in the back of her hair and pulled her to him again. Bringing his mouth down on hers in a deeply carnal kiss that rocked her to the core of her being.

She didn't know how she was going to keep this all under control.

Stopping was out of the question. Now that she had him in her arms, she wanted to savor the moment. Wanted to take her time making love to the man she'd been fantasizing about for way too long.

She groaned.

"Why did I let you start this while we were out here?" he asked. "Let's go back to my place."

"Your place is down the mountain," she said.

"Your place isn't any closer."

She rested her head against his shoulder to catch her breath. Her pulse was racing. "Okay. Your place."

She liked the idea of doing it there, and then she could leave. She had to keep things in perspective. She didn't really need romance from Bradley. Romance led to caring, which led to pipe dreams of happily ever after. Dreams that a little girl who believed in magic snow queens might buy into, but the woman she was today knew better than that.

Bradley's phone vibrated in his pocket and he ignored it until it went off a second time. "I have to check that," he said ruefully.

She arched her eyebrows at him. "Go ahead, I don't mind. But I hope you remember this later when I might have to do the same."

"Touché," he said, then stood up and walked a few feet away to check the phone.

WHEN BRADLEY LOOKED down at the screen, it showed a message from Tia. Call me.

Bradley typed, Can it wait?

Would I have said call me if it could, boss man?

He dialed Tia's number and glanced over to find that Elizabeth was checking her cell phone, as well. For a moment it had seemed they were the only two people in the world, but reality was so different.

"It's Hunt."

"I caught two kids vandalizing the back of the shop. Do you want me to call the cops or deal with them myself?"

"Define kids," he said. His company had a fairly liberal policy when it came to certain types of crime and to kids committing them. Bradley knew if it hadn't been for his business-theory teacher in high school he might have been one of those offenders.

"Fourteen or fifteen," she said. "And the graffiti is actually pretty good."

"Okay, first offense?"

She muffled the phone but he could hear the tone in his assistant's voice. She came off tough as nails, but he knew from the fact that she'd called him that she didn't want to involve the cops. The threat of Tia and the cops would be enough to keep the boys in place.

"One has a prior," she said.

"I want to see them both in my office at nine a.m. sharp tomorrow. If they don't show up and we catch them again, we'll get law enforcement involved. Do they agree?" he asked.

He heard Tia again talking to the boys and she came back a few moments later. "Yeah, they agree."

"You have to be in early tomorrow, as well."

"Crap. Maybe I should have just let the little shits go to jail," she grumbled.

"Not your style," he said. "See you in the morning."

"Better bring those bran muffins I like, boss man," Tia said, disconnecting the call.

Bradley added a note on his calendar for tomorrow morning when a photo arrived from Tia. The graffiti the kids had done was raw but showed a lot of potential. A rough version of the Wasatch Back, which surrounded Park City.

"Everything okay?" Elizabeth asked, getting up and coming over to him. He hardened in response to her ruffled hair and passion-swollen lips as he remembered what they'd just shared.

"Yes. A minor problem at work," he said. "I'm sorry that had to interrupt our evening."

"It's fine," she reassured him, but he could tell that it wasn't.

"I'm going to be busy for the next few days, but I've got a vacation day scheduled for Friday. Any chance you could take the day off and go snowmobiling with me?"

"I'd like that. I'll see how my schedule looks and shoot you an email," she said.

She put the blanket back in the hidden compartment in the stone wall and turned to look at him. "Good night, then."

"I'll walk you to your car," he said. "Unless you're going back to work."

"I do need to get some stuff from my office, and I'll be fine on my own."

"I won't be," he said. "I'd feel like an ass if I just let you walk away now."

"More like an ass than usual?" she asked.

"Definitely. I might not have had a father, but a man does know that ladies don't like a handshake and a 'see you later' at the end of a first date."

She sauntered back over to him and shook her head. "I'd forgotten how suave you could be."

"Are you challenging me, Lizzie?"

"Maybe."

He laced their fingers together and led her back up the path to the lodge where he stopped just out of sight of the front desk and pulled her into his arms. He framed her face with his hands and lowered his forehead until it rested against hers.

"Thank you for a lovely evening, Elizabeth. I enjoyed every second of it and look forward to getting to know you better," he said.

Her blue-green eyes softened the tiniest bit as he leaned in to whisper directly into her ear. "This is just the beginning for us. And I hope tonight will be the first of many magical evenings and kisses in the snow."

Then he gently brushed his lips over hers, even though every instinct in his body screamed for him to make the kiss more carnal. But he knew he had to take things slow. This was Elizabeth and not some temporary woman, he reminded himself.

She smelled good, like gardenias, reminding him of the flowers his mom kept in the house during the summer. And he wanted to close his eyes and tighten his arms around her, make sure she couldn't leave him. But he knew that was a stupid impulse.

And for Elizabeth he could tamp down his urges, because he'd been waiting since college for her. There was no hurry now that she might actually be his. If only his hormones believed that.

If only *he* believed that. He knew what he wanted—and it involved this woman naked and writhing under him. He wanted to feel her exquisite body pressed against his. But he hadn't waited so long for this embrace only to blow it by moving too fast.

And he knew he'd blow it if he gave in to his own desires, because he sensed deep down that Elizabeth was still holding something back.

6

BRADLEY COULDN'T SLEEP and he knew exactly what— who—was to blame. *Elizabeth*. She made him horny and crazy. If Tia hadn't called, who knew what he might have done. How his evening might have ended. Not alone, he'd wager.

He shouldn't have walked away. And it was totally out of character for him, since he'd built his life on taking risks and going after what he really wanted. So why, when he was so close to getting what he'd always wanted, was he hesitating?

He rolled over on his bed, his legs tangling in the sheets, and reached for his phone. It was 2:00 a.m. He knew that he probably should put the phone down and figure out another way to get some shut-eye. But instead he hit the phone icon at the bottom of the screen and his thumb hovered over Elizabeth's face.

He touched it briefly and the dialogue box opened with two icons…one of them for FaceTime. And he couldn't resist the temptation. He wanted—no, needed—to see her and it was only after midnight, when his guard was down, that he would even think of doing this.

"Hell," he said out loud, and hit the button waiting to

see if she'd answer. He put the phone down for second to stretch for the bedside lamp.

Soon a small pool of light illuminated the bed and he picked up the phone to see that Elizabeth had answered the video call.

"Is everything okay?" she asked in a sleepy voice.

"No," he said.

"What's wrong?"

"I need you," he blurted, admitting what he'd been avoiding all night. Hell, if he were completely honest, he'd admit he'd been dancing around this since the moment they met.

The sides of her mouth teased up in a smile and she tipped her head to the side. "What do you need from me?"

"The same thing you need from me," he said thickly.

"Ah, but this isn't about me," she said, licking her lower lip. "You called me after midnight, talking of needs. And I want to know what it is you want from *me,* Bradley."

He loved the sound of his name on her lips, especially when she was teasing him. And having started this, he knew exactly how he wanted it to end. "Okay, I do need something from you," he said, leaning back against the cold wooden headboard on his bed.

"I assumed so…otherwise you would have called someone else."

"I want…" Suddenly, the thought of saying it aloud freaked him out. This was Elizabeth. Not the other women he'd flirted with and slept with over the years. But the one woman he'd really wanted all that time.

"Yes…?"

"I want to see you naked."

"So you called me?"

"It seemed logical."

She laughed, and the sound loosened the knot of ten-

sion in the pit of his stomach because it was so joyful and
so relaxed. This was the woman he'd wanted to see again.

"I'm guessing logic had very little to do with it. But to
be honest, I wanted to see you again, too. Our date ended
kind of—"

"Flat," he said. "It's like we both retreated to safe cor-
ners."

"Exactly. I'm not sure what to do next," she confessed.
"I don't want to scare you off...."

He shoved his hand through his hair and looked down
at her face on the tiny screen. "You won't."

He watched her for another long, drawn-out moment
and then said, "So, about why I called...?"

She arched one eyebrow at him. "I'm not naked."

"Another dream dashed," he grumbled.

"Are you?"

He had on boxers, but knew his image on the phone
probably did look naked. He might not have the perfectly
ripped muscles of a Hollywood action-movie star, but he
was in good shape, thanks to his business, and knew he
didn't look half-bad naked.

"No," he said.

"Darn."

She moved around on her bed, pushing her pillow and
curling up on her side. Her sheets fell and pooled under her
arm, and he noticed she had on a T-shirt. He looked more
closely and realized it was *his* T-shirt. One that he'd left at
her house last summer when they'd spent the day on some
Tremoto bikes he'd been thinking of renting in the shops.

"You're wearing my shirt."

"I am."

"Why?"

"I... It makes me feel closer to you," she said. "Ever

since Marina's wedding five years ago I've been thinking of you differently."

She had? Why had it taken five years for him to find out? Because Lizzie wasn't a woman to move quickly, which was why he had hesitated earlier. But no more. If he let her set the pace he'd be on Viagra before they made love for the first time.

"I'd be happy to replace my T-shirt."

"You would?"

"Wouldn't you prefer the real me to that shirt?" he asked, stroking his hand down his abs and letting the phone follow the movement.

"Mmm…let me see a little more of what I'm missing," she murmured.

She wasn't shy about what she wanted, he thought. Just shy about letting him too close. Probably because she was afraid of being hurt again. But then, who wasn't? They both had their share of scars and he was determined this relationship between them wasn't going to leave another one.

He felt a little silly touching himself in front of her and tipped the camera up so he could see her face and she smiled at him.

"I've always liked looking at you."

"When do you look at me?"

"Whenever you aren't looking," she replied. "Do you remember that first day we met?"

He nodded.

"You had your shirt off and I thought…yum!"

He laughed. "Doesn't seem fair that you've seen me shirtless so many times and you've never returned the favor."

"I guess you'll have to up the stakes if you want to see more," she said.

"Like this?" he asked, flexing his muscles and striking a pose.

"Perhaps. But I do believe you were going to show me a little more than that...."

His voice dropped an octave. "I'll show you everything."

"Tonight?"

"Do you want it tonight?" he asked her.

"I do," she said. "I dream of you almost every night."

"Tell me about your dreams."

"Well, they involve you and your bare chest," she admitted.

"I want to hear more," he said.

She gave him a naughty look. "I'll tell you if you get naked." Get naked for Elizabeth? That was a no-brainer. "Only if you do the same."

She hesitated, then put the phone down and he heard the rustling of clothing and sheets before she picked the phone back up. She had the sheet draped over one shoulder, but the other one was naked.

"Now you," she said.

He lifted his hips, pushed his underwear off and then smiled back at her. "Now, about those dreams..."

ELIZABETH DIDN'T LET herself think too much about being naked on FaceTime with Bradley. This entire thing felt like an extension of the dream she'd been having. Another hot, sultry one where they'd been having sex on her desk in her office. But this was even better.

She hadn't been lying when she said she needed to see him naked. And by calling her tonight he had taken a step she'd been afraid to.

But then she'd always been a little more reluctant than

he was. Something that she wanted to change. She *had* to change, she thought.

"Elizabeth?"

"Yes?"

"Tell me about those dreams of yours," he said in a deep, husky tone.

She closed her eyes as he talked, letting the sound of his voice surround her. She opened them again and looked down at him on her phone. "Usually you've come to my office on a very important matter. I had to clear my calendar to make room for you."

"So I'm demanding before you even see me?" he murmured.

"Yes. Then when you come into my office... Oh, this is silly," she said.

"No, it's not. Do I lock the door?" he asked.

"Yes, you do."

"And where are you?"

"I'm sitting behind my desk. I tell you that I don't have any time," she said.

"But I'm already there, so I imagine I tell you to make time," he said.

He never did. He was never that bossy in her fantasy. "Would you do that?"

"Hell, yes. I would walk over to your desk and spin your fancy desk chair around and make you face me."

"I'm looking up at you," she said. Your shirt is pulling tight around your muscles."

"Is that so?"

"Yes," she said. "As a matter of fact, you have to unbutton it."

"Why?"

"You're suddenly hot."

"There's nothing sudden about that heat," he told her. "I've decided to put an end to your games."

"You have?"

"Yes. You like to flirt with me and keep me at arm's length, but as of today it stops," he said in a firm voice that sent a sensual thrill down her spine.

She felt the line between fantasy and reality blur, and she knew that there was more than a little bit of truth to what they were both saying.

"Yes, it does," she said breathlessly.

"I lift you off your feet and put you down on the desk."

"Then I plant my hand in the center of your chest and demand to know what you think you're doing. You put your hands on my hips and draw me forward until you're standing between my legs."

"I tell you to open your blouse. The buttons on it are straining."

She reached for the sheet as she moved around on the bed so that she was sitting up, and then slowly let the sheet drop to her waist.

He groaned. And she saw him reach out to touch her but he wasn't in her bed. He was all the way across town.

"Touch yourself for me," he commanded softly.

"How?"

"Cup your breast," he said.

She did as he asked. Her nipples tightened as she watched him watching her. "Run your finger around your nipple."

Again, she did what he requested and watched his reaction to her. She could see his pupils dilate and his breath quicken as she did what he asked.

"Slide your hand down your chest," she said.

He did what she asked.

Elizabeth leaned back and imagined it was his hand

caressing her breast and her own hand on his chest. Her pulse raced, body tightened in response.

"I push your skirt up and lift you so that I can cup your butt in my hands," he said.

"Are you surprised that I'm not wearing panties?" she asked.

"Not at all. I know you've been wanting me for a while now," he replied. "You're soft against my palms and I realize that my skin is rough from spending so much time outdoors. Is it too rough for you?"

"No," she said, hearing her voice break. "I like it. I go for your pants and unzip them, reaching inside to find your cock."

"I'm hot and hard, more than ready for you, and you did say you didn't have a lot of time so I don't hesitate to thrust my hips forward."

"I have more time than that," she said. "I slide my hand up and down your length, swirling my finger over the tip of you and then back down to cup your balls lightly."

He groaned her name again.

"You like it, so I do it again."

"You are driving me out of my mind," he rasped. "I need to be inside of you."

"I need you inside of me," she said, realizing that she'd slid her hand lower, between her own thighs.

"I put my hand between our bodies and pet you lightly until I feel your hips rocking forward against my touch. I part you and slip one finger inside."

"I tighten around it, wanting more…" she said, sliding her own finger into her body.

She noticed from his image on the phone that his hand had drifted lower, as well. "I push your hand out of the way and grasp your hips, pulling you forward, and our eyes meet."

She looked into his eyes, her breath catching as she waited. "You slip inside of me and drive in as deeply as you as you can."

His breathing was labored now and they continued to watch each other. "I can't wait too long," he warned. "I've wanted you forever…and I'm about to implode."

"Me, too," she admitted, as her fingers moved between her legs and she felt the first wave of her orgasm approaching. "You feel so thick and fill me up. I can't wait."

"Don't wait," he said. "I need you to come for me."

She felt the orgasm building, and then it washed over her as her legs tightened and her eyes squeezed tightly shut. Imagining Bradley pressed against her, thrusting deep inside, she moaned his name and heard an answering guttural cry from him.

She looked back at him and he collapsed back against his pillows. "Damn it, woman. I like your dreams."

She smiled at him. "I like having you in them."

For a second it felt as though everything was good and right between them, but then the reality of what they'd done started to sink in and she felt a little embarrassed.

"Don't."

"Don't what?"

"Take this and make it something shameful. I loved every second of it," he said.

"I did, too. But I never intended to share that."

"This is our bargain, Lizzie. We can share our fantasies."

But she wasn't sure this was real. Wasn't sure she wanted it to be. It was hard to change the dynamic between them, especially when he was capable of making her feel so much more than she'd ever expected to. They were both still playing games, as evidenced by the fact that when they were together they each kept their guard up. It was only after midnight, over the phone, when they were able to connect like this.

She sighed.

"What?"

"This isn't real," she said. "It's just an extension of the fantasies that we've both used for years to fill an emptiness."

He rolled onto his side and the camera shifted so she could see his entire body in the soft light of the lamp. She sighed again but this time it wasn't out of awe for his hot, muscular physique—this time it was because she wished he were next to her in her bed. Making wild, passionate love to her.

And that scared her more than she wanted to admit.

"I'm not a fantasy, and what happened tonight was real. I'm not about to let you shove me back into the friend zone," he said, and there was no mistaking the steely determination in his voice. She'd always known he had a strong, forceful side. He wouldn't be the man he was today if he took no for an answer.

"That's one opinion," she said, feeling as if everything was suddenly spiraling out of control.

"What's another?"

"That we just both needed to blow off a little steam." She felt a little frantic as she spoke, but she didn't want to admit that Bradley was special to her. Especially not now when she felt so raw and vulnerable.

"Lizzie, I—"

"Good night," she said, abruptly ending the FaceTime chat. She was shaking as she rolled over and flicked off the light. Then, fighting back tears, she just lay there in the dark, wondering when she going to finally feel at home in her own skin.

7

BRADLEY HADN'T SLEPT well after the call ended with Elizabeth. Park City was covered in a blanket of snow this morning and he parked his Camaro behind the Fresh Sno retail shop at 8:00 a.m., sitting there for a minute trying to figure out where he'd gone wrong.

With Elizabeth, it seemed she'd give him as much as he wanted—as long as she could still keep him at arm's length. It was as if he kept beating his head against the same concrete wall and he wasn't learning.

Any other woman he'd give up on. So why not her? What was it about Elizabeth Anders that kept him coming back? Kept him happily at arm's length, panting like a hot and horny teenager and hoping for just a glimpse of her smile? Kept him hoping for something that he sensed was still out of his reach?

When all was said and done, he was always going to be that kid from the wrong side of the tracks with a reputation for being a little seedy. It didn't matter that he'd cleaned up and made a success of his life. Inside he was still that cold, sullen ten-year-old who was never going to be good enough for his dad to actually ever meet him.

"Crap."

He turned off his car and got out. The last thing he needed to be thinking about was Elizabeth. He tried not to dwell on it as he walked around to the front of his store. Two kids were standing outside, huddled against the cold in jackets that didn't provide enough warmth. For a moment he tipped his head back to the sky and gave thanks that he wasn't a teenager anymore.

He had so much and though he never took it for granted, seeing these teens reminded him clearly of the boy he'd left behind.

"Morning," he said to the boys as he approached. One of them nodded at him and the other straightened up from where he'd been leaning against the wall. There were two spent cigarettes on the ground by their feet, and although their clothes were clearly worn, they were clean.

"Waz up?" the taller of the two asked.

"Not much," he said. He unlocked the front door even though he normally entered from the back and gestured for the boys to enter. Despite the fact that the heat wasn't on, it was warmer inside than it had been outside.

He relocked the door behind them and glanced over at the kids, who looked tough and more than able to handle anything life tossed their way. But beneath the bravado he saw a hint of vulnerability that reminded him too damned much of himself.

"I'm Bradley Hunt, the owner," he said, holding his hand out.

The kid on the right, with his cap on backward, stepped up first, taking Bradley's hand in a firm grip. "Tony Martinez, graffiti artist, and this is Hector Jones."

Hector nodded at him.

"Graffiti artist? You know what you did was illegal, right?"

"Yeah, but it's good isn't it?" Tony asked with a slight

smirk. "We talked about it last night and figured your girl musta liked it or we'd both be in jail now."

Recalling the photo Tia had sent last night, he had to fight to keep from smiling back at the kid. Tony was smart and savvy and clearly not afraid to go after what he wanted. "I did like it. You both work on it?"

Hector nodded. "I ain't no artist like T, but I can follow his sketch and do what needs to be done."

He noticed that both of the teens kept their hands in their pockets and he realized that they still had to be cold. "Let's go up to the conference room to discuss this."

The door rattled behind him and he glanced over to see Tia standing there with two fast-food bags in her hands. He went over and unlocked the door to let her in.

"Figured we'd want breakfast," his assistant said with a stubborn look on her face. "I'm not expensing it."

He shook his head at her. "Yes, you are. Go upstairs with the boys while I get the heat turned up."

"Yes, sir, boss," she said with all the smart-ass attitude she usually delivered.

He shed his coat, hanging it on one of the hooks behind the register and went over to the thermostat to initiate the heating sequence early. There was a ping from his phone and he pulled it from his pocket.

The preview screen indicated that he had a message from Elizabeth. He wanted to stay mad at her for hanging up on him last night and didn't want to let her use him. But he knew he wanted her too much—like that house he'd bought on the outskirts of Boulder that was way too big for a bachelor. But he could afford it now.

He could afford a lot of things now, he reminded himself. Even Elizabeth.

He swiped his finger across the screen and opened the message. Read it and then read it again.

Sorry for the way things ended last night. I know I look like I have it all together but I don't. Seriously I'm struggling here and I'm sorry if I hurt you. Are we still on for snowmobiling Friday?

Bradley knew she had issues. He'd met her parents before her father had his heart attack and died, and knew that Elizabeth had thought the world of her old man. In fact, from the way she always talked about him, he had sounded like a demigod who could do no wrong. Bradley knew that Elizabeth had always wanted to impress him. It must be hard on her to achieve success after her dad was gone.

He also knew she had commitment issues. It was obvious from the fact that she wanted him for sex but not dating. And even though he could kind of understand where she was coming from, he wasn't going to give her carte blanche to walk all over him.

He texted her back.

I get it. I've got issues, too. But I'm trying to trust you. Wish you could do the same. And yes, I'm still planning on seeing you for snowmobiling on Friday.

Her response came right back.

Thanks, I'm trying. Yes, snowmobiles, and I'll bring a picnic. Looking forward to it.

He didn't text back, even though he wanted to. He remembered one of the first lessons he'd learned in business and that was to give the customer a reason to come back. And if he'd ever encountered a wilier person than Elizabeth, he couldn't remember when.

ELIZABETH WAS GLAD to be back behind her desk and in the world where she had few doubts about herself. She'd always thought that when she was thirty she'd have everything figured out. Instead, it seemed the older she got the more complicated everything seemed.

She'd mentioned the charity event to the board and they had been cautious when telling her that she could explore the lodge's participation in it. Not exactly what she'd hoped for her first time going to them as GM, but she understood their reluctance.

And while she was glad that she hadn't completely burned her bridges with Bradley, the truth was that last night had scared her. He wasn't the fantasy guy she'd been dreaming of for all those years—he was a real man—and last night the line between fantasy and reality had blurred too much for her.

She didn't care for it at all because she liked things neat and orderly, and this was the total opposite.

She was jarred out of her thoughts when there was a knock on the door. It swung open and her boss walked in.

"Have you got a minute?" Lars asked. "I wanted to discuss Carter Shaw."

Uh-oh. She knew that Carter was going to be a hard sell to Lars and the board. She'd asked Lindsey, who'd been with him on the Olympic team, to talk to Carter and get an idea of the type of event he envisioned.

"Yes, sir, I do. I'm going to do a surprise walk-around in about twenty minutes, but I can be a little late."

"I won't take up much of your time. I just wanted to make sure you were aware that we are going to need you to keep a sharp eye on Carter," he said as he came into her office and took a seat in one of her guest chairs. He loosely crossed his legs and then steepled his fingers against his chest, just watching her.

"Believe me, that was the first thought I had. But the event he's proposing is one I think we'd be silly not to get involved with."

"I trust you, Elizabeth. I'm sure if you say you have him under control it's handled. How's the new position, by the way? Is it what you'd hoped it would be?"

She liked hearing the confidence that Lars had in her. She sat up a little straighter. "Good. I mean it's only been a few days," she said. "But I think I'm adjusting rather well. What do you think?"

He leaned forward in his chair. "I think you are doing a fine job. But then, it's what I expected. You have a single-minded determination that reminds me of myself."

She flushed a little. "Thank you."

"I'll leave you to your walk-around."

"Thank you, sir," she said as he stood up. Then she did the same. "I had my eye focused on this promotion for so long, I never considered what would come after I got it."

He opened the door to her office and then turned around to look at her over his shoulder "You'll figure it out, as you always do."

He walked out and she just stood there, watching him go, until her assistant, Paula, asked if she was okay. "I'm fine."

She stepped back into the office and closed the door. She knew that bringing Carter Shaw's event to the board would ruffle some feathers, but she was confident she could keep things running smoothly. *If* she focused on work and not on Bradley. This morning she'd been glad to have the distraction of work.

She rubbed a hand over her face. What she really needed was some kind of emergency at work that would stop the questions that kept whirling around in her mind, stop the images that that she saw every time she closed her eyes.

The way that Bradley had looked last night when he came. That was a vision that she'd never forget. He'd seemed so raw and vulnerable. It dawned on her that she must have seemed the same to him. And that really scared her. She wanted to ensure he never saw any of the chinks inside of her.

Even though she suspected that he already saw them all too clearly.

ELIZABETH WALKED INTO her office after her walk-around and sat there for a few minutes, warming up from the bitter cold outside. She'd felt so bold when she'd thought of her deal with Bradley, but now she questioned her own wisdom. She'd been jealous of her sister Marina when she'd gotten married before her. Jealous and afraid that maybe she'd never find the kind of partnership her sister had.

And now there was Bradley. He was fine for heating up her nights but not so good for her days. He distracted her, and she'd gotten lucky today that Lars had only wanted to talk to her about Carter Shaw.

Her being distracted by Bradley could have been noticed and the board might… No, they weren't going to change their minds. She had enough confidence to make sure they didn't.

There was something scary about thinking of living your entire life alone. She had this job, and her career had always been on the fast track. She knew it was because work was the one place where she truly felt as though she could let her guard down.

She didn't have to worry about stepping on toes or stepping out of line. In her line of work, it was important that she keep focused, be competitive and beat out the other guy. And she did it all the time. Enjoyed it more than she should, sometimes.

Her phone rang and she glanced at the caller ID. Bradley.

"It's the middle of the day. Not your usual time to call," she said, by way of a greeting.

"Trying to keep you off guard. Is it working?"

More than he could ever know. "What can I help you with?"

"Can you come to the Fresh Sno office this afternoon for a meeting with Carter and some of his folks?" Bradley asked. "Sorry for the short notice, but he's in town for some publicity."

"I'm not sure I can. How about tonight? I can do it after six," she said. This was lodge business and she wasn't going to let her confusion around him mess this up.

"I'll check with the others and text you. Are you bringing anyone else from the lodge?"

"Maybe our ski pro. I want her input on the lessons you mentioned."

"Sounds good. See you then," he said, hanging up.

She felt more confused than ever as she stared at the phone. What was Bradley playing at? He called her in the middle of the night for phone sex and now acted as though they were barely friends.

Maybe that was the point. They weren't in a relationship and weren't going to be a couple. After all, hadn't she made it abundantly clear that she didn't want anything more than sex with him? For all intents and purposes, he was simply abiding by her wishes.

So what right did she have to be upset?

Elizabeth blew out a breath. She needed to move. Clear her head. Put things into perspective. Spurred into action, she pushed to her feet and grabbed her red wool coat. Lindsey should be in her office at the ski rental shop at this time of day. She'd walk over there and chat with her about the meeting planned for that evening.

Elizabeth entered the ski shop and took a moment to make sure that everything was in order. She immediately spotted a man and woman holding hands as they looked at matching fleece pullovers with the lodge logo on them. They were cute and clearly a couple.

She felt a pang inside and wondered why.

She had everything she wanted. Her job was going really well. Bradley was turning out to be one superhot friend with benefits. And her mom had agreed to come to her house for Thanksgiving this year so that Elizabeth didn't have to travel.

Which was a huge relief, because she hated to go back home and see her dad's empty chair.

Elizabeth, her mother and sister had grown closer since her father's death almost five years ago. They'd always been a tight little family unit and a part of her realized that missing her father was part of why she worked so hard.

"Hey, Elizabeth. What are you doing in my neck of the woods?" Lindsey asked, snapping Elizabeth out of her thoughts.

"Join me for a coffee and I'll explain," Elizabeth said as the athletic blonde walked over to her.

"Make mine a hot cocoa and you've got a deal," Lindsey said.

They headed over to the après-ski area, where a fire burned in the large rustic fireplace. Elizabeth ordered drinks for both of them while Lindsey found them a table.

"What's up?"

"I need your help," Elizabeth said. "Carter Shaw has offered us an opportunity to participate in a charity event."

"Carter Shaw? Hardly seems like his kind of thing," Lindsey said, staring down at her beverage.

"The board is concerned because of the way he organized that protest for snowboarders a few years ago. I like the energy he has and I think this idea of his is a strong one. But I need someone to keep an eye on him and to make sure that he doesn't get carried away." Elizabeth glanced over at the other woman. "I'm hoping, since you were both on the Olympic team, you might know him."

"I know him. But we're not friends."

"Oh, okay. Well, forget it, then. I'll find someone else to help out."

"Hold on a second, I didn't say no. Tell me...what is he talking about doing?"

"Some sort of Thunderbolt Energy Games–style competition for kids who don't train at the competition level but have wanted to try it."

She made a face. "It's a good idea. I wish it wasn't, but I like it."

Elizabeth smiled at her. "Me, too. The board is being cautious so I want to make sure we have our best people on this. What do you think?"

Lindsey leaned back in her chair and sighed heavily "When is the meeting?"

"Tonight at six in Park City. Will you do it?"

"Yes, and I'll keep my eye on Carter. I know what he can be like."

Normally, she wouldn't pry but they were friends. "Is there something going on between the two of you?"

Lindsey wrapped her arms around her waist and looked as if she'd gone somewhere very far away. "Not really. I just don't trust him. But that won't get in the way of the charity event."

8

"You need to leave now for your meeting in ten at Fresh Sno. I've had your car brought to the front of the lodge and Lindsey said she'll meet you there. Also, the staff wants to put a gratitude bowl—a place where they can put slips of paper listing the things they're grateful for—in the staff area, is that okay?"

Elizabeth smiled at Paula as she rooted around with her stocking feet to find her pumps and slipped them on. Her assistant was very good at keeping her organized, and she planned to reward all her hard work with a generous Christmas bonus this year.

"I love the idea of a gratitude bowl. Let's make that happen. Also, how are we coming with planning for our Thanksgiving Day celebration?"

"A few of the staff have signed up. And I've ordered the turkey. We have a couple of VIPs coming in to celebrate with their families, and Chef Cruzel has prepared a special menu that I'm going to need you to sign off on."

"Okay. Can it wait until after my meeting?" she asked. Today she felt the strain of the new job. After Lars's well-intentioned talk, she'd been very aware that he was watching her to see how she handled herself. She realized that her habit of working twelve-hour days and ignoring the fact that she wanted a personal life was still her main way of operating.

But, frankly, Bradley was pushing buttons she hadn't anticipated, and no matter how much she wanted to deny it, she'd changed. She still wanted to be the general manager of the lodge, but she also wanted Bradley in her bed and in her life. Only he wasn't going to be content to stay in the corner and be her booty call. *Too bad.*

Glancing down at her clipboard, Paula nodded. "Yes, we can put that off, but then we need to move quickly because some of the ingredients on his menu are exotic and need to be flown in."

"Like what?" Elizabeth asked.

"I'm not sure. That's what Chef told me," her assistant said with a grin. "Want me to ask?"

"Yes, but only so I can tell Lars and the board if they ask. I'm sure it's going to be fab."

"I'm sure it is, as well," Paula agreed.

After tying up a few more loose ends with her assistant, she put her iPad in her shoulder bag and went down to her car. She drove carefully down the mountain to town, realizing that she was nervous.

Nervous? She had to be kidding. There was no reason for her to be apprehensive at this meeting. But it was with Bradley and she hadn't seen him since they'd had steamy phone sex more than a day ago.

Elizabeth flipped on the radio and Pharrell Williams's "Happy" blasted out of it. She wished she could clap along and make everything right in her world, but Bradley was making it difficult for her. Although she wanted him to stay safely in the sex-only zone, their years of friendship made it too easy for her to start to care for him in a way that was more intimate than just as friends.

And that was obviously a problem.

Perhaps it would be easier if they just kept up with the phone sex. That way she'd never know what it was like to fall asleep in his arms. She had the feeling that if she did, it would make it even harder to keep her emotions under control.

She parked at Fresh Sno, noticing that there were a few vehicles in the parking lot. She hopped out, determined to be all business, but that only lasted until she was directed to the conference room and saw him standing alone in the corner, looking out the window.

"Hello, Elizabeth," he said.

She felt suddenly shy and awkward. Two things she was not used to. He wore a suit and she hadn't seen him in one that often. He looked every inch the corporate raider she'd painted him in her dreams. And now that she'd been in his arms, she knew that he was just as dominant in real life. "Hi, Bradley."

He walked over to her, coming so close that she had to consciously stand her ground. But she knew there were other people coming to the meeting and did retreat a small distance.

"Scared?"

"Of course not," she huffed.

"Normally I'd agree with that, but you seem…skittish tonight. Like you're off your game."

Yes, she was. Seeing him brought to the fore a mess of emotions that she'd been struggling to keep under control, and frankly, she didn't like it.

She wasn't ready to face Bradley or the way he made her feel. Although she would never admit it to his face, deep down she feared that she had made a huge mistake in thinking that their friendship would be enough to keep her from the personal chaos that accompanied getting involved with a man. She bit her lower lip and thought long and hard about the best course of action.

"No," he said.

Elizabeth looked at him in confusion. "Excuse me?

"Whatever it is you are concocting in your head. I'm not letting you do it," he told her.

"It's not your choice."

Bradley lifted one hand and tucked a strand of hair behind her ear, his hand lingering on her shoulder as he leaned in even closer. She closed her eyes, hoping to give herself some distance, but the scent of his aftershave and another scent—something that she thought of as uniquely Bradley—assailed her. It wrapped around her with each breath she took, making her heart race wildly in her chest, and when she finally opened her eyes, she found him staring at her.

Transfixed, she couldn't help but stare back into his green eyes with those dark brown flecks that were only visible this close up. She swallowed as she felt the soft exhalation of his breath across her lips. She angled her head and gave up fighting herself. She craved his kiss. Their phone sex the other night had only whetted her appetite for Bradley. She put her hands on his shoulders, leaned in and took the kiss she needed.

He was startled for one second but then took control of the embrace. His hands fell to her waist as he took two steps forward until she was pressed between the wall and his body. She surrendered control as she thrust her tongue into his mouth, tasting him and quenching a thirst that she'd harbored for far too long.

He flexed his fingers, drawing her close to him, his hips rubbing over hers and his chest brushing against her breasts with each breath he took. He sucked her tongue into his mouth and she groaned as a wave of pure desire rocked through her body. Suddenly, he drew back, moving down the conference room as the door opened and Lindsey walked in along with Pablo Donner, one of the board members of the Lars Usten Lodge.

Elizabeth hitched in a breath and licked her lips, trying to get her head back into business, but what she really wanted to do was order Pablo and Lindsey out of the room, lock the door and finish what she and Bradley had started. Glancing across the room at him, she saw he was already making small talk with Lindsey and Pablo, as if nothing had happened moments before, while she was still trying to regain her composure.

What was Pablo doing here? She'd thought he wouldn't be in attendance. But then as other executives from lodges in the area arrived she understood why Pablo was here.

"You okay?" Lindsey asked, coming over to her.

"Yes. I was just going over the menu for Thanksgiving. I have to approve it," she said.

God, she was turning into a liar, and not a very good general manager, if a mere kiss could drive her to distraction like this. But as the other members of the committee arrived and they all settled around the table, she found that her troubles were far from over.

Bradley kept glancing over at her and she wondered if she'd ever be able to manage him and his involvement in her life, while at the same time, she acknowledged that going back to being just friends was totally out of the question.

BRADLEY HAD A hell of time keeping his mind on the meeting and off the way that Elizabeth's blouse hugged her breasts. That kiss had blown his mind, confirming for him that he craved more than just sex from Elizabeth. Part of him was happy enough to fulfill her sexual fantasies, but he had always known he wanted more. Much more.

He knew she was struggling with something—probably leaving her comfort zone—and he understood that, but he was determined to pull her out of it and straight into his arms.

The meeting adjourned and everyone was milling around. It had gone better than he'd expected and he noticed that Carter was talking to Pablo, which was key to keeping the lodge board happy and involved.

Lindsey and Elizabeth seemed to be more than just boss and employee, and Bradley wondered if the other woman would be able to help him get a list of possible attendees to Penny for the party she wanted to throw. Now he just had to get Lindsey alone for a moment.

Luckily, Elizabeth's phone rang and she had to step outside to take the call. He was tempted to follow her and keep up the pressure. To do whatever he had to in order to keep up the pressure and blur the line between the sex-only compartment that she'd put him in.

"Lindsey, do you have a moment?"

She gave him a curious look but nodded.

"I need a favor. I'm a friend of Elizabeth's—we went to college together—and I'm helping to throw together a surprise party to celebrate her promotion."

"Sounds like a great idea, but where do I fit it?" Lindsey asked.

"Well, since I'm local, I was asked if she had any friends here we could invite. But I don't really spend that much time socializing with Elizabeth, so I was hoping you'd help me."

Lindsey tucked a strand of blond hair behind her ear and nodded. "Sure, I can do that. Just give me your email. Or do you want me to text the list to you?"

"Email would be great," he said. "Then I can forward it on."

"What are you two talking about?" Elizabeth asked, coming toward them.

Bradley looked up in surprise. Damn. He hadn't been paying attention to the room. Now how was he going to—

"It's weird for a sports outfitter, but Bradley here isn't comfortable on skis," Lindsey said, barely missing a beat.

"That's right. I spend so much time in my office and away from the slopes."

"I told him to stop by the resort tomorrow and I'll give him some pointers before he checks out our facilities with the rest of the committee."

"Really?" Elizabeth asked.

Bradley didn't think she was buying the fact that he wanted a ski lesson, but he had to play along. "I haven't skied since I was a kid."

"Well, Lindsey is the best. And I think it will be interesting to see you try," Elizabeth said, flashing him a teasing smile.

Pablo waved over to Lindsey. "I've got to go. Pablo and I came together. I'll see you on the slopes, Bradley. Bye, Elizabeth."

"Bye," Elizabeth said. Carter drifted out behind them leaving Bradley alone with her.

"Skiing? That doesn't sound like you at all," she said. "You're too busy working to ever really relax."

"I have time for you."

"You have time for me after midnight," she pointed out.

"Because you haven't let me be a part of your life during the day."

"Hey, I believe we're going snowmobiling soon."

"True enough. That seems so normal. Almost like a date." Pushing her wasn't going to get him what he wanted, but at this point he wanted to know how things stood. He'd thought by bringing a level of intimacy into their relationship that he'd be closer to Elizabeth by now.

But she kept her walls firmly in place. "We're not dating, remember? Even though that's what you suggested. In fact, I have a little time tonight if you'd like to…"

"I'd love to, but I'm committed to the homeless shelter. I can't back out."

She looked at him and there was a softness in her expression that hadn't been there before. He had surprised her somehow and he wished he knew how because he'd do it again.

"I'll come with you. I've been meaning to volunteer more often."

"Are you sure?" he asked. Not that he was going to say no. He wanted to spend some time with her. Together, not on a video chat or in a meeting with a bunch of strangers.

"I'm very sure."

HE DROVE BACK to the Fresh Sno store in Park City. As he pulled around back, he saw Hector and Tony sitting on the bench near the rear of the store, smoking.

Bradley got out the truck and lifted a brow as both of them dropped their cigarettes on the ground and stubbed them out. "You can smoke when I'm around."

"Nah, dude. Tia told us you didn't like it."

"I don't like it for myself but that's because I like breathing and want to live a long life."

"Man, you sound like my pops."

"Your pops knows what he's talking about," Bradley said. "How's the mural coming?"

"I've got most of it sketched," Tony said. "But we're not sure if we can do it on canvas. We're used to concrete."

"Try it," Bradley suggested. "If it doesn't work then you

can paint directly on the walls. I'm hoping that if you do a good job maybe some of our wealthier clientele will be interested in your work."

"Dude, that'd be awesome," Tony said.

"I think so, too. But they can't cut away chunks of my retail shop," Bradley said. "So give the canvas a shot."

"We'll keep working on it. It's just different," Hector said.

"You'll figure it out."

"My mom was really proud that I owned up to what I did and volunteered," Hector said. "Thanks, man. For giving us a chance to make it right."

"No problem," Bradley said, holding his hand out to the kid and shaking it. "Everyone makes mistakes."

He knew that more than most. He thought about Elizabeth as he went upstairs to his office. He didn't want to be a mistake for her. And he was determined that he wouldn't be. He sent her a text confirming plans to go together to the homeless shelter, and she said she would stop by after she was done at work.

VOLUNTEERISM WAS SOMETHING near and dear to Elizabeth's heart. Her parents had made sure that she and her sister never took for granted the stuff they had. That was why she was going. Or, at least, that was what she planned to tell anyone—including Bradley, if he asked.

But as she purchased a pair of thick leggings and a wool sweater in the Fresh Sno retail shop and got changed in the dressing room, she knew she was going because she wanted to be with Bradley.

She took the time to let her hair down and repaired her makeup before she went to go and meet Bradley. "It's not that far. Do you want to walk?" he asked as she walked out of the dressing room.

"I'd love it." She noticed there were still customers in the store, but unlike her, Bradley didn't seem to mind blurring the lines between their business and private lives.

"Great. After you..."

The air was brisk and cold as they stepped out onto the salted sidewalks. The town was lit up for the evening with lots of lights twinkling in the windows. She shivered a little before shoving her hands in her coat pockets and finding her gloves. She put them on and then Bradley took her hand in his.

"This isn't a date," she reminded him

"Yes, it is. Even friends can go on dates," he said.

He had a point. It scared her how much she wanted to just let down her guard and relax with him. She was tempted to pull him into one of the little alleyways between the shops and kiss him. Do something carnal to prove to herself that she was just here for the sex.

But that ship had sailed. She knew that she wasn't walking through Park City holding his hand just so he'd have sex with her. She was doing it because...well, because she wanted to be here with Bradley.

"Stop thinking. For tonight let's just enjoy being with each other," he said. "Why did you agree to come with me tonight?"

She'd rehearsed this in her head in the dressing room. "All the employees at the Lars Usten Lodge have to do one hundred hours of community service each year."

"Really?"

"Yes. It's in our mission statement and in our employment contract."

"I meant you're really going to give me that pat answer instead of the truth?"

She bit her lip and stopped walking. This was it. The moment where she had to decide if she was going to be completely candid with him And, really, if it had been any other man but Bradley she wouldn't do it. But he was her friend. Her best friend.

"I agreed because when you mentioned the shelter, I saw a bit of your past in your eyes. You've never really said much about your childhood, but I know it wasn't easy for you and you went without a lot of things. I guess a part of me put two and two together and realized that you're helping feed kids and families the way you wished someone would have done for you and your mom."

He looked down and away from her, and she wondered if she'd gotten it wrong. But then he turned back and he nodded. "Damn, Lizzie. When I asked for honesty, you gave back in spades. I wasn't expecting that."

She wished she felt a flush of victory, but she could see the dark emotion in his eyes and knew that she had cut too close to the bone for him. He was vulnerable. She hadn't realized that before this moment. He always seemed so confident and so in control.

"You're a good man."

"It's about time you figured that out," he said gruffly, walking again.

Smiling despite herself, she matched his quick, easy stride. Sometimes it was too convenient to forget that there was anything else in her life but work. She wouldn't change that. She'd made her choice, but still, it was nice to be out and to have a few hours where she didn't have to worry about VIPs or broken freezers or the fact that they might not get the exotic ingredients they needed for Thanksgiving.

They walked across the parking lot of the homeless kitchen. She didn't make it down to the shelter as often as she used to, but the resort gave extra food and Elizabeth always donated generously to them.

"Thank you, Lizzie," Bradley said as he drew to stop at the corner of the building under a cone of light.

She felt awkward now. She wished she'd been able to keep things just physical between them. Right now, though, remembering that damned soulful kiss in the boardroom was making it hard for her to believe that even the carnal desires they'd shared weren't bringing them closer.

She glanced up at him; the angles of his face were sharp in the harsh light. She stood there in the parking lot of the homeless shelter wondering if she should turn around and leave.

But she'd never been a quitter. No matter how much she wanted to tuck tail and run, and that might be the smarter course of action, she wasn't built that way.

"I've been here before," she said. "This is a great shelter. Thanks for not minding that I joined you tonight."

"Are we pretending we didn't just have a moment?" he asked softly.

She sighed. "It would be a lot easier on me if we did."

"But life isn't always easy, is it?"

"Don't push," she said.

"I have to. You keep trying to slow things down or make them just about sex."

"What sex?" she asked. "We've barely kissed."

"We've done a hell of a lot more than that. And I dare you to deny that you've been running scared."

"I won't deny it," she said, meeting his eyes,

It was a canny move from him, getting her to admit how she really felt, but as they went inside and took their spots in the line of people serving food to the homeless of Park City, she was beginning to realize that it was what she needed. She was lost in trying to figure out what she needed to do in order to keep herself from falling for Bradley. But when he showed her the parts of himself that she knew he kept hidden from the world, it was really hard to keep her own emotional barriers in place

Tonight had made her realize that the little boy who'd been hungry was still a part of the successful man he was today. She wanted to pretend that it didn't matter but it did and she felt it all the way to her soul.

9

THEY WALKED BACK to the store after working at the soup kitchen. A light snow was falling around them and the temperature was plummeting. Bradley didn't talk and neither did Elizabeth. He needed time to decompress from having her by his side tonight. And even though he'd always thought he wanted more from her than to be friends with benefits, tonight had really reinforced that.

He noticed that Hector and Tony were still hanging out in front of his store when they approached it. The teens started walking toward the street and he realized they didn't have a ride.

"Hey," Tony said as they stopped next to them.

"Elizabeth, come and meet Tony and Hector. I hired them to do a mural in the shop. They're both very talented."

She held her hand out to the boys. Hector took it and brought it to his mouth, kissing the back of her hand. "What's up, girl?"

The teen's entire posture and demeanor changed and the troubled youth gave way to a confident ladies' man. He noticed the flush of color on Elizabeth's cheeks.

"Dude, she's mine," Bradley said, putting his arm around her and drawing her into the curve of his body.

"Don't see no ring on her finger," Hector said, before winking at Elizabeth.

"Are you two done for the evening?"

"Yeah. My pops was supposed to be here, but he probably got busy," Hector said.

"No problem. I'll give you a ride home," Bradley offered, hitting the button to start the SUV and get it warmed up. Then he unlocked the doors. "You can wait in the truck until I get back...no smoking in there, though."

"Cool."

The teens walked toward the vehicle and he turned to Elizabeth.

"I had planned to invite you for a drink, but I don't like the idea of you waiting in some bar for me."

She shook her head and gave him one of her haughty looks. "I might have said yes. Actually, if you feel up to driving out to my place when you're done with the boys, we can have a nightcap together."

"Really?"

"Do I ever say anything I don't mean?" she asked.

"Yes," he said. He hadn't meant to get real now, especially since he didn't want to spoil the mood, but she said a lot of things she didn't mean.

"Wow, that was harsh."

"But true. We both know that you use words like a rapper, with precision and to distract from what's really going on with you."

"Like a rapper? Really?"

"Yes. You're smart, and you're careful about what you say, and most of the time you're so clever that it takes me a while to figure out I've been played." He rested his hands on her shoulders and gazed down at her intently. "That's why I'm making sure you're inviting me to your place for the night. Because we both know it's before midnight and you don't usually lower your inhibitions until much later."

She pulled away from him. He knew he should shut up but he couldn't help but feel as if she was playing a game. The same one she'd started in college.

"You blow hot and cold and you keep me jumping at your command," he said. "This isn't a competition."

"And that bothers you, doesn't it?" she asked. "You have to be the one in charge all the time. You act all cordial and nicey-nice, but we both know that underneath you are tightly leashed and that it is only when things go your way that you're charming."

"Touché. You do the same thing."

"You're right—it's a defense mechanism. I...I didn't get to really spend any time with you tonight, and I really wanted to. But I can't ask you to let two teenagers walk home in the cold alone just so I can satisfy my own urges."

"I didn't think you would," he said. Elizabeth might be all business, but she had a big heart and would help out anyone who needed it.

"It's been a really long day for me. I want to go home, but I want to be with you, too. Inviting you over seemed like a solution. But I didn't really think it through," she admitted. "Probably by the time you've driven out to my place, I would have given in to my own doubts."

He got it. He understood that they were both afraid to trust the other, and yet they already did on some level. Well, *he* already did. "If I come to your house, Lizzie, I'm not leaving until the morning...and I don't want you to regret it."

"I won't regret it. I'm tired of just wanting and not having you," she said.

His cock hardened. God, he wanted this woman. Tonight it seemed he was finally going to have her.

"I want you, too. So much I can barely stand it. After the way you kissed me earlier, I've been in a state of arousal all day, and I haven't been so dominated by thoughts of sex since I was in my twenties." He exhaled roughly. "The truth is that I can't think of anything but making you mine. Taking you and making sure you never forget that I'm your man."

"Are you?"

"I want to be," he said. A small part of him was worried that it was simply sex that she wanted from him. Once he had her, maybe things would go back to the way they'd always been. But he wasn't sure and he had no idea how to tell until they got past this intense wanting.

"Go take those boys home and come to my place. We can play it by ear."

He gave her a heated look that pretty much said it all. "Fair enough," he said. "We both have our cards on the table."

"Yes," she admitted. "From the beginning I've always been afraid of that side of you because you are intense."

"The last thing I want is for you to be afraid, Lizzie." His hand went to her cheek and he gently stroked her face. "Let me show you that there is nothing to fear. Together we will be better than we have been before, with each of us dancing around the other."

She pulled her leather gloves from the pockets of her coat. "I'll try. But I realized tonight that I can't change to please you, Bradley."

"What do you mean?" he asked.

"It's kind of complicated," she said, wrinkling her nose at him. "Now get out of here. Tony and Hector probably think you've forgotten them."

Before heading toward his truck, he nodded as though he understood, but he didn't. That she thought only one thing about her personality was complicated was a total understatement. Everything about that woman kept him constantly guessing, but he knew that he'd made the right choice tonight. He couldn't keep letting her call all the plays. It wasn't his personality to let a woman dictate the dynamics of their relationship.

He dropped Hector and Tony off at their housing complex and waited until he saw them go inside. They had been quiet on the drive home, keeping their headphones in their ears, which suited him just fine because it gave him a chance to figure out what he was going to do about Elizabeth.

As he pulled into her driveway he realized he still had no idea what his next strategic move was going to be.

HER HOUSE WAS cold when she got home. For a while, she'd set the furnace to come on at five, but her hours weren't normal and that had made no sense. The house was quiet. She turned up the heat and listened to the sound as it came on.

She looked at the fall decorations she'd put out so that she'd feel the way she had as a child. Her parents had made a big deal of every season and Elizabeth had tried to follow that tradition.

She'd never really been the kind of woman who'd dreamed of having a family of her own because her goals had been different. She'd wanted to be like her dad. A businessman... well, woman. And she had accomplished that.

But she got the feeling from Bradley that, despite the way he was playing it cool, he might actually want a family and a wife. A traditional wife. That was something she wasn't sure she'd ever be.

Elizabeth shook her head. The house was too quiet and she felt her loneliness more keenly than before. She should get a pet. But what kind of life would that be for an animal? Spending all day alone in her house while she worked. She glanced at herself in the hall mirror and she saw the accoutrements of her own success. They were everywhere in the two-storey, 4,000-square-foot home that she'd bought.

If she was being honest with herself, the house was too big and she didn't really like it. She was still only partially unpacked and she missed the condo she'd had up on the mountain near the ski lodge. Sighing wearily, she put her purse on the table under the mirror and opened the closet to put her boots on the stand inside it along with her parka.

She flipped on the lights as she walked through the house and lit a large candle, letting the scent surround her. She wondered if Bradley was going to show up tonight or change his mind.

The thing about their relationship was that it boiled down to a game of one-upmanship. And she knew from her side of it that every time she took a step closer to him she started to have doubts.

In a way, Bradley was like this big house that she'd bought to prove that she had it all. He was helping her to remember that she was a woman and to be more in touch with those needs. "I'm an idiot."

She remembered when she was ten, she'd heard her parents in the living room talking. It had been close to midnight and she'd snuck to the hallway and watched them sitting there having a quiet moment together.

That small glimpse into her parents' life together had been enough to convince her that they'd loved each other.

The doorbell rang, and not a moment too soon. She needed to get out of her own head. But when she opened the door and saw Bradley standing there in the moonlight with his collar pulled up and flakes of snow falling on his thick brown hair, she knew this wasn't a solution.

"Hey."

"Hey, you," he said softly. "You okay?"

She nodded because words were beyond her at this point. She was so afraid that if she opened her mouth all the craziness in her mind was going to spill out. "Come in."

She opened the door wider and he stepped over the threshold, shrugging out of his coat and hanging it on one of the hooks by the door. He sat down on the bench and took his boots off, pushing them underneath.

"I haven't seen your house since you moved. It's big."

"Yes," she said. "I needed it for entertaining the board. I wanted them to see that I was ready for my promotion. You know...look the part."

Oh, God, it was bad enough she lied to herself, but now she was actually saying that nonsense out loud. To convince him that all she wanted him for was sex when deep inside she knew she wanted a lot more. She'd invited him to her home without really thinking this through.

"Good. Want to show me around?" he asked.

"No. It's not really finished yet. Only the living room, my bedroom and the kitchen are done."

"Well, I don't mind seeing your bedroom."

She felt excited. "Play your cards right and maybe you will."

"I thought that was why I was here," he said.

"You want to jump straight to the action. What about the romance? I thought you were a player from way back. I expected a bit more..."

"Seduction," he suggested stepping closer to her and wrapping his fingers around her shoulder, leaning in close to whisper in her ear. "Something more like this?"

"Yes," she said, afraid she might have taken on more than she could handle with him.

She led the way into the kitchen and her big butcher-

block table. "Sit down and I'll get us something to drink."
He did what she asked. "Cocktail or something hot?"

"Baileys on ice would be great," he said.

She poured one for each of them, then brought the
glasses to the table and sat down next to him. "It's so
weird having you here. I'm actually more nervous now
than I was having phone sex with you."

"That's because in the flesh you can't pretend I'm
something you just conjured up. You know this is real and
there's no running from me or from what you really want."

"What do I really want?"

"Me."

"COME WITH ME," Bradley said. He put his drink down and
stood up, taking her hand in his, then led her back down
the hallway to the mirror that hung over a side table. Pulling her in front of him he met her reflected gaze, but after
hesitating for a moment she looked away.

He didn't have a plan, really, he just knew that he
wanted her to see the strong, sexy, confident, successful
woman she truly was. And to admit that she wanted him.

With her chin in his hand he gently turned her face
back to the mirror. Then he lifted her arm up so that she
wrapped it around his neck and drew his hand down the
side of her body.

"What are you doing?" she asked, trying to turn in his
arms, but he held her firm.

Meeting her blue-green eyes in the mirror he let loose
all the pent-up desire that had been building for the last ten
years. He wanted this night to be perfect. But he'd learned
along the way that perfection was a trap. What he really
needed was to have Lizzie in his arms and have her realize she wanted more from him than sex.

But first he had to ensure she was out of her mind

with pleasure so that no other man would ever be in her thoughts again.

"I was thinking of getting you naked in front of the mirror and showing you every part of your body that turns me on."

She arched her eyebrows at him. He'd changed the mood and was glad. Another day could not go by without her realizing how special she truly was. Resting his head on her shoulder he fought not to clutch her closely to him. Not to hold her so tightly that she'd never be able to leave. He wanted her that badly.

Not just physically—though, in a moment, he suspected he wasn't going to be able to think of anything but her body. But right now, he wanted her in his future. He knew that he was never going to be satisfied by just something sexual between them. And he had no idea how he was going to convince her otherwise.

"Not so fast. I want you to stand in the front and look in the mirror, too," she said.

"That's not the way this game works."

"It isn't?" she mused, turning in his arms, and wrapping hers around his neck. She lifted herself up on her toes and rubbed her lips over his with the softest of brushes. He shuddered and his cock stirred to life. God, he wanted this woman naked.

"No," he said, barely keeping his wits about him to speak. "It's not."

"How does it work, then?" Lizzie asked between nibbling kisses, which she dropped along the edge of his jaw. Then she scraped one of her fingernails lightly down the side of his neck. Sensation rushed over his body, pooling in his groin. He got even harder. And rocked his pelvis against her. She closed her eyes and undulated against him.

He slipped his hands up her back, holding her carefully against him with one arm while he tangled his hand in her hair and tipped her head back so that he could stare down into her eyes. They were soft-looking, lids heavy, pupils dilated, and he could see the flush of desire under her pale complexion.

"It works like this," he said, bringing his mouth down on hers, and slowly, almost lazily, thrusting his tongue deep into her mouth. He was hungry for her, with an emptiness inside him that only being in her arms could sate. She felt so good there. Like no other woman ever had before.

He lifted her off her feet and took a step backward until he could rest against the wall while her body was pressed against his. She pushed her hands into his hair and held his head as she continued to deepen the kiss.

Her breasts pillowed on his chest and he remembered how she'd been naked the other night but he hadn't been able to really see her or touch her. He'd been frustrated then, but now that she was actually here with him, in the flesh, it was sheer torture. Gritting his teeth, he held tight to his self-control with every ounce of willpower he had, because tonight he wanted to make very sure that nothing was rushed and that everything went exactly according to his plans.

10

ELIZABETH HADN'T REALIZED that Bradley saw her the way he did. Both sides of her—the strength and the weakness. She felt lost and shattered by everything that was going through her head, but with his mouth on hers...he tasted so good. And with his arms around her she could forget for a little while that she was broken.

Even though most of the world saw her as confident and together, Bradley was the one man who always saw the real woman. And as he cupped her butt and drew her more firmly against him, she knew she didn't want it any other way.

She pulled her head back and looked up at him for a moment. His skin was flushed, his lips wet and swollen. There was stubble on his cheeks and she liked the way it felt when she ran her forefinger over it.

"Still want to see the master bedroom?"

He shifted her in his arms. "Hell, yeah. Which way?"

"Upstairs. Think you can carry me up there?" she asked. No man had carried her, ever. Maybe her father when she'd been younger, but there was something so daunting about her that her lovers had always sort of let her take the lead.

Bradley was different. And, as much as she didn't want

to admit it, he also made her want to believe in things she'd long since stopped thinking about. Things like knights and princesses and being swept off her feet romantically.

But that wasn't what they were about. He was her friend *plus*. Her sex buddy who was all about the hot nights.

"I can definitely handle you," he said.

He gave her a quick, hard kiss and then carried her up the stairs. On the landing he paused, looking at the doors that were all standing open. The hallway was dimly lit by motion-sensor night-lights that flicked on as he strode past them. He didn't stop until he was in front of her bedroom.

"This one smells like you," he said.

She sniffed the air and realized it was scented faintly with the new designer fragrance she'd been wearing lately.

"Sherlock Holmes, watch out," she said with a laugh.

He let her legs down and turned to pin her against the wall. Her wrists were clasped loosely in his as he held them up on either side of her head. "Tease me at your peril, woman."

She wasn't afraid of Bradley but she was turned on by the way he'd taken control. For so much of their relationship he'd let her set the pace, and tonight she realized he'd been biding his time.

"I'm not scared of you."

"Good, but I will get a little revenge for that teasing."

"Like what?"

"Like this," he said, while he reached for the hem of her sweater and drew it up over her head. The garment was trapped on her arms for a moment but he quickly got it off and tossed it aside.

Standing there in just a lacy bra and a pair of thick leggings, she felt a tinge of helplessness. Then it was gone as he traced his free hand down her face, rubbing his thumb over her lips and moving lower, down the very center of her body. He stopped when he encountered the delicate fabric of her bra, and as he traced its lines over the globes of each breast she felt them getting bigger, straining toward his touch. He continued stroking her, moving his hand over her skin until gooseflesh spread out from his finger and shivers started coursing through her body.

His grip was firm when she squirmed in his grasp. She liked what he was doing to her, but wanted more. And as she watched him through half-lidded eyes, she realized that he liked it, too. Seeing the way he looked at her, the gentle, almost reverent way he touched her, took her breath away. She'd had lovers but no man had ever looked at her the way that Bradley did now.

She shifted her legs, stroking his calf with her foot and then lifting her leg higher, wrapping it around his hip and drawing him closer. The ridge of his cock was hard, and she wiggled her hips to rub her center over him. He groaned as he slid his hand down between their bodies and she felt his hand on his zipper and then his erection against her. His hips thrust and she answered his thrusts with her own.

She tugged at her hands but he kept them locked above her head. Then he brought his mouth down on hers, his tongue stroking into her mouth with the same rhythm as his hips. And it wasn't enough. Just served to create an unbearable ache deep inside of her. She knew she needed more but didn't want to tear her mouth from his to demand it.

His hand on her back scraped down her spine and then flicked over her to unfasten her bra. The fabric fell away from her skin and his light touch skimmed against her side, cupping her under the fabric and holding the weight of her breast in the palm of his hand while his finger rubbed over her nipple in a small circle that drove her crazy.

She tried to increase the pressure of his cock against her center, but his hips moved in a slow steady rhythm. At that moment she was suspended in a feeling of total need and desire, and she never wanted it to end. She wanted to stay here in his arms, with his mouth on hers, forever.

He shifted his attention to her other breast, the slow, steady fondling making her wet and ready for him. She yanked her mouth from his and nibbled his jaw before he lowered his head and took her nipple into his mouth. He bit her lightly before swiping his tongue over her and then suckling gently.

"Enough games," she said, her voice sounding breathless and needy. "Let go of my hands."

"No." He licked her nipple again and looked up at her. "Not yet."

He continued moving lower on her body, kissing and caressing, but he couldn't keep her hands above her head while he traveled lower. "Guess you're going to have to let go."

Bradley just shook his head and stood up, shifting her wrists so that one was in each of his hands and drawing them slowly down her body. He let go long enough to pull her bra off and toss it onto the floor. Then he captured her hands in his again and brought them up to cup her breasts as he rubbed them against her.

"This is what I was picturing the other night. You holding your breasts, but I had no idea what color your nipples were or how you'd feel in my hands and in my mouth."

She nodded dazedly, barely able to think much less talk at this moment. He slid their joined hands lower and used her left one to grip his cock. As he moved her hand up and down over him he groaned, then suddenly tried to pull her away, but she kept her hold on him.

He was solid and smooth, and she liked the feel of him

under her hand. Liked the way he was throbbing beneath her touch. His breath coming in short, ragged gasps, he let go of her hand as she moved her fingers over the tip of his cock and then stroked him again, reaching lower to cup his balls and roll them in her fingers. She felt his free hand on her leggings as she was trying to remove them.

He let go of both her hands and pulled the leggings and her panties down, leaving them around her ankles as he stood back up and took her hands again. She stepped free and felt his cock back at her entrance.

He hesitated and she wasn't sure what he was waiting for. "Enough teasing, Bradley. I want to know what it's like to have you inside of me."

"Damn, woman, I want that, too." Then he asked, "Are you on the pill?"

She swallowed and nodded.

"Thank God."

She smiled at the relief in his voice but she felt the same desperate desire for him. She expected him to lift her up again, but instead he lowered his mouth and suckled her breast and then he straightened and leaned in, his cock finding its way to her center. She felt just his tip as he slipped a little bit inside of her. When she lifted her leg, wrapped it around his midriff and tried to force him deeper, he surprised her by grabbing her waist and lifting her up higher as he turned so that his back was pinned against the wall.

Exhaling sharply, he buried his face between her breasts, scraping his teeth over the pale white flesh. Then he let her slide down his body and she loved the feel of his chest hair as it abraded her nipples. God, he made her feel as though she was perfectly made just for him. They felt so right together.

She wrapped her legs around his hips and lowered herself onto his length, taking him completely inside of her. She braced herself with her hands on the wall behind his head as she shifted against him, riding up and down on his cock. He held her with his hands on her waist.

She bent her head and devoured his lips with her own. Responding in kind, he sucked her tongue into his mouth and then she felt one of his hands in her hair, pulling as he bit lightly on her tongue. She tightened her muscles around him and felt everything inside her demanding that she take him deeper and move faster against him.

He tore his mouth from hers and buried his face against her neck, kissing his way down her throat. The feel of his blistering breath against her body, his hot cock inside of her going deeper and deeper, drove her toward her climax. As she pushed harder and quicker against him, he thrust up into her as her orgasm exploded. She felt him stiffen. Then the warmth of his completion inside of her.

But she didn't want to stop, didn't want it to end, and continued to ride him until another wave washed over her while he held her in his arms. She collapsed against him, resting her head against his shoulder as stars danced in front of her eyes and her heart raced wildly out of control.

His chest rose and fell with each breath, and he clutched her close to him, as though he was never going to let her go. She didn't want him to.

He groaned and twisted his head to kiss her. After several long moments, he carried her over to the bed and fell down on it, still cradling her against his chest. Then he wrapped them both in the comforter and held her tenderly in his arms.

She shut down her mind and twined her arms around him, letting the closeness of the moment warm the parts of her heart that had been alone for too long. There was something so perfect about the way he felt wrapped around her. About the way he held her.

And even though a part of her was convinced this was just lust, a lonely little part of her heart denied it and wanted to claim Bradley as hers forevermore.

BRADLEY WOKE IN the middle of the night as Elizabeth shifted against him. Gently extricating himself from her arms, he tucked her under the covers and got up, cleaned himself off and climbed back into bed with her. He thought she wasn't really sleeping, just pretending so that they didn't have to talk. But since he felt raw from making love to her the way he had, he decided to just let her be.

But the house was unfamiliar. He was used to the ticking of his old grandfather clock and couldn't sleep. After lying there for what felt like hours, he wondered if he should get up and leave.

It seemed rude, but then staying didn't quite feel right, either. He was trapped between what he wanted and what he knew he should do. It almost felt to him that if he stayed here tonight he'd lose ground with her.

She just wanted him to be her booty call, not her lover— not in the sense that he wanted it. He wanted her to admit she cared for him and wanted more than this friends-with-benefits thing they'd foolishly agreed to.

When she rolled away from him, he thought *screw it* and got out of bed. He pulled on his clothes in the dim glow provided by her night-light, then looked back to find her wide-awake and watching him.

"Ask me to stay," he said.

"You don't have to go," she told him, but that wasn't an invitation and they both knew it.

"Regrets?"

She shook her head. In the faint light it was hard to read

her expression, but he felt a little bit of uncertainty. He was experiencing the same thing himself. He hadn't expected soul sex. Maybe some deep, hot lovemaking, but nothing that would touch him so deeply and make it feel as though he'd never be able to make love to another woman again.

"Confusion," she said, finally.

He almost smiled at the verbal game they were playing. There was a hint of how they'd always been with each other and he wanted to just ignore the gnawing doubt in his gut and go with it. But tonight the game was touched with a bit of sadness as well as playfulness. Because every time he thought he'd moved closer to her, he found there was a new layer of resistance that he hadn't realized he had to face.

"Fine," he said. It was late and he had work tomorrow. Also, he knew when to cut his losses. He'd made an effort—no one could say he hadn't—and it was definitely time for him to leave.

He started walking toward the door, glancing at the wall where her leggings were piled on the floor. Images flashed in his mind of how she'd looked and felt in his arms. He didn't want to leave, but really felt as though he couldn't stay.

He heard the rustle of sheets behind him and then felt her hand in the center of his back. He glanced over his shoulder and saw her standing there with the comforter draped around her.

"Don't go," she said softly.

He saw in her the same determination he'd seen at Marina's wedding when she'd told him that she'd never be able to have it all. And then he'd kissed her. And everything had changed.

"Really?" he asked, not because he didn't believe it but because he wasn't sure if she knew what she wanted. And as much as he wanted to be in her bed on this cold

November night, the last thing he wanted was to be there because she felt she had to ask him.

She shook her head. "Don't be an ass. I'm asking you to stay."

"Okay, I will," he said, turning around to face her. "Why is everything so difficult with you, Lizzie?"

"Come back to bed and I'll try to explain."

He followed her across the room, stripped down to his boxers and got beneath the blankets. She pulled a long sleeved T-shirt with a big turkey on it out of her dresser and put it on.

He started laughing when he saw it.

She just smiled. "My mom had them made for us last year."

"That's great," he said, wriggling his eyebrows at her. "Super sexy."

"I usually sleep alone," she pointed out.

"I'm glad you're making an exception for me," he drawled.

She climbed into the bed next to him. "I am, too."

The both moved around until they found a comfortable spot in each other's arms. Once they'd settled down together, their hearts beating in tandem, she released a deep breath.

"I'm so afraid that if I don't keep the two parts of our relationship separate that I might lose you," she admitted.

"How would you lose me? We might grow close enough to be everything to each other."

"I can't let that happen. I'm not really good when it comes to emotional attachments."

He gently stroked her hair, then tucked her close to him. "How do you know that? You've never been involved with anyone for long," he said.

"After you graduated, I had a very intense affair and I

almost flunked out of college. I couldn't manage both my love life and the way it dominated every waking second. My parents came down and fixed everything."

"How?"

"They got the man out of my life and helped me refocus on my studies. But it was hard at first. It wasn't love with him, but it could be with you."

She was quiet for a long time and he thought maybe she'd fallen asleep. The clock on the dresser read 2:30. The first fingers of fatigue were starting to wrap around him, as well.

"There isn't another man who's come close to taking over my emotions until now," she admitted hoarsely.

It wasn't lost on him that once again it was after midnight and he was seeing the real Elizabeth. She'd let her guard down, given him a real, genuine glimpse into her fears.

"Who was the boy?"

"Dane. That boy who looked like you," she said. "I think part of why I liked him was because of that."

Had she just admitted that she'd wanted him back then? "You're so much more mature, now. I think you could handle me."

"I don't know. Every time I think man-woman relationships aren't important to me, something usually happens to make me question that theory."

"Like what?"

"Like you."

11

ELIZABETH WOKE UP to a quiet house. Her first thought was of Bradley. She found a note on her nightstand from him, asking her to meet him for dinner that evening.

She wanted to text him and find out what he was doing right then, but she felt as though the line between sex and friendship was blurring. And that made her want to retreat. Her usual M.O.

But today she was going to try to take a step forward, to change those past behaviors. She remembered how she'd looked in the mirror when Bradley had stood behind her, showing her how much he wanted her and how vulnerable he was willing to be.

She got dressed for work and felt the same thrill as she usually did when she pulled into her general-manager parking spot. She and Lindsey were meeting for breakfast, so she braided her hair and got on her ski gear. She packed her work clothes in her bag and left her house.

It was a beautiful November morning with the sun rising and clear skies around the valley. She was really looking forward to spending some time with her friend. It would go a long way to helping her clear her head.

Lindsey was waiting for her in the employee locker

room. She found her friend examining her knee. Like most of the nation, Elizabeth had seen the film of the practice run where Lindsey had careened off the Super G course and into the protective barrier. She'd been going in excess of seventy-five miles per hour when she'd crashed, her skis and legs twisting under her body.

"Is it any better?" Elizabeth asked.

Lindsey looked up, startled, and just shrugged. "About the same. I'm going to see my surgeon tomorrow—he thinks if I have one more operation I might be able to ski more aggressively, maybe get my career back."

"That's good, right?" Elizabeth asked. There was something in her friend's tone that made her wonder.

Lindsey sighed. "I'm not sure. These last few months that I've been working here, life's been a lot different and not bad different, you know?"

"I wish I did. But I've never had anything like skiing in my life. And you are so good at it." Elizabeth paused for a long moment. "I don't like change. I could see where not knowing what was going to happen next would be hard."

Lindsey gave a rueful laugh. "Change is hard for anyone. Falling in front of millions at the Olympics was horrifying for me, because every time they mention me on one of those cable news shows they show that same clip and I'm forced to relive it again."

Elizabeth sat down on the bench next to her friend and put her arm around her in a quick hug. "That would kill me."

"That about sums it up," Lindsey said. "But as my coach told me, I'm an adult and I need to shake it off."

"What an ass. Your entire world changed—you'd think he'd have served up some sympathy."

Lindsey gave her a sad smile as she stood up and finished getting her ski gear on. "I thought so, too, but he didn't get to be the best by being nice."

Elizabeth had heard the same thing said of Lars Usten, and she understood what Lindsey was getting at, but there was a time to be a hard-nosed badass and a time for some sympathy, and it sounded as if her coach didn't get that.

"I'm looking forward to getting on the slopes today," Elizabeth said as they walked to the chairlift.

"Me, too, but I think I might have to rest my knee today."

"I wondered if you would still want to ski," Elizabeth admitted. "You know, after what happened…"

"Teaching is different from competing. I still want to push myself sometimes, and other times it makes me hungry for a race."

"I'm glad," Elizabeth said, wishing there was some way she could find the joy she'd had in her childhood. But when she thought about it objectively, she had been happy. "I guess my family does that for me."

"Really? That's great. My parents just sort of signed me over to ski training… Oh, man, I sound bitter. I mean, I am a little, because I didn't get to be a kid, but it wasn't their fault."

Elizabeth laughed a little at Lindsey. She wished she could be as forgiving about the past as her friend seemed to be. She had a good attitude toward life.

"What are you doing for Thanksgiving? Are you going home to Vermont?"

"No, it didn't work out this year."

"That's too bad. Would you like to come to my house and have Thanksgiving with us?" Elizabeth asked. Her mom loved it when they had a full house.

"Yes, you know, I think I would."

"Good. I'll text you the directions later. Have you

checked out the slopes already this morning?" Elizabeth asked as they got off the ski lift and saw members of the ski patrol gathered nearby.

Every day the ski patrol, and sometimes Lindsey, went out at dawn on snowmobiles to inspect the runs and see if there were any areas that should be roped off or dangers they needed be aware of.

"No, I didn't. I should go talk to Dan," she said.

Lindsey walked over to speak with the head of the ski patrol. Elizabeth wanted to pretend she was thinking about her upcoming run, but instead her mind was filled with images of Bradley from last night. She knew that she had to change if she was going to keep growing and she vowed to make those changes, but this morning they seemed scary.

Almost as scary as letting Bradley spend the night with her. She hadn't slept with a lover since…since Ken, the guy who'd broken up with her just before Marina's wedding. And though she hadn't mentioned it to Bradley, Ken also had found her lacking when it came to commitment and had told her in no uncertain terms that she'd make an awful long-term partner.

She wanted to ignore those hurtful words and instead thought of what Bradley had said about taking their relationship one step at a time, but she wondered if one day he'd look at her with the same disdain and disappointment every other man in her life had.

HIS DAY HAD gone downhill since he'd left Elizabeth's house early that morning. The Christmas tree they'd ordered from a family tree farm in Montana had arrived early and was about seven inches too tall for the retail floor. Tia was in a mood because her boyfriend was called back to California. And Carter had decided that he was going to spend the holidays in Park City so he could have another committee meeting to confirm who was on board for his charity event. On top of everything else, the last thing Bradley wanted to do was deal with the dang Christmas tree today. But since Tia was taking her boyfriend to the airport, he needed to do it.

"I'm open to ideas as to where to put the tree," Bradley said to his staff. He couldn't cut the darn thing since it was a potted tree, which was part of the Fresh Sno ethos of being eco-friendly. "These lumberjack guys have about forty-five minutes until they are going to head out."

"What if we put it in the center of the store where it's open to our loft offices?" Tom, his retail manager asked.

"We'd have to move the display there. Can we do that?"

"Yes," Tom said. "I can get the staff on it right now."

Bradley looked around the sales floor and that was the only place for the large tree. "Okay, let's make this happen. Tom, you're in charge. Go and liaise with the tree guys and get it done."

"Yes, boss."

Bradley climbed the stairs to his loft office two at a time, stopping when he found Carter standing by his desk. "Sorry to keep you waiting. It's one emergency after another today."

"Dude, if it's a problem I can come back later."

"Later isn't going to help. I haven't had a chance to talk to Elizabeth about another meeting."

"That's fine. I'm going to head over to the lodge later. Is there any time that doesn't work for you?"

"Um…you know it's Thanksgiving next week, right?"

"Yes. I decided to fly my family out here for the week. Have you seen the residences at the lodge? They are pretty nice. I convinced Pablo to let me stay there so I could prove I'm not the agitator I used to be."

"How's that working for you?" Bradley asked drolly. Because he knew that Carter was still as rowdy as ever.

"Not great. Which is why I'm bringing my mom here. She's about as normal as you can get."

"Maybe that will help."

"It can't hurt," Carter said.

"Since you are here...I wanted to talk to you some more about being a spokesperson for Fresh Sno," Bradley said.

Carter threw his head back and laughed. "It's cool. As I mentioned the other day, I'd love to do it if it doesn't conflict with my deal with my other sponsors. Let me check with my agent."

"Okay. Here's the name and number of my business manager. Have your guy talk to him," Bradley said, writing it down on a piece of paper embossed with his name. Elizabeth had given it to him when he'd expanded his outdoor company to Park City.

"Nice paper," Carter said.

"Thanks. I have a very fancy friend," Bradley said as he jotted the information down.

Bradley wondered what it must be like to be a golden boy like Carter. It seemed as if everything he did just came easy for him.

What was Elizabeth doing for Thanksgiving? He should see if she wanted to spend the day together. But that seemed like maybe pushing it too far. She had boundaries for the two of them that only she seemed to be aware of.

But maybe it *was* time to push them.

He hated being wishy-washy about anything, but with Elizabeth he didn't want to take the wrong step and push her away. Today they seemed even further apart than before.

"I've had a shit day. Want to join me for a drink?" Bradley asked.

Carter chuckled. "I can't, man. Gotta stay in shape, and it's not gonna be easy with Thanksgiving around the corner."

Bradley nodded. "I probably shouldn't, either."

"You seem sporty despite the whole not-knowing-how-to-ski thing," Carter said, deftly switching the subject.

"Uh…thanks," Bradley said. He couldn't believe he'd pretended he couldn't ski to cover up for a surprise party.

Carter stood. "Let's go. I've got a way to make you forget all about this crappy day."

"What?"

"Snowshoeing. There's fresh snow on the ground near the outskirts of town and a field that's just begging for someone to make some tracks on it."

"Yeah, okay, let's go," Bradley said. He left Tom in charge and followed Carter's directions to the spot just out of town, right at the turn-off leading up to the Lars Usten Lodge. He parked on the side of the road and they both zipped up their parkas and put on the snowshoes. Carter didn't talk much, just walked off in his own direction while Bradley stared at the signage for the lodge.

In his head, the lodge and Elizabeth were one and the same, and as he trudged through the thick snow in the cold weather, he realized that, just as he couldn't climb up any mountain trail in one quick burst, he wasn't going to win Elizabeth over in one easy move. It was going to take more than he thought he had to give.

He thought about the surprise party that he and Penny had planned for her on Friday, and knew that Elizabeth would feel uncomfortable with all that attention on her, but he was interested to see if she would be a little more at ease with him after last night.

Given that this was Elizabeth he was thinking about, he doubted it.

BRADLEY HAD TOO many things on his plate to be obsessing about Elizabeth, which meant that was exactly what
he was doing. But he couldn't help it. It was bad enough
that she was dodging his calls after they'd made love. It
had been a week and he'd had voicemails and texts but no
actual conversations with her. So he'd done the one thing
he really hadn't planned on: he'd shown up for a ski lesson.

He knew that Lindsey Collins was surprised to see him,
but this was the only explanation he had for being on the
bunny slope at noon with the former world number-one
skier at the Lars Usten Lodge.

"I thought that we were just making up the ski lesson
thing. Did you get my email?"

"Yes, but I thought I'd show up, anyway, just in case
Elizabeth asks. That way you don't have to lie to her."

Lame, Hunt. Really lame. Had he really stooped to this
sort of behavior? Obviously he had. The woman was making him nuts.

"Okay. But it's just that once someone reaches your
age—"

"Hey! I'm not that old," he said.

Lindsey laughed at him. She was very pretty with her
Nordic blond hair, brown eyes and slim, athletic build. He
knew that she was here because of a career-ending injury
that the entire world had witnessed in Sochi at the last
Winter Olympics.

"I know. Just testing your story in case Elizabeth stops
by."

"I'm very good at being convincing," he murmured.

And he was. He had gone over the last conversation
he'd had with Elizabeth more times than he'd ever admit,
and there was one thing she'd said that had resonated. She
didn't want their relationship to be a game.

Part of the reason he didn't normally ski was that it

seemed like the dumbest sport in the world—so dangerous. Strapping skis onto his feet and then plunging down a mountain seemed like a death wish.

He knew his argument would make no sense to anyone who knew him and how much he liked dangerous off-roading and snowmobiling into unchartered territory, but this was different. On a piece of machinery he felt more in control. As Lindsey beckoned him forward toward the assembled class, he slowly slid one foot forward and then the other.

He got into his place in line and the lesson went by quickly. If anyone had told him that he'd enjoy skiing he wouldn't have believed them, but to his surprise, he did enjoy it. A lot.

"Not bad for a beginner. If you come back I'm promoting you to my intermediate class," Lindsey said at the end of the lesson.

"Great. I have to be honest—I never got the appeal. But I think I'm starting to understand it."

"You're kidding, right? You sell the best equipment and have cutting-edge gear and you didn't get the appeal?" Lindsey said. "Skiing has always felt like freedom to me. When I'm on my skis…it's just me. There isn't anyone else who can tell me what to do. You know what I mean?"

"I do. I started out selling snowmobiles and off-road vehicles. They are the backbone of my business and I got into ski gear by accident. And now that I've tried skiing, I'm glad that I did."

"Probably because he had such a great teacher," Carter Shaw said, walking over to them with his snowboard held loosely in one hand. He slapped Bradley on the back and then did the bro-hug shoulder-bump thing.

"Definitely."

"Give it a rest, Shaw," Lindsey groused. "I already know what you think about me and skiing."

"Maybe you don't know as much as you think you do, Linds."

"Undoubtedly, but I do know when I'm getting a snow job," she said to Carter. "See you later, Bradley."

He nodded and both men watched her walk away. "What's up with you two?"

"Nothing," Carter said. "We've known each other forever and she just hasn't warmed up to me yet."

"It's hard to believe there is a woman alive who hasn't succumbed to your charm," Bradley said. His pal usually had at least three snow bunnies in his entourage. "Where's your posse?"

"On the slopes. I saw you down here and wanted to chat with you. I've had a talk with Pablo and he is scheduling a meeting for next week. I noticed that mural you're having done at your store. Do you think your graphics department could do some storyboards for me?"

"Maybe. What did you have in mind?" Bradley asked with interest. Hector and Tony could use some more work to keep them out of trouble, and getting them involved in the event would mean access to kids who might not participate otherwise.

"Just a couple of designs of the different venues and events I'm thinking of. I want to show how it would work at the lodge and in town."

"Okay. My guys are two teenagers, is that okay?" Bradley asked.

"Are they reliable? I don't want to mess this up, Brad, it's important to me," Carter said.

"I think so," he said. He hated being called "Brad," but he was a successful businessman and he wanted Carter to be a spokesman for Fresh Sno, so he let it slide this time.

Besides, Carter might seem like just an adrenaline junkie, but he knew the mogul snowboarder was much more than that.

"Okay. I'm going to bring my corporate sponsorship rep, too. If we can get the products I already endorse in on the ground level it will probably be good. I don't want to take away from your company, but they have a lot of money to invest," Carter said. "You cool with that?"

"I am. I want this to succeed, as well, and I can only do so much," Bradley said.

"Great. That's settled. What are you doing with those skis?"

Bradley groaned. "Learning to ski."

Carter looked at him. "Seriously, dude? Why?"

"Let's just say it involves a woman and leave it at that." Everything complicated in his life came back to Elizabeth.

Carter chuckled. "Say no more. I get how women are. They can make a man nuts and never even realize they're doing it."

He noticed that Carter glanced toward the ski lift where Lindsey stood talking to another instructor. How true those words were. Elizabeth was avoiding him, retreating once again to protect herself, and he had already decided he'd had enough of it. But he was pretty sure she wouldn't stand him up and they were going snowmobiling later. Still, he knew he was on a slippery slope and one wrong step could bring the entire mountain down on his head.

12

It was chilly as they left the resort and followed the trail that led away from the developed areas. Bradley had shown up for their date. It had been a week since she'd tried to avoid him and given up. There was something addictive about being friends with benefits. And she wanted to enjoy the benefits part a lot more.

A light snow had started to fall and Elizabeth let her worries about Lars and her job fall away. As the miles flew past and they got deeper into the wilderness, she even stopped worrying about her feelings for Bradley, which were still confusing her.

She'd wanted friends-with-benefits status, but her heart kept saying he was more. She woke up in the middle of the night and reached for the phone to call him, but now that they were lovers she hesitated. Calling him might make him think she wanted more. More than she'd agreed they'd have.

It hurt her to think that their friendship was suffering, but this afternoon none of that mattered. She'd always taken herself too seriously.

She'd been so lonely after he'd graduated and had decided to stop denying herself the chance to really live her life.

Bradley pulled to a stop in a copse of pine trees. She did the same. He got off his snowmobile and walked toward her.

"Are you okay? Did you lose the trail?" she asked, as he approached.

"No, to all of the above."

"What's the matter, then?" she asked, fumbling in her pocket for her phone. She had the ski patrol on speed dial.

"I need something from you, Lizzie," he said, putting his hands on her hips and lifting her from her snowmobile. He set her on her feet but didn't stop touching her and she knew what he wanted. The same thing she'd wanted since he'd left her bed.

She wrapped her arms around his neck and moved in closer so that their bodies were pressed lightly to each other. "What could that be?"

He lowered his head until their foreheads touched and he stared at her. His hazel gaze was so deep and intense that she was afraid he could see all the way to her soul. She didn't want that. Didn't want him to even get a hint that she was starting to think of him as more than her sex buddy.

She closed her eyes and kissed him. She needed to stop thinking. *Sex.* That was what this was about. And on this snowy afternoon, hidden between the pine trees, she needed to keep their focus on just that.

He held her face in his hands as he drew back, breaking the kiss. She opened her eyes and wished she hadn't. There was something in Bradley's expression that reminded her he wanted more from her than sex. She saw the longing there.

"Don't do this."

"Do what?"

"Don't start caring for me," she said.

"We're friends, Lizzie. I've always cared for you."

"Not like this. Please, Bradley, we said we'd be friends with benefits. You know what that means."

"I do," he said. "It's just that sometimes it feels like there could be more here."

She felt it, too. She wanted that, too. But she wasn't going to give in. If she ever admitted to Bradley that she cared for him, and not just as her friend…the consequences would be dire. He would continue wearing her down the way he had until they finally became lovers.

Or had this been her idea? She couldn't really remember anymore. She only knew that lovers and friends were separate for the two of them. And she needed them to stay that way.

Elizabeth leaned up on tiptoe and kissed him again, using her hands on his shoulders to balance herself. She wrapped her arms around him as she angled her head and took the kiss that she needed. He groaned but gave in to her. Opened his mouth, thrusting his tongue deep into her mouth and letting the passion that had always been between them take control. She unzipped his jacket and slipped her arms in between the heavy wool and his body. Then she burrowed closer to him, wanting this moment to never end. But as the snow fell a bit harder he pulled back. There was snow on his eyelashes and melting against his face. She looked at him, trapped between confusion and passion.

"Lizzie, don't look so sad. I'm not going anywhere," he whispered.

She nodded. But she knew he would. He had been pushing harder and harder for her to make a commitment to him. For this thing between them to be a real relationship instead of just sex. And eventually he'd tire of waiting and move on.

She turned away as she felt the sting of tears in the back of her eyes and she stumbled toward her snowmobile.

"Don't."

"I have to," she said. "I told you I don't want to lose your friendship."

"And you haven't."

"Not yet. But each time we have sex, I feel that you want more. I've caught you looking at me as if you want to say something but are afraid to. How long can we continue like this?"

"As long as we need to," he said. "I'm not going to give up without a fight."

"This isn't a war," she said. "Sex shouldn't be a war."

"No, it's not a war," he agreed. "And it's not a game, either, so there doesn't have to be a winner or a loser."

He turned away and she almost let him go. But she knew if she did, he'd never let his guard down again. He trusted her and she knew it was time she trusted him. But it wasn't that easy. She wasn't sure of herself in this intimate one-on-one setting. She'd rather be sparring with him.

"Bradley?"

He turned around and she threw caution to the winds as she ran to him and jumped into his arms. He caught her and held her closer. She kissed him when he opened his mouth.

They had done enough talking for today. "There's a cabin up ahead that I have the key to. Fancy a picnic by the fireplace?"

"Lead the way."

She got back on her snowmobile and followed the path to one of the remote Lars Usten Lodge cabins. It was a Swiss-chalet type building that had been set in this location to give privacy to celebrities. And today it was just what she and Bradley needed.

THEY PARKED THEIR snowmobiles in front of the cabin and she took the small bag she'd brought with her as she walked carefully up the snow-covered steps. She wanted to show Bradley he wasn't the only one who could be romantic.

She opened the cabin door, very aware of Bradley right behind her. The cabin had been decorated for fall with autumnal garlands around the fireplace and a pumpkin-pie-spiced candle on the entryway table.

"I'll get a fire started," Bradley said, brushing past her and going to the fireplace.

He took his coat off, tossing it onto one of the easy chairs in the main living room section of the cabin. The slim-fitting gray thermal shirt he wore was pulled taut against his broad shoulders and rippling chest, and she knew she shouldn't keep staring at him but couldn't help herself. He arched one eyebrow at her when he noticed.

And all she could do was smile and shrug. He was good-looking. It was hard to deny that fact or even to deny herself now that they were lovers.

"It's funny to see you without the phone in your hand constantly," he mused.

But, honestly, she wasn't thinking about work or phones. She was thinking about that shirt of his and how he looked without it. She wanted him. She realized it suddenly. She'd never really been a sexual person, preferring most of her encounters when they suited her schedule, but since the first time she'd had him in her bed, she'd wanted him again.

It had only been fear that kept her from calling him. But Bradley hadn't let her avoidance stop him from showing up for their date.

"This is our second date."

"What are you counting as our first?" he asked.

"The soup kitchen."

"That was a nice night. Not that you've treated me that well since."

"I'm sorry. This is harder for me than I would have guessed."

"If you were any other woman—"

"But I'm not."

"No, you're not."

He put his right forefinger in the center of her chest, right under the pendant she wore, and pushed against her. "You have been known to fib if you thought you could get away with it."

"When?" she asked, although she knew she'd done it before. But today her phone *was* off. Mainly because she'd been feeling put upon and she was entitled to some time off.

"When you told everyone in our college group that you were happy just being friends with me."

"That wasn't a fib. I was happy about it."

"And now? Do you still feel that way?"

"Now that we're lovers?" she clarified.

"Yes, now that I've held your silky, naked body next to mine, do you still want to tell everyone we're just friends?" he asked. He put his left hand on her waist, but didn't draw her closer. Instead, he just moved that one finger that was touching her in a caressing motion. She hitched in a breath, caught so off guard that she forgot what he'd asked her. Didn't even know where the conversation was going.

She couldn't think beyond the fact that this handsome, sexy man wanted her, even when she was difficult. It seemed as though Bradley was the first guy who could put up with all of her little quirks and still like her.

"When do you have to be back at the lodge?"

"Um…four o'clock," she said, but having him so close to her, touching her, distracted her.

He lowered his head, rubbing his face against hers as he whispered in her ear, "Good. So see you for dinner around six?"

"Okay."

"What's in this bag of yours?" he asked.

"Just a few things I thought might spice things up this afternoon," she said.

She handed him the book she'd brought with her. He skimmed it while she took off her coat and boots.

"This is an interesting book," he said, holding up the erotic novel. She felt the heat in her face as she noticed he'd opened it to one of the sections she'd marked by folding down the corner of the page.

"Is there bondage in here?" he asked, flipping through the pages.

There was a lot more than bondage, and while the book was spicy and pushed the limits of things she wasn't sure she wanted to experience in real life, she had always enjoyed reading about it until now. Now, she was thinking about Bradley knowing those very secret desires.

"Put that away. This might have been a bad idea."

"Not yet," he said as he used his long fingers to flip the pages of the book. Then he reached up and loosened his tie. "Maybe I'll bind your hands with my scarf...."

She walked over to take the book from him. "Why would you do that?"

He glanced down at the novel in his hands. "'Her hands were bound behind her back and he forced her to her knees, telling her to present herself to him—'"

"You don't have to read it out loud."

"Why not? Isn't that why you brought it along?" he asked. "I'm not much of a reader but I think I might really like this book. And I know you do. In fact, I'm taking it home with me."

"No, you're not," she said, trying to snatch it out of his hands, but he dropped it on the floor behind him. Then he wrapped his hands around her waist, swept her up into his arms and carried her over to the chair before sitting down and settling her on his lap. "What are you doing?"

"Taking control, just like the Master in the passage I skimmed. Do you like that?" he rasped.

She did like it. It was titillating having him all to herself, knowing he was thinking about sex. It really made her want him even more. Not that she had to try too hard to want Bradley. He was incredibly hot and there was something about the way he carried himself that always made her think about sex. Plus, it had been too long since he'd held her like this and she had missed it more than she wanted to admit.

She slowly undid the buttons of his shirt, but he put his hands over hers before she got the second one undone.

"Take your pants off," he said in a forceful voice. "Unless you want me to tie you up first."

She shook her head, feeling her long blond hair fall against her shoulders, and she wondered what he saw when he looked at her. He had told her that he saw a pretty girl with confidence, but she knew she was no Victoria's Secret model. Did she turn him on the way that just looking at him turned her on? "I like the thought of being tied up, but I'm not sure if that's just the fantasy. I mean, I don't know if I'd like it in real life."

"Have you tried it?" he asked seductively.

"No, I haven't. Have *you* ever done the bondage thing?"

He shook his head. "Nope, but I'm willing to push my boundaries for you, kinky Lizzie."

"I'm not kinky," she said, but she knew she could be with him. He made her want to try things she'd never experienced before. She felt a wave of desire course through her as she looked at the anticipation on his face.

Bradley made her feel safe with all parts of herself. Something she'd never allowed with any other man.

Elizabeth stood up and slowly removed her clothes, drawing it out the way she'd seen women do in sexy movies and heard about in the books she read late at night. She wanted him to see her body revealed inch by inch and watch the way her nakedness affected him.

"Now you undo your pants. I want to see that you want me," she said.

He groaned and unbuttoned his pants, then reached for his scarf and put it next to him. "In case I need it to keep you in line," he said with a wink.

He slowly unzipped his pants, pushing his hand into the opening. She bit her lower lip as she watched him lift his cock out. It was thick and hard. With his free hand he beckoned her closer to him.

As he reclined on the chair next to the fireplace with his shirt partially unbuttoned, she could see his taut muscular chest lightly dusted with hair. She took a step closer. He reached for her, but she kept just out of arm's length. His erection grew under her gaze and she moved closer, reaching down to touch the hard length of it. He was smooth and hot, and she wrapped her hand around him.

A shot of lust and excitement went through her, and as she looked at his face she realized how much she truly cared for Bradley. She didn't want it to be anything more than friendship, but she knew that he was slowly inching his way into her heart.

She gripped him and stroked him up and down. At first, she just watched her hand moving on him, but then a low moan escaped his lips, and she glanced up to look at his face as he closed his eyes and tipped his head back.

The first time they made love it had been so intense for her that she hadn't had a chance to see his reactions or to really enjoy his body. This time she was determined to do just that.

She wanted to see how much she affected him. It was only fair, since she'd been fantasizing about him for far too long. She lowered her head and teased him by circling the head of his cock with her tongue, swiping it over the head and then slowly opening her mouth and taking him inside. She sucked while swirling her tongue around him.

His hands came to her head, his fingers tangling in her hair, and he drew it forward, rubbing the long strands between his fingers. She shifted in his arms, letting his palms cup the back of her head. His hands in her hair tightened as his hips lifted and she tasted the saltiness of his essence.

She was excited to have him in her mouth. To taste his passion. He pulled at her head and she sucked harder as she let him pull her off of him. She looked up at him and he said her name on a desperate groan before he lifted her off her feet and pulled her over his lap. Heady with desire, she braced her hands on the wall and leaned down to kiss him.

She bit down on his lower lip, sucking it into her mouth and fondling it with her tongue. He surrounded her waist with his hands and lifted her off her feet, pulling her up over him. She didn't let go of his cock, and felt his hips lifting toward her as she settled over him. He pushed her shirt up and she loved the feel of his big, warm hands stroking down her back to her butt as he cupped her and drew her closer to him.

Bradley pushed her sweater up but it had two tiny pearl buttons at the neck that kept him from getting it off her. He struggled for a second before giving up and bringing his mouth to her nipple under her camisole. She felt a drop of moisture at the tip of his erection and smoothed her finger over it, rubbing it around the tip and then enclosing his length in her hand again. She wished she could take him in her mouth again.

He fondled her other nipple with one hand, rolling it between his thumb and his forefinger as his other hand caressed her thigh, moving up and down under the skirt from her buttocks to the back of her knee.

Then she felt him caressing his way up the inside of her thighs and his finger brushed over the center of her femininity. She spread her legs a little wider as he found the very spot where she ached for his touch. Shifting on top of him, she rubbed his cock against her center and teased them both with the hint of what was to come, but then tried to pull back.

Having none of that, he lifted his head as he grabbed her waist and drew her forward on him until his cock was poised at her entrance and she slowly lowered herself onto his length.

Elizabeth impaled herself on him, taking him as deeply as she could. She pushed her fingers into his hair and held his head while she looked into his eyes and moved up and down. His hands cupped her butt and urged her to move faster, but she tried to keep the pace slower so that this could last longer. She didn't want it to end too quickly.

She found his mouth with hers. His tongue thrust deep into her mouth and she forgot that she wanted this to last forever. He tasted so good, felt so good everywhere he touched her, and she wanted more. Needed more from him. He sucked her tongue deeper into his mouth and his hands moved, one finger sliding between her butt cheeks and making her clench with excitement as he pumped up into her with even quicker movements.

She started to move faster, rising and falling on him, tearing her mouth from his and looking down at him. His cheeks were red and flushed, his lips swollen and wet from her kisses, and his eyes were electric as he watched her.

Everything in her body was reaching and striving toward orgasm. She wanted to hold it off, to tell herself that this was like any other sexual encounter that she'd ever had, but this was Bradley and there was no denying him.

Nor could she deny how foolish she'd been. All this time she'd been trying to keep her distance from him by playing games and acting out fantasies, but as their eyes met and held, she knew what was happening between them was so much more than hot, mindless sex.

He tangled his hands in her hair and drew her head down to his, whispering dark sexy words in her ear. Telling her how good she felt and how much he wanted her in explicit terms. And then everything coalesced. She felt her orgasm rip through her as he suckled on her neck. He pounded into her two more times before she felt him spill himself inside of her.

She kept riding him, enjoying every thrust of his body until, exhausted, she collapsed against his chest. He wrapped his arms around her back and held her loosely to him as she closed her eyes and breathed him in.

She felt him all around her, surrounding all of her senses, and though she knew that it wasn't smart, she realized she was starting to fall for him. That, somehow, in spite of all of her careful planning and trying to be safe, he'd slipped past her guard and found his way into her heart.

13

Elizabeth's assistant put a pop-up meeting on her calendar for 6:00 p.m. and she had to admit she was a little disappointed that she'd have to cancel her dinner date with Bradley. But another part of her was relieved. She'd felt as if she'd just ripped a bandage off of her entire body and had to go about her day with newly exposed skin.

Most people didn't treat her any differently but she felt different. Sex today with Bradley had been more than just physical intimacy and she had to admit it.

She checked her makeup in the mirror before heading down to the conference area. She hoped it wasn't another hiccup with Thanksgiving. But as she walked through the lodge to the convention area, it struck her that the large hallways looked too big and sparse at this time of day when they didn't have any convention events going on. But the rustic holiday decorations were nice. She made a few mental notes to talk to the decorating manager to move some of the decor around.

She arrived at the long, narrow conference room with its beautiful stone columns and the sliding glass doors that opened to the patio area where a warm blaze had been lit in the fire pit. A group of chairs was gathered around it, and she saw that every seat was occupied. A table of hors d'oeuvres was set up and there was a line at the bar at the end of the room.

"Surprise!"

Startled, she froze on the spot as twenty of her friends from college and members of the board of directors, along with Lars, stood there with large grins on their faces. They all came forward and she struggled to switch gears as she took in the banner on the wall that read: Way to Go, Elizabeth!

Penny, who was her best girlfriend, was the first one to congratulate her. "I hope you don't mind all this, but you've worked so hard and I didn't want the opportunity to celebrate to pass us by."

"I don't mind at all. I can't believe everyone came for this," she said.

Penny laughed kindly at her. "Don't be like that. Everyone has always liked you. Plus, they are excited to see you finally reach your goal."

"Really?" she asked, remembering what Bradley had said, and she mentally shook herself. "I mean, of course they are."

Penny laughed and hugged her close. "I'm so happy for you."

She hugged her friend back. Penny wore her long blond hair in an updo that showed off her heart-shaped face. "Thanks for arranging all this, hon. It means a lot."

"I was happy to do it. I'm going to go get you a drink— want a caramel-apple martini?" she asked. "That is the drink we decided we'd have in November, isn't it?"

"I'd love one," Elizabeth said.

Since she and Penny were both extremely busy with their jobs, they didn't get to socialize much. But they shared a secret Pinterest board where they posted pictures of hot guys, drinks they wanted to try and dresses that they'd never be able to wear because they lived in the real world, and frankly, there wasn't much chance to wear haute couture.

"Good, but before you mingle, I got you a little something," Penny said, linking their arms and leading her to a table that had a pile of presents on it. Penny picked up a large rectangular box and handed it to her.

"Is it present time?" Hugh asked as he came over. He was part of their college group of friends. "I can't wait for you to see what I got you."

"Not yet. She has to open this first because we decided that a girl can't have a party without a new frock, right?"

Elizabeth nodded.

"Go get changed and when you come back you can mingle."

But making a getaway was harder than Penny made it seem. Everyone wanted to chat with her and she found herself putting the box down as she talked to Hugh and Ally, who'd gotten married during their senior year in college and now ran a successful bed-and-breakfast in Galveston, Texas.

They handed her a gift and she was embarrassed to have all the attention of her friends on her, but it was wonderful to see them. They hadn't all gotten together in the last three years, as everyone was much busier now.

"Who knew turning thirty was going make us all so busy," Hugh said.

"Not me," Elizabeth admitted.

She was surrounded by all the people who'd known her when she first started her career. All the kids who'd been as young and unsure as she'd been. A group of college kids who'd had goals and hopes and dreams, and as she talked to everyone, she realized how impressed she was by her friends.

"Congratulations again," Lars said, coming up to her and giving her a handshake.

"Thank you."

"Pablo is really pleased with the way you are handling Carter and the charity event."

"Thank you. To be honest, I was surprised when he showed up at the meeting. I thought maybe you didn't trust me."

"That's not the case. The board is part of the community, too. Everyone has to play their part."

Pablo came over to congratulate her as well, and they discussed Carter's event before she drifted off to mingle with others in the room.

She finished the drink that Penny had brought her and wandered over to the doors in the back of the conference room that led out to the patio. She searched the room again, looking for the one person she'd expected to see but didn't.

Where was Bradley? Was he giving her space? And then, to her surprise and delight, she saw him as he walked in from the patio. He paused, searching the room for her, and she drank him in—his thick brown hair, artfully styled, the slim-fitting gray suit with a thin black tie. He looked like a male fantasy come to life. An unattainable heartthrob who belonged on her Pinterest board instead of in this room

"Hello, Lizzie," he said, strolling over to her.

Her pulse leapt wildly in her throat. "Why are you late to my party?" she asked.

"Because I wanted to make sure you had a chance to talk to everyone before I claimed all of your attention."

"Awfully big ego you have there," she said.

He placed his hands on her shoulders, planting a soft kiss in her hair.

"Well earned, I'd say. I feel as though I have a right to *all* of your attention."

ELIZABETH HAD LOOKED breathtaking as she moved through the crowd of their friends. He'd heard laughing and talking and had stood in the corner watching her, looking for some sign that he couldn't even define.

Part of it had been pure jealousy.

Of course, he'd invited her to dinner to make sure she had the night off and could enjoy the party. But now he realized he wanted their dinner date to have been real. He wanted her all to himself. That wasn't going to happen.

At least, not tonight.

"You do have my attention now," she said, breaking into his thoughts.

"About damned time," he muttered.

"You're right," she said. "It is about time. Today has felt…different. I really enjoyed it."

He wanted to smile at the new confidence he saw in her eyes. And it wasn't that she'd been shy or unsure before—it was just that there was something more to her at this moment.

"I can't believe Penny did all this," Elizabeth said. "She's so sneaky. How did she know about Lindsey and my other friends from the lodge?"

"I helped a little bit and got Lindsey's help," he confessed.

"So the ski lessons were just a cover?" she asked.

"Yes, and an excuse to come out here and try to see you again. You were giving me the cold shoulder for a while, if you recall."

"Smart man. I always knew that you weren't just getting by on your looks," she teased.

"You think I could trade on my looks?"

He realized he wanted her to be impressed by him. Because even though he never dwelled on it, he was just as shackled by his past as she was by hers. He'd clawed out the life he wanted, but there was always someone who seemed to have it easier.

He didn't want another person's life but he wanted Elizabeth to think he was the best man in the room.

Hell, where'd that come from?

He didn't need that kind of approval. He carried his confidence like a cloak around himself. It was the one thing he'd always been able to afford—belief in himself. But Elizabeth was different and she always had been.

"Why are you watching me like that?" she asked.

"Just thinking how long it's been since I kissed you," he said, realizing that he was putting up a barrier between them and hoped she didn't figure that out. He'd been pushing her to expose herself but he was afraid to let her see the real man.

"How long *has* it been?" she murmured, tipping her head to the side and giving him a flirty smile that made his lie feel real.

He did want to feel her in his arms again. Have her mouth under his and her sexy, curvy body pressed against him. He reached for her but she stepped back, shaking her head.

"Not now."

He quirked a brow. "What do you mean?"

"When you touch me, I forget all the sensible things," she said. "I can't do that right now. I've had a martini and I still have to file my evening reports so I can't afford to let anything affect me."

He took a step closer and she stood her ground, putting her hand up to keep him from coming nearer. He was surrounded by her touch and the scent of her perfume, and he didn't have to fake the fact that it took all of his self-control not to toss her over his shoulder and carry her from the room caveman style.

As a matter of fact, that would probably be the best way of handling her. No more talking or thinking about anything but the two of them in bed. When they were wrapped in each other's arms, he didn't have to think or feel jealous or wonder if he'd ever really figure her out. Physical need was easy to read on her face and in her body.

"I don't know what you're thinking, but forget it," she warned in a low tone. "Our friends are all staring at us."

"Let them stare," he said, bringing his hand up to the one she had on his chest and wrapping his fingers around her wrist. He liked holding onto her; it gave him the illusion of control.

"Bradley! All of our friends are here and—"

"I know. But a part of me doesn't care. I'm tired of playing by all these rules. Every time I feel like we've figured everything out, I find out there is still something else we have to deal with. I sort of wish we'd never said we'd be friends with benefits. I wouldn't mind a normal relationship."

Her face fell and he knew he should have thought before he spoke. But he was on edge and hadn't really noticed until this moment. Though the way he'd been watching her since she got here should have been a huge red flag.

"So *just sex* isn't working for you anymore?" she asked, tugging at her hand and trying to pull away, but he refused to let her go.

"I'd be lying if I said sex wasn't a big part of it," he said. "But you know I want more than that from you. If I'd just been looking for an easy lay, I would have found someone else a long time ago."

"Why haven't you?" she asked hoarsely.

He looked at her. That shimmering blond hair of hers, falling over her shoulders, made her look like every image of a princess he'd had as a boy. But he wasn't about to tell her that she was the only woman he'd wanted for years. That the others he'd dated were just stand-ins for the one lover he couldn't have.

Damn. He felt bad for the women he'd dated in the past, but the reality was that he had a chance at something real with Elizabeth and he wasn't going to let her slip away.

"They weren't you," he said, touching her cheek before he turned on his heel and walked away.

ELIZABETH TRIED TO pretend that Bradley's words hadn't affected her, but she knew they had. How could he say something like that and then leave? She tried to follow him, but Penny was right next to her linking their arms together.

"Let him go."

"But—"

"No, he needs space. I'm not sure what's going on between the two of you, but I have to say that snowmobiling together must have been pretty good."

"It went well. I'm sorry I haven't called," Elizabeth said. "I've been busy."

As she said that, though, she realized she'd been busy with Bradley, not with her job. Of course, her work was still demanding, but it had been Bradley consuming most of her thoughts since he'd come back to town. "Dammit, I'm obsessed with him and I never thought I'd be."

Penny laughed in that kind way of hers. "Are you falling for him?"

Was she? She'd been trying so very hard to not let her

emotions become entangled with him, even if this afternoon, when they'd been at the cabin, she'd realized she was losing that fight. But she wasn't ready to admit it. Not even to her best friend.

"No. I don't know," Elizabeth said, as they found two seats at the fire pit. Most of their friends had broken into groups to either go for a sleigh ride or to chat among themselves.

"I always wondered what would happen if you two ever decided to be more than friends."

"Do you know what he just said to me?" Elizabeth asked.

"You know I don't," Penny said.

"That all the other women he dated hadn't been me. What does that mean, Penn? He's confusing me."

Penny looked at her, and for once her best friend seemed at a loss for words. "Love is complicated."

"I don't love him," she said. She didn't. She couldn't. She wasn't looking for love.

"Okay. Well, what do you feel? It's obvious that more is going on here than you had with Ken. And I haven't seen you this…well, not yourself ever before." Penny's eyes filled with worry. "You haven't called me, but more than that, you haven't checked your phone all evening. And when you think I'm not paying attention, you keep looking at Bradley. If it's not love, then what is it that you feel for him?"

Sighing, Elizabeth sank down farther into her chair. "Honestly? I don't know."

"It's okay not to know. But don't lie to yourself and say that nothing has changed," Penny said. "I've been doing that for years with the men I've been involved with, and I can't face it anymore."

Elizabeth realized for the first time that her friend looked really tired. "What's going on, Penn?"

"I've been having an affair with my boss and just found out that he's married."

Her heart broke for Penny. She hugged her friend close. "What are you going to do?"

"I don't know. I need to get away but really have no ideas."

"Why don't you come here?" Elizabeth asked suddenly.

Penny hesitated for just a second before she glanced out at the Wasatch Back.

"We have spa treatments and lots of places for you to relax and think. In fact, I can have my assistant book you one of our guest cottages. They're semiprivate and you'd love it." She smiled excitedly. "Plus, I'm here."

The truth was, she really missed having her closest girlfriend around. Her life felt as though it was a big, hot mess and she had no idea what to do about it. It wasn't as if she wanted Penny to tell her *what* to do, she just wanted to talk about it and not feel judged.

"Well, I do hate that we never get to see each other...."

"Then you'll come?"

"Well, I—" Penny bit her lip and Elizabeth could see the wheels turning in her head. Finally, she nodded. "Sure... why not? I suppose I could use a change of scenery."

"Yay!" Elizabeth reached over and squeezed her friend's hand. "And a fresh start is exactly what you need. Bradley is making me sort of let go of my past and look at the future with different eyes. I think you should do it, too."

"That could be because you got laid," Penny said with a wink.

"Hey! I never said we slept together." Elizabeth wasn't about to deny it, but she felt herself blushing as she glanced over at her friend.

"You didn't have to. I know you both well enough to see that the dynamic between you two has changed."

"And you're sure it's sex?" Elizabeth asked.

"Well, you said it wasn't love, so what else would it be?" Penny retorted in a no-nonsense tone that cut straight to the heart of the matter.

"Fair point," Elizabeth said.

It was kind of ironic that she thought it was better to be in a sexual relationship than in a love match. Well, not better, exactly, but safer. Sex was okay and expected. They were young and had needs that could be met by each other. But the emotional part was so much more complicated. It was easier to let him stay the night than to let him into her heart.

14

ELIZABETH'S WEEK HAD been tough. She hadn't seen Bradley since the night of the party. Penny had come back to her place and they'd stayed up all night talking. Learning that her boss was married had really thrown her friend. Elizabeth had sympathized and wanted to go find the guy and kick him where it counted.

Maybe the jerk felt safe treating Penny the way he had because she seemed like a sex kitten. The kind of girl who didn't let her feelings get involved. But over the years, Elizabeth had come to realize that it was all just an act. In reality, Penny cared too much for everyone and was easily hurt by those who saw her only as another pretty face.

Geez, who knew that relationships could be so hard?

At first Elizabeth had thought she was avoiding Bradley—something that she'd promised herself she was done with, but then she realized he was avoiding her.

He'd skipped the charity committee meeting for Carter's proposed charity event. Then, when she'd shown up at the homeless kitchen to work a shift on Wednesday, he'd slipped out after barely nodding hello to her. On top of all that, when she'd noticed his car in the lodge parking lot and tried to find him...well, she hadn't been able to.

Sighing, she forced herself to focus on work. It was the only thing right now that kept her sane.

Lars was in the boardroom when she got there, talking with a group of the other directors. She hung back when it was clear they hadn't seen her. Though their conversation was quiet she could hear what he was saying.

"We only promoted her because of my health. She's doing a good job, but I'm not really sure she's ready for it."

Elizabeth backed out of the boardroom. Her hands were shaking and she felt almost sick to her stomach. All her hard work hadn't gotten her the job? She wanted to believe she'd somehow misunderstood, but deep down feared she hadn't. As she aimlessly started walking down the hall to the big window that overlooked the Wasatch Range, a little bit of anger started flowing through her. She felt betrayed by Lars. Although she'd thought that her boss believed in her, now she knew he'd just been using her.

Elizabeth thought of the uncertainty that was going on with Bradley. How she'd been avoiding calling him because she didn't know what to do next in their complicated friends-plus thing. Yet she'd always been reassured by the fact that no matter what happened between the two of them, she would always have her job to fall back on. Now she realized that the safety she'd thought she had in her career was just an illusion.

"Ms. Anders? Are you okay?"

Elizabeth glanced over her shoulder to see one of the custodial staff standing a few feet away. She had on the uniform that Elizabeth had approved and she smiled at the other woman.

"I'm fine. Thanks for asking."

Then the second part of what she heard sunk in. Lars's health was failing? She'd had no clue. Her anger ebbed as she worried about her boss. Perhaps they'd had to promote her sooner than they had planned because of his health.

She turned away from the scenic mountains and walked back to the boardroom. She couldn't reveal what she'd overheard and she had to be very sure that she had her game face on. But she didn't feel as though she could pull it off.

She needed Bradley, but her old best friend wasn't there anymore. After changing the dynamic between them, they were both still trying to figure out what they wanted, hopefully without hurting each other in the process.

But was that even possible?

Had she made a massive mistake by making him her lover? The sex was incredible—better than even her fantasies had promised—but she needed her friend.

Especially now.

Yet, even as she picked up the phone and began to message him, she realized she had no idea what to say. In the old days she would have texted him a frowning face and been done with it. But now she didn't feel comfortable reaching out. The closer they got physically, the harder it was for her to reach out to him emotionally.

"There you are, Elizabeth. The meeting is about to start," Lars said, beckoning her into the boardroom.

Her hand trembled as she quickly texted I miss my friend to Bradley. "Sorry about that...had to finish up a text message."

"No problem," Lars told her.

She put her phone away as the meeting got started. Then, squaring her shoulders, she decided she'd carry on as if she hadn't heard why she was appointed general manager. Moreover, she'd go above and beyond from this point forward to make sure that they knew they'd put the right person in the position.

"Elizabeth, this is my nephew, Trey McAvoy. He's going to be shadowing you over the holiday season," Lars said, introducing her to the one person in the room she didn't know.

That sinking feeling was back in the pit of her stomach as she shook Trey's hand. The tall, athletic young man seemed nice enough, but as she sat there listening to the general direction of the meeting, she couldn't understand why he'd been brought in.

When they broke for coffee, Trey came over to her. "Sorry about the way Lars introduced us. I think he is still not too happy with all of the board's decisions."

"It's fine," she said cordially. "So, if you don't mind me asking, what are you doing here?"

"I've been running the Lars Usten Lodge and Spa in Antigua, but the board thought I could use some more training and brought me back here to shadow you."

"Oh," Elizabeth said. She wasn't sure why they had done that, given the fact that they had only promoted her because of Lars's health.

"You're known throughout the company as a model of efficiency and I think they want me to pick up some tips."

"Are you sure they don't want you back here?" she asked.

"Even if they did, I'd decline. I like warmer weather," he said with a laugh.

I MISS MY FRIEND.

Bradley knew immediately what Elizabeth meant because he did, too. He had never truly guessed at how much their roles would change once they became lovers.

Exhaling slowly, he put his phone away and stared out at the flurry of activity surrounding him. He was in the middle of a photo shoot with Carter Shaw wearing the Fresh Sno logo snowsuit, and so far it was going well.

Hector and Tony's mural was the backdrop and in Bradley's opinion gave Fresh Sno a unique look for the shoot. The guys had been excited to do some storyboards for Carter, which the snowboarder really liked. To Bradley it seemed like all the pieces of the charity event were coming together.

"I love this," Tia said. "Carter is perfect for our brand and our image. You did a good job, boss man."

"Thanks, Tia, I live for your praise," he drawled.

"Yeah, right. Hey, Hector and Tony are back. They finished up the storyboards and want to show them to you." She looked over at him. "I'll tell them you'll be there in... thirty?"

"Yeah, that will be good. Since this is our first time using Carter, I want to make sure everything is right."

"I get it. Fresh Sno is your baby."

She walked away and her words lingered. The company *was* his baby. The one thing that he had made for himself. And, in a way, that was what he'd thought he'd do with Elizabeth, find a way to make her his. But the reality was that he hadn't counted on how vulnerable it made him feel. He was unsure of her and of what their relationship would become, and that scared him.

And he hadn't been scared in a really long time. He didn't like it any more now than he had back then.

While the photographer and art director moved Carter around for the photo shoot, Bradley took his phone back out and thought of that message from Elizabeth. Something was up with her.

I miss my friend, too. He texted her back with a selfie of himself frowning.

She texted back a smiling face and he felt the knot of

tension in his chest begin to relax. Maybe they were both unsure of how to handle things now that they were lovers, but who they'd always been was still there beneath the surface.

And neither of them was willing to let that go. He stepped out back to look at the storyboards the boys had done and realized how truly talented they both were. "Good job, guys. Carter loves the mural you did and I'm glad we decided to use it as a backdrop."

They'd captured the Wasatch Range perfectly, the cold, pristine beauty of the snowcapped mountains with the sun slicing through the clouds. The mural was raw and rough, but so were the mountains in winter.

"Thanks, Bradley," Hector said.

"For what?"

The teen looked him straight in the eye as he replied, "For treating us like family."

"No thanks necessary." Grinning broadly, he clapped Hector on the back. "I think it was my lucky day when you decided to graffiti my walls."

"Not many people would say that," Tony said. "But you did us a solid and I'm grateful."

He watched the teens go and clean up their paints, and he thought of how often a missed opportunity could change a person's life. And he was glad, despite the fact that things were still unsettled between him and Elizabeth, that he hadn't missed the opportunity to become more than just friends with her.

A PART OF HER worried she might be obsessing a little too much about Bradley. She glanced around the boardroom trying to bring her focus back to her job. She tried to stop watching Lars to see if she could detect his health issue. She just wanted to make sure he was okay. But he acted normally at their regular meetings and she saw him out on the slopes taking a run with Lindsey.

The week of Thanksgiving started out slowly. They tested out the menu that Chef Cruzel planned to serve in the restaurant and a lot of good comments were flowing in. Carter Shaw and his mother arrived to take over one of the residences on their property, and they wasted no time inviting her and all the board members out for a cocktail party.

She'd debated skipping it. She had a lot of work to do and her mom was driving to Utah from Texas, which worried Elizabeth a little bit. But Bradley had called and asked her to be his date.

And she'd given in because, in her heart of hearts, it was what she really wanted to do.

So here she was, holding a martini as she made small talk with Pablo and Bradley.

"I think I speak for most of Park City resort owners when I say that Carter has certainly matured," Pablo said.

"And I'd wager he'd say you've relaxed," Bradley replied. "He thinks that the attitudes of you folks on the mountain are a little severe."

"He might have a point, but we know how to change with the times, don't we, Elizabeth?" the older gentleman asked.

"I've been trying to," she admitted, taking a sip of her drink.

"That's probably why you promoted her," Bradley said. "Get some fresh young blood in there."

She hadn't had a chance to talk to Bradley about what she'd overheard. The holidays were busy for both of them, and frankly, they couldn't have picked a worse time to start hooking up. She knew it and she was beginning to suspect Bradley did, as well.

"Well, not just me," she said, forcing her mind back to business. "Lars's nephew Trey is also young and full of ideas."

"He certainly is full of praise for you," Pablo remarked with a smile. "Every day I get a little more confident that the board made the right decision in promoting you."

"Thank you," she said, feeling a rush of conflicting emotions at his comments.

"You're very welcome. Speak of the devil, I see Trey now. Will you two excuse me?"

She nodded and Bradley cupped her elbow, leading her away from the crowd to a private little corner. He took her breath away when he dressed up. She was so used to seeing him ready for the outdoors and anything that nature threw at him. But tonight she was reminded of why he'd been starring in her fantasies for so long.

"What was that about?"

"I overheard something I don't think I was meant to," she said.

"About Trey. Did they bring him here to take your place? If so, they can find someone else to rent their skis from," Bradley said darkly.

She hugged him to her. "My hero. Thanks, but that's not necessary. It was about Lars's health. I don't know what is wrong with him, but the board wanted him to step down from the day-to-day running of the resort."

"Is he okay?"

"I really don't know," she said. "I've been keeping a close eye on him, but I don't think me saying I overheard a conversation is going to be the right segue. A lot of people are pretty determined to keep their health status private. Myself included."

To be honest, it felt a bit as if everything in her life was spinning slowly out of control.

He frowned. "That's a lot to take in. Are you okay? I wish I'd called you that day instead of sending you a selfie."

"It's fine."

"I think you needed me. I should have—"

"Like I said, it's fine. We're not a couple."

He pushed her back into the corner and brought his mouth down hard on hers, kissing her with the pent-up passion and emotion that she didn't want to acknowledge.

"We're more than that, whether you admit to yourself or not."

He walked away, leaving her aching for more, but she could only watch him leave. She knew she should go after him, but a part of her—the scared part—didn't want to. It would be safer to simply let him go.

15

BRADLEY LEFT THE PARTY at the Lodge and drove back to Park City and his condo. When he got there he realized how empty it was as he walked into the hallway. He wanted more from his life.

He'd worked hard in his twenties so that he'd finally be ready to settle down in his thirties and it hurt that the one woman he wanted was only interested in him for sex.

He rubbed the back of his neck and realized that he'd opened a can of worms tonight that he hadn't intended to. Was she afraid of getting hurt again—as she had been with Ken? Or maybe she didn't want more with him because of who he was.

She'd seen him flirting and playing the field. Had that influenced her against him, even though the last few weeks he'd been very careful to show her he was more than that?

But still…the million-dollar question was why she'd never let herself fall in love. He knew he'd never ask her. Not because he didn't think she'd answer him—he knew she would—but because he didn't want to reveal that he was afraid of being hurt emotionally. His phone buzzed, and when he glanced down at the screen he saw it was a text from Elizabeth.

He went into his home office and looked around the room, quietly acknowledging to himself that he was happy for his success and he had things now that, as a boy, he'd never have dreamed possible, including this house, the one in Boulder, a townhouse in London, and a ski lodge in Vermont.

He'd been thinking for years that someday he'd slow down and start a family, but now that he had the chance with her, he wasn't sure that was what he really wanted. He'd ridden Elizabeth hard to confront her own shortcomings, but now he hated doing the same thing for himself.

He dialed her number and truly hoped she didn't pick up the phone. What would he say? He was going to have see her tomorrow, and was going to have to figure out a game plan by then, but tonight he was still confused.

"Go for awesome," she said as she answered the phone.

He cracked up, and all the fears that had been roiling around in the pit of his stomach dissipated. "Hello, awesome. You wanted me to call?"

"I did. I figured out something after you left the party."

"What'd you realize?" he asked. Talking to her reminded him of how much he adored her and wanted her in his life.

At any cost.

"You've been scarce this last week. If I didn't know better I'd say—"

"I was scared," he finished for her. "But you *do* know better. Plus I knew you'd be busy at the lodge."

"I was, but not too busy for you. What's up? Have you changed your mind?"

He leaned back in his chair, propping his feet up on his desk. "Not at all. Just needed some perspective. I've waited a long time for you, you know?"

He could hear her quick intake of breath, and then there

was a long pause. Apparently, she hadn't been expecting him to fess up to that.

"Did I measure up to the fantasy of what you thought I'd be?" she asked softly.

Her insight made him uncomfortable. He had always thought that she'd be a certain way when they got together but reality had been so much more than he'd expected. And he understood now that that was part of what had thrown him off his game.

"You are more, Lizzie. So much more…and I haven't been sure that I'm enough for you. You have it all—a successful career, a good family—and you deserve a man who can be your equal in those things."

"You are that," she said. "Why don't you think you are?"

"My parents never had a relationship…I flit from one woman to the next. I've always thought it was because I was waiting for you, but what if I'm wrong? What if I can't give you what you need?"

She sighed heavily. "I'm a hot mess and you know it. Besides, who's to say either of us isn't worthy of the other. I think we both sort of anticipated that we'd have sex and everything would sort itself out. I know I never guessed that it would change the way I thought about you."

"Has it?"

"You must know it has," she said.

ELIZABETH WAS TIRED of running from what she felt, and now, lying in her bed, it was easy to see the dreams she'd built for her future had been informed by the life she was living and by her perception of everyone around her. She felt safest talking to Bradley late at night and in her bedroom alone.

Deep down, she knew that had to say something about her, but she wasn't going to look too closely at it.

At least, not tonight.

"I don't know anything about what you really think," he said. "You play your cards very close to the chest."

"You've got a good poker face, as well."

"So we both don't like to give much away. Where does that leave us?"

She rolled to her side and stared out her window. She'd left the blinds open so she could see the full moon as it shone down on the glistening snow. And she wanted to be standing fully exposed in that light with Bradley. But being that exposed…she was afraid, but at the same time understood they couldn't go any further in a relationship unless they both stopped hiding.

"I am afraid of you," she admitted.

"Why? I wouldn't hurt you."

He wouldn't intentionally hurt her; she knew that to be true. But there was that gap between who he was and who she wanted him to be, and in between, that was where she could be hurt. "I know that. But you and I both have thought about this for a long time and I anticipated…that we'd be sort of our usual friendly selves and that life would be—"

"Some sort of sexual fantasy where we stayed good friends but rocked each other's worlds at night."

"If you're going to interrupt me and be sarcastic, then I'm not going to talk to you. I thought you wanted me to be honest."

"I do. I'm sorry," he said. "Let's face it—I have no idea what you want from me. I only have my ideal of what a good relationship should be. My mom never dated."

She wondered how often he'd played the poor-little-boy-from-the-broken-home card. She knew that there was an element of truth to what he'd said, so she wasn't trying to ignore him, but she also knew that he was much stronger than he'd just portrayed himself.

"That excuse might fly if I didn't know you. But you are very well adjusted from your childhood, and it's clear that you do know how a couple should act. I think you're just pushing me for more than we agreed to—why is that?"

He said nothing and the line was silent for so long that she wondered if he'd hung up. But then she heard him sigh.

"You're right. I don't want to lose you."

His words cut to the very heart of what she herself had been thinking. "It's complicated."

She didn't know what to do. She wanted to keep Bradley in her life but work, her family and her expectations for the future were all tied together and now tied to him. "I just wish this was simpler."

"Are we making it complicated?" he asked.

"Maybe we are. Every time I try to think of breaking this off, I can't do it."

"Me, either," he said gruffly. "We can figure this out, Lizzie. We're both smart and we want to make it work. If that's what you still want."

She had no idea what she truly wanted and could only focus on the fact that even if she didn't want to admit it, she needed Bradley in her life. He was the one person who saw her with all her flaws and accepted her regardless. And that was the reason she was so afraid. He already saw her at her most vulnerable, and she didn't want him to see how much she needed him. At least, not until she was sure he needed her, too.

"Lizzie?"

"Hmm?"

"We both want this to work, right?"

Did she? The ball was in her court now. Could she have

her friend, her sexual fantasies and a normal relationship with Bradley?

"I have no idea what we're going to have to do to make it work, but I don't like the fact that I pushed you away tonight."

"Me, either," he said. "I had to step away to get some breathing room. I know that I haven't made it easy for you, but I care about you, Lizzie. I'm not going to run anymore…even though my first instinct was to do that after what you said at the party."

His words resonated through her and something in her heart made her feel as if she was really and truly starting to fall in love with him. He dominated her thoughts, and tonight, when he'd stormed off, she'd wanted to forget about her job and just go after him.

Still, she had to be careful not to let Bradley take over her life. She had to keep limits in place even though she couldn't let him go.

"I can't think of you running from anything or anyone," she said softly.

"Well, you are different, something that I think I've been reluctant to admit for a long time, but there is no use denying it now. You matter to me, and I'm not going to give up on you."

She held her breath and knew that whatever she said next would make or break the two of them as a couple. She had over a decade of friendship with him that said otherwise. Sure he'd pulled back, but then again, hadn't she? Both of them were too used to being in control and she was realizing that emotions left her feeling like a mess. It had to be the same for him.

"I've known you for ten years, Bradley, and you have always been there for me when I needed you. And I prom-

ise to always be there for you, too. At least as best friends."
She took a deep breath. "As for the rest…"

Nothing but silence met that, and she knew he must
be disappointed that she wasn't ready to say what she felt
or to really commit to him. Deep down, she still couldn't
help wondering where they stood now that she was ready
to fight to keep him in her life.

"Well, it's getting late," he said finally. "Good night,
Lizzie."

"Wait! Before you go…"

"What?" he asked.

"Come to my house on Thanksgiving. My mom and my
sister will be here. We can see how we feel about being
together…like a couple."

Again that silence buzzed on the line.

"Are you sure?"

"Yes, I am."

"Can I bring my mom?"

"Please do," she said. Might as well try it with all the
family and see what happened.

"Okay. Good night."

"Good night," she said, disconnecting the call. She
couldn't sleep at all that night, feeling as though she'd
just taken a huge leap and she was praying that a net would
appear beneath her in case she fell.

"Happy Thanksgiving!" Elizabeth said as she opened the
door. Lindsey had sent a text saying she was going to stay
at the lodge with a friend of hers who'd flown in to surprise her.

Elizabeth hugged her sister, Marina, and her brother-
in-law, Pierre, as they stepped over the threshold into her
house. Pierre was tall—about six-two—and worked as a
manager at a health-food chain in Salt Lake City. He and

Marina had met at the university in Provo and fallen immediately in love.

Her little sister hugged her close and Elizabeth realized how happy she was to see her. They didn't talk on the phone or even text much because they didn't have that kind of relationship. They all lived their own busy lives but each knew that the other was only a phone call away.

"How are you?" Marina asked. She was the same height as Elizabeth but had dark hair and pretty brown eyes like their mother. She was wearing a caramel-colored cashmere sweater with a couple of strands of different-sized pearls around her neck, a leather skirt that ended at her knees, and a pair of black leather boots that hugged her calves.

"I'm good."

"Congratulations on your promotion," Pierre said as she embraced him. "We knew you'd make general manager this year."

"Thank you, Pierre."

Despite his French-sounding name, he had grown up in Montana and had the same Midwestern twang to his speech they all did.

"I smell wonderfulness," he called out as he walked to the kitchen.

"Kiss-ass," Marina said to Elizabeth after Pierre had disappeared into the kitchen.

"Mom loves her only son," Elizabeth said.

"Yes, she does," Marina agreed. "Come with me, sis. I have some news…."

Her sister linked her arm through Elizabeth's as they walked into the kitchen where Pierre was standing next to their mother, "helping" her by sampling some of her homemade cinnamon rolls.

"Elizabeth is going to be an auntie!" Marina gushed.

Her mom squealed as Elizabeth looked at her sister and

processed what she had just said. Marina was going to have a baby. She hugged her sister tightly and kissed her cheek before her mom stepped over and the three women all hugged each other. Then Elizabeth felt another set of arms and realized that Pierre had joined them.

"This is fantastic news!"

"I'm going to be a grandma! *About time.* You two have been married for five years," her mother said. "I have to call my sister, but I don't want to leave my oven."

"I'll watch everything, Mom, go call Aunt Charlotte," Elizabeth said.

"Okay." Her mom hurried out of the kitchen and Elizabeth looked over at her sister.

"When is the baby due?"

"The middle of May," Marina replied.

She'd have to make sure she had the time off from the lodge. Unexpectedly, tears sprang to her eyes. She was just so excited for her sister and Pierre....

"Sit down. Are you hungry?" Elizabeth said.

Pierre made coffee for himself and a mug of decaf for Elizabeth from the machine in the corner, then he sat down next to her sister at the table. They joined hands and everything she'd been thinking she wanted suddenly didn't seem so great.

She sort of wanted a family of her own. But she'd already decided she wouldn't try to have an executive-level career and a family. She'd seen the strain it had put on her father trying to balance it all. Not that he'd ever expressed regrets, but she'd felt it sometimes when he'd mention the things he'd missed while she and Marina were growing up.

Last night when she'd invited Bradley to their Thanksgiving celebration she wasn't sure how it would work out. Would it be awkward because of her family? But she knew she wanted him here. She'd started out needing him to be her friend with benefits, but today she really needed her friend and her lover.

She closed her eyes as she turned back to the stove top and checked on the pots, even though she had no idea what was in them. And tried to picture Bradley holding her hand.

"You okay?" Marina said, coming up behind her.

"Yes. I'm really happy for you," Elizabeth said, blinking back the tears. How could she tell her sister that seeing her happiness with Pierre and the new family she was going to have made her question every decision she'd made? It wasn't that she thought she should be on a different path. It was so much more complex than that. She wanted what she had, but she wanted what Marina had, as well.

She embraced her sister again. "I'm going to be the best auntie in the world."

"I have no doubt."

"Why don't you two go in the living room and talk? I can handle this," Pierre said.

Her sister nodded at her husband and soon the two of them were huddled together on the couch, in their old spots from childhood. Their mom had the television tuned to NBC so they wouldn't miss the Macy's Thanksgiving Day parade.

Elizabeth turned toward her little sister and saw her for the first time with different eyes. "I envy you. A part of me wishes that I hadn't been so consumed with my career and had my own husband and family by now." She smiled brightly. "But I can't wait to put my organizational skills to good use and help you manage your pregnancy."

They sat quietly on the couch talking about different things that Marina had gone through since finding out she was pregnant, including the dreaded morning sickness. Unfortunately for Marina, it happened at all hours of the day…and it wasn't pretty. In fact, she mentioned that her sense of smell was so acute that Pierre's cologne had made her sick and he'd had to stop wearing it.

The doorbell rang and Elizabeth got up to answer it while her sister walked toward the kitchen. "Please don't mention my pregnancy—we just wanted you and mom to know."

"I promise to keep it secret," Elizabeth said. She opened the door to find Bradley and his mom standing there. Suddenly she realized that keeping it to herself was going to be harder than she'd thought.

She needed to talk about it and about how she felt. And as much as she'd value Penny's opinion, it had always been Bradley who'd been able to offer her sage advice that helped her put everything into perspective.

"Happy Thanksgiving," she said, embracing Janette and taking her coat. She hung it in the closet while Bradley's mom went on into the kitchen.

Then she turned to Bradley and didn't care who was watching or the fact that so much was unsettled between them. She hadn't realized how much she missed him until she saw him standing there. Every time she saw him her pulse quickened. That had to mean something, right? She went to him and kissed him with all the emotion she was afraid to express.

"I've missed you."

"Me, too."

16

BRADLEY HAD SPENT a sleepless night trying to figure out what his next move should be, but as soon as he saw Elizabeth, he acknowledged that he wasn't playing a game anymore.

She looked so pretty today in a sheer cream-colored top with a delicate camisole underneath it. As his eyes drifted downward, he also noted how her cream-and-tan mini-skirt, sheer stockings and heels showed her legs off. He couldn't help imagining how good it would feel to slowly undress her and run his hands up and down her silky, bare calves. To cup her full, lush breasts in his hands. To make her his all night long.

But this was about so much more than sex in his mind. This was Elizabeth and he realized that he'd missed her this morning and every other morning of his entire life. He wanted her by his side. Yet he wasn't sure he could make the concessions he needed to in order to make it happen.

"That's quite the greeting," he murmured.

"I hope it wasn't too much," she said. "But I am changing things up between us."

"You are?" he asked. He felt a little wary about that. The last time she'd altered things between them, they'd ended up as lovers and their friendship was on shaky ground. Not that he was complaining. He thought maybe they needed to spend less time in bed and more time as a couple. That would settle things between them once and for all.

"Yes. No more waiting and tentatively taking steps toward what I want. I've decided the only way to really make this work is to leap."

There was something about her this morning that he couldn't put his finger on. It was more than what she'd just said—it was that emotional, fired-up look in her eyes. Something had changed in her, but what?

"Okay, then. Glad to hear we're both on the same page...." Wrapping his arms around her and holding her more solidly against him, he lowered his head and kissed her softly but sensuously. He'd been aching to have her in his arms like this, and he hoped she'd meant it when she said she was ready to try giving this a shot, for real this time.

For the first time in his adult life he was starting something without any idea where it would end. That didn't sit well with him.

"My, don't you two look cute together," Elizabeth's mom said, coming down the stairs. She hugged Bradley and then led them into the kitchen where the rest of their families were sitting around chatting. There were only six of them altogether, but for the first Thanksgiving ever, Bradley felt as though he really got what the holiday was about. That he really had family and something—no, make that *someone*—to be thankful for.

Elizabeth made him a cup of coffee and he took a seat at the table next to Pierre, who was a stand-up guy and, like him, played fantasy football online. They were part of different leagues and discussed their teams' chances of winning this year.

He glanced over at his mom and noticed how much she was smiling, and he had the thought that she'd probably wanted something like this all along. That as he'd been shying away from finding a woman to settle down with, she might have been wishing he would find one so she could have that family they never had.

Then he began to really think about all those lofty expectations that his mother must have had for him all these years. And he felt himself suddenly pulling back as he acknowledged the pressure he had thought he'd gotten rid of by thinking that he Elizabeth were both just winging it. All at once he knew that he couldn't do it. It wasn't fair to their families. Especially since both of their moms would probably be over the moon if they settled down together.

But what if it didn't work out? What then?

Sighing, he wondered how this had gotten so complicated. He was good with details. Good with keeping everything on course and adhering to his plans. But now he knew that there was no way to plan for this. No way to keep this all going and still ensure that no one got hurt.

Because, though it wasn't his intent to hurt anyone, especially Elizabeth, he also understood that while he had his idea of how their relationship would play out, so did she. He tried to shake the feeling of insecurity that brought. He wanted to just toss her over his shoulder and spirit her away to his nicely appointed cave and keep her there until she agreed to do things his way, but he also knew he had no idea what *his way* was.

"The parade is starting. Let's go watch it," Elizabeth's mom said.

Everyone got up from the table to move into the other room, but he lingered in the doorway watching them and feeling as though he was on the outside. The same way he had as a child when he'd been at Christmas plays and other parent-kid events. He was observing this warm family gathering, and wanting to be a part of it, but he wasn't sure where he fit in.

Then Elizabeth looked over at him and held out her hand. "Come sit with me," she said.

She'd chosen a big leather two-person recliner to sit on, and again he felt that shifting and settling inside of him. As though this was right. This was the person he needed to be with for this entire situation to make sense to him.

When he went over and settled down next to her, she slipped her arm under his, twined their fingers together and looked up at him. "Together."

"Together."

AFTER THE PARADE was over, their moms went into the kitchen.

"Want to go for a walk?" Bradley asked Elizabeth as the NFL football game in Dallas was fixing to come on.

"Sure," she said.

They got their coats on, told everyone they'd be back soon, and then they were outside and alone together in what seemed like the first time in forever. He slipped his hand around hers and the simple embrace felt just as good as it had when they'd been sitting together watching the parade.

"I'm sorry if you wanted to stay in there with your family, but I needed a break," he said.

She gazed up at him, suddenly concerned by the dark, brooding look on his face. "What's up?"

"I just haven't ever been at a holiday like this before."

"Are you serious?" she asked.

"Yes. When I was growing up, my mom usually worked on Thanksgiving and we had frozen turkey dinners for our main meal. This is just a little surreal."

She wanted to hug him and go back in time and invite

him home for Thanksgiving when they'd first met. Unlike the other night, when he'd been playing his past for sympathy, she could tell that this time he wasn't. "Did you like it?"

He shrugged, then dropped her hand and turned to look at the frozen pond that was in one of the "green areas" of her subdivision. "I don't know…it was just strange. Everything seemed so perfect, you know? And that's not what I'm used to at all."

"Sorry?" she said.

"Don't be silly. You don't have to apologize because you've had a normal family all these years, or feel bad that the first time I'm with one I'm panicking," he said.

She realized he truly was out of his depth. That was so not Bradley, and she wasn't quite sure how to handle it. She walked over to him, intending to hug him—or something—but slipped on a patch of ice and careened into him, instead. Trying to catch her balance, she knocked him off his feet in the process, and they both fell to the hard ground.

He wrapped his arms around her and rolled so that he was on the bottom on the icy ground and she was on top of him. She looked down into his handsome face, staring into his green eyes, feeling the warmth of his breath on her cheeks and the scent of his woodsy aftershave around her. She leaned down and kissed him. Slowly at first, taking her time, but making a thorough study of his mouth. She'd missed this closeness and realized the things that scared her about Bradley weren't physical. She could deal with having him in her bed every night; it was the complex emotional reaction to the times when he wasn't with her that made her afraid.

His hands slid over her back and she pressed herself

up so that she could look at him. "Sorry for knocking you over."

"You've been bowling me over since we met," he said.

"Have I?"

"Hell, yeah. From the first moment you walked by me I started fantasizing about your legs."

"These legs?" she asked, slowly skimming her hands down the outsides of her thighs.

"Don't stop," he said huskily. "As a matter of fact, this is what I've been craving for days."

"Then why didn't you call me or stop by my office when you were at the lodge?" she asked. "You could have seen these and a lot more."

She noticed his expression grow shuttered and he held himself more stiffly underneath her. "I just didn't."

She pushed herself up and off him, and got to her feet. Was he hiding something from her? One of the men she'd dated had been seeing other women on the side. And while a part of her didn't think Bradley would ever do that, why else would he avoid her?

"What's going on? You ask me to be naked emotionally with you and then you pull back. You tell me that you haven't had a family holiday ever and I think that means you want us to be closer, but you aren't acting like it."

He stood, too, and ran his fingers through his hair. "Because you're an addiction for me, Lizzie. One I can't get enough of."

Addiction. He was for her, too. Suddenly she wondered if hot sex with him was clouding her judgment. "Me, too."

A quietness fell between them as he continued to touch her leg. *Stop talking and let this go,* she thought.

"Tell me more. I've seldom seen you at a loss for words. A smart guy like you can't come up with some way of explaining it?"

"Well, you're seeing me that way now, Elizabeth." He scrubbed a hand across his jaw. "The closer I get to what I want, the harder it seems to do the right thing and actually make it happen."

"Do the right thing? Why don't you just be yourself?" she asked. "That's what I'm doing. It's also really scary for me and I'm taking a huge risk and you're… What are you doing? You're hiding behind your past?"

"I'm not hiding," he said. "It's just that I don't know what I'm going to do if I ever do get everything I want." Bradley closed the distance between them, putting his hands on her face and tipping her head back so that their eyes met.

He lowered his head and kissed her with a soul-deep certainty that she'd been afraid to believe was between them. His tongue tangled with hers as he pulled her into his embrace and held her tightly against him. The cold air swirled around them but he was solid. The only solid thing in a world that was spinning out of her control.

Her job was the one place where she still had that control. Where nothing had changed. Elizabeth had left her cell phone in her handbag while they were out and checked it when they came back into the house. She saw she had several missed calls and then the phone rang again.

"This is Elizabeth."

"Elizabeth, this is Trevor. There's been an emergency and we need you as soon as you can get here."

Her heart stalled, stomach knotted as she tried to breath around the lump in her throat.

"What is it?"

"Lars. Something is not right with him. He's out of breath and he won't let us call the EMTs, but he doesn't seem right. And he won't go home until you're here."

"Okay. I'm on my way."

"WHAT'S GOING ON?" Bradley asked as she hung up the phone. She glanced over at him, so glad that he was here with her. She didn't think about it too much but she felt stronger with him by her side.

He still had his coat on and stood there as if he knew something was going on. Probably he'd heard the sense of urgency in her voice.

"Lars is having some kind of health crisis, but he won't leave until I'm there to fill in."

Everything was a little murky. This was Lars, her mentor and her friend. She was so worried about him.

"I'll drive you so you can get on your phone and find out what's going on," he said. His solution was simple and it underscored the fact that this was what it meant to be a couple. She had never been so glad to have him with her.

"Just so we're clear, I'm not choosing work over you," she said.

He kissed her quickly and pushed her toward the living room. "I know. This is the reality of being involved with a senior executive. I might have an emergency one day at an inconvenient time. This is who we are." She saw him with new eyes as he said his goodbyes and headed out the door, then she went to find her mom. "Bradley and I have got to run. There's an emergency—"

"We know," her mom said, handing her two travel coffee mugs. "Sorry, I was eavesdropping."

Her mom hugged her and Janette did the same, and Pierre waved from the sofa where he was drinking a beer and eating a turkey sandwich. Marina came over and linked their arms together. "I'm walking out with you."

"Why?"

"Because I want to know what's really going on with you and Bradley. You always said he was just a friend and you weren't interested in being a couple," she said when they were outside.

Bradley had his SUV running and was waiting for her. "I don't have time to give you a full report, but Bradley and I are sort of a couple now."

"I thought you just said it to keep Mom off your back," Marina said in that little-sister way that was almost bratty.

"Well, now you know I didn't." Elizabeth almost smiled because Marina had made her forget her worries for a moment. And she needed that. She realized how rich her life was with her family. And on this Thanksgiving Day, she gave a quick prayer of thanks for them.

"Okay, fine. I'm just worried about you," Marina said at last. "Everyone always thinks you are superhuman, but I know better."

"I'm okay," Elizabeth said, hugging her sister. "Congrats again on the baby. I'll see you again before you go back home, right?"

"Yes. Even if I have to come to the lodge and hang out there," Marina replied.

Elizabeth walked to the car and got in, clicking her seatbelt into place as Bradley reversed and drove away from her mom's house. The air was cold and the leather seat took a few minutes to warm up. "What did Marina want?"

"She didn't realize we were a real couple," Elizabeth said quietly .

"Why not?" he asked.

"I don't know, but I can't dwell on that right now." The truth was, it pained her to think her sister thought she'd lie about being involved with Bradley, but she didn't want to tell him that. "I'm going to call Trevor back. You sure you're okay to drive me? What about your mom?" she asked.

"Yes," he said. "Pierre is going to take her home."

When she dialed Trevor's number, there was no answer. She kept trying but even the switchboard couldn't reach with Trevor, and she knew that something major must have happened for him to be completely out of touch. As Bradley drove through town and up the mountain to the lodge she kept texting people and trying to call. Bradley put his hand on her thigh and patted it.

"It's going to be fine."

"Lars's health isn't the best. Remember when I mentioned it at the party?"

"I didn't realize it was so serious."

"Me, either."

She swallowed against the lump in her throat. Bradley reached over and held her hand loosely in his. The love she'd first felt a spark of in her bedroom bloomed more fully in her heart, and though it was hard to guess what would happen between them in the future, she knew that she'd never forget this day or this moment.

She jumped out of the car as soon as they arrived and ran for the lobby of the lodge. There was an ambulance at the front entrance and the duty manager was pale and sweating when she got to him.

"What's going on?"

"Lars collapsed in the restaurant."

"Oh, no. Where is he?" she asked.

"He wouldn't let them take him until you were here," the duty manager said.

She rushed over to the stretcher. It was scary seeing her boss lying there, so pale, with the oxygen mask over his face and the EMTs monitoring every function.

"Lars, I'm here."

"Elizabeth, thank you. I collapsed at Mimi's table. We need to do some damage control. And I think that the chef is doing an excellent job, but I have some notes for the

Thanksgiving service. I didn't want to leave until I knew this resort was in the best hands."

"I'm here. You shouldn't neglect your health for this resort," she admonished gently.

"The lodge is all I have," he said. And in that moment she knew that this was her future unless she learned to trust someone else—Bradley. Unless she really took a leap and trusted him with her heart and not just her body.

She squeezed Lars's hand and made him the promise she knew he needed to hear. "I will take care of everything here. It will be waiting for you when you come back."

His fingers tightened on hers for a second before he closed his eyes. "I'll go to the hospital now."

The EMTs sprang into action, putting him in the ambulance and speeding away. Elizabeth didn't dwell on the fear that had taken root in her heart when she'd seen Lars taken away. She'd let the doctors do their best to save him.

But he'd been stubborn. She felt a combination of guilt and something else that felt a little like relief. Seemed they did need her here to fill Lars's shoes, after all. She got everyone settled down at the resort and went to visit with Mimi and Paul, the VIP couple that her boss had been talking to when he'd collapsed. The wife was a best-selling author of erotica and the husband produced television game shows.

"Is Lars okay?" Mimi asked as she approached.

"He's on his way to the hospital," Elizabeth replied. "Are you both okay? He wanted me to apologize—"

"For his health? Even Lars Usten can't control that," Paul said good-naturedly.

Elizabeth smiled. The couple seemed at ease now that they knew that he'd be okay. She took a moment to check on the other guests and make sure everything was going smoothly, but then saw Bradley waiting in the lobby bar nursing a drink. Suddenly she wished she could find the right words to say to him, to find out if he cared for her—loved her—the way she realized she loved him.

But she didn't have the words and was truly afraid that, even if she did, she wouldn't have the nerve to say them aloud because she'd be too vulnerable to him.

_17_

BRADLEY FELT OUT of place in the bar while he waited for Elizabeth. He understood that she was the type of woman who always needed to manage things, and to be honest, it was very hard for him watching her try to control events and not succeed. He knew how vitally important her job was to her and he felt as though he'd pushed her too far when he'd told her to find some balance in her life.

Guilt. It wasn't the most pleasant feeling.

"Dude, happy Thanksgiving," Carter said, coming over to him and sitting down on an empty bar stool.

"You, too."

"What are you doing here? I figured you'd spend all day with your girl," Carter said, signaling the cocktail waitress.

"My girl—she's the general manager of the lodge. She had to come in and work," Bradley told him.

Carter ordered a Perrier with a twist of lime. When the waitress left, he leaned both arms on the table. "I didn't realize you went for that type."

"What type?" Bradley asked. "The kind of woman who is so busy with her career that she only has a slice of time for a man?"

"I guess you're not into the domestic scene," Carter

said. "No criticism, dude. I'm the same way. Always go after other athletes who get that training is my life. It's easier, you know?"

There was nothing easy about Elizabeth, and Bradley knew that better than most. She appeared to be all about her career, but when they'd been driving here and she'd mentioned that they'd promoted her because of Lars's health, he'd seen cracks in her career-driven facade. Saw that she was starting to question all the sacrifices she'd made.

And he wanted her to be as committed to him as he was to her, but part of what Carter said got him thinking. What if she did suddenly want to walk away and give it up, would he still want her? Was he only comfortable with Elizabeth because she was as into her career as he was into his?

He'd suggested they be friends with benefits because he'd thought it would make Elizabeth more comfortable, but the truth was he liked the way it gave him more breathing room emotionally, as well.

"Elizabeth and I have known each other since college, and back then we were just two kids who didn't know where we were going. So the career thing—it's not a type for me," Bradley told him.

"I like that. It's an Elizabeth thing with you?"

Bradley nodded. "Yeah, that's right," he said as the truth slowly sank in. It had always been Elizabeth for him, but he hadn't realized how much he'd always wanted her until this moment.

He watched her moving around, walking at a brisk pace as she made sure that the staff and guests were all doing okay. Watching Lars being taken from the lodge had been difficult even for him, and he didn't really know the man.

Elizabeth glanced over at him and he waited to see what she'd do. She started walking toward him. Carter took his Perrier and left, but Bradley was barely aware of it, could only watch her as she came closer. Her beautiful blond hair swung around her shoulders and he remembered every time they'd made love. How, when he held her tightly against him, everything seemed perfect and he felt closer to her than any other person in the world.

How could he help her find her strength in this chaos? He didn't want this event to change things for Elizabeth the way loss had colored his life. He kept moving so that he never really noticed the emptiness around him.

Now he wanted to stay put, but he had no idea if that was something he could really do or if he was just fooling himself, pretending that he could be normal like other people. When his normal wasn't like anyone else's.

"You look a bit spooked," she said, sitting down next to him.

"You do, too."

"I thought I was handling it better than that," she said.

"You are, but I can tell you're a little freaked by seeing your mentor being wheeled away with an oxygen mask on."

"Yeah, that was really strange," she said, turning toward him and putting her hand on his. "I don't want to be alone like that."

"No one does," he said gruffly.

"No, I mean it. If I don't change, I could end up just like Lars. Alone, with only other executives to notify."

"What do you mean? He has family, right?" Bradley asked. He didn't like the thought of Elizabeth alone, either. But he could see that outcome if he didn't figure out a way to be the man she needed. Grimacing, he stared down at his drink. The idea of hurting her was unimaginable, but he would never forgive himself if he ended up causing her any pain or heartbreak.

He'd walk away before he let that happen.

THERE WAS SO MUCH she wanted Bradley to know, yet she was afraid to reveal it to him. She felt scared and, for the first time in a long time, had no idea what to do next. She was self-reliant and always had been, but she had no answers inside of herself. She'd gotten what she thought she wanted and now realized it wasn't what she'd thought it would be.

And what she was really afraid to admit to herself was that she needed something more from Bradley. Elizabeth sighed. She shouldn't even be here in the bar—she was supposed to be working—but what she really wanted was to just be next to him right now. He was her comfort and her strength, and she knew that he was the only man for her.

Yet as much as she wanted to just pour out her heart and tell him she loved him, she knew that would frighten him. It didn't take a rocket scientist to realize that Bradley was carrying as much baggage as she was when it came to relationships.

What if he was happy with things the way they were? Granted, he had pushed hard to knock down her walls, but he hadn't shown her any of his own vulnerabilities. Oh, God, she felt like a mess. And she hated it. She looked into his beautiful green eyes and realized she couldn't read a single emotion in them.

What did he want from her? Could he commit to her? She really had no clue. And if she revealed her true feelings and he gave her one of those Bradley smiles, she knew she'd break into a million little pieces. "Lizzie?"

"Hmm?"

"Are you okay?"

She shook her head, but she didn't know what to say to him without coming off as too vulnerable. She'd never needed anyone the way she wanted him. She was addicted to his strength and didn't want to face her future without him by her side, but she'd done nothing to figure out if he felt the same way.

"Like you said before, I think seeing Lars like that has really shaken me," she admitted. "I don't want to keep you, so if you have to leave I'll understand. I can stay here to-night and then go get my car tomorrow—"

"Is that what you want?" he asked.

It was impossible to tell what he was thinking. His tone was flat and his mouth tight, and she wondered if he thought she'd slipped back into the safe world of her ca-reer. And despite the fact that Lars was sick, her job was still the safer place to be. Nothing could scare her the way the thought of being with Bradley did.

Nevertheless, she took a deep breath and knew that she was going to have to take the first step. She had never hesitated to go after what she wanted before. Why, then, was she doing it now?

With a bolt of insight, she suddenly realized the truth. It was because, in her mind, she still didn't think she was worthy of having it all. She had believed she couldn't have it all so she was afraid to reach out and try to get it all.

When Bradley turned his hand over in hers and linked their fingers together, she finally answered him. "I don't want you to leave."

"Good. I don't want that, either," he said. "After you're done here, do you want to go to the hospital and check on Lars?"

She nodded. "Yes, definitely. He doesn't have any close family and I told the board that I'd keep them up-to-date on his status. As soon as I get Trevor's replacement in, I think we should go to the hospital."

"Okay. Then I'll take you home and take care of you," he said.

"Why? I'm fine." Maybe, if she kept repeating that, it would be true. Maybe she would finally feel like her old self again. But she was conflicted and she kept seeing Lars on the stretcher—she had no idea what she'd do if he weren't okay.

"Today was rough. And I can tell that you aren't fine," he said with quiet confidence.

She wanted to deny it, but Bradley saw her more clearly than she even saw herself. That was humbling and shocking. And no matter that she'd been pretending ever since they'd become lovers that she didn't need him—the truth was, she did. "I—"

"Don't try to hide it. To the entire world you look super efficient and more capable than anyone else, but I can see that inside you're hurting. Lars has been like a father to you. Actually, probably better than your own father, and it has to be hard to see him incapacitated."

And if she thought she wasn't in love with him before, there was no denying it anymore. There was no way she could pretend he wasn't right and that he hadn't seen straight through her. She squeezed his hand, looked into those incredible eyes of his and wanted to confess it all. Then she wondered why she was hesitating. He had proven himself to be better than every other man in her life.

"I love you, Bradley."

SHE LOVED HIM. He had no idea how to respond to that. He felt panic at first. His throat tightened and he knew that he needed to say something. *Thank you* felt wrong and he couldn't say *Me, too*. He hadn't thought of love—not with Elizabeth—and yet, at the same time, he knew he'd been avoiding it.

This was part of a relationship, the very thing he'd

thought he wanted, but now that it was here, he didn't know how to act or what to say. He was…scared.

"I guess your silence pretty much says it all," she said, pushing to her feet and walking away.

He watched her go. He was losing everything he wanted because for the first time in his adult life he was a coward. He was taking the path of safety, afraid to risk it all on Lizzie.

Lizzie! He made himself get up.

He wasn't going to let her leave, was he? He followed her across the lobby to the employee elevator that he knew led to her office. She punched the button with barely restrained anger and he was still searching for something to say.

"Elizabeth."

She turned toward him. Her eyes were glassy, but it was her expression that broke him. She looked shattered, not angry, like someone who was one step away from losing it.

"I'm sorry."

"Don't be," she said as the doors opened and she got on. He followed quickly on her heels.

"I am. I didn't—"

"No. Please don't say anything else until I'm someplace where my staff can't see me," she said, hitting the button for the executive offices.

He stepped into the corner, hating himself for a weakness he hadn't realized he had. This stupid empty spot where other people had emotions, had a heart. He'd told himself that he wanted that from Elizabeth, but now that he'd gotten her, he felt paralyzed.

From his first memory, Bradley had known he was different, and after that he'd made sure no one could never hurt him.

And though he knew he did care for Elizabeth, love wasn't something he could even define.

He followed her down the hall to her office, closed the door behind them, then leaned back against it and watched as she sat down at her desk. She was trying to compose herself, but it was too late. He'd already seen past the facade that she wore when she faced the world. Although he knew it was really hard for her, she'd finally let him see deep inside her...and he'd hurt her. He'd never intended that. Today, especially, when everyone in America was celebrating family, he was sowing the seeds that would mean he'd never have one.

But he wasn't going to lie to Elizabeth and profess to feeling something he didn't. Something he couldn't fathom experiencing.

She glared at him. "Why are you here?"

"You can't say something like that and then walk away from me," he said.

"Why not? It's clear you don't feel the same way," she snapped. "I don't know what I was thinking. Must have been everything with Lars, and it being Thanksgiving, and the fact that I'm not supposed to tell anyone that Marina is pregnant."

"Wow. Your baby sister is having a baby." He scrubbed his hand over his jaw. "But what does that have to do with you loving me?" he asked.

The more she tried to pull back, the less he wanted to let her do it. He wanted her love. He couldn't say why. There was something about it that he didn't understand, but at the same time he knew he needed it.

"It doesn't change the fact that you don't love me," she said, looking pointedly at him. "What was all that stuff you said about seeing myself the way you see me?"

"I do see you that way," he insisted.

"Then why don't you love me, too?" she asked. "I don't pretend to know how men think, but you said some stuff to me that you probably shouldn't have."

He could see in her eyes that he'd hurt her and he hated that about himself. "I never meant to."

"That doesn't make it better, Bradley. Why change our dynamic and force me to really engage in this relationship if you knew it couldn't go any further than friends… friends with benefits."

"I didn't know," he whispered. Even to his own ears that sounded lame. But it was the truth. He'd always believed that if he were to ever be more than friends with her, she'd be the woman who'd make him want to be a better man. She'd be the one to make him fall in love.

"Whatever."

"Do you still want me to go to the hospital with you?"

"Yes," she said. "I do. I don't want you hanging around because you feel sorry for me."

"How could I ever feel sorry for you, Lizzie? You are strong and confident, and if I knew how to love, then I think you'd be the one person in the world that I would love."

She stood up and put both hands on her desk leaning forward toward him. "What kind of bullshit is that?"

"It's not bullshit, it's the truth."

She shook her head. "Are you telling me you don't love your mom? That you've never felt anything for the women you've been in relationships with?"

He thought long and hard about his answer. He'd never thought of what he felt for his mom as love or not love. He said the words to her, but he sometimes thought that was just habit because he knew she expected him to say them back. He'd never had to really confront love until now. Until Elizabeth.

"I don't know. I've always just given all I could of my time and, of course, gifts. But emotions? They are harder for me. I don't know how to really love. My mom is different, but I think we've been bound together for so long—"

"You know she'll never leave you. She's the one person it's safe for you to love. I can only guess that you really don't feel the same way about me, or you don't trust me," she said. "And you know what? I get that, because I've been afraid to admit that I love you."

_18_

ELIZABETH FELT MORE in control now that she was upstairs in her office. She realized it took nothing away from her if he didn't love her or, in his own words, _couldn't_ love her. Still, she would never be able to understand how he could have pushed her so hard to come out of her shell and then not be prepared to really commit to her.

But seeing it now, she understood that he was the one who was missing out. Today had been the strangest Thanksgiving of her entire life. She'd experienced more emotions today than she ever had before, and she realized that she relished each and every one one of them. In fact, she felt so much stronger for having experienced them and this entire day.

"You can go."

"I don't want to. Give me a chance—"

"No. I'm not going to make excuses or pretend that I don't know myself well enough to know that I really do love you, but I can't keep this relationship going knowing that you don't love me back."

"I said _can't_."

"It still sounds like an excuse to me. It took me forever to figure out that I love you, Bradley. I imagine it's going to take me a long time to fall out of love with you, but that is what will happen."

He shook his head. "I... God, Lizzie. I don't want that."

"What *do* you want?" she asked.

He looked confused and angry, and she got that. She'd changed the rules of their game without even meaning to. And still, as mad as she was about how he couldn't reciprocate her feelings, she wanted to pull him into her arms and say it was okay, that they'd figure things out together, but she had too much self-respect to do that.

She'd chased after love for so long and had never gotten it, no matter what she'd done. She'd learned early on that she couldn't make any man love her. She was smart enough to know that it would not work with Bradley.

"I want you. I want you in my life," he said at last.

"How?"

He made a sweeping gesture with his arms. "Like this. Sleeping together, hanging out together, you know, like a couple."

"But not really," she said. "Because you'll be traveling and I'll be working, and we'll never be like Marina and Pierre—and until today, I hadn't realized how much I wanted that. I want a family of my own, Bradley. And a man who looks at me the way Pierre looks at my sister. And if you can't love me, you never will be able to do that."

He shoved his hand in his hair and cursed under his breath. "Fine...whatever. I'm doing the best that I can, Lizzie. You know I never had a positive male influence in my life—" He cut himself off abruptly. "Hell, why am I still using that as an excuse?"

"Because you're scared. Believe me, I get it. I'm scared, too," she said. But the more she spoke, the less scared she was, and the more clarity she found around the future. She knew what she wanted now, and no matter how much it hurt when Bradley left, she knew she'd always have him to thank for helping her see what truly mattered in life.

And it wasn't career or family, it was both.

For years she'd worried that she wouldn't be able to handle love and a demanding job. But her love for Bradley made her understand that wasn't the case. She was ready to live life to the fullest and she wanted him to be the man she did it with.

His hands clenching at his sides, he spoke through gritted teeth. "Okay...you're right. I *am* scared to commit. But how can I do that when I'm not even sure what the heck love is?"

"For me, it's knowing that I want you by my side—not because I can't handle life on my own, but because it's better with you there," she said.

"Me, too," he said.

She shook her head. "No...not you, too. We both have to figure it out for ourselves."

"Why are you being difficult about this?" he asked.

"Because you have been pushing me to blur the lines between friendship and sex since we started this. I thought you were already there. That you already cared for me. I can't accept less than that from you."

"Are you kidding me?" he asked. "I think we both know that I've always been reaching for you and you've always been dancing just out of my reach. I wish I could just say what you want to hear, but we both know that it wouldn't be enough, would it? You're just as afraid, but of something different than I am," he said.

"Why are you lashing out at me?" she huffed. "You're the one who looked like he was facing a bear when I said I loved you. Don't turn this on me."

He moved closer, crossing the office in three long strides and stopped right in front of her desk. "But it was always about both of us. No, I can't say the words you need to hear. Words, I might add, I didn't even realize you needed until tonight. But instead of giving me the time to adjust you're ready to just push me right out the door."

"I know. It's not fair. I just want the man I love to be able to love me back. I had no idea that was important to me until you didn't," she said at last. "If you think that you can love me, I'll be here."

Pivoting on his heel, he stalked to the door and opened it, pausing on the threshold to look back at her. "Then I guess this is goodbye, Lizzie."

Tears welled up in her eyes. "Yes, Bradley, I suppose it is."

He slammed out the door and she could only watch him leave. She stood there in a sort of shock for a long time. A part of her feared she'd made a huge mistake, but she knew her heart and she couldn't be with Bradley until he figured out what he truly wanted.

BRADLEY WALKED AS SLOWLY as he could to the elevator, but it was quickly apparent she wasn't coming after him. His anger was misguided, and he knew it, but he had too much pride to go back. Plus he still wasn't any closer to understanding what love was or what he felt for Elizabeth.

He got as far as the lobby before he realized that his mom would stop talking to him if he stranded Elizabeth at the lodge. When he noticed that Carter was still in the bar, he didn't hesitate to walk over and join the snowboarder and the group of women at his table.

"Carter, can you give me a ride home?"

"Sure, dude," Carter said. "Everything okay?"

"Peachy," he said. Walking away from the table and to the front desk, he found a pen and the monogrammed note-pads that were on the counter for guests to use.

Elizabeth,
Use my SUV until you can get yours back. Be care-
ful driving to the hospital and please let me know how
Lars is—

He sounded like an idiot. He crumpled the paper up and shoved it in his pocket.

"Can I help you, sir?"

Bradley nodded at the front desk clerk. "Yes. I'd like to leave these keys for Elizabeth Anders. Can you make sure she gets them?"

"I can. Is there anything else?"

He glanced down at the notepaper and scrawled the only thing he really knew to say.

I'm sorry.

He folded the note and handed it to the attendant. He didn't bother going back to the bar. He needed to get out of here and he needed it now. With quick, angry strides, he headed for the exit and walked outside. The cold wind bit into him as he walked down the path that he'd trodden with Elizabeth after their first real date. He wished she were with him again....

"Bradley?"

He looked up to see Lindsey sitting near one of the fire pits, staring up at the ski run visible from the patio. They'd left the lights on near the lifts.

"Hi, Lindsey. Happy Thanksgiving," he said, trying to act normal but suddenly realizing that he didn't know what normal was anymore.

"You, too. What are you doing here?"

"Just dropped Elizabeth off," he said. "What about you?"

"I live near here. I have a condo up the road." She sighed. "It's weird not to be training today."

He realized she needed someone to talk to and while he

wasn't really a friend to her, God knew he didn't want to be alone with his own thoughts. He sat down next to her on the bench and she gave him a distracted smile.

"When I opened my first Fresh Sno store, I spent every second there. Lived and breathed the job. And slowly but surely, through a lot of hard work, sweat and tears, my clientele started picking up and it became a bona fide success."

"That sounds nice," she said.

"It probably seems like I'm just talking about myself, but finally, after three months of steady increases in profit, I decided I'd take a day off. I drove up here to surprise Lizzie and take her mountain biking, but only got halfway. I couldn't stand it. I needed to be back in the shop. If I wasn't in my shop, what was I?"

Lindsey nodded. "Exactly. I can't get back on the slopes, not the way I was before. When I fell at the Olympics something changed—not just with my knee, but with me, too."

"Your entire life changed in one moment, didn't it?" he asked. "I'm sorry."

"Thanks. That run was so incredible up until I skidded. I was on track to beat my world-record time. One little miscalculation and everything changed."

He was only half listening to Lindsey; what he remembered was how whenever he wanted to share something with a person, it was always Elizabeth. He didn't know if that was love, but the first seeds of that emotion had been sowed in his heart a long time ago. He'd never reached for anyone else the way he always needed her.

He couldn't define it any further than that. And he was still angry with Lizzie for giving him an ultimatum in her own way. She hadn't said he couldn't be with her if he couldn't love her, but it sure had felt that way.

Then he had a flash of insight as he realized what she'd truly meant when she'd told him she'd be there. That he had to be able to accept her love. And as he'd tried to tell her, she couldn't love someone unless she loved herself, and he realized the same was true for him.

He felt unlovable because his father had left before he was even born, and that one act had set the boundaries for a missing part inside of him a long time ago. Something that had felt like he wasn't like everyone else. He was incomplete and messed up, and there was only one person in the world who'd ever made him feel close to complete.

Elizabeth.

"I'm sorry, Lindsey. That you can't ski anymore," he said distractedly as he got to his feet. "I hope you figure out who you are now."

He waved goodbye to her and hurried back into the lodge. At the front desk he learned that Elizabeth had already left.

LARS LOOKED SMALL and pale, and so unlike his usual self that she was almost afraid to go into his hospital room. Elizabeth thought of how she'd made him into a surrogate father as he'd taken her under his wing. How he'd never told her that he was having any problems. Why had he done that?

She guessed he'd been afraid of appearing weak. It was funny the way most people tried so hard not to reveal any failings when it was those failings that led to growth and real strength.

"Are you just going to stand in the doorway all day?" he asked, sounding like his normal self despite the oxygen mask over his face. She smiled at him as she walked into the room.

"I was thinking about it," she said. "Trey is flying back

from Antigua where he went home for Thanksgiving and should be here tomorrow. I thought you'd want your family here."

"I do," Lars said, then held his hand out to her. "But you're more like family than Trey is. He just looked me up when he needed a job. We're not even that close. He's actually my cousin's kid, not really a nephew."

"Do you really think of me as family?" she asked. Feeling closer to him than ever, she sat down in the chair next to Lars's bed and squeezed his hand.

"Yes, I do. Sad, I know, since you're an employee and just here because you're doing your job."

"I'm here because I care, Lars. Not just because of my job," she said, and that was the truth. There was nothing to be gained from visiting him other than reassuring herself that he was okay. "How do you feel?"

"I've felt better."

"The doctors here are the best. Pablo texted me that his son who is a top cardiologist is coming home from his vacation early to oversee your care."

"That's nice."

She stared down at Lars and wondered if this was her future. What would happen when her mom died, and her sister and Pierre had their own life? She'd be on her own.

The anger that had been simmering toward Bradley slowly turned to determination. Just because he was afraid of love and commitment didn't mean she had to end up like this.

"Do you regret it?" she asked quietly.

"Every day. At first I used to tell myself that the work was worth it, but it's not. I imagine you already know that, since you spent the day with your family."

"I do," she said. "I'm sorry it took me so long to respond this afternoon."

"I didn't want to call you. I was trying to prove to the board that I didn't need replacing, but I can see now that I was wrong. And that I promoted the right person to take my place."

His words soothed the last of the hurt she'd felt when she'd realized they'd promoted her because of Lars' failing health. She understood much better today how much her boss must have feared stepping down. He had no one to share his life with—a path she wasn't going to follow.

She stayed with him until Trey arrived and then went back down to the parking lot where Bradley's SUV waited for her. When she got behind the wheel, she noticed his scarf on the seat, picked it up and held it to her face, breathing in the scent of him. She put her head on the steering wheel and wondered if she'd done the right thing.

She didn't want him out of her life. She wanted him next to her. She wanted to talk to him about what Lars had said and about how the things she'd always wanted for her life now seemed hollow. But he was gone.

He was gone because he couldn't love her. *Couldn't love.* What did that even mean? She had no idea. Of all the things that had happened between them, she'd finally encountered something about Bradley that disappointed her.

She wrapped the scarf around her neck and put her seatbelt on before starting the car and driving to her house. Once inside, she curled up on the couch with his scarf around her neck and a blanket over her, because if she went into her bedroom, she'd want to call him and tell him that it didn't matter if he could never love her.

That she loved him enough for the both of them.

But she knew that wasn't the way she wanted to live. She'd always feel as if she'd given up on herself, and she couldn't do that, even if she had to spend the rest of her life alone.

19

THE NEXT WEEK went quickly, with the annual tree-lighting ceremony and the opening of the Christmas village at the lodge. The pastry chef was also doing gingerbread-decorating classes for the kids who came out on the weekends, and they were already booked solid.

She tried not to miss Bradley in the midst of all this, but it was impossible. She had hit the button to call him half a dozen times and then hung up, needing him to come to her.

But now that seemed silly when what she really wanted was Bradley in her life.

She sighed. At least she had work to distract her, and she counted her blessings every day that Lars was slowly recovering.

Adding to her confidence, she'd had a meeting with the board of directors and confronted them with what she'd overheard. As Bradley had suggested, they had been trying to find a kind way to tell Lars he needed to slow down, and they'd never had any plans to replace her.

After the board members reiterated that they were very pleased with her performance, she told them that she'd like to have trained staff in place so that she could have it all— not just run the resort but have a family one day as well—

and they were agreeable. Probably because even Lars had said that he'd never pick the lodge over a family again.

She had everything she could want, but still ached every night for Bradley. She kept that note he'd left with his keys, and looked at it often, but had no idea what he'd been apologizing for.

But he wasn't the only one who was sorry. She wished she'd never really known him as more than a friend. She wished she'd always known him as a lover. She wished that things in real life could be neatly wrapped up like a Hollywood movie.

And most of all, she wished she didn't wake up with tears on her pillow in a queen-size bed that seemed too big for her now.

She wanted him back.

But she also knew she wanted him back on her terms. She'd hadn't changed *that* much and wasn't about to give up what she knew she could have.

So she knew she was going to have to just continue to live with the pain until it lessened. And she knew it would. Already she could no longer smell his aftershave in her house. And tonight when she got her Christmas tree, she was going to put it in the living room so that it dominated her view and hopefully got her mind off of what was missing in her life.

Her phone rang and she hesitated to answer it, but it was her office phone and she doubted that Bradley was calling her. Especially considering the fact that she hadn't heard from him all week.

"Elizabeth Anders."

"Hey, it's Penny."

"Hey. How was your Thanksgiving?"

"Crazy. I had to wait until this week, but I gave my notice at work," Penny said.

"What did your boss say?"

"That he wouldn't give me a recommendation. Then he begged me to reconsider. He said his marriage was rocky... We both know it's not. I can't stay here."

"You don't have to. Paula, my assistant, booked one of the chalets for you. Come and stay as long as you like. I'm letting you use my discount."

"Thank you. I definitely need to get away and figure out my messy life."

"This is the place to do it. The staff will pamper you, and you'll have a cute and cozy chalet to yourself," Elizabeth said, tucking a strand of her hair behind her ear.

"Perfect," Penny said. "Now catch me up on you and Bradley. I'm so happy you two are a couple."

Ugh. She should have anticipated this but hadn't. "Um... we're not."

"Why not? What happened?" Penny asked.

"I don't know, Penn. I mean, one minute everything was perfect. Thanksgiving was great. His mom and mine got along and everything was going well, and then I realized that I loved him."

"How is that a problem? He's been mooning over you for years," Penny said.

"Seems mooning over me was different than me saying I loved him, because he shut down. He told me he can't love or something like that."

Saying it out loud made her feel as if she was lacking. She had been telling herself for days that the problem wasn't her, but now she felt as though it was again. "Why can't he love me?"

"Ah, sweetie, I don't know what his problem is," Penny said. "You are so lovable."

"Only you, my mom and my sister think so," Elizabeth said. "I think I'm too—something, I don't know what,

for guys. I thought that Bradley might be different, but
he wasn't."

"He might just need time."

"I thought of that. But it's been a week."

Penny started laughing. "A week isn't that long."

"Penn, it feels like it's been forever."

"It will get better," her friend reassured her. "Have you
tried calling him? Or seeing him?"

"No. I don't want to. I'm afraid I'll just agree to whatever he suggests so I can have him back."

BRADLEY HAD TO fly back to the U.K. on the Sunday after
Thanksgiving, and if he thought being out of the country
would make him miss Elizabeth less, he was dead wrong.
He had one clear thought as he sat on the runway waiting
to return to the United States a week later, and that was
that he couldn't miss her more if he did love her.

He'd dreamed of her every night and had reached for
his phone more than once to try to get in touch with her,
but the words she needed from him were still stuck in his
throat. He didn't know why he was so afraid of saying
them, but he was.

He had said the words to his mom, but that was it. No
other person had ever meant as much to him, and a part of
him had wrongly believed that if he never said the words
then Elizabeth would never hurt him.

But he had been and there was no going back. He had
hurt her by his silence and she'd called him on his cowardice. The one woman he never wanted to let down, he'd
hurt the most. But he'd been unable to swallow his pride.
He'd been unable to tell her what he needed to, and he'd
paid the price for it.

He thought of the entire week, when he'd been in meetings and the only thought he'd had was getting back to her.

He didn't know if he loved her. He didn't know what that emotion was supposed to feel like, but he *did* know that he wanted her by his side for the rest of his life.

He missed her in his bed, tangled up in the sheets, her lips swollen from his kisses. He missed looking across the table at her as they shared a cup of coffee. He missed... everything about her.

When he looked to his own future, it seemed cold and empty if she wasn't by his side. And as far as he could tell, that was love. Or, at least, close to it. But he knew it was going to take more than words to win her back, and he wanted to do something to show her that he'd been losing sleep without her by his side.

So he'd found himself in front of a jewelry store in London and he'd done the one thing that he'd never thought he'd do. He'd gone in there and bought a ring for Elizabeth. Because he didn't feel alive without her and he'd waited so long for her that he couldn't wait any longer. He was determined to make her his.

Carter had pointed out that women were complicated, but if a man was truly honest with them, he could win the heart of any woman. Bradley hadn't been ready to hear that at the time, but a week all alone in a foreign city had given him plenty of time to think, and he finally had been able to truly understand what Elizabeth had been saying to him about love.

And while it was true he'd never said the words to anyone but his mother, it was also true no one had ever said the words to him. He hadn't been lying or exaggerating when he'd said that he'd been broken and felt as though he wasn't truly worthy of love, but thinking about Elizabeth made him realize that he wanted to be worthy of her.

And he didn't feel *less than* with her. He never had. From the first moment he'd seen her in front of his frat house, he'd realized that she sparked something inside of him, and now he knew he had to tell her what he'd figured out.

But first he had to actually get back to her. He was nearly jumping out of his skin with impatience, thinking about how he was going straight to the Lars Usten Lodge as soon as his plane landed. Although he expected some resistance on her part when they first came face to face, he wasn't going to leave there until he made everything right between them.

"Are you heading home?" the woman seated next to him asked.

"Yes," he said, knowing in his heart he finally was heading home. That he had a home and a family to go back to. Not to take anything away from his mom, but he needed something that only Elizabeth could give him.

"You?" he asked.

"I am. I've been gone for five years and hope my family is happy to see me." She was older and looked a little wary at the thought of returning. He realized that she might even be scared of what she would find. And he hoped that, when he was her age, he'd be happily settled with Elizabeth and no longer afraid to come home.

"Well, I'm sure they will welcome you with open arms," Bradley said.

They didn't talk for the rest of the flight, which suited him just fine. He sent a couple of emails to Tia to have her set up the things he needed in Park City.

20

"CARTER SHAW IS HERE. He says it's urgent and he needs to see you," Paula said. It had been more than a week since her disastrous confession of love and each day she'd missed Bradley more than she wanted to admit.

Elizabeth didn't want to see Carter right now. She'd delegated his charity event to Lindsey and Pablo and thought she was done with him. But she hadn't gotten to the position of general manager by ignoring VIPs, and just because she knew he was a friend of Bradley's was no reason to ignore him.

"I can give him five minutes, but then I want you to interrupt and say I'm needed somewhere else, okay?" Elizabeth said.

"Of course. I already told him you don't have time for anything today."

"The worst part is, you're not making that up. My day couldn't get any busier."

"That's what you wanted," Paula reminded her.

"I know. Thank you." Elizabeth hung up and then waited for Carter to come into her office.

He was dressed as if he'd come straight from the slopes. She knew he'd been practicing at the lodge for the last week or so because Lindsey had mentioned it. "How can I help you?" she asked as he walked over to her desk.

His brown hair was messy, but in a styled way as if he'd done it intentionally. He was clean-shaven and smiled easily at her as he settled in one of the guest chairs she had in front of her desk.

"I need you to come down to the slopes for a few minutes."

"Why? I'm busy and not dressed for skiing."

"Can I be honest with you, Elizabeth—is it okay if I call you that?"

"Yes and yes," she said.

"I'm doing a friend a favor and he's asked me to get you to the slopes," Carter said.

For a minute she felt her heart beat a little faster, but then she remembered that Bradley didn't ski, so the chance of him being on the slopes was pretty slim. "Who is this friend?"

"I can't say. All I can promise is you won't be disappointed," Carter told her.

Elizabeth hesitated. "I'm not sure that I can take the time," she said, checking her watch. "In fact I have another appointment—"

"I'm not taking no for an answer." He gave her a pointed look. "I hoped it wouldn't come to this, but you know I'm doing an interview with ESPN this afternoon from the lodge, and I'd hate to have to say how badly I've been treated here."

"That's not true," she said. She did know about the interview because he was using a pressroom they'd set up for him. "We've been very accommodating."

"I know, and I'd feel bad lying, but this is important. And I promised I'd get you down to the slopes."

She glared at him. "You like playing games, don't you?"

"Not really," he admitted. "But I do like winning, and this is a challenge. I was warned you might be difficult."

She shook her head and stood up. "I just know what I want."

"Nothing wrong with that," he said affably. "Can I assume we're going to the hill?"

"Yes. But I want a glowing report and for you to say that you think there isn't a better place to spend December," she said, figuring he wasn't the only one who could make demands. She wanted to ensure that the lodge continued to be a success. And hip snowboarders were part of the crowd that they didn't generally draw from. It wouldn't hurt to expand into that market.

"I'll make it sound like a winter paradise."

"I couldn't ask for more," she said. "How long will I be?"

"I've already talked to your assistant and let her know that we'd be a while."

"You did?"

"Yes," he said with a wink. "Ladies have a hard time saying no to me."

She shook her head as she followed him out of her office. "I want to be around when one does say no to you. You need to be taken down a peg or two."

He just laughed and blew a kiss toward Paula as they walked by her desk. Her mid-forties assistant blushed and smiled back at the devilishly charming snowboarder. "Did you tell him I had time?"

"Sorry, Elizabeth, he was very insistent."

She shook her head, but wasn't really upset with her assistant. After all, Carter was a hard man to say no to. Elizabeth took her heavy winter parka from the peg near the door and put it on, following him through the lodge lobby, which was now decorated for Christmas. She'd been thinking hard about what she wanted and she knew all of her wishes for Christmas involved Bradley. However, since she was a realist, she knew that she should switch her list to more materialistic things that she could buy for herself. Unfortunately, there weren't enough luxury items in the world to take the place of what she really wanted.

Carter led her across the wooden deck to the après-ski café and then out to the tables set around the fire pits, which were by the path leading to the ski lifts.

And then he stopped.

"This is as far as I go. But you should continue around the corner there."

"Okay," she said, feeling a little odd as she stayed on the path and then stopped when she got to the ski lifts. On the side of the building where skiers got onto the lifts was a large, graffiti-style canvas mural of her life with Bradley. It depicted all the pivotal moments they'd shared since she met him that first day of college.

She stared at it, wondering what it meant and who'd done it. It was truly one of the most breathtaking things she'd ever seen.

She stood there, just taking it all in, and as she let her gaze move from the pictures of college, to her first day at the lodge—depicted by Bradley dropping her off in his convertible Jeep—then on to them kissing in the snow and the party with her friends, she came to something that hadn't happened yet. A vignette of Bradley on bended knee in front of her.

"What do you think?" Bradley asked, coming down the path toward her. "I tried to show you what I'd spent too long denying."

"What is that?" she asked.

"That you are my life."

BRADLEY HAD SPENT the last two days working behind Elizabeth's back and coordinating many different elements for his surprise, but the one thing that he hadn't been able to plan was how it would affect him seeing her again. He had forgotten exactly how beautiful she was and how his breath always caught in his throat when he saw her again. He stepped out of the shadows where he'd been watching and waiting for her reaction.

He'd forgotten the way the scent of her perfume filled the air and wrapped around him, drawing him closer to her. He'd underestimated how much he needed her until this moment.

He'd spent the entire flight from the U.K. writing down all of the moments that he'd felt had changed his life. The ones with Elizabeth had made him realize that he'd been falling in love with her for a long time—probably from the very first moment that he'd seen her. When she'd been a pretty college freshman and he'd realized that she stood out from the other girls.

"How can I be your life?" she asked him. "What's changed between now and the last time I saw you?"

He got it. He'd known this wouldn't be easy. That's why he'd called in more favors and made more promises than he ever had before in his life. Tia had said that he deserved to have to work hard for Elizabeth because he'd been stupid to walk away from her.

And Tia's words had resonated.

"*You* did, Lizzie. When you told me you loved me, I knew that it was the beginning, but I was afraid to take that leap and follow you," he said. "I pushed you out of your shell never realizing that I had been living in one of my own for too long."

God, he hoped she believed him because he never wanted to have to blunder his way through anything like this again. He knew he had to be honest with her—his mom had said just speak from the heart—but he still wasn't sure he was doing anything right.

"All of that happened ten days ago," she said. "Why today? What's changed to make you do all of this?"

"God, you really are going to make me keep doing this, aren't you?" he asked with a grin, knowing he owed her words and actions. After the way she'd confessed her love and he'd just stared at her, he guessed he had to do more than have his friends make a mural.

"Doing what?" she asked.

"Baring my soul," he said at last, taking her into his arms and pulling her as close as he could.

She was stiff for a few moments and then she relaxed slightly against him. He pressed his mouth to her ear and whispered all the things he couldn't say out loud.

"I love you, Lizzie. I have always felt so broken inside and I didn't realize how alone I was until you told me you loved me…. And I felt that emptiness inside of myself, mocking me, warning me that I was afraid of having you and losing you."

She lifted her face to his and he gazed into her eyes, realizing that he still wasn't sure if he'd done enough to convince her. He didn't have any other words. He'd been honest and told her what was in his heart.

"Is that enough?"

"You were always enough," she said, going up on her tiptoes and kissing him. "I wasn't sure that I could love any man, really trust you, but you have always been my champion."

"And I always will be. I promise right now that I'm never going to disappoint you again. There will be times when I make mistakes and screw up, but I'm always coming back to you and I will always love you."

She kissed him, and it was long and sweet and felt like a promise for the future. "I will always love you, too."

He lifted her off the ground, hugging her close to him as if he'd never let her go, and he knew in his heart he never would.

CANDLELIGHT FLICKERED IN Elizabeth's office that evening when she entered it. Just like in her dream. She slipped off her shoes and the stone floor was cold under her feet. She glanced around the room, a shiver racing down her spine in heightened anticipation. She knew the person in the shadows.

Bradley.

Her best friend, the man who'd won her heart with his passion.

He stepped into the light and her breath caught, her eyes moving over his rippling muscles and lean six-pack abs as he strode toward her.

"I thought your meeting would never end," he said. There were a few details she noticed now...other than his rocking hot body. The picnic set up on the floor, champagne chilling on ice...

He got down on one knee next to her took her hand in his. "Lizzie, will you make me the happiest man in the world? Will you marry me?"

"Yes," she said, drawing him to his feet and throwing herself in his arms. He held her close and brought his mouth down on hers as he lifted her in the air in spun her around.

His mouth was hot, his tongue talented, and she gave in to passion, and experienced everything he had to offer.

Finally he lifted his mouth from hers. "Are you sure?" he asked, his voice deep and husky. It was a tone she'd only heard from him one time before.

"More sure than I've ever been of anything in my life."

She took his hand and guided it to her breast. He moaned her name on a long guttural sigh as he squeezed it gently.

"Take me. Make me yours," she said.

He stood up, lifted her in his arms and carried her to the desk. As her fantasy came to life, she realized that the real man, flawed and complex as he was, was far more exciting than the dream. And he was all hers.

* * * * *

Celebrate sexy reads with more HOLIDAY HEAT *stories!*
Look for UNDER THE MISTLETOE in December
and AFTER MIDNIGHT in January 2015.

COMING NEXT MONTH FROM

 HARLEQUIN

Blaze

Available November 18, 2014

#823 A LAST CHANCE CHRISTMAS
Sons of Chance
by Vicki Lewis Thompson

Snowbound at the Last Chance Ranch, genealogist
Molly Gallagher discovers just how talented custom saddle
maker Ben Radcliffe is—in the bedroom and out! But is their
scorching attraction enough to keep them together for more
than one hot night?

#824 BRING ME TO LIFE
Uniformly Hot!
by Kira Sinclair

The military told Tatum Huntley her Special Ops husband was
dead, so when he turns up three years later she can't decide if
she should kill him herself or kiss him senseless!

#825 WILD HOLIDAY NIGHTS
3 stories in 1!
by Samantha Hunter, Meg Maguire and Debbi Rawlins

Three steamy Christmas stories. Three drop-dead gorgeous
heroes. Three heroines finding out just how wild their nights
can get when they're *not* home for the holidays!

#826 UNDER THE MISTLETOE
Holiday Heat
by Katherine Garbera

Penny's thrilled to meet a hot guy to share the holiday with.
Gorgeous Will Spalding may just be the best gift she ever got!
But can she walk away from the man of her dreams after two
weeks together?

REQUEST YOUR FREE BOOKS!
2 FREE NOVELS PLUS 2 FREE GIFTS!

HARLEQUIN

Blaze

red-hot reads!

YES! Please send me 2 FREE Harlequin® Blaze™ novels and my 2 FREE gifts (gifts are worth about $10). After receiving them, if I don't wish to receive any more books, I can return the shipping statement marked "cancel." If I don't cancel, I will receive 4 brand-new novels every month and be billed just $4.74 per book in the U.S. or $4.96 per book in Canada. That's a savings of at least 14% off the cover price. It's quite a bargain. Shipping and handling is just 50¢ per book in the U.S. and 75¢ per book in Canada.* I understand that accepting the 2 free books and gifts places me under no obligation to buy anything. I can always return a shipment and cancel at any time. Even if I never buy another book, the two free books and gifts are mine to keep forever.

150/350 HDN F4WC

Name _____ (PLEASE PRINT)

Address _____ Apt. #

City _____ State/Prov. _____ Zip/Postal Code

Signature (if under 18, a parent or guardian must sign)

Mail to the **Harlequin® Reader Service:**
IN U.S.A.: P.O. Box 1867, Buffalo, NY 14240-1867
IN CANADA: P.O. Box 609, Fort Erie, Ontario L2A 5X3

Want to try two free books from another line?
Call 1-800-873-8635 or visit www.ReaderService.com.

* Terms and prices subject to change without notice. Prices do not include applicable taxes. Sales tax applicable in N.Y. Canadian residents will be charged applicable taxes. Offer not valid in Quebec. This offer is limited to one order per household. Not valid for current subscribers to Harlequin Blaze books. All orders subject to credit approval. Credit or debit balances in a customer's account(s) may be offset by any other outstanding balance owed by or to the customer. Please allow 4 to 6 weeks for delivery. Offer available while quantities last.

Your Privacy—The Harlequin® Reader Service is committed to protecting your privacy. Our Privacy Policy is available online at www.ReaderService.com or upon request from the Harlequin Reader Service.

We make a portion of our mailing list available to reputable third parties that offer products we believe may interest you. If you prefer that we not exchange your name with third parties, or if you wish to clarify or modify your communication preferences, please visit us at www.ReaderService.com/consumerchoice or write to us at Harlequin Reader Service Preference Service, P.O. Box 9062, Buffalo, NY 14269. Include your complete name and address.

HB13R2

SPECIAL EXCERPT FROM

 HARLEQUIN

 Blaze

New York Times bestselling author
Vicki Lewis Thompson is back with another
irresistible story from her bestselling
miniseries **Sons of Chance!**

A Last Chance Christmas

She stood on tiptoe, wound her arms around his neck and gave it all she had. So did he, and oh, my goodness. A harmonica player knew what it was all about. She'd never kissed one before, but she hoped to be doing a lot more of this with Ben.

Although she'd never thought of a kiss as being creative, this one was. He caressed her lips so well and so thoroughly that she forgot the cold and the late hour. She forgot they were standing in a cavernous tractor barn surrounded by heavy equipment.

She even forgot that she wasn't in the habit of kissing men she'd known for mere hours. Come to think of it, she'd never done that. But everything about this kiss, from his dessert-flavored taste to his talented tongue, felt perfect.

As far as she was concerned, the kiss could go on forever. Well, maybe not. The longer they kissed, the heavier they breathed. His hot mouth was making her light-headed in more ways than one.

That was her excuse for dropping her phone on the concrete floor. It hit with a sickening crack, but in her current aroused state, she didn't really care.

Ben pulled back, though, and gulped for air. "I think that was your phone."

"I think so, too." She dragged in a couple of quick breaths. "Kiss me some more."

With a soft groan, he lowered his head and settled his mouth over hers. This time he took the kiss deeper and invested it with a meaning she understood quite well. Intellectually she was shocked, but physically she was completely on board.

This time when he eased away from her, she was trembling. Like a swimmer breaking the surface, she gasped. Then she clutched his head and urged him back down. She wanted him to kiss her until her conscience stopped yelling at her that it was too soon to feel like this about him. "More."

Pick up A LAST CHANCE CHRISTMAS
by Vicki Lewis Thompson,
on sale December 2014,
wherever Harlequin® Blaze® books are sold.

When it snows, things get really steamy...

Wild Holiday Nights

from Harlequin Blaze offers something sweet, something unexpected and something naughty!

Holiday Rush by *Samantha Hunter*

Cake guru Calla Michaels is canceling Christmas to deal with fondant, batter and an attempted robbery. Then Gideon Stone shows up at her door. Apparently, Calla's kitchen isn't hot enough without having her longtime crush in her bakery...*and* in her bed!

Playing Games by *Meg Maguire*

When her plane is grounded on Christmas eve, Carrie Baxter is desperate enough to share a rental car with her secret high-school crush. Sure, Daniel Barber is much, *much* hotter, but he's still just as prickly as ever. It's gonna be one *looong* drive...and an unforgettably X-rated night!

All Night Long by *Debbi Rawlins*

The only way overworked paralegal Carly Watts gets her Christmas vacation is by flying to Chicago to get Jack Carrington's signature. But Jack's in no rush to sell his grandfather's company. In fact, he'll do whatever it takes to buy more time. Even if it takes one naughty night before Christmas...

Available December 2014 wherever you buy Harlequin Blaze books.

⊞ HARLEQUIN®
™

Blaze®

Red-Hot Reads

www.Harlequin.com

HTHMS1014-5

HARLEQUIN®
A *Romance* FOR EVERY MOOD™

Love the Harlequin book
you just read?

Your opinion matters.

Review this book on your favorite
book site, review site, blog or your own
social media properties and share
your opinion with other readers!

HARLEQUIN®

A *Romance* FOR EVERY MOOD™

JUST CAN'T GET ENOUGH?

Join our social communities
and talk to us online.

You will have access to the latest
news on upcoming titles and special
promotions, but most importantly,
you can talk to other fans about your
favorite Harlequin reads.

Harlequin.com/Community

Facebook.com/HarlequinBooks

Twitter.com/HarlequinBooks

Pinterest.com/HarlequinBooks

HSOCIAL